Plant Protection

Plant Protection

AN INTEGRATED INTERDISCIPLINARY APPROACH

Webster H. Sill, Jr.

THE IOWA STATE UNIVERSITY PRESS, *Ames, Iowa*

WEBSTER H. SILL, JR., *is professor of biology, University of South Dakota, and director of the Center for Environmental Studies.*

Composed and printed by The Iowa State University Press, Ames, Iowa 50010

First edition, 1982

Library of Congress Cataloging in Publication Data

Sill, Webster H., 1916–
   Plant protection.

   Bibliography: p.
   Includes index.
   1. Plants, Protection of. 2. Pest Control, Integrated. I. Title.
SB950.S54   632   81–12323
ISBN 0–8138–1665–3   AACR2

This book is dedicated by a proud father with grateful thanks to three superb children:

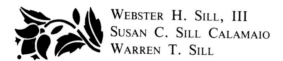 WEBSTER H. SILL, III
SUSAN C. SILL CALAMAIO
WARREN T. SILL

They have been a constant source of joy, inspiration, honest affection, and real support in a world where all of these are in short supply.

CONTENTS

PREFACE

THIS BOOK is an outgrowth of the realization that there is tremendous need for more and better cooperative efforts in plant protection (crop protection and plant pest management) and that achieving this cooperation is not only important but terribly complex. The problems associated with growing adequate food for a burgeoning human population as well as conserving and improving soil, increasing crop production, and maintaining and preserving a quality environment are so staggering as to boggle the mind of anyone seriously considering the problems. The subdisciplines of plant protection, working independently, probably cannot solve the massive pest and disease problems associated with the production and preservation of food crops throughout the world. Many have discussed this complex problem and emphasized the importance of consistent cooperative efforts among the disciplines.

In truth, we do not know whether we can solve the massive problems appearing on the horizon even when we utilize the most sophisticated team research approaches. All the disciplines involved seem willing to pay lip service to cooperation, but efforts to achieve truly cooperative research ventures often bog down in administrative detail and problems of organization, personnel, prestige, control, benefits, credits, and other human problems that are closely related to the apparently endemic "human cussedness" characteristics of humans everywhere. Unfortunately, more often than not the problems that seem to be most difficult to solve are not technical but essentially human.

This book is also an effort to compile enough information to show that the several plant protection disciplines are in fact closely interrelated and often overlap in significant ways that could be utilized more creatively in cooperative control ventures and would eventually make control techniques much simpler, less costly, and certainly far more desirable for the farmer. These interrelated and overlapping areas have not been emphasized much in the past; yet cooperative research ventures of the future should concentrate on these very areas of interface, interrelationship, and overlap.

To this end this book is written, and it is hoped that the many examples

xi

of overlapping and interrelated areas will stimulate research and give aid to efforts to combine control techniques; integrate and coordinate control activities; and eventually achieve simpler, more reasonable control methods built around systems of plant protection to minimize the use of pesticides and maximize the use of automatic control techniques (such as plant resistance and cultural and biological control techniques) that are closely related to better agronomic and horticultural practices.

This book was begun while the author was a senior fellow at the Food Institute of The East-West Center in Honolulu, Hawaii, on leave of absence from the posts of chairman, Biology Department, University of South Dakota at Vermillion, and Director for Environmental Studies, state of South Dakota. The book was completed as a labor of love at the University of South Dakota between normal administrative, research, teaching, and statewide service duties.

The author particularly appreciates the permission to go on leave of absence granted by Richard Bowen, president, and Donald Habbe, dean of arts and sciences, University of South Dakota. Hearty thanks are also due Donald Dunlap, who served as acting chairman in the author's absence, and to a patient and considerate wife who often put up with having an absentee husband.

At the Food Institute, several were most helpful in this work. Philip Motooka, research associate in pest management, gave many suggestions and much valuable help of many kinds. Nicolaas Luykx, director of the Food Institute, was a source of much appreciated encouragement, inspiration, and advice. Fannie Lee-Kai and her faithful and efficient secretarial corps were most helpful in typing and proofreading the manuscript. Rita Hong and her helpers were most useful in obtaining the necessary books and periodicals for study and perusal. The author particularly appreciates the granting of the position of senior fellow that was given to him through the approval of Everett Kleinjans, president of The East-West Center, and its board of governors.

At the University of South Dakota special thanks and appreciation should go to Mary Petersen and Lorraine Bjordal who most efficiently served as typists and proofreaders. The author also particularly appreciates the excellent editing and proofreading done by the staff of Iowa State University Press.

This book does not reflect either the official position of the Food Institute of The East-West Center or the University of South Dakota. The author bears sole responsibility for the contents, both the organization and the presentation of the ideas developed in the text. Several professional friends and colleagues were helpful in reading the text and giving creative criticisms and input. Three, in particular, deserve special thanks. These are

Joe Good, director, Everglades Agricultural Research and Education Center, University of Florida, Belle Glade; B. D. Blair, extension entomologist, Cooperative Extension Service, College of Agriculture and Home Economics, and the United States Department of Agriculture Cooperating, Ohio State University, Columbus; and Harlan E. Smith, plant pathologist, United States Department of Agriculture, SEA–Extension Service, Washington, D.C. Many others who helped are cited in the references or with illustrations furnished. The book could not have been written without their knowledgeable and unselfish assistance.

The author will admit to an unconscious plant pathology bias, but he has attempted to be fair with all the subdisciplines of plant protection. Any errors or misinterpretations must be attributed to the author alone. It is hoped that this work will prove to be useful to those who are seeking a reference that emphasizes the importance of developing interdisciplinary, completely integrated, and cooperative plant protection. This concept must be the "wave of the future" in agriculture for many important ecological and economic reasons. This text may prove to be very useful for crop protection and integrated pest management courses at both the undergraduate and graduate levels. Enough examples and illustrations are used from countries around the world that it is hoped the book will have practical worldwide application in the evolving discipline of plant protection.

The generic names of pesticides are given in the text where possible. Trade names for well-known materials, such as DDT and 2, 4-D, are used. The *Merck Index* (Merck & Co., Rahway, N.J.) and the *Pesticide Manual* (Entomolog. Soc. Am.) are the sources for pesticide names used.

FROM AN ANCIENT EGYPTIAN MANUSCRIPT—

Worms have destroyed half the wheat, and the hippopotami have eaten the rest; there are swarms of rats in the fields; the grasshoppers alight there; the cattle devour, the little birds pilfer; and if the farmer loses sight for an instant of what remains on the ground, it is carried off by robbers.

Plant Protection

1

Overview

Introduction

The first creative workers in plant protection (crop protection and plant pest management) 100 years ago were independent souls who could move in any direction in their work, unhampered by division of disciplines. Most of them were scientists by avocation; only a few were professionals. The professionals were often medical practitioners; others might now be classified as general biologists or even general scientists and, surprisingly, some were theologians. The different disciplines evolved slowly together with the closely related bodies of knowledge. It was not likely that a worker would have equal enthusiasm and talent and devote equal effort to both the study of insects and the study of fungi. Quite often individuals who studied fungi also studied bacteria, but even in that area the natural split between early bacteriologists and mycologists came rather soon. In this manner the different disciplines in plant protection evolved separately as natural disciplines containing closely related bodies of knowledge based on natural groupings of organisms and natural interests of the workers.

Entomology was early recognized as a discipline. The study of the myriad arthropods was a complex area. The science of plant pathology developed in the early 1900s, some 50 or 60 years after the first major efforts in plant pathology by such men as Woronin in Russia and Milardet in France. A few intellectual giants moved rather freely from field to field, as did the Frenchman, Anton DeBary. However, most concentrated on relatively narrow areas of work on naturally related organisms, and out of these efforts the separate subdisciplines evolved.

The subdisciplines of plant pathology came together gradually to form the basic and applied field of plant pathology, i.e., the study of bacterial, fungal, nematode, and virus diseases of plants plus the many abiotic maladies and injuries that afflict plants in the field. Weed science developed much later; until recently it was a part of agronomy and horticulture and in

3

most institutions it is still attached to one of these departments. Plant nematology emerged as a separate discipline from plant pathology and zoology only a few years ago; most nematologists are still in plant pathology departments and think of themselves as plant pathologists also. The problems with vertebrate pests, such as rats and birds, have been defined by an assorted group of individuals—zoologists, veterinarians, and various agriculturalists. Usually scientists faced with problems in the field approached them as best they could.

From the standpoint of research this evolution of disciplines is important and completely understandable. Anyone who has worked in research in any of these areas knows how complex each can be. Even though it is desirable and natural to separate the disciplines for research and teaching, unity is introduced very quickly by nature in the field situation; and one is reminded that disciplines overlap and intermingle in the field. It is not at all uncommon, for example, to see several insects and mites, several plant diseases (one bacterial disease, one fungal disease, and one abiotic malady), and nematodes all attacking one plant at the same time. Heagle (1973) summarized this point well:

> Plants often suffer from more than one pathogenic agent or a combination of pathogenic and non-pathogenic or abiotic agents. In addition, plants suffer simultaneously from insects, diseases, rats, weeds and the environment. So, the crop protection man must be broadly trained.

Because of this holistic aspect of nature in the field, applied practitioners of plant protection have tended to work as cooperating specialists at the field level. Control at the field level then becomes a decision concerning which problems are critical to the health of the crop and, particularly, which must be solved to achieve an economically successful crop of adequate quality and acceptable yield. The grower is aware that the problems of nature are complex, intertwined, and seldom simple. Those who work with the grower in the field are also aware that if their approach is too narrow they will miss important factors in solving problems of crop health. The important factors may not be associated at all with their particular disciplines and yet may be very easy to confuse with them. It is common knowledge among plant pathologists that some virus diseases and certain nutritional deficiencies look essentially identical. Often nematode infestations will produce symptoms very similar to certain fungus disease problems that are characterized by a wilting syndrome, and these can be confused with incipient drought conditions. Consequently, field workers, whether agronomists, horticulturalists, or from one of the plant protection disciplines, must have open minds and a broad approach to the diagnosis of field problems. Field workers must approach nature with great humility when working alone or have many practical, well-trained friends who represent the various subdisciplines to consult.

Nearly every field worker with long experience has traveled with a sophisticated laboratory scientist who is competent and confident in the laboratory but completely lost in the field. These people may err in judgment because of their lack of practical experience. Nature is not like a laboratory and organisms do not exist in neat, pure cultures and seldom, except in agriculture, in pure stands without intense competition. The complex, aggressive, and apparently ruthless competition occurring within natural communities is often mystifying to everyone. This is particularly true in the soil, where hundreds of different microorganisms and other microflora and microfauna compete for space and available food and produce myriad synergistic, antagonistic, or antibiotic substances to help them in the battle for survival.

Without question the plant protection disciplines are combined at the field level. However, they are only a part, sometimes a very small part, of the total problem of crop improvement, production, and management. Many would insist that the only logical approach to plant protection is made through the disciplines of crop improvement, production, and management and that any efforts in plant protection should be controlled by those who are involved with the primary problems of these disciplines. They feel that the plant protection disciplines should always serve in a subsidiary, supportive role. There is much logic in this argument. It usually fits the needs and concerns of the farmer who faces the problems of growing a high quality, high yield crop. However, occasionally severe epiphytotics and epizootics occur when a particular plant disease or pest becomes the dominant limiting factor in the production of a high yield, high quality crop. Because of this recurring reality, others insist that the plant protection disciplines should be separate from agronomy and horticulture and that the subdisciplines of plant protection should function independently and should cooperate only when absolutely necessary at the field level.

There are logical reasons for both approaches, and conspicuous successes and failures could be cited to support either. However, the most successful approaches to solving problems in agriculture—particularly in the areas of crop improvement, production, and management—have been cases where specific crops were studied simultaneously by all the people of the various crop disciplines working as a research team. Examples of success in such efforts are the work of the International Rice Research Institute in the Philippines in developing rice varieties and of the International Maize and Wheat Improvement Center in Mexico. These teams provided the major impetus toward the Green Revolution in the developing world (Borlaug 1965). As a by-product of this team research, a Nobel Peace Prize was awarded to

Norman Borlaug, longtime director of the Rockefeller Foundation Wheat Improvement Program in Mexico.

In the United States most land-grant educational institutions have scientists concentrating on the major crops of importance in their states. Workers in Illinois and Iowa are noted for their cooperative efforts in maize (corn) improvement, and those in Kansas and Nebraska for their research in wheat improvement. In the eastern United States, Georgia is well known for its outstanding work in peaches; North Carolina for its work on tobacco; New York State for its important work in apples; and Wisconsin for its work with cherries and with vegetable crops such as cabbages, cucumbers, and onions. Each state has concentrated on its crops of major importance and either by formal or informal means has achieved a cooperative approach to the improvement of the crop as well as to its production and management. In these efforts, plant protection people have usually found themselves in a subsidiary, supportive, but essential role in the overall program of crop improvement, production, and management.

Probably it does not matter whether cooperation between the various disciplines is achieved by formal or informal means but it is essential, since no discipline represents the total knowledge necessary for the achievement of the best quality crop, the highest yield, or even the most acceptable program of plant protection.

The Farmer's Point of View

The farmer or grower finds it difficult to understand the occasional conflicts in recommendations from the disciplines associated with crop improvement, production, management, and protection. At the field level it is, therefore, very important for the disciplines to present a solid front so that farmers can get a clear picture of the total problem and then make the compromises often necessary to solve problems. Growers need accurate information quickly. To them there is a single primary problem with component parts: to grow a high-yielding, high quality crop at the lowest cost for the greatest economic return. Their next most important problem is maintaining or building the quality of the soil—the preservation of the land. Normally, growers do not consider plant protection unless absolutely necessary. If a rare season comes along with no serious pests, plant diseases, or even severe weed problems, they will ignore these problems for that particular year.

In growers' minds, the priorities of plant protection range approximately as follows. (1) Every year weeds must be controlled in order to get a satisfactory crop. Consequently, weed control will constantly be in mind and is the most important aspect of plant protection to most growers in all agricultural areas of the world. (2) Growers next consider plant nutrition (avoidance of nutritional deficiencies) and the whole problem of securing a well-balanced supply of nutrients for the crop. (3) Soil conservation, basically to protect against poor nutrition in the years to come, is important. Proper management and utilization to protect, maintain, and improve the soil for the next crop and all those succeeding is a prime consideration.

In seasons with no serious pest and disease problems, farmers may not be concerned with possible minor losses. They will consider specific insects and mites only when damage is noticeable. Also, plant diseases will be considered only when they appear important enough to be considered, unless by experience they pose a serious yearly problem. In such cases, which are not too common, farmers may combine an insecticide and fungicide in a series of treatments each season, usually as a preventive measure.

Farmers will not even consider most other plant protection problems until they become visible and therefore important to them. If possible farmers will ignore them completely unless they become an economic threat. This attitude alone places most plant protection disciplines in a supportive or subsidiary role.

There is one exception to the above statement. Some large producers who have an enormous investment in the crop apply an "insurance" treatment even though knowledge is lacking concerning pests' presence or importance. The wisdom of this approach is questioned by many.

Farmers would like to be able to kill all their pests and diseases with one product in one "fell swoop." This would be less expensive, simpler, and easier—desirable attributes to good business. Consequently, combined control measures for plant diseases and other crop pests are for farmers an ideal approach toward control. Any technique that controls nematodes, plant diseases, and insects in one treatment or group of treatments will be enthusiastically endorsed by growers, particularly if the treatment is inexpensive and simple. They tend to resist or ignore any treatments that are complex, that attack only one pest or one plant disease, and that are too costly. Complex or costly treatments will be used only when disaster is near and there are no other alternatives, and they must still be inexpensive enough to allow a profitable crop.

Sometimes the recommendations of the agronomist or horticulturalist work against the recommendations of the plant pathologist and entomologist, or vice versa. When conflicting recommendations are given by representatives of different disciplines, farmers are confused and may be angered. Need for compromises is always present, and unless people working in applied research at the field level recognize that compromises are necessary, growers may become disenchanted with professional specialists.

The term *organic farming* has become popular in recent years. Actually it is the oldest type of traditional farming and has been practiced for millenia in various parts of the world. A scientific approach to its possibilities is undoubtedly overdue and it is now being researched seriously in Michigan and elsewhere (Organic farming being researched 1979). Growers will applaud this effort if it eventually means simpler, more natural, less costly, and effective plant protection methods.

Need for a New Discipline?

The general complexity of the field situation has led to the discussion of need for a general practitioner in plant protection (crop protection and plant pest management), who might be the equivalent of the general practitioner in human medicine—a person who would represent all the interests of plant protection for growers but who would also look at the crop picture from the broad standpoint of crop production and management. This person would serve as the growers' trusted "broker" in matters of plant protection.

There is no agreement concerning the need for such a general practitioner and many would oppose the notion. However, agricultural consultants in plant protection are appearing more and more in developed countries. They function as general practitioners and utilize the services of specialists in different disciplines whenever specialized knowledge is needed. The situation concerning a specific crop in a particular environment is often so complex that the generalist will find it necessary to go to specialists to obtain the information needed to solve a given problem. If the role of general practitioner for plant protection is developed, it will need all the support possible from specialists of different plant protection disciplines. The fear often expressed by representatives of different disciplines that their discipline might be swallowed up by a new plant protection specialty is completely groundless. Evolving general practitioners will find specialists' knowledge essential to their work and will need to refer constantly to basic research findings. The new discipline should stimulate the old disciplines rather than destroy them.

Browning (1977) has developed a persuasive argument for the development of a general practitioner, who he calls the "plant doctor," and more and more voices are being raised in favor of the broadly trained plant protection specialist.

Environmental Problems

The problems of plant protection have become particularly important in recent years because of the threat to people's health and the environment through the large-scale use of certain organic insecticides and a few other pesticides, particularly those containing mercury. As pointed out by Wood et al. (1969), the problems of pest control have been thrust on us in a new and much more difficult way than in the past. Some pesticides can cause death through poisoning to humans and warm-blooded animals and have caused many deaths, usually through improper or careless use. In some instances they accumulate in the human body and may concentrate in plant- and-animal food chains. Some, particularly DDT and some of its relatives, build up in the environment and denature very slowly.

Another serious problem has been the development of resistance in pest populations to pesticides and the rapid resurgence of other pests after chemical treatment. These problems, combined with the destruction of vast numbers of valuable parasites, predators, pollinators, and other useful arthropods by pesticides, make it clear that the time has come to face the threats posed by excessive use of pesticides and to develop a system of plant protection that minimizes their use and maximizes the quality of control achieved with the least cost. These control procedures then need to be presented to the grower in a simple, inexpensive system or "package of practices."

Many environmentalists are determined to see the use of pesticides virtually eliminated. These people usually are not aware that at present such a choice would create serious food shortages all over the world, markedly reduce the quantity and quality of food on the market, increase food costs greatly, and create severe political crises and even political chaos. They also may be unaware that nature is fully capable of wiping out entire species of plants and animals (and also humanity) by means of a particular pest or disease. A case in the eastern United States in the 1930s was the elimination of the American chestnut tree (except in a few research nurseries) by an accidentally introduced fungus disease, the chestnut blight, caused by *Endothia parasitica.* Despite the often legitimate concerns of environmentalists, agriculture must utilize whatever means are necessary for protecting the world food supply from destruction by various crop pests and diseases.

On the other hand, it is equally important to devise as quickly as possible ways of controlling pests and diseases that do not depend on synthetic broad-spectrum chemicals that are dangerous to warm-blooded animals and that persist and accumulate to deleterious levels in the environment.

Equally disturbing is the fact that many agricultural activities have tended to favor the incidence and development of plant diseases and pests. Yarwood (1970) estimated that between 1926 and 1960 the number of recorded plant diseases on principal crop plants increased about threefold. Activities that often tend to increase plant diseases and pests, some of which are listed by Yarwood, are as follows:

1. Plant introduction and movement from one country or area to another.
2. Vegetative propagation of plants and their movements from one location to another.
3. Practice of monoculture consisting of large acreages of a single

crop having a relatively narrow gene base and plant breeding techniques that develop these crops. (A perfect example is the 1970 outbreak of the southern corn leaf blight disease in the U.S. Corn Belt where virtually all the maize being grown contained a single gene susceptible to the southern corn leaf blight organism.)

4. Tillage practices that tend to increase the incidence of a crop pest or plant disease.

5. Harvesting practices that move plant disease propagules and pests around more than usual, such as the movement of combines or other large harvesting tools for long distances. (For example, the stinking smut of wheat was distributed all over the western United States in this way.) Harvesting may also cause wounds and damage to a crop that may encourage particular plant diseases.

6. Mass movements of storage products that distribute plant disease propagules and crop pests throughout the world and unsatisfactory storage facilities that may encourage the massive growth of certain plant disease organisms or pests attacking stored products.

7. Fertilization techniques that may increase the susceptibility of a plant to a particular plant disease or crop pest.

8. Irrigation techniques that spread plant disease propagules and crop pests from one field or area to another via the irrigation stream.

9. Use of herbicides that may favor a plant host carrying a particular pathogen, vector of a pathogen, or a particular pest.

10. Site locations for the crop that may favor the development of a specific plant disease or a given pest.

11. Use of chemicals that may be phytotoxic or cause damage to plants.

12. Use of chemicals that may be associated with the development of chemical resistance in a given pest.

13. Destruction of predators or parasites of a pest whose absence allows a particular pest to increase to huge populations.

These practices in modern agriculture greatly increase the cost/benefit ratio for farmers; but the benefits of increased yield and improved quality so far exceed the risk taken involving the possible increased incidence of plant diseases and pests that growers are usually quite willing to take those risks. The gains in production are typically much greater than the losses from plant diseases and pests (Yarwood 1970).

What is emphasized for the developed world by Yarwood is also now true of portions of the developing world as shown by the following quotation from Sun (1974):

The rapid intensification of agriculture in most developing countries . . . has vast effects on the occurrence and outbreaks of crop diseases, insects, and weeds. . . . In Taiwan, for example, disease control has largely depended on the use of chemicals in the past quarter of a century. This practice not only adds a significant amount of capital investment to the production cost, . . . but may often cause serious residue problems and harmful chemical pollution of the environment. For many diseases of low value field crops, expensive chemical control cannot be used, as the profit margin is too narrow. For the control of certain soil borne pathogens and obligate parasites, no effective chemicals are available for use at the present. Therefore, other non-chemical means of disease control, such as the use of resistant varieties and the management of cropping systems or the combination of both, have to be sought for.

This quotation and the problems emphasized by Yarwood (1970) make clear the situation that is true in most parts of the developed world as well as the rapidly advancing countries such as Taiwan. It emphasizes also the extreme importance of new research approaches in plant protection—particularly research aimed at combined control procedures that utilize nonchemical methods, or perhaps measures that combine several nonchemical methods with minimal quantities of pesticides.

Political and Social Factors

Certain plant disease and pest situations have profoundly affected the political and social conditions of a particular time. For example, one wonders how many Irish policemen would be found in Boston and New York had it not been for the Irish famine in the middle 1800s, caused by the epiphytotics of potato late blight in Ireland. Many German immigrants came to the United States at that time for the same reason. As Ordish and Dufour (1969) remind us, Great Britain was not always a tea-drinking nation. The destruction of coffee in Ceylon by coffee rust in the 1870s resulted in a changeover on the plantations to tea instead of coffee and a major shift in British customs.

Biblical plagues of locusts have occurred sporadically throughout history. Few who experienced them can forget the grasshopper plagues of the middle 1930s and 1950s in the Great Plains of the western United States, and every banker and politician in the area knew the extreme importance of those plagues to their futures. Farmers who everywhere seem to be on the bottom of the political and economic heap understood only too well. The Mormons have good reason for remembering the gulls who came in large numbers to eat the locusts that were destroying the Mormon crops in the first year of their life in Utah.

A number of human factors, political and social, determine whether good plant protection procedures are initiated and followed by growers. In addition to important physical factors such as size of plantings, types of plants, cropping systems, and dispersion of plantings, such things as the general educational level of the growers and local populace, their psychological and cultural patterns, the land tenure systems, the policies of governments toward plant protection, and the presence or absence of an effective extension system are all significant. Any one of these, or others not mentioned but equally important, may be the overriding factor that determines whether an effective system of plant protection is adopted and used in a particular place or situation (FAO 1971).

As agriculturalists we often forget that in a predominantly urban society pest control technology must be accommodated to the demands and the constraints of the society. In each culture and country certain habits, customs, traditions, attitudes, religious beliefs, land tenure structures, marketing systems, and technological patterns of organization affect the agricultural technology. Consequently, there will be a new role emerging for public relations experts in plant protection. In this role, such an expert must consider the social and political implications of actions in plant protection. This is an unwelcome prospect to most professionals in these disciplines, since they are neither oriented toward nor trained in public relations techniques and find it an uncomfortable, foreign area.

On the other hand, natural catastrophes can force society to accept drastic change to avert major and continuing disaster. We have mentioned the mass migration of Irish people to the United States because of the upheaval and famine caused by the late blight of potato epiphytotics of the middle 1800s. A recent dramatic example is the aforementioned 1970 outbreak of southern corn leaf blight in the U.S. Corn Belt. Had it not been for extreme good fortune in plant breeding, this could have been another disaster like the potato late blight (A. L. Hooker 1974, pers. commun.).

R. Smith (1969) gave an example of such a developing situation in Central America in the field of entomology:

> Insect pest control there [Central America, Guatemala and Nicaragua] is just one or two growing seasons away from the calamitous situation such as affected the Canete Valley of Peru in 1956. The bollworms *Heliothis zea* and *H. virescens* have now replaced the boll weevil as the most important pests of cotton and show increasing evidence of resistance to the available pesticides. An array of formerly minor pests has been raised to major status. The dosages and numbers of applications of pesticides have been increasing steadily with poorer control results. In several areas the average number of applications is over 30 per year. And some individuals have made over 50 treatments to a field in a single season. The possibilities of a cotton failure are very great in the next year or two if current practices are not modified. The possible social and political implications are many, especially when one considers that over 30 percent of the export dollars for countries like Guatemala and Nicaragua come from the sale of cotton fiber. It is no exaggeration to say that pest control advice which leads to an economic calamity may topple a government. The further complications are many and forbidding.

Economic Factors

Workers in plant protection often forget the overriding importance of economics. As Good (1974*a*) reminds us, "Grower acceptance is the most important factor in implementing pest management programs. Short and long term economic gain or convenience must be established." Farmers must be convinced that a new plant protection technique is less expensive and better. Even in the less developed portions of the world one can be assured that farmers will only use those practices they can afford and that they are convinced will be helpful in growing a healthy crop.

Strickland (1970) discussed the economic constraints as they occur in England and summarized them.

> The general cropping farmer is constrained by a combination of soils, climate and land values to follow a cropping system which is further constrained by the availability of capital, shortage of labor, and restrictions imposed by government (pesticides and so forth) in the national interest and by commercial undertakings in the interests of their shareholders. Within the defined (economic) framework no new pest management techniques should be introduced without clear and convincing experimental evidence that they are an improvement on the techniques already in use.

Cost/benefit ratios are always critical. Plant protection workers occasionally forget that farmers are primarily operators of a business and every other consideration must be subordinated normally in favor of the cultivation of a particular crop on a given piece of land that will bring in the largest yield and profit per acre. Van der Plank (1963) emphasized how the considerations of economics control growers' use of chemicals in Holland and Europe:

> With high priced crops control is commonly by chemicals. The cost structure supports them. But with our great grain crops, forests, plantations and pastures, we have to work more economically and attend more to the ecosystem, especially in choosing a suitable environment and resistant host plants.

Good (1974*a*, 1974*e*) summarized this situation for the United States:

> Large affluent growers or producers of high valued crops are more likely to seek pest management advisory services from private consultants than small growers with low value crops. Cooperative-type pest management associations are most likely to satisfy the needs of low-income or low-value crop growers, although this type of organization will be welcomed by more economically affluent growers in many instances.

Consequently, workers in plant protection must constantly keep in mind the economic values of the crops. It is pointless to develop a control procedure that is so costly that it seldom or never will be used. An example is the recommendation of the use of benomyl, which works reasonably well, to control Dutch elm disease. This disease has marched slowly and relentlessly across the United States primarily because the control measures suggested, including benomyl, were too expensive for most individuals and city and town councils to adopt.

The many people who have insisted that farmers must make the appropriate ecological and conservation decisions and if necessary ignore plant protection decisions have not considered the economic factors involved. Farmers cannot be expected to make the right ecological or conservation choices at the risk of going out of business. They will look at the economic costs versus benefits and ignore any factor that is too expensive to consider. An alternative for those who insist that appropriate ecological and conservation decisions must be made is the formulation of laws that make it mandatory to carry out certain practices. These practices then become fixed costs and are passed on to the consumer. It has already happened in a few cases and may happen more frequently if the problems are believed to be acute enough by society and governments and if consumers will pay the price.

Those of us who work in plant protection feel that our disciplines are important. We often forget that they are at best only supportive of economic realities and proper agronomic, horticultural, and conservation techniques in agriculture. Plant protection is always secondary in the mind of the grower unless key diseases and pests occur that must be controlled virtually every year if production of the crop is to be continued. As Ordish and Dufour (1969) pointed out,

> The farmer himself makes very little distinction between pests and diseases. They are all forces of nature which can cause him loss whether insect, virus, parasitic plant, bacteria, or fungus. For instance, the hop grower in England still uses the world "blight" to describe the hop aphis. Consequently in studying the economics of the control of their troubles, we may have to consider the whole complex in a crop, on a farm, or in a country, rather than any particular disease (or pest).

All that plant protection specialists can do is develop the most economic effective control methods possible in the hope that they will attract growers or applicators to use them. Admittedly, at times we are lucky to be able to develop any control procedure at all, no matter what its cost, but control procedures will not be used if they are so expensive that growers cannot afford them.

Palm (1972) summarized this problem for entomologists.

> An anxious and concerned modern agriculture says in effect to the entomologists, give us your best control recommendations, because we too are committed to the concept of improving the quality of the environment, but

remember that we must compete in the world of today that requires a dependable schedule of pest control that can be used economically and efficiently. . . . Too much experimentation with commercial production cannot be tolerated in our system of agribusiness.

Burges and Hussy (1971) summarized the economic difficulties in developing practical microbial control (biological control) of insects:

Unlike pesticidal chemicals, . . . biological systems are usually applicable only to a few species to localized pest problems. Among microbial insecticides *Bacillus thuringiensis* has already attracted commercial interest in manufacture for profit. Its host spectrum is relatively large, and the list of susceptible pest species in the *Lepidoptera,* and hence commercial potential, has grown apace. By contrast highly specific microbial insecticides may fail to provide a sufficient large and continuous market to be attractive to invest capital and so give a reasonable return. The microbial insecticides, together with microorganisms used for introductions, must depend on governmental or communal backing of one sort or another. Their development and use involves economics at the community level and, therefore, impinges on sociological problems.

No company will develop a selective or narrow host range material (for either biological or chemical control) if there is little possibility that enough of the material will be used to recover the cost of research, development, and marketing. The only alternative, if the material is thought to be of overriding importance, is government or private subsidy. Eventually, of course, government subsidy and/or a law that makes the material mandatory results in higher taxes or higher consumer prices or both.

Chant (1966) presented another point of view concerning the economics of plant protection.

The first and most important research need in the synthesis of a pest management program is not primarily biological at all. It is economic. A clear picture of the complex economics associated with crop production is vital. First, one must know the general economic picture and then . . . determine the margin of profit in which the agriculturalist or forester is operating so that we can calculate how much he can stand to lose to the depredations of pests. Secondly, and against this background, one must determine how much can be afforded for protection against this level of loss. This knowledge defines our problem as entomologists [other disciplines also] and sets the limits on the cost and value of the management programs we can develop.

There have been few careful analyses of the economics of crop protection relative to pest problems. . . . Principles have rarely been developed and limits clearly defined. Consequently, we are not infrequently treated to the absurd situation where more is spent to control a pest than the value of the commodity the pest would destroy, or even worse where a helpful insect is destroyed at considerable cost.

The Dutch elm disease situation has already been mentioned. Walker

(1969) outlined the two principal approaches to the control of this fungus disease, incited by *Ceratostomella ulmi*. The first control measure recommended was the detection and eradication of diseased trees, accompanied by sanitary measures—destruction of the diseased trees and spraying neighboring trees with DDT or methoxychlor to eradicate the beetle vector. The root graft spread of the disease was reduced by application of Vapam solution to the soil between diseased and healthy elms. These practices have decreased the rate of spread of the disease but have not achieved containment and are very costly.

The second approach is the use of systemic fungicides. This approach is now used more generally than the first, but even benomyl (which was mentioned previously and does the best job as a systemic fungicide) is too costly to be feasible. However, such control measures are extremely valuable in protecting the remnants of a species that can be used for research in breeding to develop a highly resistant elm equivalent to the beautiful American elm.

The importance of economics in plant protection is just as great in areas of small farms, in the developing world, and in the tropics as in the technologically advanced societies. Taiwan, for example, no longer an underdeveloped nation, is still characterized by very small landholdings and small farmers. Luh (1971) summarized many years of work and observation in Taiwan in the following statement:

> A successful crop production program cannot depend on technology alone. In addition to the technical aspects of plant breeding, plant protection, plant physiology and the like, other factors also exert a decisive influence on crop production. The most important ones are the market condition, supply and demand, price and consumer's preference and government policies. . . . In 1963 Taiwan farmers were encouraged to grow more bananas of better quality. During that time banana growers could dispose of their produce at fairly attractive prices. Thus improved farming techniques were applied extensively by the banana growers in order to boost their yields. However, this golden age of the banana trade is now a thing of the past owing to the change in the import policy of Japan and also due to the fact that Japanese importers have shifted their regular shipping channels. . . . To promote hog raising in Taiwan, restrictions on the import of feed grains from abroad were lifted by the government in 1968. As a result, production of feed crops such as corn, sorghum and soybeans, which were formerly winter crops, has suffered sharp decreases, because the prices of imported feed grains are considerably lower than those produced locally.

When such situations occur even in countries dominated by small farmers, it is easy to see why plant protection may be relegated to the bottom of the priority list under normal conditions.

In developing countries the agricultural picture usually is dominated by two facts. (1) Large plantation owners and growers, as well as many smaller growers, depend on the economic importance of a single crop. Many countries have economies dominated by a single crop: coffee, tea, coconuts, and the like. Epidemics or major outbreaks of any disease or pest in such crops can be completely disastrous to their economies. Hence, it is extremely important that plant protection procedures, equipment, and supplies be available. (2) Often, procurement and transport of equipment and supplies, training of personnel, application of pesticides, and development of practical local crop protection programs are so complex as to be almost insurmountable. The disastrous and essentially uncontrolled epiphytotics of coffee rust in earlier years are cases in point (Paddock 1967).

Many examples of disastrous plant diseases and pest problems in the tropics could be given, where the problems of control are more than economic. They are associated with the educational level of the populace, adequate transport and shipping, availability of supplies in areas remote from points of manufacture, government inefficiencies and obstruction, and all the attendant hazards and frustrations of commercial operation in the developing tropical world. This reality must be experienced to be understood and believed (Paddock 1967).

The small farmer of the tropics, who is actually the major producer, is usually left completely out of the economic mainstream. Even if plant protection techniques were available and understood, the small farmers of the developing world could not afford them. The average small farmer continues to use whatever local knowledge is available. Fortunately, these techniques, which represent the accumulated empirical knowledge of many generations of growers of a given area, are often relatively effective. It will not be possible for small farmers to improve plant protection until their economic plight is improved. New and better plant protection procedures must be inexpensive and simple. Elaborate or costly procedures, even if available, will not be used in the foreseeable future.

Another economic problem strikes at the heart of effective continuing research programs. Andres and Goeden (1971) mention two projects on biological weed control by insects. The first is the control of *Cordia macrostachya* on the island of Mauritius, and the second is the control of *Opuntia* spp. on the island of Nevis in the West Indies. They are producing annual benefits of 1000 percent and 2000 percent, respectively, on the money invested, a magnificent cost/benefit ratio. Paradoxically, the spectacular control success was the nemesis of the research. It was terminated, the annual cost/benefits were no longer tallied, and the work was essentially forgotten. By contrast, control problems such as those occurring in chemical pesticide research received far less spectacular but still satisfactory annual cost/benefit reminders. The pests kept up their constant pressure, which kept the research well supported by the government. This sad story could be retold a thousand times by research workers who have developed control methods that are inexpensive, practical, and essentially automatic—conspicuous success has meant the curtailment or elimination of the research program.

Readers who desire more information can find most of the problems discussed in this chapter in Sill (1978).

Name for a New Discipline

Although there has been a recent tendency among American entomologists to identify the disciplines in this general field as *pest management,* it is not a worldwide trend and is not accepted by other subdisciplines in the United States as the most desirable name. Through the years the term *pest management* has been associated with the control of arthropod pests that attack people, household products, farm animals, and all pests that bring to mind the pest exterminator. Thus the term does seem to have future validity as it relates to entomology, but it ignores the vast array of abiotic problems that afflict plants.

Lester (1976) made the following cogent plea for the term *integrated crop protection:* "Integrated control must inevitably broaden in scope from control of individual pathogens, pests or weeds toward the concept of the *Integrated Crop Protection* in which protection of a crop from all its major pathogens, pests and weeds will be the aim."

A combined term, *crop protection and pest management,* is often used, but in several disciplines crop protection is more significant than management of a pest population; and in other disciplines, particularly entomology and nematology, the concept of population suppression (or management) to economically acceptable levels is more meaningful.

The term (and concept of) *plant health* has been pushed by a few plant pathologists in the United States but is not accepted by many and does not appear to be used elsewhere (H. Smith 1976).

The name *plant protection* has been adopted by FAO and is being used by International Plant Protection Congresses (such as the one held in the USSR in late 1975 and the one in Washington, D.C., in August 1979) and the new Plant Protection Centers in Asia and elsewhere (jointly sponsored by FAO, UNDP, and the countries involved). In Europe, *plant protection* and *crop protection* are the most dominant descriptive names, and these names are used widely elsewhere, including the United States. The world trend seems to be toward the use of the term *plant protection* as a general designation for all the crop protection and plant pest management disciplines. It seems to be the most accepted and inclusive term in plant-oriented disciplines worldwide.

2

Plant Protection in Other Fields

Quarantines and Introductions

 One area of plant protection has always received a considerable amount of cooperative effort among relevant disciplines—the plant quarantine and plant materials introduction divisions of world governments. The people working in plant pathology, in entomology, in nematology, in weed science, and even with vertebrate pests usually cooperate rather closely in an effort to keep unwanted pests and diseases of all types from being spread from one country to another.

Often these organizations are understaffed and poorly equipped, with personnel inadequately trained and underpaid; consequently, they may labor under great handicaps in their efforts to control the movement of pests and diseases.

Many people have been critical of plant quarantine and plant introduction programs because the programs have not stopped completely the movement of all pests and diseases. We sometimes forget their many successes and concentrate on their occasional failures. Quarantine programs are the first line of defense in plant protection and they should be encouraged in every way possible in every country. Training of personnel involved should be upgraded. We should remember that the support given these programs in many less developed countries has been distressingly meager, and in developed countries it has seldom been adequate enough to achieve a satisfactory job.

There have been some conspicuous successes as well as the well-publicized failures. We can all think of the failures (such as the introduction of the chestnut blight into the United States and the spread of Dutch elm disease across the United States). However, Walker (1969) pointed out that plant quarantine has successfully prohibited the reentry into the United States of the black wart of potato from any of the countries where it occurs; and it has not reached significant levels in the United States since it was

19

originally found in Pennsylvania, Maryland, and West Virginia coal-country garden plots. The quarantine service has successfully kept tubers from being sold outside the areas in Pennsylvania, West Virginia, and Maryland where the wart was established and perhaps not yet completely eliminated (Walker 1969).

Crafts and Robbins (1962) emphasized the importance of regulatory control of seeds, plant parts, and seed certification programs to control weeds, diseases, nematodes, and insects and emphasized that these programs must be coordinated. Diseases and pests are spread by soil and plant tissues, machinery, reusable containers, animal manure, hay and forage crops, various animals, and moving water. Any of these methods can be instrumental in moving pests and propagules across state and country boundaries. Consequently, quarantine regulations and certification programs for movement of plant materials are extremely significant (NAS 1968b).

Van Gundy (1972) has emphasized that by far the most satisfactory control program for all diseases and pests is the prevention of their introduction into an area where they do not exist. He gave two examples of situations in the U.S. Pacific northwest in which little if any forethought was given to controlling their spread into new agricultural areas. Currently several million acres of virgin land are being put into production in the Pacific northwest, but very little effort has been given to controlling the introduction of soil-borne pathogens and pests via the irrigation water. Also, it has been shown that in the Columbia River basin much downstream land has been infested by many kinds of plant parasitic nematodes introduced through reuse of high quality irrigation water.

Van Gundy (1972) particularly emphasized the importance of plant quarantine in the control of nematodes. Even when relatively ineffective, such measures reduce the number of introductions and the rate of spread. For example, in 1970 inspectors in the United States intercepted some 47,000 pests, many of which were plant parasitic nematodes.

Quarantines are particularly important in weed control (NAS 1968c). The movement of seeds, all planting stock, grain, hay, straw, and manure needs to be closely monitored. These are all very important in the spread of insects, plant diseases, and nematodes as well as weed seeds and this work can best be done when the programs of the separate disciplines are coordinated completely.

There is an important weed introduction problem in world markets now because of the movement of feed grains and forage. This movement should be carefully controlled by plant quarantine programs and often has not been (NAS 1968c). State and federal laws and regulations against the importation or movement of noxious weeds or propagation parts are particularly lax in the United States and need to be updated and revised (Shaw 1973, 1974a).

A great deal of effort has been put into regulations associated with registration and safe use of herbicides but little thought has gone into preventive weed control regulations associated with control of the movement of seeds, soil, hay, straw, manure, feed grains, sod, livestock, farm equipment, etc. Actually, the Federal Seed Act and state seed laws permit rather high tolerances for weed seeds in stored grain and crop seeds. About one-third of the states have no legal limit on weed seed levels in planting seed stocks. Most states that have regulations permit 1–4 percent weed seed by weight in planting seed stocks, a huge quantity of potential weed seed. A completely revised federal noxious weed law is needed and then a complete revision and/or amendment of the Federal Seed Act and the state seed laws will be required. As McNew (1972) has pointed out,

> Before we design strategies for the future, we should consider errors of the past. We have been guilty of introducting susceptible plant varieties into an established population of pests. . . . If it [a variety] has unique horticultural attributes as a crop or has other desirable features, it may be given special care and cultivated at great expense.

A more serious economic problem exists when a parasite or pest is introduced into an established system where the climate favors its multiplication. There are many such examples that justify every effort of quarantine services (McNew 1972).

Better quarantine programs need to be developed and coordinated at the international level. The programs need to include all possible pests and diseases, and international pest and disease problems need to be considered. This might be done as an extension of present FAO programs in plant protection.

The discussion concerning quarantine programs is applicable to all national and international programs associated with the commercial movement of plant materials and breeding stock. All plants need to be screened with special care for any possible pests and diseases before entry is allowed into countries that do not have the particular plants or breeding material. Such plant introductions need to be quarantined, isolated, and observed for an appropriate time. In many countries such programs are either absent or funded and staffed inadequately.

In the United States the Plant Introduction Service with its regional centers has made a fine start in systematic collection and storage of germ plasm (Day 1972). It is particularly significant to preserve these stocks and carefully screen and certify them prior to movement within countries or abroad.

Seed and Nursery Stock

One of the most important cooperative ventures in plant protection is seed, plant, and nursery stock certification. Seed and nursery stock should be pure genetically (as pure as possible) and free of weed seed, plant disease, insect pests, nematode galls, and live nematodes (NAS 1968c). Possibly more control can be accomplished by seed certification and carefully controlled, certified planting and nursery stock than by any other single method.

New mechanical seed cleaning methods are not used as widely as they should be. They can remove nematode-infested wheat kernels (cockles) or any other plant parasitic nematode galls. They can also remove small particles of plant debris infected with stem nematodes, various insects, and weed seeds. Seed cleaning often is neglected in the United States but should be legally required everywhere. It is a valuable method of exclusion of various plant pests and diseases (NAS 1968b).

Although it is often difficult to achieve pest-free or pathogen-free planting stock, it is not impossible. The quotation following discusses some methods (NAS 1968a):

> It is essential that pathogen free planting stock be used if effective disease control is to be obtained. Use of arid areas or areas where temperatures are unfavorable for vectors are helpful in producing clean seeds. Growth of seed in areas which do not have crop diseases is also common. It is necessary in such situations to watch the use of overhead irrigation which tends to change the micro-climate and encourage some diseases which normally would not be present in significant amounts. Pathogen free greenhouses or isolated areas also can be used in seed production. Where alternate hosts are involved, as with white pine blister rust or cedar apple rust, isolation may be accomplished by eradicating the alternate host. The use of heat therapy is especially helpful in producing clean seed on both seeds and planting stock (either hot water or steam air mixtures). Many plant pathogens can be eliminated from seed by the simple process of aging the seed for two years or sometimes more. Seed infestation may also be avoided by harvesting the seed early to avoid pathogens.

As indicated above, seeds completely free of disease organisms are often grown far away from commercial plantings in arid climates using only furrow irrigation. By this means any risk of insect transmission of plant pathogens is curtailed, and the furrow irrigation discourages the development of water-splashed organisms. Certified seed crops of many vegetables, such as potatoes, cucurbits, and beans, are produced in this way (Univ. Calif. 1972c).

Clean, disease-free, and pest-free vegetatively propagated plants are important. Most people are familiar with the magnificent job the Dutch seed and bulb industry does in this regard. Most countries do not do as well. The vegetative propagation of plants is the means of spread of a great many plant viruses and other diseases by way of bulbs, corms, buds, tubers, roots, and the like. All tree fruits, sweet potatoes, strawberries, and many true seeds can carry viruses. Satisfactory control procedures need to be developed cooperatively, using the best agronomic and horticultural techniques, for the development and distribution of the cleanest possible high quality planting stock and seeds (NAS 1968*a*). Apple emphasized the importance of vegetatively clean potato plants because of the number of potato viruses and other potato diseases spread by vegetative propagation. Since many other important food crops are propagated vegetatively, preventive disease and pest control should be carried out to maintain disease- and pest-free genotypes (Apple 1972).

Many growers and nursery workers still ignore the need for clean, disease-free, and pest-free planting stock. Why are these inexpensive (and often best) control measures for nematodes (and other pests and diseases) frequently not used or required? "Cost of these practices is small, so it's puzzling that so many growers still plant infested stock. Nematode infested nursery planting stock is still shipped all over the world" (NAS 1968*b*).

Human lethargy and inertia account for much of the puzzle, but perhaps the following statement also gives at least part of the answer (Univ. Calif. 1972*b*):

> Treatment of plant and plant parts such as bulbs, corms, rhizomes and rootings is difficult because the tolerance of the plant material to treatment is often very close to the level necessary to kill the nematodes. Hot water treatments under very carefully controlled conditions have been developed for some plant materials. Thus far, chemical dips have shown an insufficient level of control for most purposes:

This brings up an important need in research. Better methods of treatment of planting stocks for the control of nematodes and other pests and diseases should be developed. This approach where applicable is one of the best, and ultimately the least expensive, methods of control. Considerable effort has been directed toward the discovery of chemicals that would control plant parasitic nematodes, particularly in a dip for bare-rooted nursery stock—this would eliminate the need for high temperatures.

Three materials have been reasonably effective thus far: Zinophos, Dasanit, and SD4965 (NAS 1968*b*). Probably it would be impossible to find a material that is equally effective on all plants and equally toxic to every stage and all species of plant parasitic nematodes. Penetration of plant tissues is different in roots, bulbs, corms, and rhizomes; and it is necessary to destroy the nematodes essentially without injury to the plant. So far the best materials are organophosphates or carbamates, which seem to be taken up rather readily by plant tissues in quantities sufficient to be nematicidal. These materials also may have important possibilities as both fungicides and insecticides. Thus far, no good seed treatment for true seeds is available for nematode control (NAS 1968*b*).

Seed treatment for insects, although not as common as routine fungicidal seed treatment for many plant diseases, has been developed for several insect situations and has achieved satisfactory control. For example, thrips, aphids, and spider mites have been controlled adequately in cotton by seed treatment. Two systemic chemicals that have given good results are Thimet and Bayer 19639. These insecticides move into the sap stream and are translocated in the cotton plant, killing the insects that feed on the plants (USDA 1957).

Seed treatment tests in 13 cotton-producing states on several thousand acres of cotton were conducted; thrips, aphids, and spider mites were successfully controlled from 4 to 6 weeks after plant emergence. For a short time there was reasonable control also of cutworms, flea beetles, leaf miners, darkling beetles, cotton leaf perforators, brown cotton leafworms, and false wireworm adults. An important economic (and perhaps environmental) bonus of insect seed treatment was the elimination of two to four sprays that usually have been applied during the growing season. Although seed treatment is not routinely used against insects, systemic seed treatment is being tried against insects in citrus fruits, onion sets, snap and lima beans, cabbage, alfalfa, and a few other crops.

This particular area needs much more research and may develop into a very effective method of insect control. Of particular significance is the fact that seed treatment tends to reduce the necessity of insecticidal sprays during the growing period (USDA 1957); however, some seed treatments may kill beneficial as well as pest insects.

The disciplines of plant protection plus the key disciplines of agronomy and horticulture should cooperate to develop better methods for producing cleaner, higher quality certified seed and nursery stock. Cooperative efforts are bound to be more effective in the long run than uncoordinated independent individual efforts.

Storage, Shipping, and Marketing

Losses in food throughout the world are very great during storage, shipping, and marketing. Experts believe that at least half the earth's food supply is eaten or destroyed by diseases, insects, rodents, birds, and other pests during storage and shipment. Control of even part of these losses might be the quickest and least expensive way of greatly increasing the world food supply (Brady 1974). Better control of storage diseases and pests in large and small granaries throughout the world could increase the edible supply of food grains immediately by 25 percent without any change in present productivity in agriculture. In India total losses of 70 percent are not uncommon.

Various researchers estimate that as much as 50 percent of all food in the tropics is lost during storage, shipping, and marketing, particularly during wet or very humid periods. Many think the losses are even greater, and, when one considers the world shortage of food, tragic (Brady 1974).

It is estimated that six rats consume or destroy enough grain to feed one person. They also store reserves, often 10 pounds or more, in a single burrow. Insects and microorganisms reduce the nutritional quality of the grain on which they feed as well as its quantity, as they preferentially consume the protein-carrying portions (Brady 1974). Many losses are easy to control by known methods, and most can best be controlled by some sort of coordinated effort between plant protection disciplines.

Bunting (1972) felt the need for greater concentration on the control of storage losses:

> A third group of pests require special mention, because they cause such extensive, discouraging and unnecessary losses: the storage pests of plant and animal products, principally insects, fungi, and small mammals. The control of these as part of improved post-harvest technology is perhaps the most immediately rewarding aspect of pest regulation in developing countries.

Anyone who has lived and worked in agriculture in any of the countries of the developing world can agree wholeheartedly with Bunting's analysis.

Plant protection disciplines can be combined in tackling storage and marketing problems. The product is usually confined and often is in a container designed to protect it from various diseases and pests. In small grains where bulk storage and handling is the rule it is rather easy to combine entomological and fungicidal control measures, particularly any that are associated with fumigation, and this often has been done.

If no bulk storage is available, as in most of the developing world, protection is a much greater problem. When not piled in a corner, most small grains are sacked, usually in jute bags. They could be fumigated, but usually fumigation facilities are not available. During the additional handling, shipping, and marketing processes in the tropics, there are many opportunities for reinfestation by insect pests and fungus spores. The fungi normally are not a problem during the dry season but are very destructive during the wet season.

Cold storage is not available in a great deal of the developing world because of the lack of or undependable electric current. Cold storage trucks and railway cars are scarce or nonexistent. The canning industry has not been developed to a point where people accept canned food readily. Therefore the only methods of food preservation are the old standbys of drying, salting, pickling, and the like.

In the developing world it is difficult to avoid bruising fruits and vegetables during shipping and marketing because of the shipping methods—bumpy roads; old, overloaded trucks and vehicles; hot and often

humid weather, and many other problems that attend the shipping of
perishable products. These problems have been for the most part successfully circumvented in the developed countries. Even so, there is still much
loss (perhaps 25 percent), often due to carelessness, ignorance, inertia, and
human stubbornness.

Each crop has different requirements for the control of storage and
marketing diseases and pests. The primary inoculum (in the case of diseases)
or the pest itself (in the case of insects and other pests) usually is on the crop
at the time of harvesting, although occasionally there is contamination during harvesting, packaging, storage, and shipping.

The most important mechanism for control of these problems is the
standardization of the storage and shipping environment (Walker 1969).
This means control of temperature (the avoidance of freezing as well as excessive heat), air movement, bruising, moisture, and particularly humidity.
Transit should be speedy and vibration minimal to avoid bruising. All of
these are combined with fumigation and spraying when possible, necessary,
and safe.

A few examples will indicate the complexity of some of these problems.
The control of fruit rots in storage and transit by the use of impregnated
wrappers and fungicide washes has solved many of the *Penicillium* or blue
mold problems of citrus and other fruits (Walker 1969). Blue mold is controlled in packinghouses by use of a 10 percent solution of borax held at
49°C as a fruit wash. Another practice, which has been even more helpful in
the citrus industry, is the use of fruit wrappers impregnated with diphenyl.
In Colorado *Rhizopus* rot of peaches is controlled by wrapping the fruit in
paper impregnated with botran. A good control for *Thielaviopsis paradoxa,*
black rot of pineapple, has been developed in Australia and the United
States—benzoic acid is applied to the cut stalk of the pineapple fruit at the
time of harvest or prior to shipping.

Rhizopus soft rot of sweet potato has been very difficult to control,
and a classic case of coordinated multiple control methods has been
developed for this disease. It begins with excellent sanitation of the storage
rooms and a complete removal of debris; disinfestation; and disinfection of
the walls, the floors, and the containers. Extreme care in handling avoids
bruises. The temperature of the storehouse is kept at 28°-32°C for 2 weeks
to encourage corking off and sealing of wounds. The temperature is then
lowered to a level that will reduce the growth of decay fungi, particularly
Rhizopus stolonifer. The storage temperatures used are slightly above
5°C—lower temperatures tend to encourage the development of non-
parasitic internal necrosis. These storage methods control rather well not
only the *Rhizopus* soft rot of sweet potato but also most other fungus
pathogens. The storage at or slightly above 5°C essentially eliminates most
biological activity in any insect pests or other pests present (Walker 1969).

Specific methods to improve grain storage facilities on farms and in villages in the developing world, where up to 90 percent of grain (in India) is stored in unprotected bags or heaped in a corner, would save vast quantities for human consumption. Some practical suggested improvements are (Brady 1974):

1. Use of sealed clay pots.
2. Burying the grain in hollow trees.
3. Use of cribs elevated from the ground with shields on the legs to keep rats out.
4. Use of hermetically sealed rubber bins. The stored grain and insects in it use all the oxygen, killing the insects and inhibiting fungus and microbial growth.
5. Pumping cool, dry air into storage bins at night and during cooler periods. This depresses insect activity, preventing or minimizing reproduction, and discourages the growth and build-up of microorganisms.
6. Storage in plastic waterproof bags under water.
7. Storage in cool, dry mines in Japan and elsewhere.
8. Partially replacing the air in storage bins with inert gases to decrease the oxygen necessary for pests and diseases.
9. Better drying of grain before storage and sealing of storage bin leaks to suppress growth.
10. Use of insect attractants in baited traps—shows promise in research but is not yet in general use.
11. Use of Malathion instead of DDT in India for stored grain treatment (Malathion is not stored in human body fat, is relatively nontoxic to warm-blooded animals, and is quickly broken down in the environment).

Fumigants and insecticides are used effectively in technologically advanced countries, but their cost and the technology prohibit their use in much of the developing world.

The United States has initiated a new approach. In 1979, extension pest management programs in Indiana, Iowa, and Kentucky used trained observers to monitor temperature, humidity, insects, and molds in grain storage facilities on farms. Farmers were then advised periodically to change storage facilities, sell, feed the crop, or treat the grain, if needed (J. M. Good 1979, pers. commun.).

The problems are legion but mostly solvable with known methods, and the time may be short. Plant protection disciplines have cooperated in the past in the areas of storage, shipping, and marketing, and their cooperation should be even more effective in the future.

3

Other Factors in Plant Protection

Economic Thresholds

 Entomologists in recent years have emphasized the importance of economic thresholds as they apply to the control of economically important arthropods. This concept is realistic for entomologists and often for those who work with vertebrate pests and nematodes, but it has not yet been particularly useful to plant pathologists or weed scientists. It has been much easier to quantify the economic threshold of a particular insect in entomology than, for example, in plant pathology, where spore or inoculum numbers may bear little relationship to disease incidence. Apple (1974) summarized this situation:

> Pest management principles cannot be applied without economic thresholds to guide in the deployment of optional management tactics. The development of economic thresholds requires biomathematical and economic expertise in the pest management team. The threshold concept has been applied widely to insects and to some extent to nematodes but has not yet been applied widely to disease organisms.

The economic threshold is more difficult to utilize practically than many entomologists would like to admit. This is emphasized by Chant (1966):

> It is difficult to determine the economic thresholds of most pests on most crops. To do so requires an ability to predict the probable consequences of continued increases in populations if controls are not exerted, in relation to the subtleties of injury levels. That is usually beyond our competence at present. . . . The major difficulty in determining the factors in an ecosystem that regulates pest populations, or has the potential to do so, is that of gathering the complex data required and analyzing them to extract the information required. One particularly useful tool is now available for this, the life table. It is difficult to believe that satisfactory control systems can be developed without understanding the dynamics of the pests of major concern.

Much has been done in the area of economic thresholds since Chant. We now measure percent defoliation of chewing insects in soybeans and count rootworm adults during the oviposition period in corn to determine whether larval infestation the following year will be at or above economic thresholds. There also are workable thresholds for alfalfa insects including the alfalfa weevil and the potato leafhopper. In high value crops such as vegetables, control measures are not used if specific insects are absent but are used if other specific insects are present. Insects in crops such as cotton and rice have measurable population and damage levels that determine controls used. These approaches represent a great advancement over procedures used in the past (B. D. Blair 1979, pers. commun.).

Monitoring

To develop a realistic economic threshold a constant monitoring of populations is required and then control decisions must be made. This is relatively easy to achieve with many insects and other arthropods.

Huffaker (1974) reported that in Michigan a satisfactory technique for the biological monitoring of the codling moth was based on the use of pheromone traps by which the population levels of the pests were estimated. This is also done with mite populations where a semiautomated system for surveying plant-feeding mite populations and their predators is being developed. In soybeans he noted that it should now be possible to develop practical recommendations for all varieties and for most growing conditions in Florida, since the indiscriminate use of insecticides previously practiced can be replaced gradually with practical management programs based on known damage levels of various soybean insects.

Light traps are now being used to predict when field scouting should occur. Ohio, Kentucky, and Indiana have initiated a program where light trap data for eight species is recorded daily on a central computer. This information is available to pest management personnel. In Ohio heat units, day degrees, etc., are used to predict certain insect life cycle events such as hatching, development stages, flight patterns, and oviposition with the alfalfa weevil, European corn borer, black cutworm, and northern and western cutworms (B. D. Blair 1979, pers. commun.).

The monitoring problem in plant pathology is very difficult and quite different from that in entomology or even nematology. It is summarized below (NAS 1968*a*):

> Since inoculum has the potential to produce disease this potential is greatest when inoculum is abundant, when it is at the infection court, when many susceptible hosts are present and when all circumstances favor infection. But increase in the instance of disease in a population is not necessarily proportional to an increase in inoculum even when climate favors disease. For exam-

ple, in a field containing 10,000 potato plants, if 9,000 are already infected with late blight, doubling of a stated number of spores of *Phytophthora infestans* will infect fewer healthy plants than when only 1,000 are already infected. Conversely, a decrease in the amount of inoculum does not produce a proportional decrease in the number of new infections.

When the floor of an apple orchard is sprayed with a fungicide more than half of the spores of *Venturia inaequalis* may be killed but the number of young apple leaves that subsequently become infected with apple scab may be only moderately decreased. The surviving inoculum may be more than adequate to cause an outbreak. This principle applies as well in the control of soil-borne pathogens by fumigation, of virus diseases by roguing infected plants and control of plant diseases by quarantines.

The increase of inoculum from the beginning of the growing season until a few plants are diseased is usually greater than the increase from this level until all plants are diseased. When inoculum increases significantly in a field of predominantly healthy plants, the danger of an epidemic of an explosive nature increases. The relation of inoculum to disease is better understood for some organisms than for others (the air-borne organisms more than soil-borne) but actually we know little about all of this. We must learn for each major disease how much of a reservoir of inoculum is needed to start an outbreak of a given disease under certain specified conditions.

Much can also be learned from aerobiological studies of the rate, directions and distance of transport of different types of inoculum and vectors into and through the upper air and of the subsequent deposition as well as the probability of establishment and spread of disease after fallout of inoculum or vectors. Here joint efforts between pathologists and meteorologists should delve deeper into the relationship between synoptic weather and weather at the ground level as a basis for more accurate and speedier prediction of disease. Future epidemiological research should be directed toward establishing a link between the ground level climatic requirements of plant diseases that have epidemic potential and the typical patterns portraying such requirements in a synoptic weather chart. For example, hourly dew points associated with large scale synoptic patterns have recently been used successfully in forecasting lima bean downy mildew, *Phytophthora phaseoli*. It would be useful to know more about the relation of the amount of inoculum to the amount of infection and the amount of infection to the extent of damage. This information would be valuable in assessing the effectiveness of disease forcasting and the success of control measures.

    This quotation shows the difficulties experienced by plant pathologists who attempt to develop a disease monitoring and forecasting system based on realistic, meaningful concepts. Only two crop disease forecasting programs of practical importance are now in use in the United States and Europe. They are associated with the apple scab disease, incited by *Venturia inaequalis,* and the late blight of potato, incited by *Phytophthora infestans.* These programs have been useful in areas where the environment favors the development of these diseases each year. New York State, in particular, has developed a system for predicting when controls need to be applied for apple scab.

Epidemiology

In plant pathology much more research in epidemiology is needed.

> Epidemiology is the study of the development and spread of the pathogens and the numerous factors affecting spread. Among the important factors are amount and distribution of primary inoculum, time required for infection, reproductive capacity of the pathogen, distance and means of dissemination of inoculum, reaction of the host, spatial distribution of the host, vector abundance, motility and distribution and especially the pervasive influence of the weather and climate on pathogen and host and the relations between them. [NAS 1968*a*]

Not all inoculum has the potential for epiphytotic development. The production of inoculum often occurs at a rate sufficient only to maintain infections at a fairly low but more or less constant level. Even if tremendous quantities of inoculum are present and weather conditions appear favorable, often no epiphytotic development occurs. As Hooker (1974) pointed out:

> Epidemics develop when three factors are favorable and occur together. These factors, often referred to as the disease triangle, are the host, the pathogen (usually a parasitic microorganism) and the weather (environment). There must be an abundance of susceptible host plants, the pathogen must be present in a virulent and aggressive form and weather conditions must be conducive to the rapid multiplication and spread of the pathogens.

As Hooker emphasized, all these factors were exactly right during the development of the southern corn blight disease in the U.S. Corn Belt in 1970. Corn rust and the northern leaf blight remained at low levels during the same period, primarily because of the availability of resistant plants developed by plant pathologists and plant breeders. This is a dramatic example of how crucial host resistance is in controlling epiphytotics.

Forecasting Outbreaks

The importance of microclimatic aspects of the environment cannot be overemphasized in the epidemiology of plant disease. Here meteorology and epidemiology merge and both macro- and microclimatological data are essential. Adequate meteorological data are seldom available. Prediction models based on both macro- and micrometeorological data need to be developed. When such data become available it will be possible to apply diffusion theory and explain much of the dispersal phenomena in progress (Waggoner 1965).

Macro- and micrometeorological factors may also be of prime importance in the relative abundance of injurious insect species during a given year. These weather factors usually cannot be influenced but a knowledge of them is important.

Some examples from entomology are given by Metcalf et al. (1951):

> (1) A winter period of very low temperature with no snow will kill most of the eggs of the gypsy moth. (2) Long periods of hot dry weather during the summer will prevent the apple maggot from ever becoming a very serious pest in areas where such weather is a rule. (3) Heavy rains during the time when the eggs of the chinch bug are hatching will often terminate a period of several years of serious destruction by this insect. (4) In Illinois during 20 years (approximately 1931-1951) fruit growers have been informed about 14 days in advance of the time when the eggs of the codling moth will start hatching. Field checks have shown that the predictions have usually been accurate to within 24 hours and that there has never been an error of more than 3 days.

Hence it is now possible to warn growers of threatening outbreaks of certain species of insects in time to apply control measures. It is apparent that accurate prediction services would be very important for both insects and diseases and would save millions of dollars each year.

Weather forecasts are crucial to accurate plant disease forecasting, and the inadequacies of weather forecasts and disease forecasting have been apparent to all who have worked with epidemiology problems. Van der Plank (1972) summarized this problem for plant pathologists and it is also true in other disciplines:

> Because weather forecasts have been inadequate, disease forecasts based on weather have generally been based on past weather. That is, disease is forecasted after a favorable weather period. With better weather forecasts disease will be forecast on weather to come. When that happens, disease forecasting will rank high in the scale of priority in ecosystems analysis.

Austin-Bourke (1970) emphasized the need for working models that contain essential relationships between weather and plant disease as well as other factors, e.g., tillage, plant growth, weeds, insects, and nematodes. Such models are not yet available in plant pathology. When good accurate disease prediction services become available, it will be possible to limit the need for chemicals to achieve adequate control. This concept is summarized also by Van der Plank (1972):

> When economic factors severely limit the number of applications of a fungicide or other chemical that can profitably be given in a season, the ap-

plications must be properly timed. If the chemical is applied too early, it may be wasted; if too late the damage may already have been done. Good timing depends on good forecasting, good knowledge of the disease progress curve, of how an application of the chemical will alter that curve and how an alteration of the curve will reduce loss from disease.

This point of view is pertinent also for insects and nematodes. The key problem of proper timing is closely related to uncontrolled weather factors that control populations. If the various parameters involved are known, it is often possible to utilize chemical control methods much more economically and realistically than in the past.

Huffaker (1974) has emphasized the importance of an on-line environmental monitoring program for certain insects at Michigan State University. Four major sites and 50 standard weather substations were involved. A national oceanic and atmospheric administration network provided daily information from 26 stations.

The American Phytopathological Society initiated a Plant Disease Detection committee in 1973 and now regional or national disease monitoring programs are under way in soybeans, maize, and wheat (Young et al. 1978). This enlarged effort undoubtedly will continue.

A national system of plant disease and pest forecasting and monitoring has been developed in Hungary. Some 100 pests and diseases are monitored and forecasts are released nationwide during the growing season. It is felt to be a vital factor in the development of integrated pest management in the country (Benedek 1979). Several other small countries have initiated similar programs.

Forecast Service for Rice Diseases and Insect Pests—Taiwan

The complexity of epidemiology as it relates to weather has tended to keep people from moving in the direction of disease and insect forecasting services even in technologically advanced countries. In most developing countries little has been done. A large and quite sophisticated program attempting to forecast rice diseases and insect pests has been developed in Taiwan and a similar program has been functioning for some time in Japan. The Taiwan program, as reported by Ren-jong Chiu, is quite effective even though the predictions concerning insect pests and rice plant diseases are not completely accurate. This program is significant because Taiwan is characterized by small farmers and small landholdings. A description of the program follows in its entirety (Chiu 1974, pers. commun.).

The network first took its present form in 1966 (in Taiwan) under a Joint Commission on Rural Reconstruction financed program. In the organizational aspect it involves the PDAF, functioning as the main station (or the headquarters for the service), the seven DAIS's functioning as substations and some observation posts (or check posts) at selected townships throughout the island. At both the main station and the substations, one specialist each, usually in pathology or entomology, is assigned as his main work relating to the forecast service. He is assisted by one or more persons with agricultural vocational school training. Upon implementing the service, recruitment was made of 50 agricultural vocational high school graduates to work full time under the program. Except 7 who are attached to the DAIS's, the remaining 43 are stationed at 43 different places throughout the island. These 50 men are serving as check post observers [for their distribution see Table 3.1].

At each check post an experiment field is contracted from the farmer each season in which a light trap is installed for daily collection of pest insects. Counts are obtained with such major insects as rice borers, green rice leaf hoppers and brown rice plant hoppers. Catching of these is also made at regular (5 day) intervals from ordinary farmers' fields by means of a power catcher. To determine the intensity of air borne (rice) Blast spores a glass slide

Table 3.1. Location of Fifty Men Serving as Checkpost Observers in Taiwan

Substation to Supervise	Hsien/City	Rice acreage* (ha)	Number of Observers Assigned
Taipei DAIS	Taipei City	6,803	1
	Yangmingshan		1
	Taipei Hsien	38,421	5
	Ilan	40,891	2
	Keelung	672	1
Hsinchu DAIS	Taoyuan	82,692	2
	Hsinchu	36,635	2
	Miaoli	37,226	2
Taichung DAIS	Taichung City	12,055	1
	Taichung Hsien	56,724	3
	Changhua	105,993	4
	Nantou	27,328	2
Tainan DAIS	Yunlin	74,747	3
	Chiayi	47,687	3
	Tainan City	3,603	1
	Tainan Hsien	51,249	5
Kaohsiung DAIS	Kaohsiung City	6,135	1
	Kaohsiung Hsien	39,632	4
	Pingtung	76,737	4
Taitung DAIS	Taitung	19,495	2
Hualien DAIS	Hualien	21,867	2

*According to the 1969 statistics.

is exposed daily in the experimental field and brought to the DAIS where microscopic examination is made. The check posts are not equipped with weather recording instruments but weather records are provided to the observers from a weather recording setup nearby for irrigation and other purposes.

One of the more important activities for these 50 check post observers is to conduct field inspections in their respective areas for early detection of any destructive diseases and insects. All information gathered by the check post observers is referred back to DAIS for compilation and analysis. Each check post observer is provided with a motorcycle as a convenient means of transportation. To help the observers in early detection of major diseases and insects in the field, a certain number of rice growers are subsidized for making field inspection, with their findings reported to the check post observers.

At the substations, besides taking the various data as is done at the check posts, some ecological studies on the diseases and insects are made in line with the forecast work. For example, dry seed beds are set up at the Taichung DAIS to determine the level of Blast incidence as affected by the seasons. At both the Taichung and Tainan Stations, laboratory rearing of borers is conducted to determine the time of emergence for these major insect pests. However, the main responsibilities of these substations have been evaluating and analyzing information and data obtained from the check posts and when necessary issuing warnings to townships, cooperative pest control teams and farmers. There are two different warnings which may be issued according to the field's situation. Attentive warning is intended to call attention to the rice growers early detection of certain diseases or insects. Outbreak warning is intended to call for action by the farmers or township extension workers responsible for pest control field programs. General information of province wide interests is compiled and released by the PDAF. In addition the PDAF also sponsors various kinds of training classes for forecast workers at different levels.

One major event relating to the forecast service took place in 1968 when regular positions were created under PDAF for those 50 check post observers who had been thus far employed as temporary employees under the JCRR-financed program. With this development, the forecast service has gained a permanent status at least in its organizational aspect.

It should be understood that the service established for forecasting rice diseases and insects in Taiwan is not comparable to that for potato late blight in some European countries and in the United States. It is patterned after what has long been adopted in Japan and functions like it. The significance of such service lies in the fact that field inspection by 50 check post observers and subsidized farmers makes early detection of certain diseases and insects possible and that through direct contacts these observers assist in the carrying out of pest control field programs, the cooperative pest control program, for instance. Although the substations issue outbreak warnings as weather data and field evidence call for such issuance, no attempts have been made to determine the degree of precision.

The ability to forecast a disease or insect incidence for a major crop can be of great importance if effective and economical control is to be obtained. This is especially so when the trend becomes evident toward using pesticides of greater safety and with a residual effect lasting shorter. In order to develop such an ability some fundamental studies are needed. A sound basis for predicting the level of disease and insect incidence can be established only after acquiring a full knowledge of the ecology of the diseases and insects concerned. Apparently such knowledge does not exist for any major rice diseases and insects in Taiwan. Accurate predictions and forecasts have become more difficult because of the much divided paddy fields to which different varieties are planted at different dates. Therefore, a meaningful forecast with any precision will await not only a full knowledge of disease or insect ecology but also uniformity in planting time as well as in varieties planted. This will not be obtainable in the foreseeable future.

The Taiwan illustration (using a Japanese model) shows that it is possible to develop a relatively practical disease and insect forecasting service even when needed data are not all available and predictions are not completely accurate. More such programs should be developed. We cannot wait for all the biological, ecological, and epidemiological data before acting; even with partial knowledge, it is possible to have a useful program. It is important to indicate the relative level of accuracy of predictions when known. When not known, we must be the first to admit ignorance. It makes sense to develop such forecasting services as cooperative ventures among all the subdisciplines of plant protection. Any other partial approach fails to face the problem of the whole situation in a grower's field, where control must occur.

Life Cycles

Of importance in all epidemiological and economic threshold analyses is knowledge of the life cycles and total bionomic picture of pests, predators, parasites, and pathogens. Even in weed control it is important to know the life cycle of each specific weed. Life cycle information is often essential for logical and economic control procedures. One constantly seeks to discover and attack the weak point in the life cycle to achieve most efficient control. Research is needed in all disciplines of this general field. Initial research must be done by specialists in each of the subdisciplines who are well acquainted with the particular organisms they are studying. It is very time consuming, often expensive, and often difficult to fund.

In plant pathology, after correct diagnosis of a disease, it is necessary to know the key characteristics of a fungus pathogen to determine the proper approach to its control (NAS 1968a). Different life cycles give different fungus pathogens varying requirements for infection, different methods of entrance into the plant, and different techniques of survival.

Powdery mildew of bean in the field can be controlled easily by the application of sulfur, but sulfur would have no appreciable effect on *Ascochyta* blight. A fungicidal spray of tomato would be worthless in controlling foliage blight, caused by root rots. If the relative humidity is kept below 95 percent, the downy mildew of rose is easy to control in the greenhouse, but *Verticillium* wilt or *Armillaria* root rot of rose would not be affected in their development (NAS 1968*a*). These control procedures are related specifically to the innate nature of a specific pathogen and its requirements for survival, growth, and reproduction.

Ecology and the Agroecosystem

Agriculturalists have traditionally been reasonably good ecologists, but professionals in the agricultural disciplines have had little or no formal training in classical ecology. This oversight is now being rectified; courses in ecology are being introduced as a basic part of agricultural training. Certainly anyone studying life cycles, the bionomics of an insect species, or the epidemiological characteristics of a plant disease is involved in agricultural ecology. However, in the past, people involved in such work usually did not consider it from the standpoint of its overall effect on a given environment.

Only recently have the environmental concerns of the public in technologically advanced countries caused agriculturalists and ecologists to focus on what is happening to the environment as a result of agricultural activities. As Bunting (1972) pointed out, "Much classical and academic ecology traditionally excludes man except perhaps as a regrettable external source of nuisance, disturbance or destruction, but we cannot exclude our own species when we consider the ecology of agriculture." We must combine traditional ecology with new considerations in agriculture and technology that relate ecology more closely to our practices as a dominant species. The ecology of agriculture is an important subject for research.

Perhaps we cannot blame agriculturalists of the past too much for their failure to analyze the agroecosystems more completely. Van der Plank (1972) stresses the difficulties inherent in ecosystems analysis:

> Progress in ecosystems analysis is closely linked with progress in other sciences. An obvious link is with weather forecasting. As weather forecasting improves, interest in disease forecasting will increase and with this interest will come the basic knowledge needed for systems of forecasting. Progress in ecosystems analysis is also closely linked with the progress of designing hardware such as computers and automatic recorders for a variety of purposes. Progress here is swift and much of it will rub off on ecosystems analysis.

People in agriculture formerly were not only naive concerning ecosystems and ecosystems analysis but also lacked training in several of the other disciplines necessary for a rational approach. Van der Plank (1972) discusses this problem as related to teaching and research patterns of the past.

> Ecosystems analysis (embracing the epidemiology of plant pathogens and the population dynamics of insects) has been a "Cinderella" in many departments of plant pathology and entomology. An imbalance between chemistry and mathematics as basic sciences in these departments may have helped make it so. Basic research is needed. For too long in some institutions basic research has been interpreted as research not inspired by farmer's need and without foreseeable application to agriculture.

The day when we can ignore the effects of our research and of agricultural activities on the environment is over. This means that several new disciplines are being introduced into the curricula in agricultural sciences, particularly in plant protection disciplines. These new disciplines include ecology, computer science, related mathematics, and systems analysis.

Before one can begin agroecosystems analyses one must understand the basic nature of the agroecosystem as it relates to a specific plant disease, insect, nematode, or other pest. This point is made for plant disease research by Van der Plank (1972):

> The general ecosystem of plant disease is a triangle. There are host plants (wheat, rice and so forth), there are pathogens (fungi, bacteria, viruses and so forth) and there is the environment (the rainfall, temperature and all the other physical and organic factors that affect disease). To these we may add a fungicide or other chemical. All parts of the ecosystem interact. Thus a high level of disease may be due to (1) very susceptible host plants, (2) very aggressive pathogens or (3) weather very favorable to disease or the absence of a fungicide.

We could substitute any specific insect, nematode, or other pest for the pathogen in this triangle and have an ecosystem triangle suitable for study, although the relative importance of the different factors involved would vary with different pests.

This research is complex and expensive. The expense is one of the reasons why not much agroecosystems research has been done yet, particularly research that concerns the environmental ramifications of a given agricultural practice. Van der Plank (1972) summarizes the complexity of just one possible ecosystem study as it relates to a specific disease and host.

> Consider the ecosystem of wheat stem rust in the Mississippi Valley. With a sequence of pictures from satellites; with aerial photographs of special film; with ground surveys recording data quantitatively; with accurate weather forecasts; with knowledge obtained both in the field and laboratory of how environmental factors and changes affect the pathogen, the host and the in-

fection process; with knowledge of air movements and the various patterns of spore dispersal by air and water; with knowledge of the host plants, their resistance, how weather influences them and how they influence the ecoclimate; with maps showing the distribution, shape and size of the fields; with knowledge of the pathogen, its races, their abundance, variance and aggressiveness in the appropriate environment—with all this; with models to coordinate it; and computers to digest it one hopes the ecosystem could be better analyzed, host resistance better evaluated and applications of chemicals better timed.

One should remember that Van der Plank is describing a plant disease that has had as much or more research effort applied to it than any other crop disease. Even so, we are not able to relate accurately most of the extreme variability characteristic of this plant pathogen as it fluctuates in an ever changing environment and with an ever changing group of possible hosts.

Ecological problems are complicated enough in the temperate zone where most of the studies have been made. They tend to be even more complex in tropical areas where many countries of the developing world are located. Wellman (1972) pointed out that in the tropics many ecological zones are present, often in close proximity, since they are determined by altitude and relationships to nearby water. He also emphasized the influence of a lack of winter and the fact that leaf spots on crops develop continuously throughout the year either on crop plants or nearby alternate hosts. Leaf spot diseases, particularly those of beans, vary markedly in severity in the tropics depending on field conditions. Such variables as temperature, relative humidity, amount and distribution of rainfall, cloudiness, and wind exposure probably affect the pathogens more than the bean plant. Wellman called for more thorough ecoanalyses, summarizing his discussion of agricultural ecology in the tropics as follows:

> No one has made the much needed exhaustive review of literature from the neotropics that deals with ecology and weather effects on plant diseases. (This is also true of insects and other pests of crops.) It seems probable that someone someday will formulate a system with special reference to disease ecology. For example, certainly there are best zones for fusarial wilts, black mildews, white mildews, algal leaf spots, tar spots, damping off, web blights, *Rosellinia* root rots and wood stain diseases. This is in many cases a more intricate kind of study than is expressed in the present tropical forester's ecology based on forest zones. In the meantime forest ecologists' findings are helpful as they very roughly define differences.

Recent criticism has been directed toward agriculturalists because of the destruction of diversity in the environment and the use of monocultures over large areas of land. It has been assumed by ecologists that any movement away from diversity would be invariably undesirable and that agriculture should move toward more diversity, such as maintenance of hedges and other noncrop areas in borderlands (FAO 1968, 1971). However, this is not necessarily true. The general problem and its implications are analyzed by Falcon and Smith (1973):

> One of the most widely accepted concepts of ecology is that the stability of a community is related to its diversity. Stability implies that both species make-up and individual species abundance remain relatively constant over a long period. A diverse natural community comprising many species of plants and animals is led to be stable because the complex web of interactions operating within and between the nutritional levels acts unerringly against any striking change in abundance of individual species.

> Apart from theoretical considerations the conclusion that diversity creates stability is based on evidence that pest outbreaks rarely occur in the most diverse communities such as tropical rain forests, whereas they are more likely as diversity is decreased through simpler natural communities such as the north temperate coniferous forest to even less diverse perennial plantation crops and agricultural mono-cultures. It has consequently been assumed that simplification is invariably undesirable and that reversion to diversity in agricultural areas should be encouraged. However, there is abundant evidence that this kind of diversity can often encourage pests. With cotton, for example, there is no doubt that in Africa the status of the species *Heliothis, Earias, Dysdercus* and *Taylorilygas* as major pests is often directly attributable to environmental diversity in the form of alternate crop and wild hosts. (This is true of a great many plant diseases in the temperate zone as well.)

The solution to this problem is the establishment of the right quality of diversity. Change might be all that is needed. In California, increasing diversity by planting alfalfa hayfields near cotton can be beneficial or harmful. It is harmful if not strip cut, because lygus bugs will leave the hayfields when they are cut and enter the cotton to cause damage. But if the alfalfa is harvested in alternate strips the lygus bugs will fly into the uncut alfalfa sections (Elton 1958).

The value of diversity in uncultivated areas adjacent to crops is difficult to assess. Minor changes in complexity may aid biological control agents. Often plant alterations can provide food and shelter for insect, parasite, and predator adults or alternate hosts; for their immature stages in the seasonal history of the population; and for alternate hosts of important plant pathogens. Emphasis should be on selective use of diversity (FAO 1971). This is illustrated by one example from Falcon and Smith (1973): "In the Cauca Valley of Colombia in recent years there has been an increasing diversity of agricultural production. The land area devoted to sorghum, maize, and tomatoes, all hosts for the cotton bollworm, has been increased greatly and the bollworm problem in cotton has increased correspondingly."

Sometimes it is necessary to decrease diversity to create an environment that lacks certain elements needed by a pest, for example, eliminating host plants that are necessary for the completion of a life cycle. At other times it may be necessary to add certain elements, for example, provide essential food plants for a beneficial predator or parasite.

Most agricultural areas and their surroundings are not natural environments. Almost all have been altered by humans and the best that we have at the moment (with the exception of the rain forest, tundra, high mountains, and other such areas of the world) is a "seminatural" vegetation, which is typically the type of vegetation that adjoins crops. It may contain elements that are either beneficial or detrimental to natural enemies, plant diseases, and other pests. When the delicate stability of climax vegetation is disturbed by humans, the vegetational system, although still complex, may be altered enough to benefit a pest or disease, work against it, or perhaps regulate it.

It is difficult to generalize, and all specific situations need to be studied. In some cases almost any form of diversity of plant species and age structure seems to decrease the damage by pests. Examples are *Pseudotheraptus* spp. on coconuts and *Choristoneura fumiferana* on balsam fir. Other examples show that the damage to crops decreases with a simplification of the plant structure, particularly if certain host plants are removed or absent. Examples are *Certitis capitata* in Israel and Tunisia, *Virachola livia* in Egypt and Israel, *Cephus cinctus* on wheat in Canada, and various birds on fruit trees in Great Britain. The same diversity can be harmful in one place and helpful in another. This situation is found in Tanzania where growing maize with cotton increases *Heliothis* damage in cotton; in Peru, growing maize with cotton helps control *Heliothis*. In one circumstance the maize is the source and cause of the damaging attacks of *Heliothis*; in the other conditions favor continuity of natural enemies and the maintenance of a stable situation or equilibrium to keep the pest scarce (FAO 1968).

Small amounts of introduced diversity may be adequate to control a particular pest. For example, a species of *Rubus* introduced into an irrigated area in California deficient in vegetation was suitable to maintain a parasite important in the control of *Erythroneura elegantula* on grapes (FAO 1968). Since this problem is so complex, each situation must be studied in the context of the immediate environmental situation (including all pertinent plants and animals). Each agroecosystem needs to be considered as a distinct manipulated system where undesirable elements may need to be eliminated and desirable elements introduced.

A review emphasizing the proper types of diversity for solving some plant protection problems was written by Way (1979).

4

Systems Analysis: Use of Computers

 With the advent of the computer and computer technology it became possible to follow easily more than one variable in a research effort. Systems analysis is coming into its own and the whole field of simulation and model building is developing rapidly.

Zadoks (1971) summarized the rationale behind all systems analyses.

> Systems analysis is a method by which complex situations can be understood and described quantitatively. A system is a chosen limited section of the real world. The aim of the systems analysis is to describe a system as a whole, the holistic approach. A model is a simplified representation of a system. The testing of ideas before starting labor consuming experiments is another attraction of simulation.

Stark and Smith (1971) discuss the importance of this new technique for pest management.

> Systems analysis is a set of techniques and procedures, mathematical, statistical and mechanical, for analyzing complex systems such as agroecosystems. It has now been demonstrated that such techniques and procedures can and should be applied to the solution of large scale problems such as ecological pest management. The rationale for such optimism is that the objective of pest management, minimizing losses caused by pests, maximizing productivity and minimizing environmental degradation, has an impressive body of pure and applied mathematical theory and techniques by which optimal management can be recognized. This has long been suggested but it was not until the development of the larger electronic computers that an investigation could reasonably encompass the complex detail and problems of broad scope such as found in any ecosystem. . . . The major contributions of systems analysis . . . are in the area of data processing, the testing of complex concepts and the role of factors. The insights gained are then used to design field research aimed at still further insight until the whole is understood. The capability of large modern digital computers to incorporate large masses of data in their "memory" and to perform complicated functions at a high rate of speed per-

mits, in principle, the ecologists to incorporate all the components, and their interactions, of an ecosystem and to subject them to analysis and experimentation as to their roles.

Most agricultural research of the past was not oriented, except empirically, toward a systems approach. Consequently, most research information, the vast body of data available, has not been used to build simulation models. This problem was summarized by Campbell (1972):

> In my opinion much of the research ostensibly directed toward understanding mechanisms . . . has in fact proceeded with no clearly defined direction whatever. . . . Our best hope I think is that in the future we will define both our goals and our operating framework clearly enough in advance that discoveries regarding the mechanisms that drive individual parts of the system can be placed in the context of that system immediately rather than hoping for that great "someday" when everything will magically fall into place.

What is needed is the separation and examination of the relatively few significant variables in a particular system from the usually much greater number of variables whose roles are insignificant. Actually, people in plant protection attempted to follow these variables long before computers appeared and from the standpoint of practical control have done rather well. Unfortunately, they ignored most of the environmental effects associated with control treatments, primarily because of a lack of adequate technology. The control programs, based on key variables that were known, have worked fairly well and only recently have the "best laid plans" broken down because of residue problems, development of resistance in pests, breakdown of resistance in plants, development of the pollution problem, and the persistence of some chemicals in the environment (Campbell 1972).

Van der Plank (1972) recognized the importance of the systems approach in plant pathology and emphasized the complexity of the problem insofar as that discipline is concerned:

> The principles of ecosystems analyses are the principles of analyzing the interaction of all the relevant organisms (including viruses) between themselves and between them and the environment. Our knowledge of the interactions considered qualitatively embraces much of our knowledge of plant pathology, entomology and related sciences. It is when one starts probing quantitatively that one becomes intensely aware of ignorance. In plant pathology particularly, knowledge of even the most elementary relations is vague and inadequate. For example, possibly the simplest relation we ought to know in the whole ecosystem of plant diseases is the relation between inoculum and disease. If 100 spores having fallen on a leaf start n lesions, how many lesions would 200 spores start? Could any question be simpler or its answer more fundamental to quantitative analysis of disease systems? But we cannot answer it.

Comparisons need to be made with the best available programmed, controlled, environmental chamber data. Atmospheric variables need to be programmed individually and collectively and the field conditions need to be documented and simulated for each specific disease. Controlled environmental equipment that would facilitate epidemiological investigations is now available for accumulation of data and for systems analyses of specific disease situations (FAO 1968).

Van Gundy emphasized that both plant pathology and nematology lag far behind entomology, wildlife management, and fisheries in the application of systems analysis and design. The present techniques developed for quantitative analyses of soil pathogens are time consuming, expensive, laborious, and in general insensitive. They need to be improved so that data may be accumulated and made available for computer programming to develop simulation models. The management of soil pathogens, including both nematodes and plant disease pathogens, depends on extensive refinement of present soil sampling analysis techniques (Van Gundy 1972).

The problem with every pest and plant pathogenic disease is obtaining enough data concerning the factors that control pest populations and/or severity of the disease to develop an ecosystem simulation model accurate enough to predict population levels of the pest and/or severity of the disease. Apple (1974) summarized this problem and emphasized the importance of accurate simulation models.

> Development of ecosystem models must be the ultimate objective for economically important agroecosystems. The development of an ecosystem model will require linkages between many submodels such as a plant growth model, pest complex model(s) and biometeorological models. These are complex processes requiring extensive biological research and sophisticated mathematical techniques but these models can also be applied in assessing crop losses due to pests, which is a critical need in establishing researchable problem priorities.

More research is needed on the use and development of models for plant disease forecasting. Empirical models based on an analysis of environmental conditions include all the records of disease occurrence and are constantly being refined through continued field and laboratory research and through the use of environmentally controlled growth chambers. When the models are developed, laboratory research has to be checked against field conditions to see whether it can be used for accurate field predictions. Such models, it is hoped, can determine the validity of experimental data under a variety of field conditions (FAO 1968). Only a few such models have been developed in plant pathology, and even fewer have actually predicted epiphytotics. None has been utilized in consistently practical ways in the field.

Waggoner and Horsfall (1969) developed a computerized simulator called EPIDEM that satisfactorily mimicked several actual epiphytotics of early blight of tomato, incited by *Alternaria solani,* based on several years of known weather data. The simulator indicated that the information available concerning the disease was adequate, and it verified what actually happened in the field during several years. The simulator was a computer program written in FORTRAN IV. It performed reasonably well in mimicking epiphytotics that had occurred and in predicting real epiphytotics, and it will be used in attempting to predict real epiphytotics in the future.

Simulation models have been developed for late blight of potato by James (1973) and for southern corn leaf blight by Waggoner et al. (1972). In the future it is hoped that these and others to be developed will actually predict with accuracy the development of disease outbreaks. When this occurs, these simulator models can be used year after year if adequate forecast data are available. Van der Plank (1975) has warned of difficulties and misinterpretations possible in model simulation techniques such as EPIDEM and EPIMAY and has warned, too, that they are not nearly as accurate as some have imagined.

Chiarappa developed a model that determines whether it would be profitable to control a specific disease by Supervised Plant Disease Control (SPDC)—whether it would be sensible to develop a forecasting system for a specific disease based on available information. It accurately predicts that many of the diseases of small grains cannot be controlled economically by Supervised Plant Disease Control. It also predicts that such a disease as late blight of potato can and should be controlled by chemicals under a Supervised Plant Disease Control system. There is a good possibility of using this type of model in plant protection advisory programs when adequate data are available each year for computer analyses. But such data can only be collected by personnel in the field and thus far not enough trained observers and data collectors are available to gather the information (Chiarappa 1974).

Chiarappa thinks the research based on information gained through the use of his model should be expanded but should concentrate on disease/crop combinations that are most suited to Supervised Plant Disease Control. As he pointed out, much more complex biological, economic, and managerial information must be obtained to help the grower determine what type of plant protection systems to use. The models developed need to take these factors into consideration, as well as factors specifically associated with the agroecosystem(s) and with the specific plant disease or pest.

Hooker (1974) also emphasized the importance of developing a systems approach in plant pathology. He particularly emphasized the importance of developing backup systems for agriculture just as for aerospace programs. He pointed out that normal cytoplasm provided a significant backup system during the southern corn leaf blight epidemic of 1970.

Good reported that it is possible to develop simulation models for the management of some nematode populations. When more information on population dynamics; cultural, soil, and environmental interactions; life cycles; and the effectiveness of various control methods is available, models may be developed through computers that evaluate complex nematode relationships rather accurately. An example in use now is a model that predicts population dynamics of the golden nematode of potato, *Heterodera rostochiensis*. This model reveals how populations can be kept below economic threshold levels by utilization of a combination of low dosage nematicides, plant resistance, and crop rotation (Good 1972a, 1972b).

Van Gundy listed four different models of host-parasite interactions that are useful in nematology: those that involve (1) nonmotile inoculum distributed around a fixed infection court on a below-ground hypocotyl; (2) nonmotile inoculum invaded by a moving infection court, for example, a growing tip; (3) motile inoculum moving into a fixed infection court; and (4) motile inoculum with a moving infection court or invaded by a moving infection court. Van Gundy predicts that "on the basis of these models . . . biological control of diseases involving moving infection courts might be difficult while biological control . . . affecting diseases might be more easily applied to interactions in which the infection courts are fixed." These models have not been adequately tested in the field. Much more needs to be done to develop accurate economic thresholds (Van Gundy 1972).

Based on mathematical theories and population dynamics, two groups of nematodes have been distinguished: (1) sedentary species that multiply in separate generations, for example, cyst nematodes; and (2) migratory or partly sedentary species that multiply continuously. These two models have been used by many nematologists to define variation in host status, i.e., good hosts, poor hosts, and nonhosts (Van Gundy 1972). Other similar models will be developed, but they must predict accurately the economically significant disease and/or population thresholds in field situations before they will be used routinely.

Problems and Dangers

The use of the computer in systems analyses and simulation model building presents not only great possibilities but also real dangers (Stark and Smith 1971).

> Confronted by the awesome capacity of the computer it is easy to forget that what is fed into the machine must be realistic, supported by real data; otherwise the computer gives results without meaning. The output of intuitive models can be grossly misleading when applied to existing complex biological processes. (Every computer should have a sign on it which reads "garbage in, garbage out.") For example, at the First International Symposium of

Statistical Ecology such a model was presented. It was developed to investigate a particular predator-prey relationship. The "machine prey" was assigned its niche and the "machine predator" was let loose against it, subject to various mathematical and statistical stipulations. The model worked beautifully but not a single prey was caught. Without including knowledge of the searching power of the predator and the dispersive or the protective behavior of the prey, based on field and laboratory studies, such games are meaningless (parenthetically, they are worse than meaningless, they are dangerous and tend to turn fiction into fact). Lastly, it must be remembered that the computer is dependent on the outside world for communication. Real data and programs have to be put into the machine (input) before it can work and its answers (output) must then be interpreted (carefully against the real world) and put to use.

Many plant protection people as well as some ecologists have tended to avoid the computer, probably because they have not been well trained in its use. They are particularly fearful of the "garbage in, garbage out" dangers and know that they can develop a model of fiction as easily as a model of fact. Van der Plank (1972) stressed this problem: "All models, all the equations, all the parameters result in meaningless analyses unless there is something to analyze." Until we get the quantitative input data that tell the computer the real story, we can expect nothing of the computer.

Therefore agricultural scientists must emphasize again and again the importance of randomized, replicated field plots and localized adaptive research, for it produces accurate empirical information that is a near equivalent to systems analysis. These adaptive research techniques often ignore certain ecological and environmental effects, such as soil and water pollution, but they do not ignore the important empirical approach to nature that is necessary for determining the adaptability and successful growth of a crop in a particular environment. This fact has been emphasized by Norman Borlaug (1972, pers. commun.) and by others who realize the importance of adaptive research for all crops.

Huffaker (1974) emphasized the importance of adaptive research in entomology:

It is important to point out that a pest management system developed for a given crop and region is not really exportable. Too many of the intricacies involved are different in different crops and regions. For example, although spider mites constitute a key problem in the apple growing areas of Washington, Michigan and Pennsylvania, a different predator species is the key potential regulating factor in each area and the pest management system in each area will be correspondingly different. The philosophies and principles are, however, exportable.

There are exceptions but this statement, in general, is true for the philosophies and principles of all adaptive research.

Simulation models that are developed using computers must conform to nature exactly and they must be tested by adaptive research through carefully designed field plot techniques. Otherwise we will not know whether the simulation models can mimic what occurs in the field. In many respects the applied research and the various empirical field plot techniques used throughout the world are natural approaches to systems analysis. They were the empirical systems research of the past. They discover what occurs in a particular environment in relation to a given crop plant and although they do not tell us about all the parameters and/or variables, the key variables are usually clear. We need to remember that we must adapt the computer model to nature and not nature to the computer model. If this approach is used, simulation models can become valuable tools in discovering the significance of variables that until now have been completely mystifying.

We cannot wait until adequate simulation models are available for all key pests, predators, plant diseases, and the like. We must do the best we can to control pests and diseases now, particularly in the developing world where it is not likely that simulation models will be used routinely very soon. This again emphasizes the importance of applied research and the best empirical field plot techniques. It also emphasizes the importance of knowing and studying the key pests and predators and the dominant factor(s) in the control of any plant disease or pest. Huffaker (1970) particularly emphasized that we must seek the key component of the pest and disease problem, whether systems analyses are available or not. In many cases when the key(s) to a specific problem is (are) known, systems analyses (via simulation models) only confirm what we already know.

The entomology department at the University of Nebraska has developed a number of computer teaching "games." When students plug in field data, they receive control alternatives. More practical computer training programs in plant protection are needed.

Spedding (1975) attempts to carry out a systems approach and outlook to all aspects of agriculture. Many of the systems analyses given are incomplete but this is a meaningful effort in the right direction.

5

Chemical Control of Insects

 The term *biocide,* although not often used in plant protection circles, is more inclusive than the term more generally used, *pesticide.* Biocides include insecticides, fungicides, herbicides, nematicides, miticides, rodenticides, etc., and all other chemicals designed to control organisms not of interest or concern in plant protection. The term pesticide is employed here because of its more common usage in agricultural disciplines.

Pesticides

Most pesticides developed since 1940 are synthetic chemicals. A few have posed problems because of their persistence in the environment and because of their capacity to be stored in fat and accumulate in natural plant and animal food chains. Some chlorinated hydrocarbons, especially DDT, have these undesirable characteristics.

In spite of recent adverse publicity, pesticides are our most important tool in the management of pests and probably will be for many years (R. Smith 1970). In fact, Mrak (1969) suggested that "our need to use pesticides and other pest control chemicals will increase for the foreseeable future." Falcon and Smith (1973) have emphasized this point:

> Chemical pesticides are useful and powerful tools for the management of pest populations. Many are effective, dependable, economical and adaptable for use in a wide variety of situations. Indeed use of chemical pesticides is the only known method of control of many of the world's most important pests of agriculture and public health. No other tool lends itself with such comparative ease to manipulation and none can be brought to bear so quickly on outbreak populations.

> While it is recognized that pesticide chemicals have been and will continue to be an essential part of crop protection, current practices in pesticide use have not always been sound either in terms of food production or from the stand-

point of human health and environmental quality. The proper use of pesticide chemicals depends mostly on the continuing program of research and education. Each use of the pesticide should be judged on the basis of the potential positive values to be achieved as weighed against the possible negative values.

R. Smith (1970) summarized the negative aspects or disadvantages of pesticide chemicals: (1) development of resistant strains of pests; (2) consequent development of larger populations of pests after treatment; (3) hazards from residues remaining on the crop and moving to areas nearby; (4) increase of secondary pests because of the destruction of their natural enemies; (5) destruction of nontarget organisms such as parasites and predators of important economic insects, fish, birds, other wildlife, honeybees and other pollinators, and (potentially) domestic animals and humans.

McNew (1972) summarized the essential position of most professional agriculturalists:

> The use of chemicals to disinfect, to suppress, to destroy the pest or to permit the crop to escape the most extreme ravages will remain a potent force. Without this form of crop insurance, most agricultural practitioners cannot afford to invest in expensive equipment, precise fertilizer components and tailor made crop varieties. . . . These chemicals of the future are going to be more expensive because they must be more specific so as to avoid adverse side effects, must meet rigid standards of environmental safety and must be distributed and used with better control than at present. The general pesticide will probably give way to the more specific types as demands for safety gain prominence.

Although the supposed dangers of using pesticides have been emphasized, most fears appear to be unwarranted. Edwards (1970), after an analysis of the dangers of pesticides, gave the following report:

> To summarize, it does not seem that the present situation concerning pesticides in the environment is too serious. Many resources are being expended to develop alternative chemicals or methods of pest control and the environment is already being monitored for residues. Investigations into the hazards to animal and human populations by insecticide residues in various parts of the environment are proceeding. Many governments are taking action to restrict the use of chlorinated hydrocarbon insecticides. It seems, however, that the monitoring program could well be improved and made uniform and (more) extensive.

A more recent summary by McEwen (1978) corroborates the conclusions of McNew and Edwards. However, McEwen still emphasized the extreme importance of improving all other methods of plant protection so as to minimize our dependence on pesticides.

More careful selection of environmentally acceptable pesticides is needed in the future. Hassall (1969) pointed out that the majority of pesticide manufacturers are now keenly aware of the problems and their urgency. Enlightened self-interest, moral responsibility, and government regulations have demanded that manufacturers avoid release of pesticides on the market before adequate testing for potential toxic hazard and pesticidal efficiency has been completed. This testing is very expensive but is now a standard practice. (It is erroneous to suppose that untested materials are being marketed.) In many countries before any pesticide is marketed it has to comply with voluntary industry requirements and also compulsory governmental requirements, registration, testing, and approval. Usually the manufacturers' data are checked through an independent testing body to confirm the manufacturers' tests and determine the relative levels of safety and field efficacy of new materials.

Research on new materials does not end when clearances have been obtained. It moves from manufacturers' research laboratories to governmental laboratories and then to many other research organizations. It involves practical utilization in agriculture or may be associated with the mode of action of the pesticide. Also, it now typically moves into possible long-term ecological and residue research problems. All this research is feedback; if new hazards are revealed, routine tests in the future include the new information and become a part of the preclearance investigations. In Great Britain, the United States, and many other developed countries, additional research is sponsored by universities and private organizations such as those interested in the protection of wildlife (Hassall 1969).

The manufacturer also has the responsibility of proper labeling and packaging in containers that will not leak or corrode. Substantial improvements in such matters have occurred in recent years but some countries still do not take these responsibilities seriously. In Great Britain each label must now carry the chemical name and also the trade name of the product (Hassall 1969). Many feel it should also carry in bold type a Frazer scale assessment of acute oral toxicity. The containers should be returnable to avoid dumping of empty cans and drums that are potential hazards to children, fish, and wildlife. Users often are careless of the warnings on labels and ignore the information provided. The return and/or proper destruction or storage of empty cans and drums should be solved via legal channels in all countries where pesticides are used.

Pesticides in the Developing World

In the developing world the need for pesticides is so great and the difficulty in utilizing those that require advanced technology is so insurmountable that FAO continues to support the use of DDT where necessary. This position is summarized in the following statement (FAO 1973*d*):

> FAO recognizes that pesticides have sometimes been applied without sufficient studies of needs, alternative methods of control and possible ecological effect. It is recognized as particularly pertinent in the case of DDT which is of low cost, of low toxicity to man and therefore relatively safe for application by untrained persons, and which is active against a broad range of species. It is also recognized that this and certain other organochlorine pesticides are more persistent than is necessary to control some pests and their residues have become widely distributed in the environment. However, many published references and extensively reported statements on this subject have been found to be without valid basis, misleading or quite erroneous when examined objectively and in relation to facts. Some statements, although genuinely inspired out of honest concern, have been misinterpretations due to lack of critical studies in reading chemical analytical data or through use of inadequate procedures of identification of residues or through other similar causes. Since in many situations, too, residues occur at only low level, it is rarely possible to draw firm conclusions regarding any likely biological effects.
>
> For these reasons, FAO considers it essential, first to collect information on such matters from all reliable sources, then to assess it critically, using an interdisciplinary approach to provide a sound basis for subsequent action. Acknowledging that residues of certain organochlorine pesticides (including DDT) have become widely distributed in the environment, that their effects have been shown to be harmful in certain (very limited) circumstances, FAO considers it desirable to apply restraints in their use. This is in accordance with the recommendations of the 1969 joint FAO/WHO Meeting of Experts on Pesticide Residues ("that the use of DDT should be limited to those situations where there is no satisfactory alternative"). For certain pest situations, satisfactory alternatives to these compounds (organochlorine) are not available at this time.

When one considers the extreme gravity of the world food situation, FAO's position is easy to understand and approve. FAO has developed an official policy statement on this whole matter (FAO 1973*d*):

> The Food and Agriculture Organization of the United Nations (FAO) is fully aware that an ever increasing world population and a constant search for higher living standards carry great risk of over exploitation of natural resources and that the spread of technologies may eventually prove harmful. The organization is very conscious of the need to include broad ecological criteria in long term development plans.
>
> Pesticides have made very substantial contributions to the expansion in agricultural productivity that has occurred throughout the world in recent years. That is indisputable. Pesticides frequently offer the only means of arresting disastrous crop losses and in many areas production would be quite unprofitable without them. If drastic curtailment of productivity with its consequences on human welfare is to be avoided, then it is inevitable that

pesticides will continue to be widely used for many years to come. However, growing reliance on chemicals to increase agricultural productivity brings special problems in its train.

Most pesticides are toxic to a range of species other than those against which they are used. Some can be hazardous to man and over the years there have been numerous poisonings and deaths. These instances have often (in fact, usually) resulted from failure among packers, distributors and users to follow simple precautionary measures and a realization of this has in many countries led to stricter supervision and control by the authorities. The occurrences of residues in food for men and animals has caused doubt and hence research, and has led to the introduction of residue tolerances and similar restraints. In turn the need for exporting countries to comply with tolerances has produced problems in international trade and this has meant that scientific research and routine technical supervision have had to be expanded. Among pests, strains have developed which are increasingly resistant to pesticides formerly used and the farmer (and scientist) has had to take account of them. More recently, it has become evident that residues of certain of the more commonly used and persistent compounds are widely distributed in the environment and in certain situations with deleterious effects.

FAO considers that solutions to environmental problems for developing countries must not ignore the need to assist the growth of agriculture, ensure the employment of rural people and ensure that pollution and waste that decrease the production and quality of food and other agricultural products are rigorously controlled. As far as pesticides are concerned, FAO accepts the possibility that use of specific or otherwise valuable products or methods of application may have to be restricted or forbidden on the grounds of unacceptable contamination of the environment. In applying this principle, however, likely gains and losses must be carefully evaluated bearing in mind that agriculture and the developing world should not be unnecessarily denied the tools known to be required to develop productivity and improve human (physical) welfare.

Ecological and integrated approaches to pest control problems have been (and are being) fostered. Activities designed to avoid excesses of all kinds and to raise the standards of supervision, of marketing and application of pesticides have been pursued both from headquarters and in developing countries. At the same time the controlled application of useful materials has been assisted rather than denied.

This policy, endorsed by the nations of the developing world, will be continued by FAO in the foreseeable future. A particularly important point is emphasized by Hassall (1969):

We forget the indirect benefit of pesticides in the underdeveloped world which gives people the new strength and ambition to begin to work their land creatively. Mortality statistics do not describe fully the effect of pesticides on the probability of human survival. Thanks to better nutrition and to the rapid advances in medical science the expectation of life nowadays is higher nearly everywhere than it has ever been before. In this respect it must be recalled that pesticides have contributed to increased production, so these, and many other types of toxic chemicals, have greatly reduced the risk of early death and disease. In India, for example, the death rate has been halved since 1947 while in Ceylon it fell by 34 percent in one year. It is no coincidence that this rapid improvement in health in developing countries has occurred during a period of rapid expansion in the use of pesticides. The fall in the death rate in Ceylon can be ascribed very largely to the spray of houses with DDT.

Furthermore as the following extract from a pamphlet issued by the World Council for Welfare of the Blind so poignantly illustrates, health is an essential prerequisite to adequate, let alone efficient, farming. "In certain parts of Africa near streams in heavily infested areas we find villages in which every adult is blind. In these villages children are precious things for they alone can see to lead about their elders for a few years before they themselves turn blind." The Simulium fly which carries the organism responsible for river blindness, like the mosquito, tse-tse flies and other insect vectors of debilitating diseases, is readily controlled by insecticides (particularly DDT). Since such diseases sap men's strength and destroy both their will to work efficiently and their desire to plan for the future, the use of pesticides for medical purposes may in some areas contribute as much to agricultural efficiencies (and hence to yield per acre) as their use to protect crops from predations of insects (and diseases). This indirect contribution of pesticides for agriculture has often been given too little attention, perhaps because most authors do not come from countries infested with the insect vectors of extremely unpleasant and debilitating diseases.

The foregoing observation is most important. Admittedly, other materials and methods should be sought to give adequate control of these pests, but thus far no other materials are as inexpensive, as safe to use, or as effective.

A major basic difference emerges concerning the use of pesticides in the developed and the developing worlds in the future. Their use will probably be stabilized and reduced gradually in the developed world but probably will increase markedly in the developing world (Ivan C. Buddenhagen 1975, pers. commun.) Many pests and diseases of crops can be controlled only by pesticides, although many can now be controlled by materials other than DDT.

It has recently been shown that chlorinated hydrocarbons, including DDT, denature much more rapidly in the tropics than in the temperate zones, particularly during the hot, rainy seasons (Talekar and Chen 1979).

Insecticides

Some insects that can only be controlled by insecticides are listed and discussed by Metcalf et al. (1951). Spray programs are essential for fruits and vegetables, such as apples, peaches, and pears, that must have a cosmetic quality to be acceptable in the modern world market. The following fruit insects must be controlled via spray schedules, no alternatives now being available: spring cankerworm, fall cankerworm, fall webworm, eastern tent caterpillar, yellow-necked caterpillar, red-humped caterpillar, apple leaf skeletonizer, leaf crumpler, the various bud moths, fruit tree leaf roller, red-banded leaf roller, apple flea weevil, San Jose scale and other scales, all apple aphids and apple leafhoppers, European red mite and other mites, plum curculio, codling moth (requires many sprays), apple maggot, and others.

On legumes the alfalfa weevil can best be controlled by insecticides, although now a parasite of the alfalfa weevil is being used with some success. The lesser clover leaf weevil is not controlled well by any known insecticide; insecticides combined with clean cultural practices are required for adequate control of various lygus bugs (Metcalf et al. 1951).

The rice crop in the tropics is subjected to heavy pressure from about 15 insect species that infest it from seedling stage to maturity and often occur in overlapping generations throughout the year (Pathak and Dyck 1973). In a series of experiments conducted in farmers' fields by the International Rice Research Institute in collaboration with the Bureau of Plant Industry and the Agricultural Productivity Commission of the Philippines, it was revealed that plots protected from insect damage yielded on the average 1 ton more rice per hectare than similar unprotected plots—an increase of 20 to 25 percent in the yield. Pathak and Dyck (1973) emphasized that the use of insecticides is the only practical method to achieve immediate reduction in insect and arthropod populations. However, they urge that pesticides be used only when absolutely necessary.

Brady (1974) pointed out that the average yield of rice in Asia could probably be doubled by the use of insecticides. However, their high cost, their relative scarcity, and the difficulty of application cause them to be considered only partial solutions to the field pest problems in developing countries. Other methods of control are greatly needed, particularly those applicable to small farms in the tropics.

Some insecticides (and also herbicides) affect the incidence of fungus diseases of plants. For instance, lindane (gamma benzene hexachloride), isodrin (compound 711), and 2, 4-D increased the incidence of early blight of tomato. Other chemicals decrease the incidence of some plant diseases. For example, dalapon (a, a-dichloropropionic acid), demeton (Mercaptophos), aldrin (Octalene), IPC (propham), dieldrin (Octalox), endrin (compound 269), MH (maleic hydrazide), NPA (prajmaline), binapacryl (dinoseb methacrylate), DDT, and TCA (calcitonin) decreased the incidence of *Fusarium* wilt of tomato (Richardson 1959).

Nine insecticides and ten herbicides were tested on root rot infection incited by *Helminthosporium sativum* in the soil on several hosts. The root rot infection was reduced and the seedling growth was unaffected by aldrin; endrin; chlordane (toxichlor); NPA; 2, 4-D; Monuron (Telvar); DNBP (Dinoseb); and dalapon. Other chemicals tested had no apparent affect on the fungus (Richardson 1957).

Resistance to Pesticides

The development of resistance to insecticides by many insect species is an important phenomenon. Pest species change genetically under regular use of pesticides (Whitten 1970). Resistance develops in populations possessing resistant genes. These individuals survive, propagate, and repopulate the species (Burges 1971). Georgopoulos (1969) stated that 137 species of mites, insects, and other arthropods had been reported as developing resistance to insecticides as early as 1960. The changes developed very fast in some species. This phenomenon was probably more important than any other factor in convincing entomologists to move to integrated pest management programs that minimize the use of chemical pesticides where possible.

Fadeev (1979) has reported a technique to partially circumvent the development of resistance to specific pesticides by insects and mites. He recommends alternating the use of as many pesticides as are effective to avoid constant use of one. He reports much less development of resistance by this technique.

In Asia only a few examples of insect resistance to insecticides have been reported (R. Smith 1972). Most are based on circumstantial evidence alone and the documentation is not as careful as it should be. Several chemicals used against the diamondback moth, *Plutella maculipennis* (*xylostella*), which attacks cruciferous crops, are now becoming ineffective.

Another attendant result of prolonged pesticide use has been the buildup of previously minor pest species. Several well-documented reports are available on cotton in Aisa and on tea in Sri Lanka (Danthanarayana 1967).

The development of resistance is an important possibility in plant disease organisms and other pests. Thus far only a small number of fungi are known to be resistant to fungicides. Horsfall (1972) summarized the resistance to fungicides: "In the field, fungi have rarely developed economically important resistance in farmers' crops. In the laboratory they often do. The general theory for this is that most fungicides have a broad spectrum of activity. Some fungicides seem to have a limited spectrum of activity and resistance has developed to these."

Farkas and Amman (1940) first reported resistance of fungi to fungicides when the *Penicillium* mold of oranges became resistant to diphenil. Georgopoulos (1969) listed two other cases of field resistance—bunt of wheat to hexachlorobenzine and *Helminthosporium* on oats to organic mercury. Schroeder and Providenti (1969) reported that cucumber powdery mildew had become resistant to benomyl (Benlate); and Szkolnik and Gilpatrick (1969) reported that *Venturia inaequalis,* the incitant of apple scab, was becoming resistant to Dodine (cyprex) in New York. Webster et al. (1970) reported that *Botrytis cinerea* on stone fruits was becoming resistant to 2, 6-dichloronitroaniline (dicloran) (Botran) in California.

Georgopoulos (1969) emphasized that resistance to fungicides in fungal diseases has developed only rarely and that the problem is minimal, probably because of the nonspecific nature of most fungicides. With the development of more selective fungicides he felt the fungi would develop more resistant strains and predicted that fungicide resistance will be more frequent and more serious in the future. Erwin (1973) concurred and gave a specific example of serious cases of resistance that have developed in blue mold, *Penicillium italicum,* and in green mold, *P. digitatum,* to the fungicide thiabendazole (TBZ). TBZ can no longer be used prior to the storage ripening period in fruit packinghouses. In 1976 Dekker (1976) was still able to say that the development of resistance to fungicides is rare, possibly because they are usually multisite inhibitors.

Resistance of nematodes to nematicides has not been a field problem thus far but potential for development should be of concern to nematologists (NAS 1968*b*). Since most fields are treated only once a year against nematodes, there is not a great deal of selection pressure against field nematode populations. Also, nematicides have come into general use only since 1950. Perhaps tests should be developed to discover whether some of the more important nematodes can be put under enough selection pressure to develop resistance to nematicides.

Weeds until recently had not developed genetic types resistant to herbicides. Weeds reproduce much more slowly than insects (generally only once a year) and herbicide treatments are applied just once a year, so selection pressure is much less than on insects. According to Arnon (1972), no report had appeared of weeds resistant to herbicides in the field. Since that time resistance of two common weeds, lamb's-quarters and pigweed, to atrazine (Aatrex) have been widely reported and several other weeds may show resistance.

Watson and Brown (1977) summarized the general knowledge concerning resistance to pesticides developed among various pests and diseases.

Selectivity in Pesticides and Use

Problems that were developing because of the use of persistent insecticides and some other pesticides largely brought about the integrated pest management movement some years ago by entomologists concerned about the excessive use of pesticides. Metcalf (1972*a*, 1972*b*) summarized the problems and emphasized the importance of developing more selective methods of using insecticides in more efficient, smaller dosages.

> It must be remembered always that pesticides are applied to the environment as purposeful contaminants. Consequently, the benefits from their use must greatly exceed any damage to environmental quality. Adequate pest control can be achieved in most cases with lower volume of applications more precisely timed and placed.

> For reasons difficult to explain evolution in the insecticide area seems to favor the widescale use of compounds highly toxic to man while their more innocuous relatives are relegated to minor applications or back to the shelf. [By contrast] from the acute toxicity viewpoint, DDT obviously provides no hazards to the human population as proved by extensive worldwide use for a generation in human habitations for malaria and typhus control and eradication without evidence of ill effects. No *human* fatality has been attributed to DDT. The vast majority of pesticide poisonings and fatalities in the United States result from exposure to organophosphorous insecticides, especially parathion.

Metcalf (1972*a*) was also concerned that there are many safer, more selective, and well-tested pesticides that are kept on chemical company shelves because they cannot be developed economically. He suggested directions in which chemical companies might move in the development of more selective insecticides.

> The selectivity of the methyl parathion analogues provides an appropriate example of the possibilities for the design of better pesticides through understanding the biochemical nature of the selective process. It seems that a small additional cost per pound is a small price to pay for a substantial saving of human life and for a much better public attitude regarding the use of insecticides. It should be evident that there is urgent need to replace DDT and other persistent nondegradable (hard insecticides) with persistent yet biodegradable substitutes.

Metcalf (1972*a*) suggested that methoxyclor might be a satisfactory substitute for DDT and he suggested two ways to find selective pesticides that are safer, biodegradable, and not stored in animal fat. (1) He suggested concentrating on analogues of parathion to improve their general selectivity and make them safer for humans and warm-blooded animals while retaining parathion's high toxicity to insects. (2) He suggested developing biodegradable analogues of DDT that are not stored in animal lipids or concentrated through food chains and are reasonably, but not dangerously, persistent in the environment. He feels that the most profitable research for good selectivity and reasonable biodegradability is to hunt for analogues of already effective insecticides that retain the desirable characteristics and eliminate or minimize the undesirable characteristics.

Falcon and Smith (1973) recommend the development of narrowly selective chemicals for ideal pest control. The efforts for many years have been to develop materials with high toxicity to invertebrates and low toxicity to mammals, but now Falcon and Smith think that much more effort should be made to seek differential toxicity within the phylum Arthropoda. Effective materials are needed that are specific not for species but for groups of pests, for example, aphids, caterpillars, weevils, locusts, and muscoid flies.

Metcalf (1972a, 1972b) defined selectivity in pesticides "in terms of maximum effect of the insecticide on the target organism with minimal effects on humans, domestic animals, wildlife, beneficial invertebrates and to the quality of the environment." No matter how it is defined, it is agreed that (1) a reduction in the amount of insecticides used is important and (2) these insecticides should be more selective in their effects. Metcalf compared the selective chemical approach to the use of a surgical scalpel in place of a broadsword. Another analogy would be to compare the selective use of insecticides (including selective materials) in pest management to the careful use of pharmaceuticals in the practice of medicine. Selective use, then, is a matter of placement, minimum amount, timing, and use of materials poisonous to only one group or species.

Some examples of effective selective placement of insecticides are available (USDA 1972). For example, in Texas the lesser cornstalk borer, *Elasmopalpus lignosellus,* is a major pest of the peanut. Foliar spray techniques of the past developed insect resistance problems, destroyed beneficial insects, and encouraged the development of secondary pests. A directed spray technique that places the insecticide in the solid zone exactly where the borers feed and avoids treatment of the leaves and branches has been developed. The arthropod fauna on the foliage are not destroyed and the number of insecticide treatments has been reduced to at most two per season, with equivalent control.

Metcalf (1972a, 1972b) gave other examples of placing the insecticide in the pest's most vulnerable niche or in the place most suitable for best control. An example is maize silk or ear treatment for corn earworm larvae control. Another example is precise spraying of tree branches for tsetse fly control. For control of the European red mite, *Panonychus ulmi,* a single spray of a suitable acaricide is applied to the tips of the branches to suppress overwintering mites. This does not kill many of the predaceous fallacis mites, *Neoseiulus fallacis,* that overwinter on the trunks of the tree. Later the predator mite, as its population increases, moves up the tree from the trunk and is able to control the phytophagous mites for the rest of the season. The net result is much less spray used for equivalent control. Metcalf (1972b) suggested that sufficient knowledge concerning microhabitats and ecological behavior is not yet available to take advantage of possibilities for control of other pests by similar techniques. More research is needed in this area to develop control procedures based on selective placement of minimal amounts of insecticides.

Good (1979) points out that selective insecticides used when an economic threshold is reached must be very powerful and give quick kills before significant plant damage commences.

The new microencapsulated insecticides have many advantages— increased residual activity, reduced mammalian toxicity, superior insect control, increased crop yields, fewer applications, less active ingredient used per acre, reduced phytotoxicity, greater efficiency, and reduction of pesticide loss due to volatilization (Advani and Koestler 1979).

Pest management programs can minimize overtreatment of pesticides in other ways. Metcalf (1972b) emphasized the importance of seed treatments and future research in that area. Application of insecticides to seeds can occur at the time of planting. Applications are minimal in dosage and cause little disturbance to the environment. Also, savings in costs are considerable. Some examples given by Metcalf (1972a, 1972b) follow: A wide variety of field and vegetable crops have been treated with dieldrin (Detalox), endrin (compound 69), aldrin (Octalene), lindane (gamma benzene hexachloride) and heptachlor (Vesical 104) with as little as 7 grams (0.245 pounds) per acre with excellent mortality of wireworms. This is a reduction of more than 99 percent of the usual dosage of up to 1.35 kilograms (3 pounds) per acre. Oats seeds have been treated successfully with propoxure (Baygon) at 4 ounces per 100 pounds of seed or 2.8 ounces per acre. This has given excellent kill to the cereal leaf beetle, *Oulema melanopus,* and has persisted for up to 50 days after planting. The reduction in amount of insecticide used is about 83 percent.

Van der Plank (1972) has emphasized the importance of timing in minimizing the number of chemical treatments used. His discussion concerns fungicides but is equally applicable to other pesticides.

> When economic factors severely limit the number of applications of a fungicide or other chemical that can profitably be given in a season, the applications must be properly timed. If the chemical is applied too early it may be wasted; if too late the damage may already have been done. Good timing depends on good forecasting, good knowledge of the disease progress curve and of how an alteration of the curve will reduce loss from disease.

This statement implies a rather complete knowledge of the bionomics and life cycle of the disease organism, insect, or other pest to be controlled. Then the possibilities for reducing the number of chemical treatments are very favorable.

Another point emphasized by Van der Plank (1972) that has not received much attention thus far is the beneficial interaction of plant resistance and chemicals. It has been known empirically for a long time but little research has been done. First it would appear important to stop the competition and antagonism between those who breed resistant plants and those who favor the use of chemicals. These two groups are properly not rivals at all but should be cooperating to minimize the use of chemicals and maximize the use of outstanding resistant plants. As Van der Plank (1972) suggested, both methods of control will probably be necessary in the future.

Benz (1971) emphasized the possibility of utilizing the synergism of microorganisms and chemicals in disease control, which would greatly reduce the quantity of chemicals used. An interesting report concerns the healthy larvae of the codling moth (*Cydia pomonella* or *Laspeyresia pomonella*), the tent caterpillar (*Malacosoma disstria*), and some other species that were not infected with spores of the muscardine fungus (*Beauveria bassiana*) unless the insects were first treated with weak doses of DDT or HCH (lindane). Such weak doses of insecticides combined with insect control via fungi may eventually have some practical potential.

In another example of synergism reported by Benz (1971), the nuclear polyhedrosis disease of larvae of the gypsy moth, *Lymantria dispar,* is activated by sublethal doses of endrin, dieldrin, or aldrin. Benz and several other authors report the activation of latent viroses by some other chemicals, for example, NaF, H_2O_2 and hydroxylamine. These synergisms have not yet been used in any practical way but need more research and consideration.

Pheromones and Other Attractants

The extensive use of pesticides in the more affluent nations has stimulated the search for more natural alternative means of control. Wood (1970) summarized this effort:

> One of the most promising alternative methods of control is the use of naturally occurring organic compounds that influence insect chemosensory behavior as attractants, repellents, stimulants, deterrents and arrestants. . . . Utilizing this biochemical approach remains painstakingly slow because of our primitive understanding of insect behavior, problems associated with mass rearing and with isolation and identification of compounds occurring in minute amounts in complex mixtures, synergism and masking, synthesis and the problems of developing control protocols that utilize synthetic compounds.

An attendant problem is profitable manufacture and sale of these new, usually selective, compounds.

The term *pheromone* was coined by Karlson and Butenandt in 1959, as reported in Kilgore and Doutt (1967). It concerns chemicals secreted into the external environment by an animal that elicit a specific reaction in a receiving individual of the same species. These materials have also been referred to as *ectohormones*. As summarized by Jacobsen (1972), these materials are produced by a wide variety of insects and mites, often by both males and females. They may be odorous and they act directly on the central nervous system to give a specific behavioral response such as dispersal and territoriality, aggregation, sexual activity, alarm and flight, and trail following. Jacobsen documented the success of sex pheromones used to bait traps in insect surveys of particular species. These surveys have shown whether species are present and have indicated the relative abundance of the species.

The use of pheromones in insect control has only had serious research in recent years and few practical controls are available as yet. Beroza (1970) said,

> Many insects depend on chemicals for survival, for finding a mate, for defending themselves, for maintaining their social organization, for finding food (or rejecting it) and for appropriate placement of eggs. Clearly the key to insect control in many instances may very well be the key that unlocks the structure of their secretions or of chemicals that attract or repel them. In effect, we wish to utilize the survival mechanisms of insects in order to destroy or control them.

Research in pheromones is expensive. Progress is slow. Often thousands of compounds have been tested and synthesized and tested again before a single practical attractant has been found. Yet, as Beroza emphasized, when one considers the fact that the control method will be safe and will be available for all future time, the search for attractants giving practical control is worthwhile.

Practical employment of sex attractants and other attractants in insect control has been achieved for some of the Lepidoptera (Jacobsen 1972). Males of certain species of moths can be lured to their deaths by use of even crude extracts of the females. These lures are placed in traps with insecticides or on sticky boards. Demonstration of the effectiveness of these lures has been achieved with the cabbage looper, the gypsy moth, and the red banded leaf roller. So far attempts to control the boll weevil in the same way have failed but chemosterilant–sex attractant mixtures appear to be more potent in the newer boll weevil management programs.

All the known attractants need to be identified and synthesized—it has been done in a few cases. Attractants are often effective in the laboratory but ineffective in the field (Jacobsen 1972). Often there has been success in areas of light infestation but failure in areas of heavy infestation. There have been successes in local areas under special conditions but failures under more widespread generalized conditions.

The development of pheromones and related hormonal materials as possible insect and mite control measures was originally an outgrowth of basic research. Williams (1970) tells that "the possibility of using insect hormones as insecticides arose fortuitously as a by-product of studies of insect physiology from a research effort sufficiently pure and impractical to scandalize any Congressional committee."

Juvenile Hormones and Other Plant Products

A new, exciting possibility for research and practical insect control appeared a few years ago—the discovery that some plants produce chemical materials that are identical to the juvenile hormones produced by certain insects in the corpora allata (Williams 1970). These hormones keep insect larvae from becoming adults; when absent, metamorphosis proceeds and the insects become adults. The result of using the juvenile hormone in insect control is the formation of creatures that undergo only partial metamorphosis and never become adults. Williams commented that "until a few years ago the hormonal approach to the selective control of insects appeared to be a novel concept. Now we know that the strategy appears to be an ancient art invented by certain plants and practiced by them for tens of millions of years."

The "paper factor" research concerning juvenile hormones, which opened this door, is a classic example of an important discovery made as a secondary aspect of a primary research project. The juvenile hormone had been found earlier in insects. By accident it was found in paper products made from evergreen trees in American paper pulp but it was not found in European paper pulp. The active juvenile hormone was eventually isolated as a normal plant constituent of the balsam fir, the eastern hemlock, the Pacific yew, and the tamarack and may be at least part of the reason why these trees are so resistant to insect attack.

Japanese workers have reported 54 plant species that produce equivalent materials called *phytoecdysones* (Williams 1970). They are like the *ecdysones* synthesized by insects to stimulate metamorphosis. They are particularly abundant in the Polypodiaceae (ferns), ancient plants that evolved long before insects appeared.

These discoveries raise challenging and significant questions. Could these materials be used routinely to control metamorphosis and hence control insects? It is known that large overdoses of juvenile hormones produce nonviable insects and in the laboratory they appear to be effective in dosages much lower than any known insecticide. Also, phytoecdysones may act as potent insect deterrents and antifeeding agents (Williams 1970).

Other intriguing questions can be raised. Will other similar materials be found in plants that may control a plant's natural immunity and/or resistance to insects and other pests and diseases? Might it be possible to discover and isolate enough of these hormonal chemicals in plants to make them available to confer immunity and/or resistance on other agricultural plants where desired? If so, they eventually may be utilized to control insects and vectors of plant diseases as well as the plant diseases themselves. Then those who emphasize the importance and use of plant resistance and those who emphasize the primary significance of chemical control or pesticide techniques may cooperate closely. Most early insecticides were natural plant products, i.e., nicotine, pyrethrum flowers. Maybe we shall again have our basic arsenal of chemicals from natural plant products.

Wood also emphasized the possibilities inherent in other natural materials found in plants that have potential significance in the control of insects. The volatile organic sulfur compounds, the mustard oils, and the sulfides and mercaptans, all natural plant products, are attractive to some insects and may account for feeding selection and host preference in many specific cases. Chemicals that inhibit insect feeding (antifeedants) but do not kill the insect directly have been found in plants. For example, most insects (according to Japanese workers) will not feed on the plant, *Cocculus trilobus*—an exception is the Japanese fruit piercing moth, *Orgyia* spp. (Wood 1970). The soft leaves of *Clerodendron tricotomum* are not attacked by insects and compounds from this plant sprayed on rice plants may prevent insect attack. A very strong housefly attractant is found in a mushroom, the fly agaric, *Amanita muscaria* (Wood 1970).

It is known that catnip (nepetalactone) is closely related to the cyclopentanoid monoterpenes that have been isolated from insects. Both are insect repellents and it is thought that the adaptive function of nepetalactone in the catnip plant may protect it against destruction by insects (Eisner 1964).

Much of the foregoing research is being done in Japan (Wood 1970). Much more research of this type should be encouraged for "natural" chemical control of insects.

Sterilization

An important control now being developed is the sterilization of insects and particularly the production of male-sterile individuals. This is now being done on a large scale (Kilgore and Doutt 1967). A variety of chemicals have been found that can interrupt the reproductive cycle of a large number of insect species, and both chemosterilants and ionizing radiation have been used to produce male steriles. Gamma and/or X rays have been most useful thus far; usually cobalt 60 is used, producing gamma rays. Certain chemosterilants, including several alkylating agents and antimetabolites, have also been used with some success (Proverbs 1969). Of particular interest is the use of genetic manipulation to achieve sterility. Males that carry recessive lethal genes are utilized (Proverbs 1969). This research is centered in the U.S. Agricultural Research Service, Metabolism and Radiation Laboratory in Fargo, North Dakota (Knipling 1972).

Whitten (1971) has reported the beginning of genetic development and release of laboratory-created strains of insects that differ from field populations. They should create unstable situations that lead to the rapid replacement of undesirable field populations. Genes for all sorts of characteristics such as insecticide susceptibility, cold sensitivity, and even sterile hybrids, could be introduced into the natural insect populations by these manipulative techniques. In the future some of these developments may be of great practical value in control.

Sterile males are used in two methods for control of native insect populations. (1) Insects are reared in the laboratory, sterilized, and released into native insect populations; and (2) a proportion of the native population is captured, sterilized, and then restored to the local population. Some examples of effective control programs follow. The Mediterranean fruit fly has been controlled in Israel, Hawaii, France, Costa Rica, and Tunisia; and a control project was sponsored via a United Nations Special Fund program in 1965 in Central America. The same pest was virtually eliminated from the island of Capri in 1967 (Proverbs 1969).

The Mexican fruit fly, *Anastrepha ludens,* of northwestern Mexico has been a threat for many years to the California citrus industry. From 1954 to 1963 a 2–5 mile strip was sprayed along the California border. Starting in 1964 tepa-sterilized male flies were released. Later, gamma-ray sterilized flies were employed. The results have been good. No flies had appeared in California by 1969 (Proverbs 1969), and the control still seemed to be effective in 1972 (Knipling 1972).

In 1968 an attempt was made to halt an incipient bollworm infestation in cotton in the San Joaquin valley of California. Metepa-sterilized males of the pink bollworm, *Pectinophora gossypiella,* were released (Proverbs 1969). This control program also was still effective in 1972 (Knipling 1972).

Two effective small control programs of the codling moth on apple have been reported. In British Columbia from 1962 to 1965 radiation-sterilized codling moths were released in two abandoned apple orchards. The result was excellent control. In 1966 tepa- and radiation-sterilized male codling moths were released in a 93-acre orchard in the Yakima valley of Washington, giving control equivalent to that obtained with insecticides in a control orchard (Proverbs 1969).

Recent experiments in sterilizing the cotton boll weevil, *Anthonomous grandis,* with Dimilin (difluron) are promising. It has virtually no adverse effect on the beneficial insect complex, i.e., *Georcoris* sp., *Nabis* sp., and *Orius indieasus* in North Carolina. This sterilant must be applied to cotton plants at least 5–7 days before the females lay eggs to be effective. Since female boll weevils are not killed, multiple applications are required to maintain female sterility and are quite expensive. More research on the use of Dimilin against the boll weevil is needed (Jack S. Bachelor 1980, pers. commun.) but it appears to hold great promise. For example, 90–99 percent control of bollworm reproduction by Dimilin has been reported (Ganyard et al. 1977; Ganyard et al. 1978).

Radiation-induced sterilization of insects is discussed also in Chap. 10.

6

Chemical Control of Other Plant Enemies

Vectors

 Insecticides might be expected to be the most effective means of control of the vectors of plant diseases, particularly viruses, but satisfactory entomological control of the vector insect or mite seldom controls the disease (Walker 1969). The only explanation is that enough vectors still survive to bring about disease epiphytotics. Good insect control may eliminate 90–95 percent of the population and the remaining vectors, if they are active, can still introduce the disease and even bring about a bad outbreak. Vectors of plant viruses and other diseases, mostly mycoplasmal and bacterial, may be leafhoppers, aphids, white flies, thrips, beetles and other chewing insects, mites (particularly eriophyid mites), and others. Most of these cannot be controlled adequately by insecticidal sprays.

There are some exceptions. In greenhouse aphid control, fumigation can prevent the spread of cucumber mosaic; Pound and Chapman as reported in Walker (1969) used DDT sprays on carrot to control aster yellows, a mycoplasma disease. They were able to control the leafhopper vector well enough to reduce the percentage of diseased plants and increase yields by 20 percent or more. Aster yellows on lettuce has been controlled satisfactorily in the same way.

Another example is curly top of sugar beets, carried by a leafhopper. The leafhopper overwinters on virus-infected weed hosts in foothill areas in California and moves out into spring plantings of sugar beets and tomatoes in the interior valleys. An extensive spray campaign used on overwintering populations has been reasonably successful in controlling this virus disease. Also, the leaf-feeding beetles, *Diabrotica* spp., that spread the bacteria causing bacterial wilt of cucumber have been controlled reasonably well by spray programs and the disease has been minimized by this method. Since the bacteria overwinter in the bodies of the adult beetles and primary infection occurs when they feed on young leaves and cotyledons, the organism is

67

completely dependent on the insect for its survival. Hence, control of bacterial wilt hinges on control of the cucumber beetle (NAS 1968*a*; Walker 1969). Another example is control of the flea beetle, vector of Stewart's wilt of sweet corn, by insecticides (B. D. Blair 1979, pers. commun.).

Vectors often can be controlled via chemicals more easily and cheaply if their life cycle and ecological requirements are known. An example is the control of the vector of the beet western yellow virus, the green peach aphid, *Myzus persicae* (Tamaki et al. 1979).

Fungicides and Other Disease Controls

In plant pathology the first line of defense has seldom been chemicals. Chemicals used have been generally protective and preventive rather than therapeutic. Consequently, the general point of view toward chemicals in plant pathology is quite different from that in entomology.

Fungicides generally have not been as dangerous to the environment as insecticides. Most are not highly toxic to mammals and break down rapidly in the environment. One known conspicuous and potentially dangerous group of exceptions is the mercury compounds, most of which are used for seed treatments. Most mercury seed treatments have now been eliminated or are very closely controlled and monitored.

Plant pathologists in general have not felt as much pressure from environmental groups as have entomologists to alter their techniques. In the major field, forage, and forest crops the primary control techniques used have not been chemical. In fruit, vegetable, and ornamental crops chemical controls have been much more important and commonplace.

Fungicides and some other chemicals are important in plant disease control, however, and this point is emphasized in the following statement (NAS 1968*a*):

> Chemical control is often the feasible means of attacking a disease problem. It is often more economical and effective than any other measure. Many diseases cannot be controlled by any other means. Ultimately, the development of satisfactory resistant varieties and a better understanding of the environmental influences on pathogens which will permit wider utilization of environmental and cultural means of control may provide measures to supplant or supplement many of the chemical controls in use today.

Chemicals used in plant disease control are classified according to the group of organisms affected. Fungicides are used against fungi, bactericides against bacteria, and so forth. No chemicals are registered now as working against viruses (viricides) although these have been sought by many researchers (Univ. Calif. 1972*c*). Occasionally insecticides control disease vectors in a satisfactory manner. Herbicides control some plant diseases in which the key is the control of weeds that serve as alternate hosts of pathogenic organisms or vectors. Bactericides, particularly antibiotics such as streptomycin, satisfactorily control several important bacterial diseases of crops. Occasionally the research associated with these chemicals has been done cooperatively by plant pathologists and representatives of other pest management disciplines. Usually this has not been true. Such cooperative research should be encouraged because combined chemical controls are typically less expensive than separate chemical controls and also save time and labor. In some cases, also, potential deleterious effects on the environment are reduced markedly.

Copper compounds have served as fungicides and also as bactericides. A few fungicides have also functioned effectively against mites as miticides, for example, binapacryl (dinoseb methacrylate) and dinocap (Karathane). At least one fungicide, lime sulfur, has functioned effectively as an insecticide and a miticide. Some other sulfur compounds have both fungicidal and insecticidal value.

Quite a few nematicides have fungicidal properties, particularly against soil fungi. For example, dichloropropene and several other soil fumigants are as effective against soil fungi as against nematodes and are also effective against many other soil microorganisms that are very difficult to control (Univ. Calif. 1972c). Chloropicrin, for example, controls the fungus, *Verticillium alboatrum,* and carbonbisulfide and methylbromide control the fungus, *Armillaria mellea* (NAS 1968a).

This area of interdisciplinary research needs much more attention. Cooperative efforts between the disciplines should be the order of the day.

The protective contact fungicides used most in control of plant diseases are typically applied to seed, soil, or foliage to keep the disease organism from entering the plant. Such fungicides usually need to be applied frequently (Turgeon et al. 1973). Protective fungicides are particularly important in fungus diseases that are very hard to control or that must be controlled thoroughly because of the commercial cosmetic requirements of the crop, such as diseases of apple, peach, plum, many small fruits, potato, and tomato. Protective fungicides now work very effectively in achieving cosmetic control required for these crops but costs are becoming prohibitive, and more effective, less costly, foliar fungicides with eradicant properties that can be applied less frequently are needed (NAS 1968a). There is also need for less expensive and more efficient soil fungicides. Many aspects of research in chemical control of plant diseases need to be expanded even though reasonably satisfactory measures are now available.

An example of a plant disease that is difficult to control is apple scab, incited by *Venturia inaequalis.* It is a classical fungus disease, controlled only by protective fungicides since the early days of Bordeaux mixture. A complex spray schedule, including Glyodin (Crag fruit fungicide 341), captan (Orthocide 406), and Dodine (Cyprex) used as eradicants and protectants and Elgetol (4, 6-dinitro-o-cresol) used as a ground spray, is followed. It requires spraying every week to 10 days or after every heavy rain, a very expensive process (Walker 1969).

Some other plant diseases can only be controlled by fungicides. The only good method of controlling white rot of onion, incited by *Sclerotium cepivorum,* is to treat the soil with dicloran (Botran). Peach leaf curl, incited by *Taphrina deformans,* can be controlled rather easily by a single fungicidal application in the fall or early spring (Walker 1969).

The problem of controlling plant diseases in the tropics is compounded because of the nature of the tropics. Wellman (1972) summarized this problem and emphasized the need for more careful studies in the tropics:

> It is not wise for the tropical man to go unhesitatingly to temperate zone tried-and-accepted chemical treatments. There are special problems in the tropics, the effects of such matters as the non-winter, epiphytic bacteria and fungi occurring as natural but invisible growth on leaf surfaces, foliage that never dries, tree crops with no truly annual dormant period, soils with massive numbers of bacteria and fungi, that nevertheless change disinfection problems. In some places in the tropics rain may fall almost every day in the year. There are seeds that need disinfection that are never truly dry or dormant and there are difficulties in chemical storage and transportation and spray machine maintenance.

Often in the tropics, as well as elsewhere, growers find that spraying for the control of a specific disease has secondary helpful or harmful effects. Some fungicides greatly reduce the amount of mosses, algae, leafy liverworts, and lichens that cover leaves and limbs of many trees, the coffee tree, for example. In these cases spraying for one disease results in reducing (if not curing) a secondary disease or malady (Wellman 1972).

Some fungicides have been shown to have considerable insecticidal value in specific cases, either alone or in combination with specific insecticides. This area deserves more research (Phillips and Todd 1979).

Harvest-aid Chemicals

Harvest-aid chemicals and defoliants are often helpful in disease control, and sometimes in insect control even when not designed for this purpose. Aid in achieving early total harvest and cleaning of fields often helps in disease and insect control. Defoliants and desiccants may accelerate the destruction of stalks and encourage early deep plowing, both of which tend to be beneficial in reducing disease carryover from year to year. Effective harvest-aid treatments have been important in controlling cotton insects as well as cotton diseases. The growth of the cotton plant is stopped, which reduces the damage from late season buildup of any pests that are over-wintering, such as aphids, leafworms, and white flies. This is another area where more cooperative research between entomologists, plant patholo-gists, and agronomists might lead to less costly disease and insect control (Univ. Calif. 1972 *a*).

Chemotherapy in Disease Control

Chemotherapy is relatively new in plant pathology. Most systemic fungicides have been used to treat established infections, but attempts to protect plants from invasion by pathogens via chemotherapeutants will become important (NAS 1968*a*). Systemic fungicides are absorbed and distributed within the plant and can destroy established infections and con-trol diseases for weeks or even months. Typically they are absorbed via the leaves or roots and hence can be applied through drenches or in granular form (Turgeon et al. 1973). The granular form is easily applied without ex-pensive application equipment—particularly important for small growers in the developing world.

Not many effective systemic fungicides are available. Those effective under various circumstances are benomyl (F-1991 or Benlate), chloroneb, thiabendazole (TBZ), and ethazole (Turgeon et al. 1973). Generically they are either oxathiins, pyrimidines, or benzimidazoles (Erwin 1973). They share the ability to move through the cuticle and translocate through the vascular system and across leaves.

Thus far according to Erwin (1973), "benomyl has the widest spectrum of fungitoxic activity of all the newer systemics and is the most effective benzimidazole fungicide, but Phycomycetes, some Basidomycetes and dark spored members of the Deuteromycetes are insensitive to benomyl." Both the powdery mildews on cucumbers and other crops and brown rot of stone fruits have been controlled by benomyl. Biehn and Dimond (1971) reported a 97 percent reduction of foliar symptoms in Dutch elm disease by benomyl, which remained in the tissue of the trees in measurable amounts throughout the growing season. Others also have reported benomyl control of Dutch elm disease. Unfortunately, it is so expensive and difficult to apply properly that most potential users have not been able to afford or use it consistently to control Dutch elm disease.

There are several examples of benomyl suppressing oxidant air pollu-tion. On bean plants in field plots, benomyl sprayed once a week gave 80 percent suppression of foliar oxidant injury (Manning and Vardaro 1973). Seem et al. (1972) have reported two systemic fungicides, triarimol (EL-273) and its monochlorophenyl cyclohexyl analogue, that suppressed ozone in-jury in the greenhouse. This research should be pursued, particularly with extensive and severe air pollution damage in agricultural areas near large cities.

Benomyl also may be effective against a microsporidial disease of the alfalfa weevil. Since microsporidia are the most important group of protozoan parasites attacking insects during the mass rearing of insects in the laboratory, this may be a lead toward practical microsporidian disease control (Hsiao and Hsiao 1973). Benomyl is relatively nontoxic to mammals. If it can be shown to be significant in the control of certain insect and plant disease problems, it may develop into a more useful material.

The fungicide benomyl is very toxic to the predatory mite, *Amblyseius fallacis*. Consequently, it should not be used on apple trees when these mites are controlling the prey mite pests of apples (Nakashima and Croft 1974). Also, many people in the United States are concerned about the adverse effects of the use of benomyl on another control agent, *Spicaria rileyi* (B. D. Blair 1979, pers. commun.).

There have been recent U.S. government hearings concerning the continued registration and use of benomyl and a carefully controlled set of rules has been established to protect workers who handle benomyl.

The seed-borne loose smut of cereals, incited by *Ustilago tritici,* has been controlled in wheat seed in England by carboxin (Vitavax), an oxathiin, with a 6-hour soak. *Ustilago nuda* has been controlled by seed treatments alone. Using the pyrimidines, control of powdery mildew of wheat, incited by *Erysiphe graminis,* has been achieved with ethirimol in England; and apple scab, incited by *Venturia inaequalis,* has been controlled by triarimol (EL-273). This compound also has eradicated both stripe smut, *Urocystis striiformis,* and flag smut, *U. agropyri,* on bluegrass sod (Erwin 1973).

Two synthetic antifungal systemic chemotherapeutants, Vitavax (carboxin) and Plantvax, have been effective against Basidiomycetes, the rusts and smuts (Fawcett and Spencer 1970). Purines and pyrimidines, for example, Blasticidin-S, are used rather extensively in Japan to control rice blast disease. Several antibiotics that are produced by *Streptomyces* spp. have been considered as systemic antifungal, antibiotic chemotherapeutants. An example is the cycloheximide, actidione. It has been effective in the control of certain bacterial diseases of plants. Unfortunately many compounds that show excellent antifungal activity in culture studies or against spores in vitro are quite ineffective as systemic fungicidal materials in the field. The glowing reports of in vitro studies must be tested in the field and treated with considerable skepticism until field analyses are made (Fawcett and Spencer 1970).

Systemic insecticides, such as Systox (demeton or mercaptophos), have been more effective overall than systemic fungicides. In the chemotherapy of plant diseases, the investigator is typically dealing with two types of plants, the pathogen (fungus) and the host, which may often have similar metabolic systems and respond similarly to the fungicide. Systemic insecticides, by contrast, typically act against the nervous system of insects; the host plant has no comparable system and therefore is not killed.

Nematodes

Most nematicides degrade rather rapidly by biological, chemical, or physical processes and are not a serious threat to the environment. Their residues have seldom been a problem and rarely approach legally established tolerances. Alkyl halides such as bromine have left residues at times but rarely above legally safe levels except in muck soils (Good 1972*a*). Like plant pathologists, nematologists have usually used chemicals only when all other methods have failed or have been only partially satisfactory—the reverse of the typical situation in entomology.

However, use of nematicides has increased dramatically in recent years. Good (1972*a*) reported this increase and its effects:

> Suitable application methods have been devised for applying about 20 highly effective nematicides and soil fumigants. When nematodes were controlled with nematicides an average yield increase of 37.4 percent was obtained for 20 crops in the United States. Such remarkable yield increases are primarily the result of nematode control.

Chemical control of nematodes has definite limitations and has never replaced standard control methods such as crop rotation, fallowing, and use of resistant varieties (NAS 1968*b*). When these methods do not work or are not practical, nematicides often have proved to be the only effective means of reducing nematode populations below economically damaging levels. Careful research is necessary for a definite host, a particular environment, and a specific chemical and nematode before dependable control procedures are developed. Few, if any, techniques have been devised that work under all situations (Univ. Calif. 1972*b*).

Examples of nematodes that must be controlled by nematicides follow. The citrus nematode, which is a sedentary exposed endoparasite, cannot be controlled well by standard methods. It requires a nematicide preplanting treatment with dichloropropene fumigant at 70–200 gallons per acre. This nematicide is injected into the soil by chisels or applied in irrigation water (Univ. Calif. 1972*b*). Nematode species that are involved with virus transmission are difficult to control, since a control that approaches eradication must reach the roots of the previous planting, sometimes 8–10 feet. This control has only been achieved by summer-to-fall applications of dichloropropene fumigants at 250 gallons or more per acre to depths of 3 feet or more (Univ. Calif. 1972*b*).

Nematicides are also effective in controlling some plant disease organisms and other organisms in the soil. Interdisciplinary research wherever nematicides are being tested would be wise. Some examples follow. Chloropicrin, an older soil fumigant, is valuable when serious nematode problems are combined with serious soil fungus problems. Also, the compounds Trapex (methyl isothiocyanate), Vapam (metham sodium), and propargyl bromide are nematicidal but are usually used to control disease and pest complexes where fungi, bacteria, insects, and weeds in addition to nematodes are involved. These materials are potentially very practical. Good (1968) has reported several cases in which the fumigant, ethylene dibromide, has been effective in controlling the *Fusarium* wilt organism, *Fusarium oxysporum,* and root-knot nematodes, *Meloidogyne* spp. Materials such as Vorlex and Trizone are also combination nematicides, fungicides, and herbicides and may control some soil arthropods.

Some organic phosphates are nematicidal but they are primarily considered insecticides. Examples of these are diazinon, phosphorothioate, and Thimet (Phorate). Methylbromide, although expensive and having a high vapor pressure similar to chloropicrin, is valuable in high value per acre plant beds and in nurseries. It destroys most deleterious microorganisms in the soil and is quite effective in weed control (NAS 1968b).

Counter (terbufos) and Furadan (carbofuran) are both nematicides and corn rootworm insecticides. Much initial research was done independently. Nematologists reported yield increases that may have partially resulted from insect control and entomologists probably reported findings that may have been the result of nematode control. A joint venture would have eliminated confusion, increased efficiency, and produced more credible results (B. D. Blair 1979, pers. commun.).

Weeds

Herbicides are relatively new and only recently have they been used in large quantities for weed control. Now their use in developed countries is mushrooming. In 1950 there were only 15 basic herbicides. By 1974 there were more than 180 with about 6000 formulated products (Shaw 1974a). They are second now only to insecticides and are gaining fast. Weeds, next to weather, are the worst enemies of crop plants year after year and *must* be controlled to have satisfactory crops. The old methods of weed control are time consuming and expensive. Herbicides, consequently, are becoming more important, in many cases, than other plant protection chemicals. Growers do not always know whether they will have diseases, insects, or nematodes but they know they will have weeds. Consequently, little persuasion is needed (if herbicides are available) to convince growers to use them.

Shaw (1974*a*) has summarized the effects, direct and indirect, that the development of herbicides has had on modern agricultural practices.

Advances in chemical weed control technology have had far reaching impact on all phases of crop production, including the selection of crops and varieties, seedbed preparation, methods of seeding and seeding rates. They have made possible a wide choice of row spacings, plant spacing in the row and plant populations. They also influence fertilizer practices, including time of application and placement.

Tillage and cultivation techniques have been revolutionized. For many crops chemical weed control now makes minimum tillage possible. Even zero tillage now seems feasible for a few crops on certain soil types. Control has had a major impact on irrigation practices, harvesting, seed-cleaning operations and erosion control.

New herbicides have tremendously increased the efficiency of fallowing practices for weed control. The use of chemicals has greatly reduced tillage in some of the fallow-farming areas. The adoption of minimum tillage and chemical fallow practices greatly reduces wind erosion; improves moisture conservation; reduces sheet erosion; improves fertilizer utilization; improves soil structure and drainage and increases yield and quality of crops.

Chemical weed control has also improved the effectiveness of various practices directed to the control of diseases, nematodes and insects. Herbicides have increased the effectiveness of pasture renovation techniques. They have also improved the productivity of pastures, rangelands and forests. The use of farm water resources for irrigation and recreation and the maintenance of reservoirs, drainage ditches, ditch banks, irrigation canals and farm roadsides have been significantly improved by the use of herbicides.

Shaw's statement implies that nearly all crop production efficiency would be markedly improved if all known modern weed control practices, particularly use of herbicides, were used. For example, hundreds of thousands of acres of maize are now being produced using zero tillage, thanks to herbicides (B. D. Blair 1979, pers. commun.).

Controversy has developed in recent years over the use of herbicides, particularly 2, 4-D and 2, 4, 5-T (TCDD) in Vietnam and elsewhere. Most people are aware of the effects of 2, 4-D drift on many plants and have seen the apparent plant monsters created by such drifts. This phenomenon is often disconcerting. Plant disease clinics are bombarded every year by questions from suburban home owners concerning herbicidal drifts.

The arguments have waxed long and loud both for and against the use of herbicides and articles on both sides have appeared in scientific journals. In his 1971 study of Vietnam, Westing came to the following conclusion: "The herbicidal agents in Vietnam have a significant and long term impact not only on the land but also on the many human beings only coincidentally involved." He suggested an immediate halt to military spraying of herbicides. Galston (1971), after studying many scientific papers concerning 2, 4-D and its related compounds, gave a somewhat neutral report. He wrote that many workers feel that these compounds are potentially damaging to health and the environment, while other equally competent workers report that the compounds degrade rapidly and are actually very safe to use insofar as the environment is concerned. Galston concluded, "The ecological consequences of the widespread use of herbicides in natural communities have been largely unassessed." By contrast, Johnson (1971) summarized his study as follows: "The widespread use of phenoxy herbicides has produced no demonstrable evidence of potential harm to man. The herbicides used most widely are degraded and do not bioconcentrate."

The 2, 4, 5-T controversy continues (Wendell R. Mullison 1979, pers. commun.). A conference of 60 scientists representing all sides and aspects of the controversy was held in June 1979 at Arlington, Virginia. The consensus was that 2, 4, 5-T is not carcinogenic or mutagenic in animal test systems, that there are no adverse effects on human reproduction, that there is no long persistence or accumulation in the environment, and that the material is safe as an herbicide when used according to directions. Perhaps it is best to let continued extensive herbicide research and use settle these arguments.

Most herbicides to be efficient must have a certain amount of persistence in the soil. Hassall (1969) summarized the problems associated with using an herbicide with the proper persistence to do a particular job.

> The varying chemical stability and physical properties of different herbicides are such as to provide a wide range of persistence in the soil. Care must therefore be exercised in the choice of herbicide for any specific purpose. The use of an herbicide of too low persistence may result in the unnecessary work and extra costs of multiple applications, whereas the use of one too persistent can prove financially disastrous by putting land out of commission for a season or more.

A new development in herbicides (and insecticides), *controlled-release technology,* would control the amount of chemical available at a specific time and thus extend residual time as long as desired but no longer, avoid use of excessive amounts of herbicides on a given crop, avoid environmental contamination and/or damage, and decrease total cost of purchase and application (Shaw 1974*b*). This development is summarized by Shaw (1974*a*):

> The effectiveness of most herbicides is reduced by their inadequate residual activity. To overcome these limitations, more is usually applied initially than needed. In our future strategies, we shall need to develop herbicide formulations with controlled-release characteristics. These would permit the slow release of the active ingredients uniformly over a predetermined period of

time. Successful development of such technology would revolutionize chemical weed control. Initial rates of application could be reduced. Losses from volatility, undesirable downward movement through the soil profile, sheet erosion, drift and other environmental problems could be reduced.

Intensive research is needed to develop the controlled-release characteristics of polymerized herbicides, copolymers, encapsulation, and related formulation techniques (Shaw 1974a).

Controlled-release herbicides, insecticides, and other pesticides should be important in controlling various aquatic pests and have already resulted in improved mosquito control (Shaw 1974b). Controlled-release technology would also improve effectiveness and safety of many agricultural chemicals, soil conditioners, antibiotics, seed protectants, attractants, repellents, chemotherapeutants, growth regulators, nematicides, fumigants, fungicides, insecticides, and defoliants. Controlled-release preparations of volatile fumigants for nematodes, soil-borne plant pathogens, weeds, seeds, and harmful soil arthropods are needed. If toxic concentrations could be maintained in the soil for 24 hours without use of gastight covers the control of soil-borne pests could be improved dramatically. Fungicide seed treatments with longer effective residual activity would also revolutionize the efforts to control seed and seedling diseases of plants. Shaw pointed out that "many of the agricultural chemicals introduced in the 1950's and 1960's can be substantially improved in effectiveness and safety through controlled-release technology."

Controlled-release technology may be less expensive and more effective than developing new, more selective chemicals. For example, a polymeric microencapsulated formulation of methyl parathion was introduced by the Penwalt Corporation. It has improved insecticidal activity, has a much longer residual control period, and is only about 1/100 as toxic as conventional parathion (Shaw 1974b). However, problems have arisen with encapsulated methyl parathion because bees often carry the small granules back to the hive (B. D. Blair 1979, pers. commun.). Hence, controlled-release technology is being viewed with some caution and concern. A book by Scher (1977) summarizes controlled-release technology.

Effective weed seed germination stimulants would greatly improve weed control technology. Most such materials are not effective because they denature very quickly in the soil. Improvement of their residual activity characteristics would be a big boon (Shaw 1974a).

In modern agriculture the fields sometimes show evidence of cases in which too high concentrations or too persistent herbicides were used. Destructive effects sometimes can be seen in the current crop. Herbicides by their very nature must be selective since they are designed to kill some plants but not others. Their primary characteristic is the differential phytotoxicity. Most of them are relatively innocuous to animals. There are a few exceptions—for example, the substituted dinitrophenols, used to control weeds in cereals, are highly toxic to mammals—but most herbicides are characterized by low levels of mammalian toxicity (Hassall 1969). To assure proper usage of weed control technology it is wise to obtain the annual *Weed Control Manual.*

Not enough research has been done on the effects of herbicides on soil microflora and microfauna. Soil-borne pathogens are important to agriculture and soil microorganisms are essential to the decomposition of organic matter, the maintenance of complex systems of antagonism and synergism, and the maintenance and development of soil fertility. Sufficient observations have been made of most herbicides to show that the usual field applications are not developing any serious hazards as far as soil microorganism populations are concerned. Several herbicides have no known effects on any species of soil microorganisms, a few herbicides have transitory effects at the rates used for weed control that may be either stimulatory or inhibitory, but none have had a demonstrable lasting effect (NAS 1968c).

In laboratory surveys, herbicide concentrations that far exceed normal use have had no adverse effects on soil microorganisms or soil microbial processes such as nitrification, nitrogen fixation, and cellulose decomposition. In some cases rates of application several times greater than those used in the field have been stimulatory to the growth of some microorganism species studied (NAS 1968c). In laboratory studies, concentrations of 2, 4-D up to 200 times the amounts normally used have shown no appreciable effects on populations of bacteria, actinomycetes, and fungi—a finding that would question whether it is dangerous in the soil environment.

Some common herbicides have been reported to inhibit the growth of plant pathogens in the soil, although typically the concentrations have been much higher than would be employed in the field. Some herbicides—PCP (Santobrite), DNPB (Dinoseb), amitrole (aminotriazole), CIPC (chlorpropham), and EPTC (Eptam)—are toxic to certain specific groups of soil microorganisms at usual rates of application. However, the effects are short-lived; soon after degradation of the herbicide, they grow back to their original numbers, often achieving temporary population counts higher than before the application of herbicide. The population typically returns to a lower level in the normal cyclic pattern characteristic of competing microorganisms in the soil (NAS 1968c).

Altman and Campbell (1977) have summarized the effects of herbicides on plant diseases and plant disease propagules. Some diseases and organisms are stimulated by specific herbicides, some are inhibited, and some do not appear to be affected in any way; the problems do not appear to be severe. However, each new herbicide will need to be tested for its effects on plant diseases and pests.

The interactions between soil microorganisms and herbicides have just begun to be explored. The soil is so complex that opportunities for studying the effects of various herbicides on different species of microorganisms are legion. The research associated with other possible deleterious environmental effects of herbicides also needs to be encouraged.

Herbicides are far more important than generally realized in the control of plant diseases and pests. When large populations of weeds are destroyed, the attendant populations of arthropod pests, including vectors, may starve or be forced to migrate. The use of herbicides around the base of trees to control weeds may destroy predator breeding locations (B. D. Blair 1979, pers. commun.). Weed populations often function as alternate hosts or inoculum sources for specific plant diseases; when they are destroyed, the local reservoir for specific diseases is destroyed also. Likewise, weeds are often hosts of important species of plant parasitic nematodes.

The herbicide atrazine (Aatrex) has been shown to have a selective effect on the growth of certain soil fungi. It suppresses the growth of *Sclerotium rolfsii, Rhizoctonia solani, Fusarium oxysporum* f. sp. *vasinfectum,* and some other *Fusarium* species. By contrast, it stimulates the growth of *Trichoderma viride, Fusarium roseum, Gestrichum* spp., *Penicillium* spp., and several species antagonistic to *Fusarium* spp. It was felt that the resultant shift in the fungal balance in the soil might reduce the incidence of soil pathogens because more saprophytes than pathogens appeared to be tolerant of or stimulated by atrazine (Richardson 1970).

It has been predicted that weeds would soon develop resistance to herbicides. However, there is little evidence to show that resistance has actually occurred. Resistance to triazine herbicides has been reported in a few localities in North America on a few annual weeds, i.e., *Chenopodium album* and *Amaranthus retroflexus,* but in most situations where herbicides are used no weed resistance has been reported (Putwain and Holliday 1979).

7

Compatibility of Pesticides; Toxicology

 Pesticides are designed to do a specific task. The present trend is to develop more selective chemicals that will do a specific job with minimal or no effect on the environment. Several pesticides can be combined, however, in the same spray, dust, or application. Insecticides and fungicides have been combined in spray programs, particularly on crops requiring cosmetic control such as apples, peaches, and pears. Combined spray mixes or dusts are the rule rather than the exception in some control schedules. Combining pesticides saves time, is more economical, and is more convenient.

A problem with this practice is that some chemicals are not compatible with others. A complex group of charts has been developed that must be used religiously in any attempt to combine chemicals in control programs. These compatibility charts are available in various industrial handbooks and through most agricultural extension services. The annual *Farm Chemical Handbook* produces a group of compatibility charts that are the result of the combined studies of chemical companies, university research, extension programs, and others. This handbook includes not only spray compatibility charts but also manufacturers' product recommendations for each chemical and for each mixture—whether insecticides, fungicides, herbicides, nematicides, or something else. The research required to find out whether chemicals are compatible with each other is tremendous and expensive. Many pesticides come with a compatibility chart on the package and recommended dosages. Users must appreciate the significance of these charts and follow them carefully (Sharvelle 1961).

In the general area of compatibility there has been complete cooperation between the plant protection disciplines. It is very important to know which chemical materials can be mixed and in what concentrations for safe utilization. Only interdisciplinary research programs can yield such information. Such interdisciplinary cooperation, often on an informal basis, has been characteristic of plant pathologists and entomologists associated with fruit and vegetable spray programs in the developed countries.

80

The compatibility of fungicides and bactericides is quite variable (Univ. Calif. 1972c), ranging from combinations that are desirable to others that are essentially impossible because of chemical reactions in the spray tank or extreme phytotoxicity after application. Bactericides should be combined with other pesticides only when compatibility studies are favorable.

A number of commercial products are available that contain a mixture of ingredients—insecticides and fungicides or fungicides and bactericides, and so forth. They are the result of many years of testing under a variety of environmental conditions (Shurtleff and Petty, no date). These mixtures often cost more than the separate ingredients.

Many herbicides are compatible with other pesticides and even with fertilizers. Herbicides are sometimes but not usually used together because normal economic use does not encourage mixtures. Herbicides usually are used at times when insecticides and other pesticides need not be applied. There are exceptions, however, and more interdisciplinary research is needed in this area and particularly in the possibilities of applying preemergence herbicides with preemergence fertilizers and, at times, nematicides (Sharvelle 1961). Shaw (1974a) emphasized this point also: "The cross contamination of herbicides and other pesticides is a growing problem and research is needed to solve it." One interesting example of this problem arises when Di-syston (disulfoton) and Thimet (phorate) used as soil insecticides are used with Sencor (metribuzin), an herbicide. This combination will eliminate soybean plants (B. D. Blair 1979, pers. commun.).

The new microbial control agents need to be tested for compatibility with chemical pesticides. *Bacillus thuringiensis,* a microbial control, is now known to be compatible with 26 fungicides, insecticides, herbicides, and acaricides (Burges and Hussey 1971) besides 35 supplements, emulsifiers, adhesives, wetting agents, and so forth. This compatibility will make *B. thuringiensis* very helpful in coordinated control programs. Better control often may be obtained with combinations of biological and chemical control agents, with the additional advantages of less chemical use and usually minimal environmental damage (Burges and Hussey 1971).

Microbial insecticides have several advantages. They are typically innocuous to vertebrates and plants and they tend to be specific in their pathogenicity to insect species. Even insect pathogens such as *B. thuringiensis,* which have rather wide host ranges, normally do not upset existing host-parasite relationships and do not create secondary pest problems as chemical insecticides often do. The fact that microbial pesticides seem to have potential for outstanding compatibility with chemical insecticides will prove to be most advantageous in integrated insect control programs (Kilgore and Doutt 1967).

On occasion reduced or even sublethal quantities of chemical insecticides mixed with microbial pesticides have achieved effective control, reducing costs and residue problems. This research deserves more interdisciplinary attention (Kilgore and Doutt 1967). One must remember, however, that specific pesticides must be used according to the limitations and requirements on the label.

Phytotoxicity

The problems of phytotoxicity in the use of chemical controls is seldom emphasized sufficiently. Shurtleff and Petty (no date) say that "in light of the many hundreds of pesticides, soluble fertilizers, growth regulators, sticking-wetting agents and other chemicals that can be sprayed on plants it is a wonder that plant injury (phytotoxicity) does not occur more often." Improper or accidental application of agricultural chemicals is a major cause of plant injury. These materials are subject to misuse and the salespeople, researchers, growers, and all who are involved with their use need to be familiar with their potential for hazard and their legitimate limitations.

Before an agricultural chemical is approved by the U.S. federal government it must meet stringent requirements. This seldom means that the approved material is completely harmless to plants, animals, humans, or the environment. It is safe—giving minimal, temporary, or directed damage—only if the directions are followed carefully (USDA 1972). Incorrect use occasionally causes serious problems.

Classic examples of plant damage result from the use of severe toxicants along roadways, for example, the excessive use of road salt on highways; the effects of automotive pollutant gases accumulating in toxic quantities along confined, heavily traveled roadways; or excessive use of certain herbicides to kill noxious weeds along roadsides.

Since so many different kinds of chemical materials are involved, there is no simple set of principles concerning phytotoxicity. Each potential case must be studied separately. In addition to industrial chemicals already discussed, natural phytotoxic materials such as sea spray and volcanic ash occur in the environment. Many other industrial chemicals are phytotoxic when present in high concentrations. The potential phytotoxicity of each of these materials must be considered for different plant species and under varying environmental conditions. For pesticides this research is a standard part of U.S. federal registration requirements (NAS 1968a).

Most commercial nematicides are too phytotoxic to be used immediately before a crop is planted. Nematicides and soil fumigants, for example, carbon bisulfide; EDB (ethylene dibromide); 1, 3-D; and chloropicrin, are applied several weeks or even months prior to planting. The resultant phytotoxicity is influenced very much by temperature, moisture, soil tilth, soil type, and the kind of plant. Some plants are very susceptible to injury by certain nematicides; others are very resistant. Fortunately, most nematicides and soil fumigants can be used in ways that minimize phytotoxic potential and still control nematodes and be safe for use in the environment (NAS 1968*b*).

Plants vary a great deal in their response to chemicals. This characteristic is the basis for the whole herbicide industry, where specific phytotoxicities are the key to control of certain weeds while the crop plant is essentially undamaged. Phytotoxicity is often more severe under slow drying conditions when plants are in a low state of vigor. They may also be predisposed to greater damage by such things as herbicide injury, winter injury, waterlogging of the soil, poor soil, diseases, insect damage, drought, and imbalance of nutrients (Shurtleff and Petty, no date). Quite often chemicals may be more damaging to plants when applied during hot weather. For example, sulfur applied above 32°C (90°F) is much more toxic than at lower temperatures (Univ. Calif. 1972*c*).

Metallic ions that are very phytotoxic in one form may be quite safe to use in other forms. For example, copper ions are highly toxic to all plant life but safe, selective fungicidal action has been obtained by applying copper in insoluble compounds. Such compounds as copper oxychloride, copper carbonate, Burgundy mixtures, and cuprous oxide (all insoluble materials containing copper) are routinely used as fungicides. The best known of all these insoluble copper fungicides is the oldest, the still excellent Bordeaux mixture (Hassall 1969).

The relationship of weed control to phytotoxicity is interesting because herbicides are designed to be phytotoxic to particular species. Their phytotoxicity is the key to their use and also to their abuse. Consequently, a complicated lexicon of information has been developed concerning proper use of materials to achieve desired weed control. When properly used, herbicides kill the weeds only (Crafts and Robbins 1962). The widespread feeling, particularly during the Vietnam War (see Chap. 6), that herbicides such as 2, 4-D are potentially hazardous to warm-blooded animals has less credence when one realizes that essentially all common herbicides are safe for mammals because they are designed to be toxic to plants. Their toxic potential has never been aimed at animals. The notion that herbicides should be toxic also to animals and people indicates a complete misunderstanding of the chemical goal for herbicides, which is differential phytotoxicity.

The overriding consideration in phytotoxicity with all chemicals and materials is dosage. Research for specific instances will determine acceptable dosage for a given plant species during its various stages and under specific environmental conditions. The specifications for use must be followed as carefully as the recommendations for human and animal medicinal materials and are the result of just as much careful research.

Many materials are potentially phytotoxic. An old and favorite teacher once remarked in his flat and raspy voice, "The most toxic material in your spray tank is water, the lack of it is called drought and always causes death in plants, an excess of it is called flooding and usually causes death rapidly in all but aquatic plants. The secret of proper usage of all potentially toxic materials, including water, is dosage." He was a great teacher and a true sage.

Pesticide Application Equipment

Pesticide spray equipment that can utilize any spray materials and dusting equipment that can utilize any available dusts are desired. Compatible mixtures usually can be handled satisfactorily in standard spray and dust equipment. It is important in developing pesticide application equipment to consider the requirement of mixtures as well as of specific individual materials.

The recirculating sprayer, a recent development, takes advantage of the difference in height of weeds and crop plants. For example, in many U.S. Corn Belt river bottom fields maize was grown continuously because it could compete with Johnson grass, a weed. This continuous cropping meant that northern and western rootworms usually became a problem on maize. Now, with the recirculating sprayer, soybeans can be grown and Johnson grass can be controlled with an herbicide. This new maize-soybean-maize-soybean rotation eliminates the need for soil insecticides for rootworm control, controls Johnson grass much better than was possible previously, gives a good soil building rotation with a legume, and probably reduces the incidence of a maize virus disease that overwinters on Johnson grass (B. D. Blair 1979, pers. commun.).

More research is needed to develop simple equipment for the application of pesticides and mixtures in the developing world. More granular materials that can be spread safely by hand are greatly needed. The small farmers of the developing world now have few pesticides that can be spread simply and safely by hand and often have no satisfactory simple, effective, and safe application equipment.

Toxicology: Chemical Residues and Tolerances

The problem of chemical residues on foodstuffs and other commodities as well as residues accumulating in the environment is relatively new. We have only recently developed adequate analytical methods to determine the safe use of agricultural chemicals that may affect humans and the environment deleteriously. Palm (1972) summarized this matter:

> A growing awareness of problems related to these residues in the field during the time of application, crop production, and harvest, as a human health

hazard, compels us to direct more attention to avoiding contact with certain classes of pesticides and their residues. This aspect of environmental safety is of constant concern.

As Matsumura et al. (1972) pointed out, these environmental contamination problems are for the most part the result of urbanization, modern industrialization, and technologically advanced agricultural practices. They have become serious in the technologically advanced countries— the United States, Western Europe, and Japan. When we examine the use of pesticides in the United States as compared to Japan there are several very interesting differences. These are summarized by Matsumura et al. (1972):

> The major concern in the United States has been with pesticide residues in food for human consumption as well as mammalian toxicity of pesticidal compounds. Only recently has serious attention been focused on other problem areas such as effects on wildlife, water quality and environmental alteration of pesticides. Particular emphasis has been placed on the chlorinated hydrocarbons, with DDT singled out as the principal target of public and scientific concern.

> In Japan the major concern has been the development and study of chemicals for rice production including insecticides, herbicides and fungicides for rice blast control. Organomercurials used in controlling rice blast have been the major factor in increasing rice yields. In addition, they have created severe environmental problems. As a result, studies on the effects of the organomercurials on higher animals, as well as their action in the environment, have been in progress in Japan for many years. In addition, the widespread use of BHC for control of the rice stem borer created problems somewhat similar to those caused by DDT in the United States. Japan has been quick to suspend the use of these chemicals and her scientists have been highly successful in developing alternate means such as the use of biological control, antibiotics and other chemicals with less undesirable properties for pest control.

When pesticides are applied, some of the residues stay in the soil or in soil water or both. It is important for us to know what happens to these chemicals after they arrive in the soil and groundwater. In particular, we need to know the time scale of physical and chemical degradation of the materials. Most pesticides begin to break down immediately on application. Only a few have been shown to be quite stable. The physical and chemical properties of the pesticide determine how rapidly its degradation takes place. Generally they break down in one of three ways: (1) by photodecomposition (degradation by sunlight), (2) by biological decomposition (degradation through the action of some living organism, usually a microorganism), and (3) by chemical decomposition (any chemical reaction that changes the chemical form of the pesticide). The speed of degradation varies with several factors: (1) surface runoff, (2) volatilization or evaporation into the atmosphere, (3) leaching through the soil, (4) capillary action, the upward movement through the soil (nearly the opposite of leaching), and (6) adsorption (on soil particles). The degradation process varies and needs to be studied specifically for each chemical. The problems involved are usually complicated and the quantities of the elements being assayed are minute (Weber et al. 1972).

The first major effort to solve these residue and toxicology problems in the United States was initiated in 1945 by the federal Food and Drug Administration (FDA). A tolerance of 7 parts per million set for DDT on some food crops was the first residue tolerance set for any pesticidal chemical in the United States (Sharvelle 1961). This first effort to develop reasonable and safe tolerance was urged not by the general public but by industries involved with manufacture of the products and by professional users. Their efforts primarily brought about the passage of the federal Insecticide, Fungicide, and Rodenticide Act of 1947.

Various organic chemicals began to be popular about 1948. In 1950 hearings held by the FDA to discuss safe and sensible tolerances and residues on food crops lasted for a full year. Over 200 experts were heard. A congressional select committee in the House of Representatives also investigated the use of chemicals in food production from 1950 to 1953. During these committee hearings 220 experts, key witnesses, and representatives of the general public were interviewed; and at that time pesticides received essentially a clean bill of health although careful residue and tolerance levels were recommended for each. The Miller Pesticide Residue Amendment to the Food, Drug, and Cosmetic Act (P.L. 518) was passed by Congress in July 1954, largely as a result of these hearings. This law requires that manufacturers test materials for their toxicity to all warm-blooded animals, including humans, and that acceptable residue levels be recommended by the manufacturers. Again, these laws primarily were developed through the activities of concerned industrialists and professionals working with plant protection chemicals (Sharvelle 1961).

The United Nations has also had a group of experts working on pesticide residue recommendations through the Food and Agriculture Organization (FAO), Rome. Their recommendations concerning residues and tolerances are distributed throughout the world (FAO 1973c) and their approach to residue problems is summarized:

Only residue data from trials carried out in conformity with registered or approved use patterns are employed as a basis for recommendations. Attention, however, is paid to the effect on residue levels of the number of applications, application rates, and the interval between final application and harvest.

The uses of any compound against a pest on a particular crop vary considerably from region to region owing to differences in ecology, climate and culture practices. The residue levels at harvest consequently vary over a range. The minimum interval permitted between the last application and harvest varies considerably from country to country. This does not necessarily mean that the residue level at harvest varies to the same degree.

Considerable attention is paid to the question of metabolites, degradation products and impurities that might appear as residues in plant or animal products and significance of each is considered. Where available, data on disappearance during storage, processing and cooking are considered and reference is made in the monographs and recommendations. However, since it is necessary to base the proposals on levels to be found in raw agricultural products the tolerance levels normally recommended are much higher than those of the residues actually present in the prepared food eaten by the consumer.

To guide regulatory authorities in their examination of commodities moving in trade at some stage later than harvest, information on the rate of reduction during storage is provided, where this has been determined. Likewise, information that indicates the location of the residue on or in the commodity (on skin, shell, leaves, husks, or in fat, meat, juice, pulp and so forth) is provided when available.

Long lists of acceptable residue levels on different commodities come with the FAO monographs and have developed into an extremely useful body of information for the chemical analyst involved with regulatory activities of chemical residues and tolerances.

The analytical residue chemist is a new breed of analyst who is in the business of looking for the proverbial needle in the haystack. Often the analyst is searching for a 1 part per million (or even less) residue in a food material. This means that 1 microgram of residue has to be detected in 1 gram of material being examined.

For each new compound that is registered a tough 2-year research program that includes feeding several species of test animals is undertaken. Despite the difficulties, the success has been remarkable. In the United States no reported illness or death has been attributed to pesticide residues or food additives occurring on food since the development of the first legislation in 1938 (Zweig 1963). This speaks very well for the concern of manufacturers and growers and for the quality of the personnel in the regulatory agencies.

For the toxicological chemist the most difficult matter is legal and not scientific. It concerns the laws associated with residues that include *zero tolerance* or *no residue* registration. Taken literally, it means that not a single molecule of a given pesticide is anywhere in the food product. This condition is not possible to achieve or even measure at present and is not even sensible to consider. In practice this concept is expressed as *nondetectable amount*. It always brings into question the sensitivity of the analytical technique that is used (Zweig 1963). A few analytical techniques are so sensitive that a relatively small number of molecules can be detected.

More important than the presence or absence of a few molecules is to know the safe tolerances for a given material. It is hoped that sometime the concept of zero tolerance will be eliminated and that a more realistic legal concept of safe tolerance or acceptable tolerance level will be written into laws involving pesticides and other potentially dangerous chemicals. Some tolerance levels now demanded are much lower than necessary and others are probably higher than safe limits should require. This problem will eventually be solved as more accurate and complete data are developed.

In the developing world few good residue and toxicology laboratories exist; this has not been significant until recently, since very small amounts of pesticides have been used except in localized areas. In Asia there has been a concern about the hazards of pesticides and their residues on food crops only in recent years. Very few pesticides are used, typically in relatively small amounts. According to FAO statistics, in all of Southeast Asia in 1967 less than 1.2 million pounds of insecticides of all kinds were used in agriculture. Many more were used in public health control of human diseases, such as malaria and typhus, particularly by various agencies of the United Nations.

In Southeast Asia, meats, tobacco, and other products being shipped in international trade have special residue problems (Smith 1972). These problems will increase in the future and a movement is now under way in some of these countries to develop toxicology laboratories to deal with them. It is hoped that these laboratories may begin to monitor the environment for long-term effects as well.

The most serious residue problems have been associated with insecticides. DDT and other chlorinated hydrocarbons have been the principal insecticides incriminated.

Fungicide residues have not yet been a serious problem. Most fungicides are characterized by low toxicity to warm-blooded animals (NAS 1968a). The mercurial fungicides, the only important exception, have for the most part been taken off the market, particularly those used for seed treatments. Increasingly stringent government regulations concerning chemical residues have made it crucial to search for fungicides that are even more safe and effective (NAS 1968a). Plant pathologists have not been under the pressures from environmentalists that entomologists have and consequently have had more time to develop safer fungicides.

Plant pathologists usually have used something other than chemical control wherever possible, such as in field crops. The chemicals used typically have been protectants rather than therapeutants. Residue problems generally have not been severe enough to cause alarm, although they cannot be ignored and far more study of these problems is needed.

Since herbicides are primarily developed to be toxic to plants, their residue problems have not been as serious as those of insecticides. Usually they are nontoxic or have very low toxicity to mammals. There has been concern over possible environmental effects, particularly in the Vietnam War, and some concern over possible deleterious effects on humans and animals in cases of excessive use (see Chap. 6). Generally the evidence available gives herbicides a relatively clean bill of health in the areas of residue levels and environmental effects.

Herbicide residues are usually greater in arid than in humid areas and greater in rainfed than in irrigated agriculture. When moisture is slight or erratic it is difficult to predict the time required for herbicide degradation to safe or innocuous levels. Long dry periods may permit persistence in the soil, which may interfere with the cropping pattern in the next or subsequent crops. In Nebraska in dry areas phytotoxic concentrations of simazine (Gesatop) and atrazine (Aatrex) have been reported in the subsoil for 16 months after treatment (Arnon 1972).

Plants vary tremendously in their response to herbicides. For example, applications of diuron (Karmex Diuron Herbicide) or monuron (Telvar) in California have been applied for a total of 8 consecutive years on irrigated cotton and have not resulted in a buildup of residue toxic to cotton. By contrast, after a single year's application, subsequent cereal crops are adversely affected and the herbicide is phytotoxic (Arnon 1972).

Most herbicides break down very quickly into innocuous materials. This degradation may be encouraged by dilution (by tillage or irrigation), by sowing crops that are not affected by a given herbicide, by accelerating the time of breakdown (by adding organic matter, irrigating, or both), by more careful crop planning so that succeeding crops are resistant to herbicides used, or by some other technique. Breakdown of most herbicides is complete enough by harvesttime that the residue is minimal (Arnon 1972).

Most nematicides have until recently been highly volatile; the remaining residue typically either breaks down quickly or leaches out, leaving minimal traces in the soil (NAS 1968b). Recently the trend has been toward more stable, less volatile nematicides that present some danger of excessive residues in the soil and on plant roots. In fact, long residual action may in some cases limit the use of certain compounds that are highly toxic to nematodes—compounds that otherwise would be used in considerable amounts in nematode control programs.

There are a few records of nematicidal residues causing minor problems. There are cases of "off taste" or "taint" in crops occurring after the application of chemicals to the soil, but usually they have been associated with an overdose, some other misuse, or applications made when soil or weather conditions were unfavorable for chemical breakdown (NAS 1968b). In a few cases, nematicidal residues on root crops grown in treated soil have caused them to be unpalatable or potentially harmful to humans or animals.

Tolerance levels for nematicides are not as significant, generally, as tolerance levels for insecticides or the mercurial fungicides. Chemical break-down usually occurs before the consumption of the crop because the usual time of application of nematicides is far removed from the harvest date.

In the developed and also in some of the developing countries, the trend is to build special laboratories in which toxicology, residue, and phytotoxicity analyses and environmental monitoring are done on all biocides (pesticides)—whether insecticides, fungicides, herbicides, nemati-cides, rodenticides, or others. The chemical analyses are essentially identi-cal, hence it makes sense for a toxicology laboratory to concern itself with all the biocides. It is less expensive and much more efficient for cooperative efforts of various disciplines to be gathered in one central well-staffed and -equipped toxicology and environmental monitoring laboratory. Any effort to create independent laboratories in the subdisciplines should be discour-aged except in special cases where specific research programs require in-dependent laboratories. Laboratories of government regulatory agencies, which have the responsibility for toxicology studies, residue and tolerance level analyses, and environmental monitoring, should be large cooperative laboratories where the interests of all the plant protection disciplines can be coordinated.

A major toxicological problem associated with pesticides, which until recently received little consideration, is the safe disposal of excess materials and containers. Shaw (1974a) discussed this:

> Faulty disposal of unused pesticides, pesticide wastes and pesticide containers is a threat to a quality environment. Disposal practices of the past will not be acceptable in the future. A significant expansion of research for the develop-ment of better disposal technology will be essential to the effective and safe use of herbicides (and other pesticides). Unless better disposal techniques are developed, constraints on current methods will undoubtedly be imposed that will inhibit expansion in chemical weed control (and the use of other pesticides).

Need for cooperative research in this area is great. If it is not initiated soon by plant protection personnel, legislation enacted concerning disposal prob-lems may be unrealistic and biased against legitimate agricultural objec-tives. A book edited by Kennedy (1978) reviews the state of the art for disposal of pesticides; another book on this general subject was written by Watson and Brown (1977).

8

Cultural Controls

For centuries farmers have had ways of reducing pests and plant disease damage. The methods used were built around cultural control measures such as time of planting, plant spacing, choice of location, irrigation, green manuring, crop rotation, sanitation, and roguing. Often farmers were not quite sure why they followed these time-honored procedures but were convinced that they were helpful in disease and pest control; in many cases this was true (Univ. Calif. 1972c). These control measures were the only methods earlier generations had. We are now going back to them, perhaps in a somewhat more sophisticated manner.

We sometimes forget as plant protection specialists that agronomic, horticultural, and economic aspects of farming are more important than plant protection. Plant protection is employed only when necessary and may or may not be necessary in a given year or on a given crop, whereas good agronomic and horticultural techniques and careful economic analyses are absolutely essential every year.

We cannot change the demands of economics. The best plant protection programs must be worked out in conjunction with the best agronomic and horticultural techniques available and must always be subservient to economic necessities. This point is emphasized by several entomologists (Metcalf et al. 1951):

> The importance of good husbandry as defined by agronomists, horticulturists, entomologists and plant pathologists working in cooperation cannot be overstressed. The use of good seed, excellent preparation of the seed bed, conservation and regulation of soil, moisture, proper pruning and thinning when necessary and the judicious use of fertilizers all offer possibilities of stimulating plant growth in such a way as to make possible the growing of profitable crops where the neglect of one or more of these factors may result in a loss or disaster.

Another entomologist, Petty (1972), also emphasized the primary im-

91

portance of the agronomic and economic aspects of agriculture where growers are concerned.

> Activities in related fields such as weed science and plant pathology affect insect control and vice versa. We must be knowledgeable about the production practices which involve crops and soils. Our efforts toward insect control and all other pest management must be compatible with sound agronomic programs and must not deter an otherwise profitable practice unless the pest is so devastating that the problem cannot be ignored and changes in agronomic practices are dictated. Our recommended practices must be economically sound. The applied entomologist is therefore at the mercy of sound agronomic practices and sound agricultural economics.

Because of the problems raised by the massive use of pesticides there has been a recent return by entomologists to a reexamination of cultural control techniques and their possibilities in the light of modern agricultural knowledge. Apple (1974) discussed this trend.

> The need for more ecologically sound, effective and economical methods for pest control has prompted renewed interest in cultural methodology. This methodology will become increasingly important and effective in pest management systems as we gain a fuller understanding of the ecology of major pests. This understanding will open new opportunities to suppress pest populations through cultural means. There must also be closer collaboration between agronomists and crop protection specialists because changed agronomic practices may alter significantly pest dynamics. As an example there is increasing evidence that minimum tillage practices enhance the severity of some pest problems.

Because of the extensive and almost exclusive use of insecticides for most insect control problems since World War II, we sometimes forget that cultural methods of insect control were once all the farmer had. Insects were controlled by sanitation, time of sowing, crop rotation, pruning and thinning, distribution or control of weeds or alternate hosts, tillage and seedbed operations, strip cropping, sowing trap crops, and multiple cropping or mixed cropping (Metcalf et al. 1951; Arnon 1972). These methods of insect control are still good and when used in proper combinations with other methods, particularly resistant plants, often are quite efficient in maintaining relatively low levels of insect and mite populations.

Cultural practices are usually used in combination with other techniques for suppression of pests. Often they can be used very well with minimal chemical control. More research would result in more judicious and minimal use of chemicals combined with suitable cultural control methods. To be most effective it is often necessary to carry out cultural control practices through growers' cooperatives (USDA 1972).

An example is the cultural control of the pink bollworm in Texas, which is based on the seasonal incidence of diapause, and supplemental chemical control is only used when necessary. Legislation in Texas to minimize pink bollworm populations enforces compliance of all cotton farmers with the necessary cultural control methods. Part of this practice is chopping and plowing under stalks and residues of the cotton crop after harvest, which alone destroys about 85 percent of the larvae of the pink bollworm. Of course the remaining 15 percent may at times be very efficient in reestablishing the insect populations.

Many specific cultural practices control certain insects rather well. In Israel early spring sowing of sorghum is the most effective way of controlling the sorghum shoot-fly, *Atherigona exigua.* In the Near East *Syringopais temperatella,* a most damaging pest of wheat, is controlled by plowing to the depth of 15 to 20 centimeters (Arnon 1972).

Most wheat in the midwestern United States is seeded in the fall after all adults of the Hessian fly have died. If early volunteer wheat is also controlled, the result is a Hessian fly–free crop. For many years this control has been practical, cheap, and effective (Painter 1958).

Plant pathologists have given primary emphasis to cultural and other nonchemical controls even during the advent of more sophisticated fungicides. Consequently, they do not feel threatened by environmental concerns. Cultural controls have been used alone and in combination with suitable host-resistance and other nonchemical techniques. At times they have been combined successfully with minimal chemical control (NAS 1968a). Particularly with low value per acre crops such as forage, timber, and small grains, farmers have been for economic reasons forced to rely largely on nonchemical control methods.

Cultural control offers an opportunity to alter the environment, the condition of the host, and the behavior of pathogenic organisms in ways that adequately control a particular disease. If no good cultural methods are available, new cultural methods are sought. More research is needed on disease dynamics related to cultural or agronomic activities. This research often is needed on specific crops at specific locations as related to particular diseases (NAS 1968a).

As in most plant pathological practices, cultural control techniques are largely preventive. They reduce the quantity or the activity of the inoculum by means of crop rotation, deep plowing, sanitation, green manure crops, and roguing. Cultural techniques also may be used to avoid disease organisms by changing locations, patterns of seedbed preparation, plant spacing, nutritional levels, time of planting, and so forth (NAS 1968a).

Cultural control is increasingly important for nematodes and is being used constantly in combination with resistant varieties and minimal chemical treatments. Van Gundy (1972) pointed out that every manipulation of the soil affects the level of activity or balance of its microbial population including nematodes and thereby the fundamental basis for a nonchemical control program. True management of soil pathogens including nematodes and insects requires thorough understanding of the dynamics and ecology of populations. Intelligent application of cultural control depends on the knowledge of the life cycles of the pathogen nematodes and the primary factors that influence growth, reproduction, survival, and pathogenesis in a particular ecological setting.

In the tropics many pest and disease problems are associated with intense heat, lack of cold temperatures, excessive humidity, and so forth. One of the commonest and oldest methods for controlling pests and diseases has been to move away from the old infections (Wellman 1972). The slash-and-burn agriculture typical of the primitive tropics is partially built around this principle. Another technique, often not practical in the temperate zone, is the repeated plowing of fields during hot dry seasons. Small farmers tend to grow food in small isolated clearings surrounded by more or less natural forests or semiwild areas; this isolation in itself is helpful. Planting mixed species is common and avoiding long rows or any rows at all is typical. If severe pest or disease attacks occur in a bed of plants they are often cut down or pulled and allowed to rot in place, often with weeds piled on top of them. This infested area is then given time to purify and is not planted again for several years. Roguing of diseased or infested plants is also routine, and the movement of virgin soil from nearby forest areas into planting holes is a common practice that tends to avoid accumulation of soil pests and diseases. All these measures are useful for small farmers but are difficult if not impossible to use on a large scale by plantation operators. Also, these methods typically achieve at best a minimal, satisfactory, inexpensive control.

Crop Rotation and Related Practices

Crop rotation has probably had the longest history of use and success of all cultural control methods. It was used in the past in developed countries more than at present (Pimental 1970):

> The increased reliance on pesticides has resulted all too often in growers abandoning several cultural practices which were helpful in insect and plant disease control. Also, the sound practice of rotating crops has decreased. Often growers plant the same crop on the same land year after year, allowing pests to increase and increasing needs for pesticides.

Multiple cropping by crop sequences or by intercropping has always been important in insect control; specific sequences or patterns may increase or decrease insect damage, depending on the insects involved (Sun

1974). To omnivorous insects such as *Heliothis armigera,* which attacks cotton, maize, sorghum, and many other crops, multiple cropping and many crop sequences actually increase the populations and infestation. By contrast, it is possible to utilize a rotation to control insects—in the Philippines, cabbage grown close to tomato or in alternating years with tomato is a rather good control technique for the diamondback moth, *Pluetella xylostella.*

Falcon and Smith (1973) gave some examples of how crop sequence can control the level of pest infestation. In central Texas, alfalfa, maize (corn), and cotton in the same river valley are beneficial to the bollworm. The overwintering population attacks alfalfa in the spring. This feeding does not harm the alfalfa significantly but the alfalfa serves as a bridging host until the appearance of the favored host, maize. The next generation of the bollworm then becomes very abundant on the maize. As cotton comes into prominence during the summer it becomes the main host; and the bollworm returns to alfalfa, the bridging or least-favored host, again in the fall. By contrast, the tobacco budworm in the same area of central Texas lacks any important bridging host. Its only important host is cotton and it is not able to maintain nearly as large a population as the bollworm. Development of a favorable crop sequence in the areas where the bollworm is important would do much to reduce its population.

Many commercially significant insects are controlled by crop rotation or by crop rotation in combination with some other related nonchemical technique. For example, wheat stem sawfly and wheat stem maggot are controlled by rotation with immune crops (Metcalf et al. 1951). Unfavorable crop sequences for certain insect problems are also known; for example, maize-soybean rotation in the Corn Belt appears to be increasing black cutworm losses in maize (B. D. Blair 1979, pers. commun.).

Crop rotation can often be used to break life cycles for insect pests and nematodes—it is particularly important with some nematodes and is a desirable way to control corn rootworm (Wilcke 1972).

Crop rotation is important in the control of plant diseases, especially soil diseases. Four important results are helpful in disease control if proper crop rotation sequences are carried out. (1) Some pests and diseases will be reduced by starvation. (2) Rotation encourages replenishment of organic materials in the soil. (3) There is a stimulation of antibiosis or competitive symbiosis against pests and disease organisms. (4) A ''conservation bank'' of nutrients is created with high organic matter and moisture can be captured more easily and held in the soil (McNew 1972).

Crop rotation is one of the most effective ways to control plant disease pathogens that invade the soil and survive in plant debris for a relatively short time. Usually only one or two crops of nonhost plants grown in an infested area greatly reduces the pathogen population, making it possible to plant a host crop again. An outstanding example is the take-all disease of cereals, incited by *Ophiobolus graminis*. This fungus persists almost entirely as mycelium in infected plant tissue and does not compete well as a soil saprophyte. It is destroyed with the decomposition of plant residues. A year of summer fallow or a single nonhost cropping season generally gives satisfactory control (Sun 1974). In Taiwan, the head-and-neck blast, incited by *Pyricularia oryzae,* and *Helminthosporium* leaf blight, incited by *Helminthosporium oryzae,* are much less severe on rice that is alternated with nonhost crops such as sweet potato, potato, sorghum, or maize (Sun 1974).

The continuous cropping of cotton often results in decreasing yields, which are often caused by an increase in species of *Verticillium* and *Fusarium* or by increases in nematode populations. If beans are grown year after year in the same soil, root rots often develop, specifically *Fusarium, Rhizoctonia,* and *Thielaviopsis* spp., often becoming quite destructive and reducing yields. Often they can be corrected by crop rotation with suitable poor host or nonhost crops (NAS 1968a).

Potato scab, a soil-borne disease, can be reduced considerably by growing soybeans as a green manure alternate crop. The use of barley as a rotation crop is quite effective in the control of *Fusarium* root rot of bean. The use of a field pea–cotton rotation limits the severity of *Phymato-trichum* root rot of cotton. This control measure has been used for many years.

Often long rotations are needed. For example, Walker (1969) reported long rotations were quite effective when used with resistant varieties against the club root of cabbage, a soil-borne disease that is difficult to control. Control of *Fusarium* diseases is more easily obtained by long-term than by short-term rotations (Sun 1974). In Taiwan, watermelon wilt, incited by *Fusarium oxysporum* f. sp. *niveum,* is an indigenous disease of watermelon occurring on sandy or sandy loam soils. The pathogen is widespread and farmers in Taiwan cannot grow watermelon every year on the same land without severe losses. A long 3-year cropping rotation system with watermelon has been quite effective in control. This rotation includes nonhost crops of sugarcane, sweet potato, and peanuts or other legumes. Another disease controlled by long rotations is *Aphanomyces* root rot of pea (Walker 1969). Dukes (1970) reported that either clean fallow or a marigold-weeds rotation for 3 years reduced to 2 percent or less the disease incidence of *Phytophthora parasitica* var. *nicotianae,* the causal agent of black shank of tobacco. Several other crops in 3-year rotations reduced the disease incidence to 15 percent or less as compared to control plots. These rotations in order of effectiveness were rye, weeds, peanuts, cotton, and soybeans.

Some fungus pathogens may require a much longer rotation than 3 years. For example, the Panama disease of banana, incited by *Fusarium ox-*

ysporum f. sp. *cubense,* requires much longer rotation periods combined with water fallowing for reasonably adequate control (Sun 1974).

As mentioned before, not all crop rotations are beneficial (NAS 1968*a*). For example, *Rhizoctonia solani* is a serious fungus on sugar beets. A rotation with beans does not reduce the inoculum level because the same organism attacks beans also. An extensive study in Ohio by Williams and Schmitthenner (1962) demonstrated that crop rotation produced a much richer and more variable soil fungus flora than monoculture.

Plant disease control by crop rotation is economically sound but it is seldom complete. Throughout the world crop rotations can be used more intelligently and effectively with better ecological knowledge of the crop and pathological organisms. More research is needed in combinations of control techniques that include crop rotation (NAS 1968*a*).

Crop rotation prevents the buildup of damaging population levels of plant parasitic nematodes and was used by growers long before they understood what they were controlling (NAS 1968*a*). Good (1968) calls it the "oldest and best" cultural means of controlling nematodes. Years of monoculture may precede dangerous levels of nematode buildup, but once present the high populations are difficult to reduce. Consequently, crop rotation systems as a preventive measure are practical. A high population of destructive nematodes also restricts the choice of crop in control rotations. Hence, for nematodes it is always better to use crop rotations as preventive rather than curative measures.

An example of satisfactory control of the sting nematode on maize is shown in Fig. 8.1. The sting nematode population builds up when cotton is in the rotation and decreases when peanuts and millet are in the rotation. Both the cotton and the peanuts were treated with ethylene dibromide. Another example is the control of the nematodes, *Trichodorus* spp., on celery grown immediately after maize (see Fig. 8.2).

For crop rotation to control nematodes effectively, the nematodes must have a relatively narrow or specific host range. Some of the worst nematode pathogens, the golden nematode of potatoes, *Heterodera rostochiensis,* the stem nematode of alfalfa, *Ditylenchus dipsaci,* the soybean cyst nematode, *Heterodera glycines,* and several species of root-knot nematodes, can be controlled quite easily because they are, relatively speaking, host specific. The growing of a nonhost crop from 2 to 4 years will usually reduce the population of these species dramatically by starvation but 1 year is usually not enough. To use crop rotation to control nematodes, therefore, it is necessary to take a susceptible crop out of production for several years, which is sometimes difficult for growers. The alternate crop may encourage other species of nematodes that are very harmful to the crop being protected. Often, too, the nonhost or resistant crops have relatively low economic value (NAS 1968*b*).

Van Gundy (1972) stated that despite the value of crop rotation in

Fig. 8.1. Effects of different crop rotations in control of the sting nematode, *Belonolaimus longicaudatus,* on maize in Georgia. Left: Stunted maize following 2 years of cotton. Right: Good yield following a rotation of peanuts and millet. Both the cotton and the peanuts had been treated with ethylene dibromide. (Courtesy J. M. Good)

nematode control, growers tend to use the easier chemical methods. He suggested that crop rotation is more likely to persist in the developed countries in combinations with other control methods. He also stressed the disadvantages of crop rotation: the time required, the fact that the nematodes are never completely eliminated, and the frequent low value of the alternate rotation crop.

Crop rotation to control nematodes has a lasting future in crops of low economic value that can be alternated in a long rotational system with other resistant or nonhost crops. In some cases it is the only economically acceptable means of control (Nusbaum and Ferris 1973). It is wise to use as an alternate resistant crop a cover crop for soil conservation, to provide forage

Fig. 8.2. Control of the nematode, *Trichodorous* spp., by crop rotation. Left: Celery grown immediately after maize. Right: No rotation. (Courtesy J. M. Good)

for livestock or cover between fruit trees in orchards, or to plow down as a green manure. Since many common plant parasitic nematodes have wide host ranges, crop rotation has definite limitations (Univ. Calif. 1972*b*).

Cyst nematodes are the nematodes most easily controlled by crop rotation systems, and when combined with resistant varieties very effective control systems have been developed. Chemical control has never been very satisfactory with cyst nematodes. The combination of alternate nonhost crops and resistant varieties is also very helpful in the control of the golden nematode of potato (Univ. Calif. 1972*b*). In Taiwan, crop rotations are utilized to control *Meloidogyne* spp., its most important plant parasitic nematodes. Crop rotations do not eliminate the nematodes but they keep them at a relatively low level. An example of a good rotation is tobacco or jute with rice, which minimizes the damage of *Meloidogyne* spp. infestations in tobacco and jute.

Weed populations can be greatly reduced by proper systems of crop rotation, particularly when they involve well-adapted crops such as silage, maize, or alfalfa that are often more competitive than the weeds. When combined with desirable tillage, suitable rotations often bring weeds under adequate control. Careful cultivation of row crops tends to reduce the grassy weed populations in the next planting of small grains (Janick et al. 1969). Rotations that use crops with different life histories often help control weeds, especially if the life cycles of the weeds are not adapted to the cultural practices necessary for growing the crops (NAS 1968c). Rotations also allow a wider choice of herbicides. For example, problem soybean weeds in maize may be controlled with an herbicide several years before being planted to soybeans (B. D. Blair 1979, pers. commun.).

Cropping systems that take into account the effect of crop rotation on weed control are used in Taiwan and elsewhere in the developing world. For example, maize and grain sorghums, which are very competitive when well established, shade out weeds. In Taiwan, these crops are used in rotation with soybeans, peanuts, sweet potatoes, and low growing vegetable crops that do not shade out weeds. The use of the tall, competitive grains is helpful in preventing excessive buildup of weed populations. When certain weeds are associated with specific crops, rotations can be built around crops that have life cycles different from those of the weeds or different cultural requirements, as indicated earlier. An example of this in Taiwan is the rotation of rice with dry-land crops. The rice culture greatly reduces the dry-land crop weeds and the dry-land crops and their culture greatly reduce the rice crop weeds (Sun 1974).

Cropping Patterns

Cropping practices or patterns are important to the presence of insects, diseases, and other pests. Changes in cropping patterns are more often the result of economic factors than of plant protection requirements, but they may dramatically affect the overall pest and disease population (Petty 1972).

Some examples from the state of Illinois follow. The oat acreage at present is about one-fourth that of 20 years ago. At that time oat fields planted on cornstalk ground produced at least 80 percent of the European corn borer moths for flight and egg-laying on maize during June. Wheat favors armyworm, wireworm, and chinch bug populations. Wheat acreage is down 60 percent from 20 years ago. Clover and grass acreages, down about 70 percent, favor development of wireworms, cutworms, seed-corn beetles, white grubs, seed-corn maggots, corn root aphids, and cornfield ants. In short, the principal maize insect–producing crops dropped during the past 20-year period from 6.5 million acres to 2 million acres and the estimated maize insect pest production decreased 67 percent. At the same time soybeans, alfalfa, and maize (which are essentially nonproducers of maize insects except for northern and western corn rootworms) increased in acreage from 10,000 to 16.8 million. It is easy to see why maize insect problems are much fewer than they were 20 years ago (Petty 1972).

Sun (1974) showed how cropping patterns influence specific insect populations in Taiwan. For example, with an omnivorous or wide host range insect such as *Heliothis armigera,* which can attack cotton, sorghum, maize, and many other crops, few cropping patterns can be helpful in reducing populations. By contrast, in the Philippines when cabbage is grown close to tomato (a nonhost of the diamondback moth, *Plutella xylostella*) the pest has been controlled rather well. Cabbage plants interplanted with tomatoes had fewer adults and eggs than cabbage planted alone; the odor of tomato plants apparently acts as a repellent to the *Plutella* adult. Intercropping corn and peanuts also greatly reduces the damages from the corn borer, *Ostrinia furnacalis,* in the Philippines. In this case, predators are provided a very good habitat in the peanuts and move out into the maize to reduce borer populations.

Mixed cropping (intercropping) is not always favorable. For example, olive trees are very susceptible to *Verticillium* wilt but in general the disease incidence in established plantings is quite low. The inoculum builds up slowly in olive but increases rapidly in tomato and cotton. When tomatoes are grown in young olive orchards, the inoculum in the soil increases rapidly and the disease becomes much more severe in olive. *Verticillium* wilt is also increased in other orchard crops such as apricot, almond, and avocado when tomato is grown as an intercrop. Currants and gooseberries grown commercially near white pine cause white pine blister rust to become much more severe, since currants and gooseberries are the alternate hosts. A similar situation occurs with cedar-apple rust, which may be controlled by elimination of the alternate hosts, cedar or juniper (NAS 1968*a*).

Strip farming, another valuable cropping pattern, also must be approached cautiously. Depending on crops and environments, pests and diseases may either be encouraged or discouraged by strip farming.

A diversification of crops may limit the food source for certain species, but it also may provide alternate food sources for other insect pests or natural enemies. Hence, crop diversification patterns need to be studied before being recommended for a given pest or disease situation as the net result may either be helpful, harmful, or neutral. If the natural enemies of a pest can be encouraged through alternate hosts, it often can be controlled satisfactorily via such methods (USGPO 1972).

Continuous cropping of a specific crop is not always damaging.

Cereals may be grown continuously in some areas without decreasing crop yields and without increasing diseases or pests significantly. For example, the *Cercosporella* disease of wheat has reached an equilibrium with the crop in one area after many years of continuous culture. Many pathogens eventually achieve an acceptable balance with a specific crop in this way although losses may be high initially (NAS 1968a).

Elimination of weeds or of alternate crop hosts is often important in pest and disease control and should be practiced where appropriate. Some plant diseases that can be controlled by the control of alternate hosts are the downy mildew fungi (which overwinter in perennial weeds), cucumber mosaic (which overwinters in perennial weeds, particularly milkweed and pokeweed), wheat streak mosaic (which overwinters in several native perennial grasses and volunteer wheat), yellow bean mosaic (for which sweet clover is an alternate host), cabbage mosaic (for which peppergrass and shepherd's purse are alternate hosts), and wheat stem rust (for which the common barberry is an alternate host) (Walker 1969). The important point is the economic cost of controlling alternate weed, volunteer, or crop hosts. In some cases (such as cedar-apple rust) the control is quite easy and economically feasible. In others it is too expensive or time consuming to consider.

Trap Cropping

Often trap cropping and/or the use of toxic plants can be used with crop rotation for effective nematode control. The use of plants in which the nematode larvae enter the roots but are unable to develop into adults is especially helpful; the nematodes are trapped within the tissues and die when the crop is harvested early or plowed under. Roots of several plants contain chemicals that are toxic to some plant parasitic nematodes in the soil; an example is *Crotalaria* used as a toxic trap crop for root-knot nematodes. The French marigold interplanted with susceptible crop plants or used in a rotation is valuable in the control of lesion nematodes (Van Gundy 1972).

An example of using a trap or decoy crop to control a fungus disease is the control of club root of cabbage, incited by *Plasmodiophora brassicae.* The decoy crop induces the fungal resting spores to germinate but is actually resistant to the fungus (MacFarlane 1952).

Time of Planting and Plant Spacing

The agronomic or horticultural techniques associated with time of planting and spacing of plants are important in plant protection. In cotton the time of planting is most important. Planting is usually timed to coincide with the best soil temperature and moisture so that the seed will germinate rapidly, young plants will grow quickly, and harvesting can be done during the dry season. Anything that extends the growing season exposes the crop to more possibilities for insect damage (Falcon and Smith 1973). Early planting is important in helping to control the corn leaf aphid (Metcalf et al. 1951). By contrast, delayed planting is used routinely in the control of Hessian fly of wheat.

Planting time is important in avoiding insect vectors of plant diseases, particularly virus diseases. Late planting of winter wheat helps the plants to emerge late enough so that they escape fall infection of wheat streak mosaic via the eriophyid mite vector, *Aceria tulipae*. Spring infection of winter wheat seldom causes severe wheat losses in the Great Plains of the United States (Fellows and Sill 1955). By contrast, early sowing of winter wheat in the Palouse area of Washington and Idaho is recommended as the higher temperatures of the soil are unfavorable for the germination of bunt teliospores (Walker 1969). Cool weather crops (for example, spinach and peas) germinate poorly at high temperatures and often the seedlings are attacked by *Pythium* and *Rhizoctonia* spp. By contrast, warm weather crops (maize, melons, and lima beans) require higher temperatures for good germination and growth; otherwise they will be attacked by these same soil fungi (NAS 1968*a*).

Nematode damage also is affected by planting time in certain situations. A classical example is the planting of early potato varieties in Great Britain to control the golden nematode. The potato develops and grows at soil temperatures below those at which the nematode eggs will hatch and the larvae develop. Winter potatoes are seldom attacked by the root-knot nematode because they are grown at cool soil temperatures. Potatoes grown in the same field in summer when the soil temperatures are warm often are badly attacked. In North Carolina the root-knot nematode rarely damages the spring potato crop because of the cool soil temperatures. Later potatoes, which grow during the summer months and are harvested in the fall, have serious infestations of root-knot if not controlled by other means. Yields of California sugar beets are much higher if the beets are planted in January or February rather than in March or April, particularly where the fields are heavily infested with the sugar beet nematode, *Heterodora schachtii* (NAS 1968*b*).

In recent years a movement (for agronomic and economic reasons) toward closer spacing of plants has been helpful in some weed control because of the denser shade and it has been important in some plant disease control. If a disease that does not normally spread from plant to plant within the field is introduced, denser stands are helpful. For example, *Verticillium* wilt of cotton is less damaging in dense stands. In the heteroecious fusiform rust of pine, close spacing of pine in nurseries reduces the disease.

By contrast, in hemlock an autoecious twig rust can spread from plant to plant in hemlock seedlings very easily and losses are greatly increased by denser stands.

Diseases that are more severe at high humidity tend to be more severe in dense stands. For example, *Botrytis* blight in tomatoes and *Sclerotinia* rot of beans are usually worse in dense plantings where the humidity remains high for long periods and the plant surfaces remain moist. This is also true in rubber plantations with *Corticium salmonicolor*. In forests, proper spacing to facilitate early branching and pruning typically reduces infection by decay fungi and tends to reduce rusts and dwarf mistletoe infections (NAS 1968*a*).

Plant populations are also important in control of insects. High plant population in cotton tends to shorten the period of time when reproductive tissues are available for insect feeding and often results in lower pest control costs. Since the fruiting period is shorter, boll weevils, pink bollworms, and other midseason or late-season pests are less important and it may be possible to eliminate one or more insect generations each season. The earlier crop harvest associated with the dense stands aids in early stalk destruction and results in a longer host-free period. This reduces overwintering populations of the pests (Falcon and Smith 1973).

More research is needed on the effect of plant spacing on pests and diseases. Specific knowledge is needed about each crop and specific pests and diseases prior to changing the density of a stand (NAS 1968*a*).

Fallowing

The use of fallow periods is a valuable mechanism of long standing, particularly in arid or semiarid areas, and is often useful in the control of pests and diseases. Fallowing cropland often reduces pathogen carryover because of the decay of tissues that harbor the pathogen. A good example is the control of *Ascochyta* blight of pea by fallowing. In the case of western celery mosaic a long fallow or crop-free period limits the aphid vector population. Several virus diseases of lettuce and crucifers are controlled in the same way (NAS 1968*a*). Vector buildup on weed hosts is often reduced by chemical means in California, and thus infection from the curly top virus is reduced in sugar beets; when these vector weed hosts can be largely eliminated by fallowing, it also effectively controls the disease (Univ. Calif. 1972*c*).

In hot climates with minimal summer rainfall it is possible by repeated tillage during the hot months to expose the surface of the soil to both heat and drying to control some nematode populations. It also is effective in the control of some soil fungi, for instance, take-all disease of wheat, incited by *Ophiobolus graminis,* and in some insect species, particularly where eggs are laid on or near the soil surface. If fallowing soils are tilled periodically during dry periods, surface soil moisture is reduced and maximum aeration occurs, which decreases food reserves in the surface soil and nematodes may be starved. The combination of aeration, desiccation, and heat is quite effective in the control of some nematode species (Univ. Calif. 1972b).

Fallow periods are useful in the control of some weed seeds, particularly in semiarid regions. In Canada, for example, fallow periods are important in the control of Russian and Canadian thistles (NAS 1968c).

In his tropical nematology review Good (1968) emphasized that summer and winter fallows are effective in controlling some nematodes, plant diseases, weeds, and insects, especially during hot, dry weather.

Flooding and Irrigation

Apart from its effects on pests and crop diseases, flooding is an important abiotic disease of crops. For most plants, 48 to 72 hours of flooding in midseason is permanently damaging. This is true of potato, cabbage, turnip, and field crops such as maize (Walker 1969). Nothing is more damaging to the growth of plantation crops in the tropics than "wet feet." Most roots soaked in water for prolonged periods deteriorate more rapidly in the tropics than in temperate zones—particularly coffee, banana, and citrus. Hardpan situations also encourage flooding. Some volcanic hardpan layers in the tropics may become completely impervious (Wellman 1972). Occasionally subsoil plowing or dynamite blasting has been used to break up these hardpans, particularly in perennial crops (orchards) to promote better drainage and eliminate more or less permanent flooding and poor drainage problems (NAS 1968a).

In the tropics the disease organisms characteristically found in roots of plants suffering from "wet feet" are fungi such as *Rosellinia, Fusarium,* and *Phytophthora* spp., particularly on such crops as coffee, banana, and citrus (Wellman 1972). After serious flooding damage, facultative parasites that normally are not able to initiate serious diseases usually appear (Walker 1969). Good drainage tends to reduce root diseases. By contrast, flooding has been reported as controlling the inoculum quantity of a few soil-borne plant disease organisms, *Sclerotinia sclerotiorum* and *Fusarium oxysporum* f. sp. *cubense* (Rotem and Palti 1969).

Flooding can be used quite effectively in the control of upland weeds, particularly where dryland crops are grown as an alternate crop with paddy rice. Flooding is used routinely in the control of upland weeds in rice and taro and can be used in certain situations where water is normally used for flooding purposes in the tropics (NAS 1968c).

Flooding techniques are infrequently used in the control of insects.

Cranberries in cranberry bogs and a few other crops that will stand flooding are protected from insect enemies by flooding at certain times (Metcalf et al. 1951).

Since nematodes are semiaquatic (they typically live in water films in the soil), one would suspect that flooding would be ineffective in their control; however, prolonged flooding has worked rather well in some cases. For example, in Florida 66 days of flooding during the summer reduced the root-knot nematodes on a celery crop significantly. In the delta area of California, 12 months of flooding controlled root-knot nematodes in the egg stage (Univ. Calif. 1972b). Good (1968) reported several examples where 10 to 12 weeks of flooding achieved good nematode control. In Taiwan, flooding conditions in rice cultivation are considered unfavorable for the survival of several species of nematodes.

Irrigation is sometimes a factor in the development of crop pests and diseases—it not only has been incriminated in the increase of levels of certain pests and diseases but also has been associated with satisfactory control measures. It is necessary to analyze the effects of irrigation on specific crop pests and disease situations.

Irrigation techniques are important in the control of weeds. Most irrigation waters carry large numbers of weed seeds and severe weed problems are often found on ditch banks and in laterals. Ditch irrigation is the worst offender in spreading weed seeds, but sprinkler irrigation may occasionally spread rather large quantities of small weed seeds. In the new drip irrigation, screens trap weed seeds and keep the drip irrigation orifices from clogging, reducing the need for herbicides. In Hawaii drip irrigation has been effective in helping to eliminate weed problems along irrigation ditches and in sugarcane fields (Robert Osgood 1974, pers. commun.).

In general, irrigation favors the spread and incidence of crop diseases. It spreads spores and other propagules and alters macro- and microclimates and soil microflora. In most countries where new large-scale irrigation projects (especially sprinkler irrigation) have been developed, diseases that previously were absent or scarce have become common and at times epiphytotic (Rotem and Palti 1969). Diseases tend to be more severe with sprinkler irrigation than with surface or ditch irrigation, particularly bacterial leaf diseases and aerial fungal diseases in which moisture on the leaves is of significance in infection. An example is the late blight of potatoes in arid regions, which normally would not develop with furrow irrigation. This is also true of the *Cercospora* leaf spot of peanuts (Arnon 1972) and the water molds such as *Aphanomyces, Phytophthora,* and *Pythium* spp. The water molds are particularly favored by free water on the surface of plants and are usually serious pathogens where water is in contact with the susceptible portions of the plants. Again, furrow irrigation is less likely to stimulate disease than sprinkler irrigation.

Excessive overhead watering (heavy rain or anything that leads to water soaking of leaves) favors the entry of bacterial pathogens. For example, wildfire disease of tobacco is much more severe under these conditions. Late season irrigation tends to increase the development of *Verticillium* and *Fusarium* wilts and the danger from *Botrytis* neck and bulb rots in onions and other bulb crops (NAS 1968*a*). On the other hand, a controlled furrow irrigation may reduce root, fruit, flower, and foliage diseases in certain crops (Univ. Calif. 1972*c*).

Most airborne diseases are increased in severity by irrigation but a few are reduced. For example, the incidence of *Sclerotium bataticola* on sorghum and of *Alternaria sesami* and *Corynespora casiicola* on sesame were reduced by irrigation (Rotem and Palti 1969). Irrigation must be used carefully where important plant diseases are concerned. More research on given diseases, specific crops, and proper agronomic procedures is needed.

Irrigation also may favor insect pests, particularly if it increases the number of available hosts for the insects. In general, insect levels increase with the advent of irrigation, and insect problems become more severe (E. Smith 1972). Intensification of agriculture, particularly in arid or semiarid zones, is inevitably associated with large increases in the number of insects and insect species attacking crops. Native predators and parasite insects of native insect pests are also typically increased by irrigation. Imported pests that do not have predators or parasites are more difficult to control.

Occasionally irrigation reduces insect populations. For example, sprinkler irrigation may reduce thrips populations by as much as 50 percent (Arnon 1972). In Egypt, the cotton leafworm, *Spodoptera littoralis,* which attacks several important crops and has many generations each year, overwinters almost entirely on clover; when the clover is not irrigated after May 10, leafworm mortality increases and the number of leafworms moving to cotton is reduced greatly (Falcon and Smith 1973).

Control of irrigation water is one of the most effective ways of controlling nematodes and some of the soil pathogens. Both nematodes and soil pathogens are moved rather easily, particularly via furrow irrigation. Root-knot control is often achieved by reduced irrigation, which prevents root-knot eggs from hatching (Van Gundy 1972). Irrigation often increases nematode populations (Good 1968). An example of *Pratylenchus brachyurus* on peanuts is given in Table 8.1.

Often major climate and environmental changes and also major changes in cropping and plant varietal patterns are due to large-scale irrigation developments. Their effects on plant protection are particularly important. This phenomenon has been documented carefully for the Wu-Shan-Tau reservoir in Taiwan (R. Smith 1972).

Table 8.1.   Increase in Population of the Nematode, *Pratylenchus brachyurus,* on Peanuts after Irrigation (Good 1968)

Year	Variety	Number / 10g Shell Sample	
		Nonirrigated	Irrigated
1960	V.B. G-2	93	1017
1961	V.B. G-2	176	1161
1962	V.B. G-2	73	984
1963	V.B. G-2	250	1060
1962	ARG. SP.	240	2705
1962	ER. RUN.	27	1057
1962	V.B. 67	45	886
1962	NC-2	104	1830
Mean		126	1338

The complicated changes that resulted in the Chia-nan area of Taiwan when the Wu-Shan-Tau reservoir was built about 1960 illustrate in more detail these changes and how rapid this agroecosystem evolution can come about. The new irrigation water impounded by the reservoir made possible a greater intensification of agriculture in the Chia-nan area, which was formerly limited by the availability of water, particularly in the nonmonsoon periods of the year. There were changes made in the rice varieties and a great reduction in the number of varieties grown. Previously, the first crop was almost entirely *japonica* type rice and the second crop about 50 percent *japonica* and 50 percent *indica.* Now both crops are essentially all *japonica* and 60 percent of the acreage is devoted to the single variety Tainan 5. With this varietal simplification, it is quite significant that the variety Tainan 5, while somewhat resistant to rice stem borer and rice blast, is quite susceptible to plant hopper and sheath blight.

This intensification of agriculture with multiple cropping (at least two good crops of rice plus a dry-land crop each year) required increased use of fertilizer. Previously in this area they had used only manure and rice straw compost but under the new system they applied high levels of commercial fertilizer to the fields. With all these changes in the rice agroecosystem the pest complex changed significantly as might be expected. The rice hispa, *Hispa armigera,* and the rice beetle, *Oulema oryzae,* which formerly were major pests were essentially eliminated through the use of insecticides. The yellow rice borer, *Tryporyza incertulas,* decreased in importance because of a combination of partially resistant rice varieties, insecticidal control and better land management. With irrigation it was easier to plow fields at the right time, hence harder for *Tryporyza* to overwinter.

At the same time, presumably because of multiple cropping and high use of fertilizer, the striped rice borer, *Chilo suppressalis,* increased in importance. Leafhoppers, *Nephotettix* spp., and plant hoppers, *Sogatella* and *Nilaparvata* spp., were greatly favored by the new microhabitat in the rice paddies, particularly as a result of the new plant type, closer plant spacing and fertilizer use. As a result, their feeding has caused severe damage but more importantly they are vectors of viruses and mycoplasma. Yellow dwarf, Tungro virus and a new disease called transitory yellowing are especially important. At the same time, rice blast was declining in importance through the development of varieties with moderate to high resistance and the use of fungicides. Finally, sheath blight of rice, caused by *Thanatephorus cucumeris,* was increasing in importance and none of the rice varieties in Taiwan possess adequate resistance to this disease.

Similar stories could be documented concerning many recently developed large-scale irrigation projects and all pose complicated interdisciplinary control problems for plant protection.

Trickle irrigation, being developed in Israel on a large scale, has many practical advantages and helps in several aspects of plant protection. Trickle irrigation is often used with polyethylene strips laid over the plant rows. This innovative system deserves more study and use, particularly in areas where water is precious (Palti 1979).

Tillage

Tillage is important in the control of many diseases, insects, and nematodes and even more important in the control of weeds (NAS 1968c). Tillage is not always helpful. Yarwood (1968) recorded instances in which tillage may increase or decrease plant diseases and he felt a principal task of research agriculturists was to develop tillage patterns that favor crop growth and health without encouraging diseases and pests.

Since tillage is primarily an agronomic procedure, its effects must be considered from the standpoint of agronomy and horticulture before being considered in disease and pest control.

One of the principal purposes of tillage is weed control. Weeds compete with crop plants for soil nutrients, sunshine, and water. Historically, tillage has been the principal method of weed control and today is the main method of control in most parts of the world. In Asia weeds are controlled mainly by hand weeding. Experiments in five Asian countries have demonstrated that careful hand weeding of rice increased yields by an average of 45 percent. Since herbicides are typically too expensive or unavailable in these countries, the value of hand weeding is clear (Brady 1974). Weeds also may be controlled by other tillage techniques—smothering in various ways, mulching, or using polyethylene strips or other shading (NAS 1968c). Parenthetically, weed control may be very helpful in controlling certain pests and diseases by the destruction of alternate hosts.

The arguments for and against minimum tillage, a fairly recent development in developed countries and very important from an agronomic and economic standpoint, have waxed and waned. Agronomic or horticultural practices take precedence in the minds of growers over plant protection procedures. Minimum tillage is used because it is less expensive, uses less energy, is more convenient, takes less time, and minimizes wind and soil erosion and soil moisture loss. It keeps organic matter on the surface and gradually produces an improvement of soil tilth for nutrient reserves over the years. The disadvantages are that it often does not destroy pests, disease organisms, or other propagules as do burning and sometimes deep plowing. Deep plowing returns organic components to the soil quickly and usually improves soil physical structure but increases soil erosion and moisture loss.

Burning quickly returns nutrients to the soil but does not give the soil the benefits of rotting organic matter and the attendant improvement of physical soil structure. However, burning is often quite effective in destroying pests and diseases (Pimental 1970).

The arguments for and against minimum tillage, deep plowing, and burning prior to plowing and after harvest will continue. The trend will probably continue toward minimum tillage in the developed countries because economic, agronomic, and soil conservation considerations favor minimum tillage. Plant protection personnel probably will need to develop control procedures that fit successfully into minimum tillage practices.

Recently, minimum tillage agriculture has been given the sobriquet *ecofarming* in the Great Plains of the United States. The trend is definitely in the direction of ecofarming in this area. A book by Phillips and Young (1973) summarizes the arguments concerning minimum tillage.

There are many examples of insect control by means of tillage. One of the most dramatic in the United States is the destruction of grasshopper eggs by fall plowing or disking and exposure of the eggs to weather and to birds. Minimum tillage works against this control and is much less effective than deep plowing. European corn borer populations can be reduced quite well by deep plowing and the consequent destruction of crop residues. Minimum tillage again is much less effective.

Black cutworm moths are associated with certain annual winter weeds at oviposition time in the spring. Consequently, weed control by tillage (and by chemical means) may have considerable bearing on black cutworm populations in maize (B. D. Blair 1979, pers. commun.).

Some plant diseases are decreased by tillage, others are increased, and others are apparently not affected. Specific host-disease situations are affected by tillage (Yarwood 1968). The take-all disease of wheat, incited by *Ophiobolus graminis,* is increased by tillage. There was 53 percent infection after conventional tillage and only 17 percent infection after the wheat was seeded directly into land where herbicides had been used to kill the previous vegetation. In tomatoes, the *Sclerotium* disease is increased by conventional tillage. The infection percentage was 69 after conventional tillage and only 23 when plastic covers were used on the soil to control vegetation. The powdery mildew disease of the California coastal chapparal broom, *Baccharis pilularis,* incited by *Erysiphe cichoracearum,* is greatly increased under cultivation but is almost free of the disease when grown on undisturbed land (Yarwood 1968).

Decreases in other plant diseases due to tillage have been reported by many workers (Yarwood 1968). Two examples follow: the *Verticillium* wilt of mint is controlled by deep plowing, which buries the inoculum on the soil surface and brings soil fairly free of inoculum to the top (NAS 1968a). The *Sclerotinia* disease of vegetables also is controlled by deep plowing; again, the inoculum is effectively destroyed by being placed far below the soil surface (Univ. Calif. 1972c).

By contrast, some forest diseases are very severe on undisturbed land, for example, chestnut blight. Many plant diseases are apparently not affected by tillage methods (Yarwood 1968).

Cultivation equipment, other objects, and workers moving through fields during wet weather can be important in the movement of aerial pathogens, particularly in diseases spread by a bacterial ooze. *Anthracnose* spore masses may be distributed to healthy plants while the foliage is wet and *Septoria* late blight fungus of celery is moved in the same way. Several plant virus diseases, particularly tobacco mosaic and other mechanically transmissible viruses, can be moved easily through wounds by equipment and workers. Dry spores of various rust fungi are moved and deposited the same way. Minimum tillage decreases diseases that may be transferred in this manner. Anything that minimizes physical activity during plant growth will also minimize the spread of such diseases (NAS 1968a).

Good (1968) gave several examples of nematode control by tillage practices. The destruction and removal of tobacco roots after harvest by tillage significantly reduces *Meloidogyne incognita* populations in soil. Root-knot is more severe on young tobacco plants in flatbeds than in raised beds where the soil has been sun and air-dried. Moldboard plowing gave partial control of *Pratylenchus brachyurus* in peanut and also partial control of pod rot. (See Table 8.2.)

Sanitation

Sanitation techniques such as the destruction of crop residues or the destruction of border weeds and trash are useful in plant protection. Infected residues from previous crops provide the overwintering or season-to-season carryover for many plant pathogens and are the strongest arguments for agricultural burning and deep plowing.

Examples of plant disease control by sanitation measures follow. Brown rot of stone fruits can be partially controlled by pruning diseased portions of plants and brown rot mummies from the trees. Disking infected

Table 8.2. Effect of Land Preparation Methods on *Pratylenchus brachyurus* in Peanut Shells and on Pod-rot at Harvest (Good 1968)

Previous Crop	Average Number of Nematodes Recovered from 10 g Shell Samples	Average Pod-rot Index*
Moldboard plow with concave disk (surface soil buried)		
Rye	151	2.3
Corn	117	1.9
Soybeans	73	1.7
Cotton	159	2.3
Mean	125	2.1
Disk-harrow (surface soil not buried)		
Rye	321	3.0
Corn	204	3.5
Soybeans	263	3.2
Cotton	839	3.7
Mean	407	3.4

*Pod-rot index: 1 = clean, 2 = trace, 3 = light, 4 = moderate, 5 = severe.

apple leaves on the ground helps reduce the amount of apple scab inoculum in the spring (USDA 1972). The inoculum of *Verticillium* wilt of mint can be controlled rather well by burning the remaining organic matter after harvest (NAS 1968a). In Kansas a good control for wheat streak mosaic is the destruction of volunteer wheat, which carries both the virus and the eriophyid mite vector, a week or more prior to planting (Somsen and Sill 1970). In Taiwan, Sun (1974) has emphasized the importance of destruction of postharvest wastes and trash in the control of several crop diseases that survive on or in dead host tissues on the soil surface.

It is easy to control ring rot of potato, a bacterial disease, by decontaminating or sterilizing crates, sacks, knives, planting equipment, hands of workers, and the surface of the seed pieces. A classic case of control by sanitation is the destruction of potato cull piles to control the potato late blight fungus (Walker 1969). Peach yellows disease, a mycoplasma, is controlled by the eradication or burning of infected trees, control of alternate hosts, and the production of certified nursery stock. Quite often sanitation procedures are used in combination with other cultural techniques (Walker 1969).

Early mowing and cutting of weeds before they can produce seed controls weeds effectively and minimizes some plant diseases also. One cannot make a blanket statement, however, concerning the favorable effects of such practices. For example, destruction of some weeds may cause mass migrations of insect vectors and pests to susceptible crops and also may cause predators and parasites to migrate and become less helpful.

Control of insects by sanitation is important. The greenbug is partially controlled, especially on oats and some other grains, by the destruction of all volunteer or overwintering oats or susceptible grains. This is also true for the English grain aphid and the Hessian fly. These control procedures are combined with other nonchemical measures. Sanitation is important for control of the wheat stem sawfly and the wheat jointworm (by burning stubble soon after harvest and cutting the wheat low to remove all insects in the straw) and the wheat stem maggot (by destroying or baling the straw and destroying all adjacent or volunteer small grains). Sanitation via community-wide cotton stalk destruction is important in the control of the pink bollworm in Texas. It is part of a large-scale cultural control program (Falcon and Smith 1973).

Sanitation is also important in controlling nematodes. A good example of this follows (NAS 1968*b*):

> Because of sucker growth semiannual crops such as tobacco continue to live several weeks after the harvest is completed. This sucker growth is sufficient to keep the root systems alive and consequently parasitic nematodes present in the roots continue to reproduce. One or two additional generations may develop between the end of harvest and the time the plant is killed by frost. If the stalks are cut soon after harvest and the root system of the plants then turned out and exposed, the population of the nematodes, especially of the root knot nematode, is reduced through the drying action of the sun and the wind. Two control principles are utilized in this practice, the destruction of the host plant by cutting the stalk and uprooting the plant thus preventing further reproduction of the nematode and the killing by desiccation of large numbers of nematodes concentrated in the soil around the root system and inside the roots.

Organic Manuring

The use of green manure, organic residues, or other manures is important in much of the world's agriculture. Organic manuring has many advantages; one is associated with the partial control of pests and diseases. A complex pattern of antagonism and antibiosis is initiated by the introduction of organic matter into the soil. This phenomenon is poorly understood but extremely significant in the maintenance of certain plant pathogen propagules at relatively low population levels.

Intensive cultivation of crops and failure to restore organic materials affect soil structure deleteriously and also affect the numbers of soil microorganisms and the resulting types of available antibiosis (McNew 1972). In the tropics the antibioses and antagonisms produced by organic matter are important in the control of some plant diseases. Wellman (1972) gave an interesting example of this.

Coffee fusarial wilt, incited by *Fusarium oxysporum* f. sp. *coffeae,* and also
the coffee root-knot nematode, *Meloidogyne* sp., increase when shade is
removed. . . . It was finally concluded that shade trees not only furnish shade
but also furnish extra leafy soil mulch that . . . appears to retard certain
diseases. When a coffee planting with its shade taken away and showing
declination from *Fusarium* and *Meloidogyne* diseases is replanted to shade
the diseases are reduced. . . . Heavy loads of weed and grass mulch materials
are cut and carried into their fields by peasant and Indian growers of Central
America. . . . Field visits and collecting trips have shown by examination
that root troubles, especially for fusaria, are more prevalent in unmulched
than in mulched plants of beans and tomatoes.

Many investigators have shown a reduction in plant pathogenic nematode population levels after the addition of organic matter or manures to
the soil. Increased activity of microorganisms in the soil typically follows
these treatments. It has been assumed that nematode populations were
reduced by the increase of organisms that destroy nematodes in the soil;
however, the specific reasons for the reduction are essentially unknown
(NAS 1968*b*).

Antagonisms and antibioses, which are not understood well, need to be
studied to clarify a confusing picture in plant protection that often develops
after the use of organic manures.

9

Environment and Nutrition

 Knowledge of the effects of environment on plant diseases and pests is the first line of defense in control for agronomists, horticulturalists, and plant pathologists. Plant pathologists have always felt that environmental and nutritional knowledge concerning crops and their diseases was most significant in developing control programs. Colhoun (1973) emphasized that study of effects of individual environmental factors is the first step in understanding a disease. The interaction of the environmental factors is significant and often complicated. The environment usually is a predisposing factor to various pathogens in the air and soil and is critical in the growth and susceptibility of the crop.

The key component in effective disease forecasting is a complete knowledge of environmental factors and their effects on a given pathogen and crop. The interactions of environmental effects on crops and pathogens determine whether large outbreaks of the disease occur (Colhoun 1973). McNew (1972) also emphasized the practical importance of a knowledge of environmental effects on plant disease control.

The major environmental factors that affect the development of plant diseases and their hosts, particularly pathogenic microorganisms, are moisture, aeration, temperature, and the mechanical properties of the soil. In addition, nutritional diseases are obviously affected by the chemical characteristics of the soil, particularly as they relate to plant nutrient levels, availability, and possible toxic materials present (NAS 1968a).

Wellman (1972) discussed the tropical environment:

> That diseases of crops show distinct dependence on the environment is perhaps clearer to experienced tropical plant pathologists than to temperate zone workers. Where causal organisms are involved there is no question about their effects but where, as is often the case in the tropics, one can see marked variations in soils short distances apart coupled with often quickly reached differences in climate, environments in the tropics may be considered to have

almost an exaggerated, certainly a leading role in the presence or absence, or relative severity, of disease. The soils themselves are new in many cases, are easily disturbed, and are being continually influenced by leaching from abundant rainfall coupled with unfailing warm temperatures.

Climate and Weather

Climate determines whether a pathogen will flourish or can even persist and whether insects, nematodes, and weeds can survive in a given location. Climatic effects are complex, and consequently recommendations for given crops differ because of differences in climate. Recommendations that are appropriate in one location are not at all appropriate in other macro- and microclimatic conditions. Important climatic or weather elements are temperature, moisture in its various forms, air movement, evaporation, light, radiation, and atmospheric pressure.

Climatic changes not only affect the severity of diseases but essentially create new disease problems. Weather patterns can determine whether a pathogen-host relationship will be economically unimportant or develop into an endemic or severe epidemic disease relationship. The biotic plant disease is actually an interaction between the environment, two living entities (the host and the pathogen), and often a third such as a vector. All of these tend to be very sensitive to changes in climate and weather.

The microclimate adjacent to the plant host and the causal organism is often the most important factor in disease development and may be quite different from the macroclimate of an area (NAS 1968a). Macroclimatic examples are well known. The forecasts of late blight of potatoes are based primarily on the weather, which controls the infection rate. If the weather conditions are right, the causal fungus can increase a millionfold during a season. If weather conditions are wrong, even large quantities of initial inoculum will not increase rapidly and hence no severe outbreak will occur. Also, susceptible crops are not planted to soils known to be infested with root-knot nematodes in very warm climates because it can be forecasted with great accuracy that the root-knot will become severe (Van der Plank 1972). Byerly (1972) reported a case in which the hoja blanca disease of rice, established in the late 1950s, never became severe because of an extremely severe winter that apparently destroyed all the insect vectors, *Sogata orizicola*. Another example is the destruction of the fungus *Ophiobolus graminis* in most of the wheat soils of the high Great Plains of the United States by the hot dry weather of the middle 1930s (Hurley Fellows 1958, pers. commun.).

Apple scab is rare in California owing to the lack of rainfall to disseminate conidia during the growing period. Bean anthracnose does not exist west of the continental divide in the United States because the pathogen requires soft spattering rain for the dissemination of spores. In the Pacific coast states blackleg and black rot of cabbage are very rare; dissemination of the pathogen of these diseases depends on extensive rainfall. Some subtropical and tropical diseases seem never to move out of the tropics. Examples are those incited by *Pellicularia rolfsii* and *Pseudomonas solanacearum* (Walker 1969). Other organisms do not thrive in areas with relatively severe winters. For example, the root rot diseases of cotton and other plants, incited by *Phymatotrichum omnivorum,* rarely get north of southern Oklahoma.

Weather and climate are important also in integrated insect control. Messenger (1970) illustrated how treatments can be quite successful in one area under certain weather conditions and fail completely in another area because of different weather patterns. A classic example of an insect affected by climate is the case of the greenbug. This aphid can be a serious problem when the preceding summer is very cool and moist; mild winters and cool springs produce very bad outbreaks (Metcalf et al. 1951). These conditions of course are not controllable hence are often ignored, but heat, cold, wind, rainfall, flooding, drought, and the like are extremely significant in the natural control of insect and mite populations.

Storms, high winds, and jet streams are very important in transporting spores, various propagules of plant diseases, and many of the smaller insects. Some transport of nematodes and weed seeds in this way also occurs although these are not considered to be major mechanisms of spread (Univ. Calif. 1972c).

Lightning causes more damage than would be expected to plants, trees, and various vegetable crops and is also a major cause of forest fires (Walker 1969). Hail and ice sometimes cause wholesale loss of small grains, particularly in the Great Plains of the United States, and cause destructive plant lesions and fruit damage in many parts of the world. This damage is often predisposing to secondary pathogenic organisms, particularly on fruit and vegetable crops (Univ. Calif. 1972c).

Air movement—particularly dry, hot, and rapid air movement—is very much underrated as a cause of plant damage. It is particularly important in increasing evapotranspiration, which in dry climates such as the Great Plains is often called *atmospheric drought.* Wind affects the physiology as well as the morphology of plants. The evapotranspiration rate is related to sunlight, temperature, wind speed, and relative humidity. Strong, hot, dry winds can rapidly desiccate and destroy plants. Even plants that have adequate soil moisture may be destroyed when such conditions are severe and prolonged (Univ. Calif. 1972c).

High winds coming constantly from one direction can radically change plant form and structure. Whipping of plants by wind leads to severe root injuries that lead in turn to root rot infections. Strong winds carry smaller insects, weed seeds, spores, fungi, and other microorganisms long distances, particularly the winds of warm summer storms and the jet streams. The nature and character of the dominant vegetation of the world is partially controlled by the effects of strong winds.

Severe air pollution problems are associated with the phenomenon of air stagnation caused by temperature inversions over large cities. Strong winds rapidly remove the gases and suspended solids of air pollution, which is not a problem in regions with constant air movement across vast areas (NAS 1968a).

One of the most obvious ways of regulating crop diseases via climate is to select growing sites where the environment is unfavorable for the disease and the disease or vector insect is unknown or is present in low levels. Examples are the growing of certified seed potatoes in the northwestern tier of states; growing of cabbage, turnip, and rutabaga seeds in the Pacific coast areas; and the shifting of pear culture to California and Oregon from the eastern states to avoid disease, particularly fire blight (Walker 1969).

Air and Soil Temperatures

People in plant protection as well as people in agronomy and horticulture should understand the effects of air and soil temperatures on plants, plant diseases, and insects. Unfortunately, this area of training often is neglected and may result in major misunderstandings. The annual cycles of air and soil temperatures are crucial in the planting and growth of crops. It is necessary to know mean temperatures and typical high, typical low, and extreme temperatures at any given time of year.

During dormancy many deciduous plants need an accumulation of a minimum number of hours below a specific temperature or they will not flower and fruit normally the next season. The bud drop of stone fruit trees that follows a warm winter is an example of inadequate winter chilling (and is sometimes mistaken for a severe abiotic or even pathogenic disease).

Very low air temperatures during blooming or early fruit development can nearly eliminate a crop because of embryo abortions. Late frosts in the spring can lead to russet rings on pome fruits and surface cracks on stone fruits that can be confused with insect and spray damage. The wide variety of symptoms from frost damage need to be learned and recognized. In the fall early frosts can damage succulent plants, especially if the fall weather has been warm. The injury is worse under drought conditions.

Sunscald damage occurs during hot summer weather and is usually seen where there is excessive water loss due to high temperatures and direct sunlight. This condition also produces leafscorch or tipburn that can be confused with plant diseases and insect damage (Univ. Calif. 1972c).

High and low air and soil temperatures often affect insects, plant diseases, and nematodes, also, and overall effects on pest and disease populations as related to a specific crop in a particular environment must be determined before understanding the total effects. A good plant protection observer must also be a good agronomist and horticulturalist (or work must be done in coordinated team efforts) so that the effects of climate, weather, and other environmental factors can be appreciated. For example, it is important to know that maize is a warm weather plant and cabbage is a cool weather plant. The growth requirements of each plant must be known by individuals working with the plant. Each plant shows a different symptomatic effect from freezing as well as from sun and high temperature injury (Walker 1969). The yearly temperature cycles of air and soil determine which plants can survive in a given place and which can be grown commercially. All the physiological processes of a plant are directly or indirectly influenced by air and soil temperatures (NAS 1968a).

Some types of plants, particularly those adapted to the tropics, are very susceptible to chilling at temperatures well above freezing. Sugarcane is often damaged by chilling at altitudes of 1500 meters and above. Bananas also are very susceptible to chilling (Wellman 1972). Chilling can be serious in the temperate zone to such crops as tomatoes and cucumbers, causing surface and internal necroses, surface pitting, increased susceptibility to decay by weak parasites, and failure to ripen. Warm season crops may be badly hurt by chilling during the seedling stage. Chilling also tends to make seedlings susceptible to damping-off organisms and other similar organisms in the soil. Many plants can be hardened gradually to withstand very low temperatures. Most of the winter small grains as well as temperate zone deciduous trees are in this category. When tissues are actually frozen, particularly when they are succulent, they tend to become pithy and lose water. This is very common in lettuce, peas, celery, and citrus fruits (NAS 1968a).

Plants vary tremendously in their capacity to withstand heat. Repiration rates increase with rising temperature up to 30°–40°C. Some plants can withstand these temperatures for prolonged periods; others cannot. No plant survives long when food loss from respiration exceeds food gain from photosynthesis. Best photosynthesis temperatures for plants range from 10° to 35°C. After prolonged hot periods, trees and many other plants lose foliage through wilting, leaf scald, tipburn, and leaf scorch.

High temperatures after spraying are very damaging to plants. The application of chemicals on hot, sunny days often causes severe phytotoxicity, which would not occur at all on cooler, more humid, or cloudy days (NAS 1968a).

Soil temperatures are very important in governing the rate of moisture absorption, which varies with different plant species and cultivars. Some plants grow very well at low soil temperatures; others must have high soil temperatures. High soil temperatures can cause basal or stem lesions or heat canker—a zone of dead tissue on the plant stem at the soil level, particularly in black or dark soils that absorb heat easily. It occurs quite often in flax in the northern central states, particularly in the black soils of North Dakota (NAS 1968a; Walker 1969).

The most severe effects of extreme soil temperatures are on the nutrient and water relations in plant roots, which affect all metabolic processes and plant growth. Soil organisms and their biological processes are also affected. The marked changes that occur are often underestimated or even ignored (Univ. Calif. 1972c). For example, unseasonable or consistently low soil temperatures typically stunt plants because chemical processes slow and growth slows commensurately and often nearly stops.

Very low soil temperatures can kill the roots of tender plants and even of some hearty plants. Severe damage can occur in the spring when temperatures have been warm for a short period and then drop markedly. The sturdiest plants usually are those that are hardened well in the fall and those that produce new growth late in the spring. Soil that is very cold or frozen cannot yield water to the roots of plants. A common and very damaging situation develops in the spring when the earliest warm weather arrives and warm, often dry, winds stimulate transpiration in plants with young leaves. If the roots are still in very cold or frozen soil that does not yield water, the result is a foliage browning and killing often referred to as *winter drying* (NAS 1968a; Univ. Calif. 1972c).

Pathogenic disease organisms are also affected by changes in air and soil temperatures. Some pathogens, which seem to be capable of causing diseases throughout the world wherever susceptible plants are grown, tolerate wide ranges of environmental conditions. Most pathogens are less tolerant of variations in temperature and are usually restricted in distribution. One pathogen that is restricted because of temperature is the onion smut organism, *Urocystis cepulae*. It is well established in the northern, cooler onion-growing areas of the United States and Europe but it is absent in the large onion-growing areas of the southern United States (Colhoun 1973).

Some pathogenic diseases are delayed or prevented by low temperatures. For example, Brussels sprouts can be grown economically in the *Fusarium* wilt infested soils in the western coastal areas of the United States because temperatures typically remain too low for *Fusarium* wilt to develop; if seasons are very warm there may be occasional severe wilt losses. Seedlings in Southern pine nurseries are planted in late spring after the warm temperatures arrive to avoid rust sporidia of *Cronartium fusiforme,* which typically are present on young oak leaves during earlier cool weather (NAS 1968*a*).

Soil and air temperatures can be used in the control of nematodes also. In California the cyst nematode on sugar beets and the root-knot nematode on Irish potatoes are controlled by planting these crops early in the spring when soil temperatures are still too low for significant nematode activity. By the time nematodes begin to be active the plants have grown beyond the point where they normally will be damaged (Univ. Calif. 1972*b*).

Few insects except some tropical species are killed by low temperatures. Insects in hibernation often stand temperatures of −30° to −40°C or lower. In normal winter temperatures from −18° to 5°C, little damage occurs to most insects although they become inactive at temperatures somewhere between 12° and 18°C. Consequently, insects may cause only minor damage at cool temperatures that are well above freezing. Stored products can be protected from insect damage by cooling. Clothing, food products, or any perishable materials held in freezing or cold storage are safe from insect damage, although the cold usually will not kill the insects.

Changes from low to high to low temperatures are quite effective in killing insects, particularly if the changes are made rapidly. Most insects are susceptible to extreme and prolonged high temperatures coupled with drought and may be destroyed rather easily by heating (Metcalf et al. 1951). The use of fire to destroy pest and plant diseases is an ancient practice that deserves more attention, particularly since the advent of minimum tillage. Many arthropods, weed seeds, and plant disease propagules can be destroyed by burning (Hardison 1976).

Light

Many maladies of crop plants are associated with inadequate light. Agronomists, horticulturists, and plant pathologists are constantly concerned with plant phenomena associated with light. Light provides the energy for photosynthesis, but the requirements are different for each plant species. The importance of light is summarized in the following statement (NAS 1968*a*):

> The intensity, wave-length, duration and periodicity of light affect the germination of seeds; growth, form, and color of plants; time and abundance of flowering and fruiting, the size and form of organs; and therefore, crop yields. Insufficient light leads to etiolation, stunting, reduction in flowering and other abnormalities. High light intensities can scorch or roll foliage, dry up flowers, accentuate spray damage and bring about injuries from photochemically formed air pollutants. Light governs so wide a range of

plant responses that its causal role in plant abnormalities should be suspected whenever plants are grown out of their native habitat, or in artificial culture or to a light regime different from that to which they are adapted.

Light is equally important in the growth of weeds. Some important control measures are associated with light exclusion, i.e., mulching; use of black plastic sheets or strips; and shading given by fast growing, thickly planted crop plants. Shading is essential for the proper growth of some plants or it may kill other plants or portions of them. Seedlings may not grow properly and may be predisposed to other debilitating agents such as fungus pathogens if the light is not correct (Univ. Calif. 1972c).

Ultraviolet light is sometimes quite damaging at high altitudes (Walker 1969).

Most maladies of plants associated with light are due to light effects alone, but light intensity, quality, and photoperiod are sometimes related to the successful development of pathogenic organisms and plant disease situations. For example, low light intensity reduces the level of club root of cabbage, incited by *Plasmodiophora brassicae,* unless the soil is very heavily contaminated with the organism. Short days are more favorable than long for the development of take-all of wheat, incited by *Ophiobolis graminis.* Barley plants are resistant to the rust *Puccinia striiformis* when the day length exceeds 12 hours but may be completely susceptible at very short day lengths. Light tends to encourage sporulation in most pathogens on plants, but can have the opposite effect. For example, low light intensity or short day length prior to inoculation makes tomato plants more susceptible to *Fusarium* wilt (Colhoun 1973).

Shade (an overhead cover) is used routinely for the coffee tree. It reduces the incidence of *Cerospora* leaf spot and has other protective characteristics (NAS 1968a). It also is useful in controlling the Sigatoka disease of banana (Lopez-Rosa and Bonata-Garcia 1979).

Light is also important in the annual growth and maturation of insects and all arthropods. However, few experimenters have attempted to control insects in the field by alteration of light. One by Hayes (1970) extended the day length by artificial light in selected field plots. This prevented 76 percent of the European corn borer larvae and 70 percent of the codling moth larvae from entering diapause, which made them unable to survive the hard winter. This treatment, however, probably cannot be utilized in general field practice.

By contrast, lights to lure and destroy insects, i.e., light traps, are often effective. They fix the candlepower or control the exact color of the light spectrum that is attractive to specific insects. Many insects are attracted by the blue and ultraviolet portions of the spectrum. Some species can be lured very easily to their deaths by light traps (Metcalf et al. 1951).

However, B. D. Blair (1979, pers. commun.) states that in only one well-documented case has light controlled insects of economic importance effectively. Light traps have been used in Alabama for satisfactory control of the hickory shuckworm in pecan groves.

Water and Soil Moisture

Too little or too much water is probably the source of more plant growth problems than anything else in agriculture. Sandy soils lose water too quickly. Heavy clay soils may hold water to the point of damaging the plant. Plants that are very lush from irrigation and heavy fertilization often suffer severely from pathogenic diseases and also from drought should it occur. Low soil moisture tends to increase the buildup of toxic ions to a level that damages plants (Univ. Calif. 1972c). Some plant diseases are more serious in wet soils, others are more serious under dry conditions, and nearly all plant diseases are affected by the level of moisture. The germination of most pathogenic organisms depends on atmospheric humidity and often on a film of water on the plant surface. Spore dissemination is often achieved by the splashing of raindrops or the movement of water droplets in the air, on plant surfaces, or on the ground (Colhoun 1973).

Low soil moisture increases the accumulation of toxic ions, particularly boron and manganese, and encourages the closing of stomates and, if prolonged, the movement of carbon dioxide into the plant. The resultant reduction of photosynthesis then becomes significant. Low soil moisture causes wilting, both temporary and permanent, and in vast areas of the earth the most important continuing malady of plants is that of drought, either incipient or severe (NAS 1968a).

At high soil moisture levels, carbon dioxide and toxic products of anaerobic metabolism tend to accumulate. Soils become poorly aerated and movement of oxygen and other gases important to the growth and functioning of roots is restricted, encouraging the development of fungus root rots and tending to make plants so succulent that they become sensitive to invasion by many pathogens.

Anoxia, or lack of sufficient oxygen in plant roots, is far more serious than generally recognized, particularly when the condition is chronic in perennial plants, trees, or shrubs. The small feeder roots die back first from lack of oxygen, followed finally by the larger roots. After prolonged anoxia the plant foliage begins to thin out and die back. Any situation that creates a high water table—excessive irrigation, excessive rain, a perched water table owing to a hardpan, or any impervious subsoil layer—may result in anoxia (Walker 1969; Univ. Calif. 1972c). An important anoxia disease of rice in the second and third rice crops of the year in Taiwan is the suffocating disease. It is easily controlled by aerating the soil during growth of a dryland crop (Ren-jong Chiu 1974, pers. commun.).

In sandy soils or in soils lacking adequate humus heavy precipitation or excessive irrigation may cause severe leaching, which removes most of the nutrients from the soil and causes nutrient impoverishment and hence nutritional deficiencies. This too is far more important than generally recognized (NAS 1968a).

Most plants can stand short periods of flooding. However, prolonged flooding in land plants inevitably leads to death of roots, primarily from lack of oxygen, and when flooding occurs during hot weather the increased rate of respiration increases the damage. Overall losses to agriculture from flooding, drought, and all the attendant abiotic effects of adverse soil moisture are staggering and more attention should be given to this essentially agronomic and horticultural problem.

Some plant pathogenic diseases are made more severe by excessive soil moisture or irregular water supply. Examples are the *Aphanomyces* root rot of pea, which is incited by a water mold and requires high soil moisture levels, and other water mold diseases such as those caused by *Pythium* spp. The most effective measures of control are adequate drainage and avoiding poorly drained soils (Walker 1969).

An example of how temperature and moisture levels control a disease is the powdery scab of potato. It is completely controlled by environment. The organism persists in the soil for long periods but only develops when the temperatures are below 14°C and soil moisture levels are high. It was introduced into the United States many years ago but is not of much significance except in New England. The disease is so severe in Germany and Russia where the environment is more favorable that attempts have been made to control it with resistant varieties. In the United States this effort has not been necessary. A few plant diseases are more severe when water levels are low and the environment is generally dry. The powdery mildews are classic examples (Walker 1969).

The greatest damage done by weeds is to use scarce soil moisture—they typically use twice the amount of water consumed by the crop. One of the most important reasons for control of weeds is to make sure the crop gets the available water (Janick et al. 1969).

Nutrients, Minerals, and Toxicities

A large number of essential plant nutrients are known. A few of these, such as nitrogen, phosphorus, and potassium, are classified as major elements. Plant pathologists always have been concerned with plant maladies associated with mineral deficiencies and excesses. Plant pathologists must know the symptoms characteristic of the various plant deficiencies and toxicities, since they can be easily confused with many other plant diseases—particularly virus diseases (Walker 1969). Probably most agricultural soils are deficient in one or more of the essential elements, especially if they have been cropped for long periods or if they are light, sandy, and have been exposed to abundant rainfall. For these reasons alone, plants may be stunted, discolored, and weak in growth. The malady is a case of deficiency usually of nitrogen, phosphorus, potassium or one of the other essential elements. Nutritional problems and pathological diseases form exceedingly complex relationships, and a basic understanding of plant physiology and the effects of all the major and minor nutrients on plants is needed (Univ. Calif 1972c).

The field of plant nutrition is closely related to plant pathological maladies and is involved with and often related to damages caused by other pests. The problems are too complicated to be expressed well by a few principles but those that follow are helpful.

1. Many elements are essential for plant growth and good health.

2. The elements need to be in an available form and in appropriate amounts.

3. The nutrient balance is as important as the absolute amounts available and is expressed in ratios of one nutrient to another.

4. Deficiencies vary with genetic constitution and stage of plant development.

5. Soil salt content, soil pH, temperature, moisture, microbial activity in the soil, and other soil characteristics greatly affect nutrient availability (NAS 1968a).

Nutrient imbalance in plants can cause mosaics, mottling, chlorosis, necrosis (large and small necrotic spots), yellowing, etiolation, leaf curl, dwarfing, and mottling of various types, all of which can be confused with specific plant diseases.

Two examples that often cause confusion follow. Manganese deficiency in sugar beets often looks like insect damage. Copper deficiency in Sudan grass may look like eriophyid mite damage, causing the tips of the growing leaves to be caught in the leaf whorl. It is most important for workers in plant protection to be trained in plant nutrition and to cooperate with specialists in soil science and plant physiology (NAS 1968a; Univ. Calif. 1972c).

Several diseases cause wilting phenomena that can be confused with nutritional disorders. Nematodes cause wilting at times and also cause plants to have a light green, unthrifty appearance, indicating generally poor growth. Damage associated with flooding, drought, and some of the feeding and egg-laying effects of insects, such as tipburning, marginal necrosis, various galls and distortions, can be confused with specific nutritional disorders. Nutritional deficiencies and toxicities predispose plants to diseases in many complicated ways.

One would hope that optimum nutrition would provide defense against disease but this often is not the case (NAS 1968a):

> Optimum nutrition provides no defense against most virus diseases or other obligate parasites, nor against fungus or bacterial vascular wilts. Plant vigor is not necessarily correlated with health. In many forest tree rusts cultivation and optimal nutrition consistently increase rust incidence.

People with experience know that breeding plots (where nutritional conditions theoretically are ideal) seem to have the most diseases. C. O. Johnson, plant pathologist and plant breeder, said that "if you want to see which diseases are in the area go to the breeding plots." McNew (1972) summarized this situation well:

> Many soil management practices have intensified pest control problems. One, forced feeding of plants renders them more susceptible to the attack of highly specialized pathogens such as the downy mildews, powdery mildews, and rusts. Two, an excess of nitrogen is almost uniformly deleterious to disease-escaping and disease-resistant attributes.

The powdery mildew of cereals and grasses, incited by *Erysiphe graminis,* is far more severe when high levels of nitrogen are used. Apple orchards with high levels of nitrogen are more susceptible to the bacterial disease called fire blight—the healthy, well-nourished, succulent tissue is more susceptible than the less succulent growth. Proper use of nitrogen fertilizers in apple orchard management is required (Walker 1969). High nitrogen levels also increase the severity of Stewart's wilt of maize and the bacterial disease of tobacco called wildfire.

In the tropics, heavy fertilizer applications in the rice growing areas have greatly increased the incidence and severity of sheath blight of rice (S.H. Ou 1974, pers. commun.). Excessive amounts of nitrogen also make the rice plant more susceptible to rice blast, incited by *Pyricularia oryzae.* Formerly, little fertilization of rice was done in the tropics and this disease was not nearly as important (Feakin 1970). High levels of nitrogen also are favorable for more severe development of leaf scald of rice, incited by *Rynchosporium oryzae* (Peregrine et al. 1974).

In a few cases nitrogen fertilizer tends to reduce disease severity. An example is the fungus disease incited by *Pellicularia rolfsii,* which attacks sugar beets in California—high nitrogen levels tend to reduce the damage from the disease (Walker 1969).

Potassium deficiencies are associated with severe disease situations. For example, potassium deficiency tends to make plant tissues more readily water-soaked and thus more susceptible to some diseases. Cotton wilt, incited by *Fusarium oxysporum* f. sp. *vasinfectum,* tends to be more severe when plants are growing on potassium-deficient soils (Walker 1969).

McNew (1972) indicated that proper balance of nitrogen and phosphorus may help plants escape excessive damage from some of the less highly specialized parasites, particularly root rot disease organisms. McNew also reported that optimum potassium levels not only tend to stimulate good crop growth but also to increase resistance to parasites. Proper nutrient balance is, in all likelihood, more important for good plant growth and disease resistance than very high levels of a specific nutrient.

Many severe deficiency diseases and also some toxicity diseases are associated with the minor nutrients of crops, such as boron, calcium, manganese, magnesium, and copper. These deficiencies are most common in sandy soils that leach rapidly under heavy rainfall or irrigation conditions.

In some cases, heavy metal ions, i.e., iron, are unavailable for plant nutrition when the soils are alkaline. This type of iron deficiency is very common in the Great Plains of the United States.

Boron deficiencies are common in some areas, resulting in poor growth of tops and roots, blackened necrotic vascular tissues, and breakdown of other internal tissues. Pecan rosette, citrus mottling, and little leaf of stone fruits and grapes are the result of zinc deficiencies. They may easily be confused with certain virus diseases. High levels of calcium may make plants more resistant to wilt pathogens and soft rot organisms (NAS 1968a).

Minor element deficiencies, such as iron, manganese, zinc, and boron, are significant in certain portions of the tropics. On heavily farmed volcanic soils with good drainage and abundant rainfall, minor elements are likely to be leached away. Usually the minor element problems develop on tropical soils after several harvest seasons on new land have been completed. They also seem to be most severe in tilled land that is not mulched and is not kept under protective cover from the sun (Wellman 1972). Minor element problems also tend to be quite common in the temperate zones in muck and alkaline soils. The necessary nutrients actually are often present in the soil but are not available or are in an insoluble form (Walker 1969).

Deficiencies of minor or trace elements can usually be corrected by annual applications of the required salts applied in available form as soil amendments or as dilute leaf sprays. Manganese chlorosis on beans is corrected in the Florida Everglades muck soils by a manganese sulfate spray solution. Zinc sulfate is added to soil or incorporated into a spray to correct zinc deficiency in pecan and also in citrus. Along the U.S. Atlantic seaboard area dolomitic lime is often used as a soil applicant to correct magnesium deficiency. In some cases (particularly on potatoes) the lime used in Bordeaux mixture is sufficient to correct magnesium deficiency problems. Copper deficiency is typically corrected by the addition of copper sulfate to fertilizers. Occasionally copper fungicides provide sufficient copper for a crop. When manganese, boron, and zinc are fixed in alkaline soils, adding sulfur or acid-forming fertilizers to the soil lowers its pH sufficiently to make the minor elements available to the crop (Walker 1969).

Nematode damage can be reduced somewhat by proper nutrition although nematode populations are often increased at higher levels of nutrients (Good 1968). High nitrogen levels tend to reduce losses by root-knot and lesion nematodes (Van Gundy 1972). Soil populations of several nematode species have been altered by host nutrition and, in general, levels are lowest where plant nutrients are in short supply (Good 1968). Also, nematode infestations have been shown to cause both increases and decreases in concentrations of minerals in leaf and root tissues. These interactions between host and parasite as they affect and are affected by nutrition are complex and the design of fertilizer programs to minimize damage to crop plants caused by nematodes is just beginning (NAS 1968b; Van Gundy 1972). Good (1968) has reported good nematode control after heavy applications of anhydrous ammonia in some situations.

Residues from nematicides, namely EDB and DBCP, have altered the uptake of bromine in certain crops, e.g., peanuts and citrus, and caused some problems. The uptake of halogens from several fumigants has altered adversely the burning quality of stored tobacco (NAS 1968b). Excesses of chlorine can usually be controlled by a reduction of chlorine in fertilizers that are applied.

In general, well-nourished plants are more subject to attack of causal organisms than poorly nourished plants. Pimental (1970) pointed out that this is true also for insects and some other pests. Plants that are well fertilized tend to be more attractive to insects and hence more vulnerable. Well-fed plants produce larger populations of well-fed insects.

An example of well-nourished plants receiving excessive damage is the injury to rice plants caused by the stem borer larvae. The damage is much greater in rice that receives high rates of nitrogen fertilizer (Ishii and Hirano 1959). The larvae are bigger and more numerous, the adult females lay more eggs, and the plant appears to be more attractive to the females for oviposition. The rice gall midge is more severe on rice when nitrogen levels are high (R. Smith 1972). Also, high levels of nitrogen have been shown to result in higher populations of corn leaf aphids in maize (B. D. Blair 1979, pers. commun.).

Occasionally excessive use of pesticides on a crop will alter the availability of nutrients. A nitrogen deficiency disease of sugarcane was reported in Puerto Rico by Dubey (1970) in which excessive use of pesticides apparently changed the soil microbial population so much that the soil nitrogen was mineralized, resulting in nitrogen starvation of the sugarcane crop. Such cases appear to be rare.

Weeds compete for mineral nutrients. Hence, indirectly they can cause mineral deficiencies in crop plants and reduce crop quality and yield.

Absence of weeds assures a better yield and better nutrition for all crop plants because crop plants get the available nutrients (Crafts and Robbins 1962).

Soil pH and Salinity Problems

Hydrogen ion concentrations and salinity problems are adverse for plant growth in many parts of the world. Some plants accept or even grow better in an acid soil and others must have neutral or basic soils; but no agricultural crops can survive well at extreme soil pH levels, whether acidic or basic. So many plant maladies are associated with pH and salinity that it is essential for workers in plant protection, particularly plant pathologists, to recognize these problems.

Severely reduced yields are typical in saline situations. In a few saline-alkali soils the salts at the surface may be so concentrated that they create cankers at the crown level of growing plants (NAS 1968*a*). Acid soils often make nutrients unavailable, and salts accumulating in irrigated soils may become so concentrated as to hinder plant growth. In irrigating alkaline or saline soil, the important factors are the composition of the irrigation water, the leaching characteristics of the soil, and the methods of irrigation.

Toxicity problems are essentially salt problems and they are rarer than deficiency maladies. The most common toxicities are associated with excessive amounts of boron, manganese, aluminum, and iron. A toxicity example called crinkle leaf of cotton has been severe in some cotton growing areas (Walker 1969).

Modification of soil pH, where possible, often reduces the incidence of certain plant diseases. A high pH reduces the severity of clubroot of cabbage. A high pH tends to induce copper and zinc deficiencies in citrus infested with citrus nematodes (Van Gundy 1972). The potato scab, incited by *Streptomyces scabies,* is greatly reduced when the pH is below 5.2—many potato soils along the Atlantic seaboard from Maine to Florida are in the pH 5.2 range. Scab has been controlled rather well in this area by use of acid-forming fertilizers, somewhat acid tolerant cover crops, and avoiding the use of lime (Walker 1969). Sweet potato soil rot, which is really sweet potato scab, incited by *Streptomyces ipomoea,* is severe in Louisiana where the soil pH is 5.6 to 5.8 or above. Sulfur applied to the soil changes the reaction to pH 5 or lower and practically eliminates losses from this disease.

By contrast, clubroot of crucifers is controlled by keeping the pH at 7.0 or above. The addition of lime to the soil to control clubroot has been used for two centuries or more (Walker 1969). Iron chlorosis is often seen in California trees and shrubs when there is an excess of lime in the soil. The soil becomes alkaline and makes the iron in the soil no longer available to plants. Yellowing appears in the interveinal areas of the outer leaves and looks remarkably like some virus diseases. High pH conditions also tie up manganese and zinc. Such lime-induced high pH–deficiency symptoms occur in various woody plants (Univ. Calif. 1972c).

Salt accumulations may cause retarded seedling germination, slow or little growth, small leaves, weakened shoots, chlorosis, burning of foliage, tipburn, and premature defoliation. High concentrations of boron, calcium, magnesium, sodium, and other elements can be responsible for unusual toxicity symptoms if present in excessive amounts. Some irrigation waters, quite often from underground water supplies, have a high concentration of salts that may build up rapidly in soils (Univ. Calif. 1972c).

10

Abiotic Maladies and Controls

 Abiotic problems, often not considered important by other plant protection disciplines, are extremely important to plant pathologists. They probably will become more troublesome (NAS 1968a).

In the future plant pathologists must work with scientists in related disciplines to learn more about the nature and effects of the many noninfectious agents that cause plant diseases and in particular to develop a better understanding of the influence of abiotic factors on the development of pathogenic diseases. It is obvious that the amount of noninfectious damage to plants will increase with increases in population, intensification of agriculture and industry, and the use and reuse of available water supplies.

In recent years many plant pathologists have been involved with the increasingly severe problems of air and water pollution and their effects on agricultural crops.

Air Pollution

Nearly every environmental change affects plants either physically or physiologically. The effects are largely interdependent and often controlled by the plant's genetic makeup. An example of genetic difference in plant response is the degree of sensitivity to industrial stack gases shown by trees of the same species. In the same area one tree may be symptomless, a tree next to it may be dead, and others nearby may show all ranges of foliage damage. By contrast, within a single picked clonal line of the same species, the response to the same air pollution usually will be uniform. This genetic response is significant and indicates great possibilities for breeding for resistance. It also makes the importance of air pollution problems difficult to assess (Rich 1964; NAS 1968a).

Many types of urban and industrial air and water pollution are present, and several are harmful to plants. Sulfur dioxide, one of the commonest industrial pollutants, has severely damaged cotton, alfalfa, and forest trees. It is converted in moist air to an acid aerosol and is characteristic of the eastern industrial areas of the United States and of London. It recently has been called "acid rain" in the press and business magazines such as U.S. News & World Report (The growing furor over acid rain 1979) have carried long articles on the subject. Acid rain or snow is now falling on much of the industrial eastern United States. The pH values have averaged about 4 but vary from 2.1 to 5. As indicated by Likens and Bormann (1974), little is known about short- or long-term effects of these acid storms.

The Los Angeles smog, by contrast, is the oxidizing smog found in and near big cities that includes the photochemical production of ozone and peroxyacetyl nitrate (PAN) (Rich 1964). The damage from the photochemical oxidants is the result for the most part of emission of huge quantities of partially burned materials and unconsumed hydrocarbons from internal combustion engines. These materials produce recognizable symptoms on host plants. Smog damage to citrus, tobacco, and other crops has been severe. Auto exhaust fumes have also caused severe dieback of redbud along highways in recent years (Parris 1968), and "roadside decline" of citrus in Florida is associated with automobile exhaust fumes.

Several other atmospheric impurities affect plants. One of the most interesting is associated with apple scald. In this case, volatile by-products produced by the apple tissue itself, particularly when the fruit is confined during packing and shipping, create the scald.

Another common source of damage is illuminating gas. This damage occurs with houseplants, in florists' establishments and greenhouses. Many plants are sensitive to ethylene gas; carnations are particularly sensitive (Walker 1969), and damage has been reported in orchids. Also, damage from fluorides has been reported on azalea, gladiolus, and pine (NAS 1968a).

Control of air pollution problems in plants has been confined largely to the selection of plants differing in resistance. Some breeding programs have been initiated. Moyer et al. (1974) reported that benomyl and thiophanate greatly reduced ozone injury and stress when applied as liquid soil amendments to annual bluegrass, *Poa annua*. Several other cases in which benomyl reduced damage from ozone have been reported. This is a potentially important area for plant pathological research.

Relatively little is known about the effects of pollutants on various pathogenic diseases of plants. Different plant species and even different cultivars of the same species vary in sensitivity to particular pollutants. Also, environmental conditions such as temperature, moisture, humidity, and sunlight alter the sensitivity of plants to air pollution. Reports show that sulfur dioxide emissions can affect fungus diseases in the field. Wheat stem rust was reduced in polluted, heavily industrialized areas in Sweden. Decreased parasitism has been reported for species of *Cronartium, Melampsora, Peridermium, Pucciniastrum, Puccinia,* and *Coleosporium,* all rust pathogens, where plants have been injured by sulfur dioxide in heavy industry areas. In Czechoslovakia, heart rot and other Basidiomycete tree diseases have been reduced near the smelter areas as compared to areas farther away. Sulfur dioxide in general has apparently decreased disease severity.

By contrast, in ozone areas, where the rusts and powdery mildews also seemed to be decreased in severity, *Botrytis* infections were more severe. Moreover, tobacco mosaic virus infections were more severe and occurred in greater numbers in ozone areas. Conflicting evidence of other virus diseases has been reported (Heagle 1973). These studies open a new door in research efforts. We are only beginning to understand the significance of air pollution as related to plant diseases, plant growth, and development.

Trees injured and weakened by air pollutants are more likely to be attacked by certain insects that require weakened trees for reproduction. In other cases feeding of insects is decreased or not affected. Insect damage is probably associated with feeding habits of the larvae and depends on whether the larvae are shallow or deep feeders and whether they normally attack weakened or healthy trees.

Bark beetle and weevil populations are decreased in fir trees damaged by fluoride, possibly because of toxic levels of fluoride in the plant tissues. Insect air pollution research has been done almost exclusively on forest insects (Heagle 1973). Virtually nothing is known about the effects of air pollutants on the feeding habits of food crop insects. This area is also potentially significant.

Of particular interest is the recent documentation of plant species that have developed highly resistant plant types under air pollution pressures (Bradshaw 1976). Recent publications give more detail concerning air pollutants (Naegele 1973; Mansfield 1976).

Injuries

Many diseases of plants are associated with or initiated by injuries, which are particularly important in plant pathology. Many pathogens are spread by handling plants and by pruning, especially when the plants are wet. Pruning shears should be sterilized before touching each tree when pruning for fireblight cankers, a bacterial disease of apple and pear that is easily transmitted by tools. Young tomato plants need to be pruned without the shears touching the rest of the plant. Mechanically transmitted virus diseases can be shifted from plant to plant very easily by small injuries. There are many examples of this phenomenon and more research is needed (Univ. Calif. 1972c). It is also discussed in Chap. 2.

Sweet potatoes that are injured or damaged at harvesttime are susceptible to *Ceratocystis fimbriata* and *Rhizopus stolonifer,* serious diseases either in storage or transit. Strawberries and other perishable fruits must be picked at the proper time of day and packed with extreme care if fruit rots, initiated primarily by injury, are to be avoided (NAS 1968a).

In forest trees as well as in fruit and ornamental trees, extreme care must be exercised in pruning, handling intermediate cuttings, and handling or moving young trees to reduce wounds and decay hazards. The virtual elimination of basal wounds in forests by fire control has reduced the butt rot disease of eastern U.S. hardwood forests from 15 to only 1 percent (NAS 1968a).

In the tropics (and sometimes in temperate zones) there are many so-called sterile leaf spots that contain no fungus or bacterial pathogens and for which causes are often unknown. Many are associated with sunscald or sunburn. Many are the result of dry winds, blown sand, or injuries from being beaten together in storms. Insect punctures, injuries from leaf miners, air pollutants, and sea spray may also cause injury spots. Occasionally they may be the hypersensitive, local lesion spots from virus infections. Necrotic spotting may come also from minor element deficiencies. Wellman (1972) estimated that one-third of the spots brought to pathologists for identification are sterile spots. These spots may be susceptible to invasion by weak plant pathogens and may become infection courts for certain diseases. Workers in plant disease clinics know how numerous, frustrating, and mystifying these spots often are.

Mechanical Barriers

The use of mechanical barriers in controlling insects has been important in specific cases. Special mechanical measures are (1) hand destruction; (2) mechanical exclusions such as linear barriers, tree banding, fly nets, and screens; (3) traps such as collecting machines and suction devices; and (4) dragging, grinding, or crushing machines (Metcalf et al. 1951).

Use of inert, protective plant covers or protective buildings (greenhouses and screenhouses) to make plants unavailable to insects are common. Also, certain inert materials are used to make plants unpalatable to insects (Delthier 1970).

Many pathogens that spread from plant to plant by their root systems can often be prevented or delayed by physical barriers or nonhost plant barriers. An example is the Moko disease of banana incited by *Pseudomonas solanacearum.* Control is achieved by destruction first of the infected plants and then of the healthy plants immediately adjacent to them to create an effective barrier. Movement of the oak wilt fungus is controlled by digging trenches between the trees to break the root connections so the fungus cannot move by way of root grafts. The use of such barriers, ditches, or root-free zones will also stop the spread of *Fomes annosus,* a root rot disease of conifers incited by this fungus (NAS 1968*a*).

Aerial barriers are also used. For example, vein-banding mosaic can be reduced significantly on pepper by locating the plants at least 150 feet from any source of the virus disease. For the fungus disease cedar-apple rust the cedars and apples should be at least 3 miles apart. Vertical barriers between plants, such as tall nonhost plants growing between lower host plants, have also been used successfully (Simons 1957).

Barriers have been used in nematode control also. A good example is the "push and treat" and the "buffer zone" controls of the burrowing nematode, *Radopholus similis,* cause of the spreading decline of citrus. A combination of plant destruction, fumigation, and buffer strips is used to create the physical barriers (Poucher et al. 1967).

Geographical barriers to the spread of insects, plant diseases, and other pests are very important. They may be rivers, mountains, oceans, lakes, deserts, and the like. Arid regions can be effective barriers for certain insects. The pink bollworm was in Egypt for perhaps 50 years before it crossed the desert to the south by way of infested seed samples that were sent by mail. Canals that cross desert areas are important routes of spread. The cucumber beetle, *Diabrotica balteata,* spread rapidly in California along irrigation canals (Arnon 1972).

Weeds are also kept from spreading by the larger geographical barriers, while the larger canals and irrigation channels spread weed seeds through arid regions that otherwise would serve as effective barriers. More careful analysis of the ways in which physical barriers can be used to control and prevent the movement of crop pests, diseases, and weeds should be made.

Electromagnetic Waves, Radiant Energy, and Sound

Various types of energy have been utilized in insect control. Important developments have been made in the area of radiation-induced sterilization of insects. For example, the male pupal stage of the sugarcane gray borer, *Eucosma schislaceana,* has been irradiated successfully in Taiwan (Renjong Chiu 1974, pers. commun.). Electromagnetic energy has been used to control insects and mites, mostly in light traps or disinfestation of confined areas or storage bins (Kilgore and Doutt 1967).

Insects in stored products have been exposed to high frequency electrostatic fields and large currents between two electrodes at high voltages. Sufficient heat is thus generated within their bodies to kill them before they can damage the stored products. This technique has been successful in stored grains and has considerable potential. There are accounts also of insect control by means of light or other radiant energy and by the use of sound waves, although these procedures are not used routinely (Metcalf et al. 1951).

Electrical energy applied at radio wave frequencies, somewhat similar to diathermy, has been successful in killing encysted golden nematodes, *Heterodera rostochiensis,* in burlap bags and bails. Nematode disinfestation via electrical energy should be tested further as a possible barrier mechanism against nematodes and against other soil-borne pests (NAS 1968*b*).

Davis et al. (1971) has suggested the use of ultrahigh frequency electromagnetic fields for weed control and has shown that some species of weeds are highly susceptible and others are resistant. It has not yet been used in a practical application.

Little successful work in this area has been done in plant pathology. Microorganisms can generally survive heavier doses of ionizing radiation than higher plants and their seeds. For this reason it would appear that direct control of pathogenic organisms by ionizing radiation is not feasible. Gamma irradiation has been given favorable reports concerning control of brown rot and other molds on peaches but other control methods have been superior (Willison 1963).

Heat

Various forms of heat have been a longtime treatment of some plant pests and diseases. Traditional methods that go back hundreds of years involve burning, especially the use of forest and brush fires. The burning of crop residues and stubble destroys pests and many plant disease propagules that overwinter or survive the dry period on plant debris or survive in the shallow soil layers. However, few insects, nematodes, or disease organisms in the deeper soil layers are affected by this treatment (Univ. Calif. 1972*b*).

Solar heat, used in dry climates where fallowing is practical, has been reasonably effective in controlling soil nematodes and a few insects. Using this method, fallowed soil is plowed or disked periodically to expose the soil to the hot sun. Again, it is not effective against organisms that survive in the deeper layers of the soil over considerable periods of time (Univ. Calif. 1972*b*).

An exciting development in the use of solar heat for the tropics is reported from Israel by Grinstein et al. (1979). Transparent polyethylene sheets laid over moistened soil cause the temperature to rise enough through the greenhouse effect to destroy weed seeds and soil fungi. Good control of the soil-borne *Sclerotium rolfsii* and weeds in peanuts is reported by this technique.

Heat treatments of planting stocks and seeds have been used for a long time. They include treating seeds with hot water, hot air, or steam-air mixtures or growing plants at prolonged high temperatures that destroy the microorganisms or pests but not the plants. Heat works reasonably well because many pests and pathogens are more sensitive to high temperatures than host plants. The various heat techniques are often used on virus-infected, vegetatively propagated plants and fruit trees and for treating various other pests and diseases in rhizomes, corms, bulbs, root stocks, and seeds. Most heat treatments have been on vegetables, ornamentals, and fruits, but occasionally field crop pests and diseases have been partially controlled by heat (Univ. Calif. 1972c).

A number of virus diseases of perennial plants have been controlled in planting stocks by dry heat held at or slightly below 100°C for specific periods of time. For example, Guengerich and Millikan (1964) reported eliminating viruses in apple clones by growing the plants for relatively short periods at 100°C. Strawberries and other clonally propagated plants have been cleared of virus infections by similar techniques. Dry heat applied to bulk and container soils causes physical and chemical changes in the soil, often resulting in unsatisfactory plant growth. Steam heat is better than dry heat, but even then the temperatures held at 82°C (180°F) or above often destroy physical and chemical soil characteristics of value to plant growth.

Often hot water treatments are used to control nematodes and other soil pathogens and are the only practical way to control nematodes in some plants. They are sometimes made more effective by the addition of formalin to the treatment baths. In some cases viruses and other plant pathogens have been controlled at the same time (NAS 1968b). The water is kept at carefully controlled temperatures and plants or plant parts are immersed in it for various lengths of time, depending on the thermal death point of the nematode or organism being controlled. Since the heat tolerance of each plant varies, studies must be made with each plant and pest or disease combination before successful control is possible.

Recently the development of soil pasteurization with steam-air mixtures at somewhat lower temperatures has been successful. Temperatures held at 39° to 53°C for relatively long periods are sufficient to kill most nematodes and many pathogens. Most of the beneficial organisms survive and the phytotoxic effects of the higher temperatures are avoided as well as the effects on physical and chemical soil characteristics and structure.

In the nursery business, steam-air mixtures that selectively kill plant soil pathogens by holding the soil at 50°-60°C for 30 minutes have been used recently. Live steam has been used for many years to sterilize potting benches in greenhouses. Van Gundy (1972) suggested that waste energy from power plants or perhaps geothermal energy might be used for steaming field soils, particularly in such areas as the Imperial valley of California. Thus far such ideas have not been utilized effectively in the field.

Another source of heat used with some success has been electricity. Cables are buried in the soil and a current is passed between electrodes, generating heat. This technique has worked well in greenhouses and in confined soil beds (Univ. Calif. 1972b).

Heat methods are useful for the control of some insects. Experiments show that most insects cannot survive when exposed to temperatures of 60° to 66°C; most are killed by 3 hours at about 55°C and with longer exposure at this temperature most stages of most insects are destroyed (Metcalf et al. 1951). Heat has been helpful in destroying insect infestations in mills and storage bins. It is far less expensive and safer to destroy insects by superheating than by fumigation. High temperature techniques have been employed against insects in cereal, coffee beans, and other seeds; insects in clothing, bedding, baggage, bails of cotton, and other fibers; insects such as the Mediterranean fruit fly in oranges and grapes; insects infesting logs; insects and mites infesting oil; and insects and mites infesting bulbs. In the dry tropics, sun rays have occasionally been utilized effectively to control insects where fallow soils are turned frequently (Metcalf et al. 1951).

In the area of heat treatments and therapy, the plant protection disciplines have cooperated; combined efforts should be made routine to minimize the treatments and maximize the control against various pests and diseases associated with planting stocks, seeds and stored grain, and plant products.

Remote Sensing

Infrared and related aerial photography was first used to identify plant diseases from a distance with some success by Colwell (1973). Others have used the techniques with varying success, but practical field results have been disappointing. The problem of all remote sensing has been the development of accurate and quick ground truth data for interpretation of the data obtained.

Satellite remote sensing techniques have been developed and efforts have been made to use them in the identification of crops, plant diseases, crop stress situations, etc. Remote sensors are unable to identify plant stress conditions as such but do show variations from normal patterns. The particular stress agent can be pathogens, pests, mineral deficiencies, salinity, drought, flooding or excess water, or something else (Robert H. Miller 1974, pers. commun.).

Infrared photography has given more useful data than satellite or other remote sensing techniques. It is possible to determine density and distribution of hosts, location and extent of stressed plants, early detection of presence of stress, effects of various control measures, ecological or other factors causing stress, possibly better and safer use of control measures, and more efficient and cheaper surveys (Robert H. Miller 1974, pers. commun.). Bleiholder and Rittig (1979) have reported the successful monitoring of the effects of fungicide and nematicide treatments by densitometric evaluation of aerial false color infrared photographs. Such analyses do not stand alone but give a valuable addition to the usual trial evaluations.

The problem of procuring quick and accurate ground truth data in remote sensing techniques remains to be solved, as do most adaptations for practical use.

11

Biological Controls

 Biological control has in recent years received much publicity, particularly from entomologists who have rediscovered it since recognition of the problems associated with the use of pesticides. Burges and Hussey (1971) say that "the development of resistance to pesticides is largely responsible for the current interest in biological control."

A great deal of disagreement and misunderstanding concerns what constitutes biological control. This is emphasized by Burges and Hussey (1971) in the following quotation:

> Biological control in its commonest sense means the influence of predators, parasites, and pathogens introduced or applied by man. Some authorities include the activities of naturally occurring biological agents in the term. But here these activities will be distinguished as "natural biological control." The classical approach to biological control has mainly encompassed predators and parasitic arthropods so that a new term "macrobial control" is proposed to distinguish these conveniently from "microbial control," i.e., the activities of microorganisms.

One definition of biological control is given by Beirne (1967): "Any living organisms that can be manipulated by man for pest control purposes are biological control agents."

Although some entomologists insist that biological control concerns only the activities of predator and parasite insects, representatives of other disciplines feel that biological control is involved with the activity of any biological species that functions as a control mechanism for any economically significant pest or plant disease organism. Others include the whole area of antagonism, antibiosis, and toxins—the production of any natural product that is metabolized by pests, plants, or microorganisms and can function as a control mechanism. Still others feel that the whole area of disease or pest resistance in plants is a part—the most important part—of biological control and that the goal of all research should be to discover not only resistance but also immunity to pests and plant diseases in key crop species.

Biological control—whether considered in the narrow entomological sense or in the broadest possible way to include plant resistance—is potentially the most important area of research in plant protection. Huffaker (1971) emphasized the importance of biological control used in conjunction with other control methods:

> If we are to reverse the trend toward an ever intensified overloading of the environment with polluting and highly toxic pesticides we must show that biological control, combined with restricted uses of selective chemicals, use of resistant varieties and other integrated measures can, in fact, solve many of our pest problems without resort to such disturbing and polluting chemicals. Biological control, where effective, is cheap, usually persistent, without need for recurrent expense, entails no significant genetic counter-attack in the pests in nature, does not occasion the rise to pest status of forms normally innocuous, does not add to the ever growing problems of man's pollution of the environment, and is not attendant with serious toxic hazards to the workers using the methods, to consumers of the products, or to our cherished and declining wildlife. Moreover, because of the expense in the use of other methods, it is often the only method available in underdeveloped countries, a contributing reason why the International Biological Program is sponsoring this method. Biological control, moreover, is compatible with enlightened integrated control programs wherein restricted use of chemicals combined with cultural and other ecological methods are employed. In fact, biological control is usually a key aspect of integrated control programs, for this technique is manipulatable and augmentable, whereas other major aspects of natural control, for example, the weather, are not.

Biological control in agriculture is particularly attractive because it is economical. This point is discussed by Kilgore and Doutt (1967):

> Although it requires a substantial investment in talent and facilities, this is amply repaid by the benefits that accrue from the results of biological control. It has been conservatively estimated that in the 36 years between 1923 and 1959 the net savings from major biological control projects amounted to over 110 million dollars in the state of California alone. The numerous projects which failed should also be charged against it. . . .

> Biological control has always been of special value to crops with small margins of profit and to areas where food and fibre must be produced by workers who do not have the expensive equipment or necessary training to apply safely the modern highly toxic chemicals.

Biological control also has many detractors. DeBach and Huffaker (1971) summarized this aspect:

> The use of biological control is essentially the antithesis of chemical pest con-

trol. . . . There are still some few ecologists who consider that natural enemies rarely if ever regulate prey populations. Climate is often proposed as the key factor by them, on the basis of circumstantial evidence and poor deductive reasoning.

It seems apropos here to reaffirm our considered conclusion that experimental analysis of the prey—natural enemy population systems, involving paired comparisons of plots having enemies present with plots where enemies are absent (or inhibited)—furnishes the only satisfactory proof of the control and regulatory power of natural enemies. Such analyses simultaneously permit experimental isolation and evaluation of other parameters, including weather and competitors. . . .

The fact that considerable disagreement remains is sufficient evidence of the need for adequate assessment of the efficiency of enemies. Precise means of evaluation are needed for several reasons: (1) to illuminate basic principles of population ecology, especially the role of biotic and abiotic factors; (2) to furnish a sound ecological basis for manipulation of natural enemies either by demonstrating the need for the importation of new ones or by showing that the established ones are rendered ineffective due to interference phenomena, including pesticides, weather, or cultural practices; and (3) to provide the proof of effectiveness of natural enemies that is necessary in applied biological control in order to justify needed increased research and development support.

Much of the basic research needed to assess the effectiveness of parasites and predators has not been done. Probably this is the reason why the arguments wax furious at times. Varley and Gradwell (1971) emphasized this dilemma and discussed what can be done to correct it.

The part played by parasites and predators in the dynamics of natural populations has been one of the most elusive and controversial problems of population ecology. Although natural enemies have been successfully used for the biological control of insect pests, the properties of these animals have neither been sufficiently well known beforehand to forecast the degree of success nor have the studies after the introduction revealed the mechanisms involved. Theoretical ideas based on simple assumptions about the form of the interaction between parasite-host or predator-prey populations have largely been ignored and measurements necessary to test these ideas remain unmade. In our opinion these theoretical ideas are of prime importance, since we can claim to understand a process only when measurements conform to some theoretical model which shows how they might have come about.

Another problem in biological control is that many plant protection workers are not particularly good systematists. Biological control must be built around exceedingly accurate systematics. Kilgore and Doutt (1967) discussed this problem:

Biological control is very much dependent upon good systematics, and specialists in biological control can often furnish valuable information to taxonomists. Of all the various fields of entomology, probably no two could mutually benefit from cooperative studies more than biological control and systematics.

This problem cannot be overemphasized. One must be able to recognize species, variety, biotype, and so forth; be able to grow it in large numbers; and control it under laboratory as well as field conditions before biological control can be a practical reality in most cases. The large numbers of possible species, subspecies, biotypes, and strains make this task exceedingly difficult. Researchers interested in biological control must cooperate with systematists in research programs. When one adds climatic factors, other environmental factors, and the variability inherent in hosts to the biological control picture, the complexity is "mind boggling." This picture is summarized by Sabrosky (1955):

> Biological control workers are dealing with complex biological problems, with the interactions of one to many parasites, with one to many species of hosts, and with each other and with hyperparasites, and all with populations of predators, and all in turn with climate and other environmental factors. Likewise, the taxonomy in biological control problems can be a complex matter, involving identification and classification of all those categories.

In plant protection disciplines other than entomology various types of biological control have been standard practice (although not often labeled as such). The terminology is complex because of the different approaches taken by different workers and disciplines and because the term *biological control* has been emphasized recently by entomologists to describe for the most part old techniques. In most cases the phenomena involved have not been well understood. This problem is discussed by Kilgore and Doutt (1967):

> In the field of biological control parasitism is such a protean phenomenon that its continued usefulness as a unit concept of this work has become doubtful. The symbiotic relationship by which one species obtains its energy requirements at the expense of another is surely parasitic, and offers a system to be exploited at every opportunity in biological control. Yet the terminology presents some problems in proper communication. While a scientist will speak of entomophagous insects that develop at the expense of a single host as parasites, he actually has less justification for this than does his colleague who speaks of the phytophagous insects employed for weak control as parasites. In microbial control, the problem is avoided by simply calling the useful organisms pathogens.
>
> In actual practice, the procedures for exploiting parasitism have become so remarkably specialized that the technology required for one aspect will bear little resemblance to the skills, equipment and techniques used by scientists in

another field of biological control. Even their respective philosophies may be distinguishable. It is unlikely that the same scientists could with confidence manipulate species of fungi belonging to the hypomycetous Moniliales to suppress plant nematodes, and with equal facility test phytophagous insects imported from Turkestan for their effectiveness in controlling noxious weeds on Nevada sheep ranges. This necessary specialization and compartmentalization of effort reflects the manifold nature of the disciplines contributing to biological control and demonstrates the high level of technical training required by practitioners in this field.

Until recently the framework of the biological dimension of this field was primarily formed by the nutritional requirements of natural enemies of arthropods. Research was largely focused on the necessary interrelations, adaptations, and behaviorisms of entomophagous species in obtaining these essential sources of energy. Now, however, newer aspects of the biological dimension are being presented by the increasing use of parasites to control noxious weeds and by the recent stimulating emergence and development of biological control as an integral part of plant pathology.

Most plant pathologists would object to the notion just expressed that biological control has only recently emerged as a part of plant pathology, but it is true that the term has not been utilized as such. The report of the first international symposium on the biological control of soil organisms (Baker and Snyder 1965) demonstrates that the equivalent of biological control has always been utilized by plant pathologists. Many people tend to forget that host resistance, crop rotation, and other crop management and cultivation practices often owe their success to biological control phenomena. As late as 1971 the American Phytopathological Society sponsored a symposium entitled "Biological Control—Mission Impossible?" at its annual meeting (Baker and Cook 1974). Too few current plant pathologists have been involved in empirical field studies where biological control phenomena could be observed and often utilized in practical control methods. The well-equipped laboratory and the ivory tower syndrome have held their attention and diverted their minds. (Baker and Cook feel that we would now know more about biological control for plant disease if as much effort and expense had been placed on finding and utilizing antagonists of plant pathogenic organisms as was put into the discovery of antibiotics for use in human and animal medicine.) Plant pathologists have routinely used cultural practices, sanitation practices, and breeding for resistance for disease control, and many have surmised rather uncritically that these non-chemical controls owe their success to resident antagonists (Baker and Cook 1974).

Working with microorganisms is usually more difficult than working with macroorganisms such as insects. The complexity of the soil environment for microorganisms has presented unique problems, which are summarized in the following statement by Baker and Snyder (1965):

Soil microorganisms present one of the most complex, difficult and rewarding present areas of exploration. Contact with this frontier has been established by the disciplines of plant pathology, microbiology, soil science, plant physiology, plant anatomy, biochemistry, bacteriology, nematology, mycology, virology, and zoology. Penetration in depth has, however, awaited the overcoming of this departmentalization of the scattered, diffuse, isolated and uncorrelated knowledge in these fields. It is increasingly clear that a mastery of the soil microflora will come only when we understand the obscure complex of non-parasitic organisms, even though the pathogens have seemed the logical point of attack.

The interrelationships, antagonisms, synergisms, and other interrelationships between organisms in the soil must be understood before the biological control of any pathogenic organism can be achieved by competitive or antagonistic organisms or antibiotic chemical metabolites produced by such organisms.

Again, as in the case of the biological control of arthropods, biological control in plant pathology is just one facet of the total control program and when possible it is combined with other control methods, including the best cultivation practices and resistant varieties. For example, at least one large fungicide manufacturer is studying the possibility of combining fungicides (in small quantities) with tillage and biological control measures to control plant diseases (Baker and Cook 1974).

Baker and Cook have emphasized the importance of using nature and the environment in biological control. They stressed the importance of carefully planned, applied, empirical research for control programs.

Nature has achieved astoundingly successful biological control which man only dimly perceives and does not understand. It is, therefore, not necessary and usually not desirable to await complete knowledge before making the control attempt. Biological control should be confidently approached with the idea of putting it to work. . . . Isolate the phenomenon, make it work, then study it carefully to perfect its accomplishment. . . .

The environmental effects in biological control are typically indirect. When they are direct they kill the insect, nematode, weed, or pathogen with cold, heat, desiccation, flooding and the like. This is an ecological (weather or climate) rather than biological control. By contrast, in biological control the indirect effects of the environment may increase the capacity of the host to resist, escape or tolerate the pest or pathogen by increasing the effectiveness of the predator, parasite, or antibiotic producer or the capacity of the antagonist as a competitor or it may weaken the capacity of the predator, parasite, and pathogen to attack or affect the host or, perhaps, to resist any antagonists. [Baker and Cook 1974]

Most breeding work has aimed to increase the resistance of hosts. Few workers have attempted to improve the effectiveness of organisms used in biological control although there is as much potential genetic variability in the predator organisms as in the hosts. This topic has been discussed for many years, but the only achievement has been in laboratory selections with changes in attributes such as diapause, pesticide susceptibility, and temperature tolerances (Hoy 1979). More research might be profitable.

For additional general information about biological control see Huffaker and Messenger (1976).

Arthropods

Metcalf et al. (1951) defined biological control of insects as "the introduction, encouragement, and artificial increase of predacious and parasitic insects, other animals and diseases." The following species have been or could be utilized in biological control of insects: (1) domesticated fowls and mammals; (2) parasitic and predacious insects, mites, birds, worms, fishes, toads, and other animals; (3) insectivorous wild birds and other related animals; (4) plants grown to destroy, prevent the growth of, or repel insects or their damage; and (5) the use of bacterial, viral, fungal, and protozoal diseases of insects and the growing, manipulation, and liberation of insects infected with these diseases.

The first successful use of biological control in entomology was in 1889 in California (Kilgore and Doutt 1967) when a predacious ladybird beetle (Coccinellidae) was imported from Australia to control the cotton cushiony scale, *Icerya purchasi*. This vedalia beetle did a remarkable job and established biological control as a viable method for entomologists. (This beetle continues to be as effective now as when it was introduced.)

Several other examples of biological control of scale insects and mealybugs include control of the citrophilus mealybug, *Pseudococcus fragilis*, in California; Green's mealybug, *Pseudococcus citriculus*, in Israel; red wax scale, *Ceroplastes rubens*, in Japan; the coconut scale, *Aspidiotus destructor*, in the islands of Mauritius, Principe, and Fiji; and the coffee mealybug, *Planococcus kenyae*, in Kenya (Huffaker 1971).

Insect biological control techniques are particularly valuable in crops of low value per acre. Control of Rhodes grass scale, *Antonina graminis*, has been successful in Texas. This scale attacks Rhodes grass, *Chloris gayana*, and at least 94 other species of grasses in North America, some severely. The scale parasite, *Neodusmetia sangwani*, introduced from India in 1959, has been effective in the control of the Rhodes grass scale since that time (Huffaker 1971).

The winter moth, *Operophtera brumata*, was accidentally introduced into Canada from Europe and rapidly became a serious defoliator of hardwoods. It has been controlled effectively by the deliberate introduction of two parasites, a tachinid fly, *Cyzenis albicans*, and an ichneumonid wasp,

Agrypon flaveolatum. Both were introduced from Europe, where they are endemic (Huffaker 1971).

Huffaker (1971) reported that biological control has been attempted with at least 223 (usually introduced) insect pest species and at least some success has been achieved with over 50 percent. Coccids have accounted for more than half of the partial successes against insects and about two-thirds of the complete successes (Hodek 1970).

It is always hoped that native predators, parasites, or diseases will achieve adequate control of a given pest, but this is not often the case. Petty (1972) reported that in maize in Illinois the native predators, parasites, and diseases, although helpful, had not produced economic control that satisfied the farmer or consumer. He feels that foreign biological control agents or entirely new techniques are needed to achieve success. This point has been made also by many other workers who have had disappointing results using native species.

The utilization of the environment to maintain satisfactory levels of natural predators or parasites has been successful in a few cases. In an outstanding example from California, planting and harvesting of alfalfa fields are timed so that the natural control insects will be kept at the highest possible population level. Harvesting is done by strip cutting; only a fraction of the crop is harvested at any one time so that natural enemies can be maintained in the unharvested portions. The cut areas are allowed to produce new growth for maintenance of the natural enemies before the uncut portion is harvested. Strip cutting used in this way appears to have considerable potential, particularly in perennial crops such as alfalfa (USGPO 1972).

In some cases beneficial insect fauna seem to be effective in pest insect regulation only during a portion of the year. Then, particularly in the tropics, predators may be helped by other techniques, such as chemical pesticides. An example is given by Falcon and Smith (1973). In the cotton crop in Nicaragua the beneficial insects do very well from January through September. But during October, November, and December, when cotton is at peak production, rainfall is heaviest, and other pest problems of cotton are most severe, then the beneficial insects are nearly absent. During this period it is necessary to utilize chemical control methods.

Different growing areas for a given crop may have entirely different native predatory and parasitic species and their relative importance may vary greatly. An example is the egg parasite, *Trichogramma* sp.; during the growing season of desert cotton in southern California it may destroy from 40 to 50 percent of the bollworm and cabbage looper eggs but it will seldom destroy eggs of the same insects farther north in the San Joaquin valley (Falcon and Smith 1973).

Kilgore and Doutt (1967) have emphasized the importance of an ecological approach in research on biological control—the management of populations and the manipulation of the environment to encourage natural control by helpful insect species. DeBach (1964) has suggested importing ecological homologues that would not be pests for competitive displacement of other pest species. An example is importing a fly that does not attack people to replace one that does. This approach has worked with several species of flies in various parts of the world (DeBach 1964) and is a form of competitive displacement of species.

Successful efforts to grow and distribute natural enemies of arthropods in the field are summarized in a book edited by Ridgway and Vinson (1977).

Like other animals, insects suffer from disease organisms and disease epidemics. Pathogenic organisms and diseases that will eventually be available to use against insects will include bacteria, viruses, fungi, protozoans, the rickettsial diseases of insects, and the nematodes that attack insects in the soil (Burges and Hussey 1971). The use of arthropod diseases gives a relatively new dimension to insect control and the study of these diseases has expanded rapidly in recent years (Metcalf et al. 1951; Burges and Hussey 1971).

There have been a number of efforts to use insect diseases to control insects. Some have been successful or partially successful. The brown, red, and yellow fungi that live on the bodies of white flies that attack citrus in Florida have been used to control the white flies. Spores of the fungi are mixed with water and sprayed over trees infested with the white flies. Control of the Japanese beetle, particularly the larvae, can be achieved under some circumstances by inoculating the soil with spores of the milky disease of the Japanese beetle, incited by *Bacillus popilliae*. A bacterium, *Coccobacillus acridiorum,* has been used in Africa against grasshoppers that are susceptible to it.

Different groups of insects are affected in different ways by various microbial control agents. For example, surface-feeding phytophagous caterpillars, particularly colonial moths and sawflies, are vulnerable to bacterial and viral diseases contracted by feeding on contaminated leaf material. They are less likely to be attacked by fungal diseases because their feeding habits do not normally include the long periods of high humidity required for fungal spore germination. By contrast, bark beetles often succumb to the entomogenous fungi that live and thrive in the humid environments inside their galleries but they are much less likely to eat bark that is superficially contaminated by bacteria and viruses. Many such ecological barriers in the manipulation of insect disease organisms must be understood before it is possible to use them (Burges and Hussey 1971). For example, we know that in soybeans the interaction of plant feeders, microbial pathogens, bacteria, fungi, and viruses are very important as population regulators but in most cases little is known about their intimate biology. This information is necessary before adding these organisms to ecosystems as pest or disease regulatory mechanisms (Huffaker 1974).

The potential for microbial control of cotton insects is great. All arthropod cotton pests, including spider mites, are infected by one or more pathogenic diseases. A variety of viral, fungal, bacterial, and protozoal diseases and some nematodes attack insects. Development of the use of these pathogens and nematodes as control agents of insects has been slow. Most efforts have been restricted to the laboratory and there have been relatively few field evaluations. Insect pathogens are inexpensive to produce and safe to use and they might eventually emerge as the ideal pest control for developing countries.

To use insect pathogens for pest control it is necessary to find the suitable pathogen, to develop techniques for routine field collection and artificial mass culture of the pathogen, and to develop techniques for mass dissemination so that the greatest number of insect pests are destroyed. There have been only a few cases of satisfactory production and preparation of insect pathogens for use as microbial insecticides. Several insect pathogens have been mass-produced by industry and a few microbial pathogens have been produced commercially (Falcon and Smith 1973).

The knowledge of bacteria-caused diseases in insects actually began in 1870 with Pasteur's study of flacherie of the silkworm and a little later with Cheshire and Cheyne's study of European foulbrood of the honeybee. At the present well over 90 species and varieties of pathogenic bacteria are known to attack insects but only a few have been developed for commercial pest control purposes. The most important are the causative bacteria of types A and B milky disease in the Japanese beetle, *Popillia japonica, Bacillus popilliae* and *B. lentimorbus,* respectively. The most important crystal-forming bacterium is *B. thuringiensis,* which attacks many species among the Lepidoptera. Concentrated efforts have been made to develop *B. thuringiensis* as a broad-spectrum bacterial insecticide. It has been used successfully in Europe against the European corn borer, in Egypt against the pink bollworm (Burges and Hussey 1971), and in Canada via aerial spray techniques against the spruce budworm (Smirnoff 1979).

The microbial method of insect control has received considerable emphasis in Russia because the preparations are harmless to plants, humans, and farm animals, and can be used until the time of harvesting without any danger. Several commercial preparations are already used. In the Ukraine good results have been obtained with Beauverine for Colorado beetle control; in Leningrad province Entobacterine has been used successfully against caterpillars and some butterflies and moths; farther south, Dendrobacillin, Tuverine, and some other preparations are being used successfully in the control of forest pests (Kalyuga 1968).

A large number of virus diseases of insects are known and more are found every year. Only a few have been studied carefully insofar as their natural distribution, dispersal, and possible utilization as biological control agents are concerned. The nucleopolyhedrosis viruses (NPV) have been studied the most and they have been used in a few cases to control insect pests. Two other viruses that appear to be significant are granulosis viruses (GV) and cytoplasmic-polyhedrosis viruses (CPV).

The gypsy moth and several other species of Lepidoptera have been controlled on an experimental scale in the field but not in commercial operations. The European spruce sawfly and several other sawflies have been controlled successfully in commercial operations in Canada, but the techniques have not been approved officially in the United States (Stairs 1971). In California the nucleopolyhedrosis virus of the cabbage looper, *Trichoplusia ni,* has been used to control this insect. The infected larvae are obtained from cotton fields during epizootics and are ground and prepared in a suspension with a wetting agent. The mixture is then applied with conventional spray equipment (Falcon and Smith 1973). The nucleopolyhedrosis virus of the gypsy moth, *Lymantria dispar,* is being used to control the gypsy moth in forests in the northeastern United States and appears to be a good alternative to chemical insecticides (Mazzone et al. 1979).

The first product from an insect virus that can be used as an insecticide has been approved for use by the Environmental Protection Agency (EPA) in the United States (First natural virus insecticide registered by EPA 1976). It is effective against the cotton bollworm and tobacco landworm. It is a very specific material because the nucleopolyhedrosis virus has a narrow host range. The trade name of the new product is Elcar.

Insect viruses have been isolated from more than 400 species of insects and mites, including the codling moth; many species of cutworms, armyworms, and other noctuids; grasshoppers; several species of sawfly and defoliating caterpillars that attack forest trees; and also some mites such as the citrus red mite (FAO 1973a).

Insects may have more than one disease simultaneously. The net effects may be additive, synergistic, or antagonistic. The use of combinations of diseases in the microbial control of insects is in its early stages and is potentially valuable (Krieg 1971).

Many species of nematodes are parasitic on insects, such as moths, cockroaches, grasshoppers, and beetles. Species of nematodes that attack the striped cucumber beetle and the Japanese beetle have been relatively important in the control of these pests, and there has been some effort to use those that attack the Japanese beetle in a biological control program (Metcalf et al. 1951). No evidence so far shows that entomogenous nematodes cause damage to plants or vertebrates. Even though nematodes have been associated with most insect orders and with most mites, it is not usually known whether effective nematode control is possible. Nematodes as agents for biological control of insects pose many difficulties: the mass rearing of nematode species, the successful control of environments in the field, the determination of desirable or acceptable environmental situations for effective nematode activity, and lack of other important information.

Moisture is probably the most important limiting physical factor in the use of entomogenous nematodes as biological control agents. It is necessary to know precisely the most favorable conditions under which a nematode will attack the insect. The microclimate of the plant leaf and the first few inches of the soil surface are very important. Nematologists and entomologists need to collaborate to work out the necessary ecological and biological details concerning each species combination (Poinar 1971).

A commercial corporation in France has invested much money in the effort to mass-rear some nematode species of the genus *Neoaplectana* that have been quite effective in controlling rape (*Brassica* sp.) insects. In Italy tests conducted with the nematode genera *Neoaplectana* and *Heterorhabditis* have given satisfactory control of click beetle larvae attacking the roots of maize (Certain groups of nematodes attack only insects 1979).

Few attempts have been made to manipulate protozoan parasites of insects as possible microbial insecticides, although large-scale natural infections have been seen and reported. A great deal of fundamental biological and ecological information is needed concerning the intimate host-parasite relationships and the effects of various environments on these relationships. Protozoans are likely to be useful in giving the first measurable degree of microbial control and may also be used in combination with other biological control measures or possibly even with chemical controls. Thus far, a degree of control by protozoans has been described against seven insect species. None of these have been demonstrated in the field under controlled conditions (McLaughlin 1971). The protozoan, *Perezia pyraustae,* has been used against the European corn borer in the United States (Metcalf et al. 1951) but not regularly or on a large scale under controlled conditions.

Fungi appear to be the principal cause of disease in aphids and scales. Virus diseases have not definitely been demonstrated, pathogenic insect bacteria seem to occur rarely, and there are no known serious bacterial diseases. Many fungi from several orders occur on aphids and scales (Gustafson 1971).

Attempts have been made to use fungi as practical microbial control agents of citrus scales. *Cephalosporium lecanni* has been used for scales and has produced reasonably good results in Florida and in some other citrus-growing areas of the world. Suspensions of field-collected diseased insects are sprayed on the trees. For the most part the fungi have not been isolated or cultivated and the research has largely been empirical field work. It would appear that research on species in the Entomophthorales might result in large-scale practical control of citrus scales (Gustafson 1971).

A large number of publications on insect mycoses involve species from the following genera: *Entomophthora, Beauveria, Metarrhizium,* and *Aspergillus.* Other genera are less common causes of insect diseases. Mycoses are frequent in some taxonomic groups of insects, for example, *Hymenoptera, Coleoptera, Diptera, Lepidoptera,* and *Homoptera.* In other groups no fungus diseases have been reported. It is not known in most cases whether the fungi kill insects by toxins or by other methods, but some very potent toxins are produced by fungi. For example, the nearly universal toxins such as the aflatoxins are produced by a species of *Aspergillus.*

Most entomogenous fungi have not been examined for possible toxins. Before pathogenic fungi can be used as control measures for insects it is necessary to develop life tables for both and to learn the ecological and biological details associated with their lives, including the environmental requirements for disease development—particularly the necessary microenvironment (Roberts and Yendol 1971).

Many attempts have been made to utilize entomogenous fungi to control important insects. Roberts and Yendol reported 41 successful attempts among 28 groups of insects, but few fungi are utilized in practical control programs at this time. Kilgore and Doutt reported 52 successes in about 98 attempts all over the world. Most successes have been obtained with the white muscardine fungus, *Beauveria bassiana;* the green muscardine fungus, *Metarrhizium anisopliae;* and various species of *Entomophthora.* Some workers minimize or deny the successes reported with these fungi (Kilgore and Doutt, 1967).

In the Soviet Union a preparation called Boverin that contains conidia of the fungus *Beauvaria bassiana* is used primarily against the Colorado potato beetle, *Leptinotarsa decemlineata.* In Brazil the preparation Metaquiono that contains conidia of the fungus *Metarrhizium anisopliae* has been used against several insect pests. Other countries, including the United States, are attempting to develop similar useful commercial materials (Ferron 1978).

Various commercial fungicides that inhibit or essentially control entomogenous fungi theoretically could control or partially control some insect populations; i.e., the fungicides used on plant pathogenic fungi are also effective against the fungus parasites of insects. This phenomenon often has been reported but it is not known how well the fungi can actually control insect populations in nature. Also it is not known just how completely the fungicides control or inhibit the entomogenous fungi. More research on this subject is needed (Roberts and Yendol 1971).

In practical field control only one case in which a fungus disease seems to hold an insect population in check throughout most seasons is reported. This is the case of the clover leaf weevil. The larvae are often infected, turn yellowish and brownish, and remain curled around the tips of the clover leaves. It is one of the best practical controls for this insect and is often combined with cultural controls or chemicals (Metcalf et al. 1951).

In Taiwan, Cheng and Chen (1962) reported a field insect mortality of 65 percent for the black beetle, *Alissonotum* sp., and 78 percent for the top borer, *Scirpophaga nivella,* on sugarcane after treatment with the green muscardine fungus, *Metarrhizium anisopliae.* Wang and Leu (1974) reported treatment of 156 ha of sugarcane in Taiwan with 100 flasks/ha of mixed cultures of the entomogenous fungi, *Isaria sinclairii* and *M. anisopliae.* The resultant mortality of nymphs of the grass cicada, *Mogannia hebes,* varied from 19 to 22 percent during the first year following the application. Mortality was highest in ratoon cane and was still high 2 years later.

Information concerning microorganism diseases that attack mites is sparse. No bacterial disease of mites has ever been recorded and few viral diseases are known. Naturally occurring pathogens have reduced populations of mites markedly so it is known that epizootics do occur in the field. Some fungus diseases of mites are known and several *Entomophthora* species attack and kill mites. The fungi *Aspergillus fumigatus* and *Penicillium insectivorium* kill laboratory cultures of ticks of the species *Hyalomma scupense* and *Dermacentor marginatus.* Eriophyid mites have been killed in large numbers in nature by the fungus *Hirsutella thompsonii;* this fungus seems to be a key factor in the control in nature of the citrus rust mite, *Phyllocoptruta oleivora* (Lipa 1971).

Successful field experiments in mite control have been demonstrated, particularly when combined with low dosages of acaricides. Fine results were recorded when the fungus *Beauveria bassiana* was applied in combination with the acaricide, demeton. This fungus was also applied to citrus trees 4 days after spraying with lime sulfur at half the usually recommended dosage, with excellent control results. More combinations of pathogenic fungi that infect mites with acaricides hold promise for the future (Lipa 1971).

Natural epizootics of fungus diseases of mites typically occur after heavy rains that favor fungi development. Severe natural epizootics have been reported of fungus diseases and also of virus diseases of mites. Successful field control experiments have been conducted with the noninclusion virus of the citrus red mite *Panonychus citri*. This virus was sprayed on the plants in experimental plots for several months at 6-week intervals. Heavy mite populations were reduced well below damaging levels and were kept there for at least 1 year following the spray period. Large numbers of virus-infested mites have also been released into citrus groves having heavy populations of healthy mites, causing epizootics of the disease and significant reductions of mite populations.

Interesting attempts have been made to combine microbiological preparations for insect and mite control. For example, *Bacillus thuringiensis* has been combined with the nucleopolyhedrosis virus to control the alfalfa caterpillar (Steinhaus 1951). Kalyuga (1968) reported in Russia a successful combination of *B. thuringiensis* and the fungus *Beauvaria bassiana* in a control technique.

Combinations of two or more microbial control agents with a chemical pesticide also offer possibilities. By contrast, the combination of two or more such pathogens, instead of producing a synergistic or helpful situation for insect or mite control, may prove antagonistic and hence deleterious (Burges and Hussey 1971).

An interesting development is the use of microbial insecticides with commercial chemical insecticides. Beauverine (a fungal preparation) and Entobacterine (a bacterial preparation) have been combined with small doses of a chemical poison to produce considerably better results against rutabaga insects than Beauverine alone, and only 10 percent of the amount of chemical poison normally used was necessary. This joint use of fungal and bacterial preparations has been more effective than their separate use, particularly in Russia. Combining bacterial preparations alone, such as Entobacterine, with chemicals has not given synergistic effects in control efforts thus far (Kalyuga 1968).

Benz (1971) reported an increased effectiveness of bacterial pathogens of insects combined with low doses of DDT and suggested that the two toxicants may have synergistic effects. Several studies of synergism between chemical sprays and bacterial insecticides have been made, mostly with materials obtained from *Bacillus thuringiensis* (BT), with about as many reports of antagonism as of synergism. Some have concluded that it may be as complicated to combine bacterial insecticides with chemical pesticides as to combine chemical pesticides. The problem of compatibility appears to be significant.

Under natural conditions insect diseases occurring as epizootics may be very severe. Weather conditions are most significant in the spread and development of insect diseases. Not much progress has been made in the artificial spread of insect diseases for insect control and no extensive epizootics have been produced. This may be possible in the future, however (Metcalf et al. 1951).

Many substances that are highly toxic to insects are produced by various microbial organisms. Their significance as important factors in insect control is usually not known. For example, *Clostridium tetani* and *C. botulinum,* which produce the most lethal toxins known, are natural soil inhabitants and their toxins are normal bacterial products. Other toxins, such as the aflatoxins produced by *Aspergillus* spp., are also exceedingly potent. It would be naive to suggest that they have no ecological role even though it may be unknown at the moment. Some toxins may be associated with the control of other organisms in the soil environment.

Bacterial toxins that are harmful to insects have seldom been defined scientifically as toxins because of inadequate knowledge concerning their biochemical structure and mode of biological action. Lecithinases and proteases are bacterial toxins that have been shown to kill some insects. The crystalline parasporal bodies, the endotoxins, produced by *Bacillus thuringiensis* and *B. cereus,* are examples of toxins (Lysenko and Kucera 1971).

Some fungi produce several toxic compounds that destroy insects and may act simultaneously to cause a variety of toxic effects. The aflatoxins are effective against certain insects. Destruxins are toxins produced by the fungus *Oospora destructor,* and other toxins from other fungi have not yet been defined chemically. The only practical commercial preparation used is the microbial insecticide obtained from the crystalline toxin produced by *B. thuringiensis.* Although this toxin is very potent against certain insects, it can be applied with complete safety to human foodstuffs (Lysenko and Kucera 1971).

More insect pathogens that produce insect-destroying toxins are found each year. It is hoped that some of these toxins will be synthesized and utilized as specific insecticides. Eventually, microbial insecticides probably will be divided into two groups—those containing living organisms or spores and those containing only the toxins that destroy insects.

Variation as a factor in microbial control of insects will probably be important in the future. This aspect is often misunderstood or ignored. The problem is summarized by Burges and Hussey (1971).

Variation is . . . experienced in microbial control more severely than in most other forms of control. In addition to variation common to all methods of control, such as variation in the susceptibility of insects and the imperfect distribution of materials, other variations stem from the complexity of the host pathogen relationship, the production of toxins and the fact that pathogens (and their hosts) are living organisms and consequently variable. This variability makes the standardization of pathogenic preparations not only difficult, but also important, if predictable control is to be achieved.

Application of pathogens as microbial insecticides requires large quantities of the active agent, consequently preparation must be relatively easy and storage qualities must be good. In view of the frequent occurrence of acquired resistance to chemicals, the possibility that pests will also acquire resistance to microbial agents must not be ignored, particularly since "resistance to disease" is a phrase constantly used by pathologists and epidemiologists in all fields of pathology.

The general phenomenon of cannibalism within species may be at times important in control. With specific insects cannibalism occurs at certain times of the year and under certain circumstances. An example of natural control by cannibalism is found in the larvae of the corn earworm (Metcalf et al. 1951).

Many insect control factors, essentially biological, are not yet controllable. The predators, parasites, and insect diseases naturally present are examples. In addition, birds, reptiles, amphibians, and some mammals that occur naturally often function to control insect and mite populations at least partially. They may be very important under some conditions—in certain environments at specific times of the year—but they are not consistent enough to be regarded as a regular control procedure (Metcalf et al. 1951). More thorough investigations of these natural phenomena might reveal ways in which they could be manipulated in the control of insects and mites.

Great variation occurs between closely related species of insects and mites and their resistance to biological control agents. One insect can be susceptible while a closely related subspecies or biotype may be resistant or even immune. These attributes do not remain static, so selective development of insect and mite resistance to biological control agents must be considered a constant potential problem. There is no record of resistance of insects to microbial agents in the field; since these microbial agents have not been in use long, it is doubtful whether any resistance should be expected as yet. In the laboratory, however, there has been a 14-fold increase in resistance of the housefly, *Musca domestica,* to the toxin produced by *Bacillus thuringiensis* (Burges 1971). Only one example was found by Burges of the development of resistance in a macrobial insect control program. In about 27 years the larch sawfly, *Pristiphora erichsonii,* developed an immunity to the introduced ichneumonid, *Mesoleuis tenthridinis.* The parasite is encapsulated in the body of the host and made harmless in that way.

Investigations by Altieri and Whitcomb (1979) have shown some possibility of partially controlling insect populations through control of the composition and abundance of specific weed species. They feel that weeds have great potential as biological components of pest management systems if maintained at tolerable population levels.

Some common weeds in maize produce large colonies of aphids that are eaten by beneficial predator insects. If the weeds are eliminated, the food supply for the predator insect species is also destroyed (B. D. Blair

1979, pers. commun.). More research is needed if weed manipulation is to become practical.

Diseases

As indicated earlier, the term *biological control* has not been utilized as much in plant pathology as in entomology although the concepts involved often have been used by plant pathologists. The term actually was suggested in 1956 by a plant pathologist, Garrett (1965): " 'Biological control' implies the control of disease by living microorganisms under either natural or artificial circumstance."

Baker and Cook (1974) gave the following definition of biological control as it relates to plant pathology:

> Biological control is the reduction of inoculum density or disease producing activities of a pathogen or parasite in its active or dormant state, by one or more organisms, accomplished naturally or through manipulation of the environment, host, or antagonist, or by mass introduction of one or more antagonists.

They would insist that any control of plant disease in which antagonists play a major role is biological control and resistant varieties can be considered a form of biological control

Two hundred sixteen plant pathologists working with soil-borne pathogens were surveyed by Baker (1975) concerning their definition of biological control. The results showed strong disagreements and differences of opinion. Forty-nine percent preferred Baker and Cook's (1974) very broad definition; 34 percent preferred Garrett's (1965) rather narrow, restricted definition; and 17 percent felt a good definition was not yet available.

Many plant pathologists would insist that biological control must also include use of toxic products produced by various microorganisms, particularly those in the soil. It is often not known whether control effects come from the organism, from a toxin or metabolite produced by the organism, or from a combination of both. Yet other pathologists insist that it is unrealistic not to include the whole area of plant breeding as being the quintessence of biological control (Roane 1973). If these last two groups of natural control phenomena are accepted as biological control, plant pathology has an enormous body of known effective biological control techniques.

It is difficult to follow the activities of one particular organism exercising biological control over another, because most of the organisms involved are microorganisms and most persist naturally in the soil or on plant debris.

Various cultural control techniques have been developed empirically that are very useful and are known to be the result of some type of biological control—usually the details concerning the exact phenomena involved are not known.

Arnon (1972) has summarized several areas in plant pathology where some knowledge of biological control exists:

1. The control of plant bacterial diseases by bacteriophages.
2. The suppression of virulent bacterial pathogens by other bacterial species that are indigenous to the host.
3. Cross protection utilizing a mild virus to protect a plant against a severe strain.
4. The parasitization of pathogenic fungi by other fungi.

He pointed out that thus far there are no good practical applications of any of the first, second, and fourth techniques. In the United States the use of a mild strain of potato virus to protect against infection by severe strains illustrates example 3.

Many bacteriophages that destroy bacterial plant pathogens have been described, but as far as is known none has been developed as a practical control measure (Okabe and Goto 1963). In one hopeful effort reported by Civerolo and Keil (1969), the bacteriophage that attacks *Xanthomonas pruni* protected the foliage of the seedlings of the Elberta peach from infection by the bacterium. Leaf infection was significantly reduced when the *X. pruni* inoculum was mixed in a suspension with the phage and also when the phage was applied as a spray and allowed to dry on the leaves prior to inoculation with *X. pruni*. The phage was stable and effective in protecting the plant against *X. pruni* for 24 hours. The utilization of bacteriophages against plant pathogenic bacteria deserves more research.

The influence of soil on plant diseases is complex; understanding and manipulating it in practical disease control situations is difficult. Not many details of these phenomena are known. Katznelson (1965) summarized this problem as follows:

> For purposes of biological control of soil-borne plant pathogens, more information is required on simple means of altering the rhizosphere's population, quantitatively and qualitatively so as to render the root zone inimical to the pathogen. Although such changes can be affected by manipulating environmental factors (light, temperature, moisture), this is obviously difficult under field conditions. Soil amendments with organic and inorganic materials are of some value in this connection, although it is frequently not clear whether the suppression of the pathogen is due to effects on the soil population in general, on the rhizosphere population in particular, or both. Foliar treatments with selected substances capable of altering the microbial popula-

tion and equilibrium in the rhizosphere is another approach to biological control.

Baker and Cook (1974) emphasized the importance of saprophytes:

> The vast majority of antagonists are saprophytes. Antagonists exert their influence through competition, parasitism or antibiosis. Mycorrhizae, which may protect plant roots against root pathogens, are not saprophytes, nor, perhaps, are the hyperparasites which can attack the living pathogens. Except for these examples nearly all are saprophytes (obligate). In a sense, biological control is pitting saprophytes against parasites.

Despite the fact that we do not understand the details of biological control phenomena functioning against soil pathogens, there are many examples of effective biological control techniques. For example, when alfalfa meal is mixed with soil that is infested with the causal organism, *Phytophthora cinnamomi,* at the rate of 1 to 5 percent, good control of *Phytophthora* root rot of avocado seedlings and also root rot and stem canker of *Persea indica* is obtained. Great increases in microbial populations occur after the addition of alfalfa meal (Zentmyer 1963).

In California, soybeans grown in the fall after potato harvest and turned under in preparation for spring planting effectively control the soilborne actinomycete disease called potato scab, *Streptomyces scabies.* Barley is rotated with beans and plowed under prior to bean planting to control the *Fusarium* root rot of bean. It is believed that the bacterial decomposition of soybean plants in the first case produces toxic substances that are destructive to *S. scabies.* In the second case, the bacterial decomposition of the barley straw seems to tie up the available nitrogen, thereby depriving the *Fusarium* fungus of an essential nutrient for germination and reducing infections in the bean plant (NAS 1968*a*). Some would argue that biological control does not involve nutrients and toxic materials, but others would insist that these are the very essence of biological control.

Other examples have been recorded by Baker and Snyder (1965). In the southwestern United States an immature crop of peas is disked into the soil in the spring before cotton is planted to control root rot of cotton, incited by *Phymatotrichum* spp. In Great Britain and elsewhere the severe fungus disease of wheat called take-all, incited by *Ophiobolus graminis,* is controlled effectively by rotating the wheat crop with a nonhost such as oats. In the southern United States the top few inches of soil are kept free of undecomposed organic litter to control the *Sclerotium* stem rot of peanuts. In Malaya a legume is grown as ground cover between the rows of rubber trees to control a serious *Fomes* rot that attacks the crowns and roots. The legume is also susceptible to the pathogen and is attacked by it; this is believed to dissipate the energy of the pathogen in its attack on the rubber tree.

The effect of certain tolerant and intolerant soils on the presence and effective pathogenicity of plant pathogens is interesting. The fungus, *Fusarium oxysporum,* is often prevalent in forest nurseries and damages pine seedlings but it disappears when the seedlings are transplanted into native forest soils. It is absent in the rhizosphere of pine seedlings in natural stands (Toussoun et al. 1969). *Fusarium* root rot of bean, *F. solani* f. sp. *phaseoli* is active in some soils but not in others in irrigated portions of the Columbia River basin in the state of Washington. The pathogen persists well in one soil and quickly forms chlamydospores and conidia. In the other soil it makes extensive mycelial growth but typically does not form chlamydospores and endolyses (Burke 1965). A classic example still not fully understood is the gradual decline of the take-all disease of wheat, *Ophiobolus graminis* (now *Gaeumannomyces graminis* var. *tritici*), with continuous wheat cultivation. This phenomenon was first observed in Kansas in the 1930s by Fellows and his associates and has been confirmed and carefully recorded many times in England, France, Yugoslavia, Switzerland, Denmark, and Australia (Baker and Cook 1974).

Numerous competitive "weed molds" bedevil the mushroom industry. They have been controlled effectively by improving aeration during the process of composting and by careful manipulation of temperatures during spawning and pasteurization. This manipulation of soil microflora is essentially biological control (Baker and Snyder 1965). The fungus hyperparasite *Ampelomyces quisqualis* has been used in Israel experimentally in greenhouses to control several powdery mildew diseases (Sztenjnberg 1979). Recently there has been some success in controlling chestnut blight by the use of hypovirulent strains of the causal fungus, *Endothia parasitica*. It is comparable to the use of mild virus strains to protect against severe strains. This phenomenon deserves more attention (Hebard and Griffen 1979).

The above examples and many others used for plant disease control for the most part are results of empirical knowledge. These measures are often combined effectively with other plant disease control techniques. This situation is discussed and summarized by Baker and Snyder (1965):

> Although it is generally recognized that interactions of microorganisms constitute an important limiting factor to survival of disease organisms in soil, widespread utilization of such biological control awaits greater understanding of the processes involved. As clearly indicated, effectiveness and dependability of biological control of root pathogens are enhanced when they are integrated with other control procedures such as cultural manipulations, soil disinfestation, crop sequence or fertilizer practices (and also resistant varieties).

An even more complex combination of biological phenomena occurs in mycorrhizae in the soil (Marx 1972): "Feeder roots in the ectomycorrhizal condition are so physically or chemically altered that they resist infection by pathogens. They are also beneficial to plant health as biological deterrents to feeder root infection by such pathogens as *Phytophthora, Pythium* or *Fusarium* spp." For example, it has been reported that tree seedlings with ectomycorrhizae are much more resistant to feeder root infections by fungi than the seedlings with few or no ectomycorrhizae. Although the reason for this phenomenon is not known, it is clearly biological control of a root disease. Several investigators have reported that ectomycorrhizae decrease the incidence of feeder root diseases and nonmycorrhizal plants were uniformly more susceptible to root diseases (Marx 1972).

Several mechanisms by which ectomycorrhizae might protect plant feeder roots from disease have been suggested (Zak 1964):

1. They provide a physical barrier, the so-called fungal mantle.
2. They may secrete antibiotics that are inhibitory to plant pathogenic fungi.
3. They may use the surplus carbohydrates in the roots, thus reducing the amount of available stimulatory nutrients available to plant pathogens.
4. They may help support a protective microbial population in the rhizosphere.

Marx suggested also that inhibitors may be produced by symbiotically infected host cortical cells and may limit the infection and spread of root pathogenic organisms.

In a recent effort to control root diseases in three crops with biological seed treatments (Kommedahl et al. 1979), several fungi and bacteria were applied to the seeds of corn, peas, and soybeans with surprising success. Fungus genera used were *Chaetomium, Trichoderma,* and *Penicillium* and the bacterial genus *Pseudomonas* was used.

Many species of nematodes in the soil attack and feed on soil fungi. The exact effects of their feeding on fungus populations, its influence on rhizosphere fungi, and its possible effect on mycorrhizal interrelationships are not yet known but eventually this area may be significant in biological control of plant pathogenic soil fungi (NAS 1968*a*).

Nematodes

Biological control of nematodes occurs but it has developed slowly, probably because of the complexity of the soil environment in which nematodes thrive. Although some investigators are optimistic about the potential of biological control, no practical controls of nematodes by predacious fungi, toxic substances from plant decomposition, or other biological agents are known.

The problems associated with biological control of nematodes are summarized (Univ. Calif. 1972*b*):

> Naturally occurring predators and parasites of nematodes, including predacious nematodes and small arthropods, parasitic fungi and protozoans, are already present in almost all soils. Modification of the soil environment to allow these organisms to increase to the numbers necessary to provide a significant level of control has not been practical except under laboratory conditions. At present biological control cannot be applied successfully under field conditions.

Knowledge of the ecological factors involved and the problems associated with biological equilibrium and the competitive potential of predators and other organisms is limited. Before dependable biological controls can be developed, far more understanding of soil ecology and the microhabitat requirements of each of the competing species are needed (Van Gundy 1972).

Some empirical cropping techniques help in the control of nematodes. The addition of organic matter by turning under green manure crops increases populations of nematode-trapping fungi and their predacious activity, increases population levels of predacious nematodes and of internal parasites of nematodes, and increases nematicidal substances such as butyric acid in the soil. Butyric acid is produced in rather large quantities by the decomposition of both rye and timothy (grasses). However, it has not been possible to correlate any of these phenomena or organisms with the rise and fall of plant parasitic nematode populations and their relative importance is not understood (NAS 1968*b*). Good pointed out that some control of nematodes can be achieved through the addition of organic matter to the soil, especially biodegradable soil wastes. The natural enemies of nematodes usually are increased or maintained in organic matter and some chemical decomposition products or organic matter are toxic to nematodes (Good 1972*a*).

Biological control of nematodes alone is rarely effective enough for modern farming; but when known empirical techniques are combined with other control methods they are useful supplemental measures. Good suggested that it will be impossible to control nematodes by biological methods until it is possible to regulate the biotic community of the soil, which is far beyond present knowledge (Good 1972*a*).

Even though consistent effective field control of nematodes has not been achieved by biological control techniques, a number of experimental efforts have been promising. By 1972, over 50 species of fungi; 2 protozoans; and numerous carnivorous nematodes, tardigrades, and other small invertebrates in the soil had been reported to destroy or feed on nematodes (Van Gundy 1972). There are also examples of strong competition between soil feeding insects and nematodes, e.g., corn rootworm and nematodes (B. D. Blair 1979, pers. commun.).

A large number of carnivorous nematode species attack and destroy plant parasitic nematodes. Many of these belong to the Monochidae. They may be very important and are the least studied of the predacious organisms that attack plant parasitic nematodes. The small predatory nematode, *Seinura* sp., feeds voraciously on nematodes. There are many predators in the nematode superfamily, Dorylaimoidea. Essentially all the information concerning these predacious nematodes has been derived from observation, not experimentation; more experimental work is needed (Christie 1960; NAS 1968*b*).

Other invertebrates also attack nematodes. Tardigrades are small animals found in water films, on leaves of terrestrial mosses and lichens, and in the soil; they have been seen to feed on nematodes. Very little is known of the population dynamics and biology of these organisms. A soil-inhabitating turbellarian flatworm has also been seen consuming large numbers of root-knot nematodes in the laboratory (NAS 1968*b*).

A sporozoan parasite, *Duboscquia penetrans,* that has been seen parasitizing plant parasitic nematodes occurs widely in the soil and has considerable ability to destroy the reproductive organs of nematodes. A large amoeboid proteomyxan organism, *Theratromyxa weberi,* has also frequently been observed consuming nematodes. The biology and ecology of these sporozoans are largely unknown (NAS 1968*b*). In the laboratory the free living stages of mermithid nematodes are often attacked by parasitic protozoans, causing trouble in rearing these nematodes (Burges and Hussey 1971). One of the most interesting reports of nematode control by a sporozoan parasite is that of Prasad and Mankau (1970) who reported that in a greenhouse test a sporozoan parasite of the root-knot nematode was quite effective in controlling two plant parasitic nematode species, *Pratylenchus scribneri* and *Meloidogyne incognita.*

Duddington (1960) has reported about 50 known species of predacious fungi that either capture or kill nematodes in the soil, and there are also internal parasitic fungi that attack nematodes. None of these are understood well enough to know their potential in the biological control of plant parasitic nematodes. The predacious fungi that attack and kill a great many species of nematodes are common in soil and organic matter and are not host specific. Consequently, they seem to have great potential. Most of the nematode trapping species are in several genera of the Hypomycetes and the Zoopagales (NAS 1968*b*). Fungi in the Chytridiales and the Saprolegniales have also been seen attacking mermithid nematodes in the laboratory (Burges and Hussey 1971). A report from NAS (1968*b*) states that "greater fungus populations may be difficult to obtain in view of demonstrated biological antagonisms to such introduced predacious fungi."

In the laboratory bacteria have been seen attacking and destroying nematodes. In the field only one report—a bacterial infection of a dagger nematode—has appeared. No knowledge is available concerning the significance of bacterial infections of nematodes in nature.

A transmissible and presumed viral disease of root-knot nematodes, *Meloidogyne* sp., was observed but again no knowledge of its significance under controlled conditions in the laboratory or importance in nature is available. It would appear desirable that nematologists, bacteriologists, and virologists cooperate in studying bacterial and viral diseases of plant parasitic nematodes (NAS 1968*b*).

Weeds

Biological control of weeds has been of economic significance for some time and is a natural phenomenon of importance. Crafts and Robbins (1962) say that

> the conscious use of the method by man to control weed pests is of fairly recent origin. The natural processes of biological control are part of the process of evolution. . . . Complete eradication is impossible by the biological method. The best result is an equilibrium in which the weed, though present, is no longer an economic pest.

Goeden et al. (1974) lists some 70 research projects on biological control of weeds. Control by phytophagous insects appears to be important for the future. Andres and Goeden (1971) said that "weed control with insects is not a dangerous, untested, unproven pipe dream but rather a well-documented accomplishment."

Note that biological control of weeds with various host-specific insects does not eradicate the plants. The reproduction of the insect is closely related to the presence of the weed hosts. An equilibrium level is reached when the weed's average population density falls below its level of economic importance. Since the introduced insect itself is usually host specific to the weed, other plants in the immediate vicinity are not harmed but are often assisted because of the suppression of the competing weed (Andres and Goeden 1971).

The first practical biological control of a plant by insects probably was made in Hawaii. The thorny shrub, *Lantana camara,* an introduced plant that became a pest, has been reasonably well controlled by several introduced insect species obtained from Mexico around 1902. Later several other species were introduced to obtain even better control (Perkins and Swezey 1924; Crafts and Robbins 1962; Andres and Goeden 1971).

Another classic example is the control of prickly pear, *Opuntia* sp., in Australia. Biological control efforts started in 1912. Eight species of insects were brought in from the Americas to attack and feed on the introduced *Opuntia.* The most successful insect was the cactus moth borer, *Cac-*

toblastis cactorum, introduced from Argentina in 1925 (Crafts and Robbins 1962).

The control of the prickly pear cactus in California was also achieved by introducing natural enemy insects. The cacti controlled were *Opuntia littoralis* and *O. oricola* and their hybrids, which were infesting rangeland areas on an island about 25 miles off the coast of southern California. Substantial biological control of these cacti has been achieved by the cochineal insect, *Dactylopius opuntiae,* which was introduced from Hawaii in 1951. Other species of cactus insects were introduced but none were particularly effective. The biological control efforts were combined with range management practices to encourage the forage plant species that compete with the prickly pear on the formerly overgrazed rangeland. This combination of practices has brought the cactus population down to an acceptable economic level (Andres and Goeden 1971).

Other good examples of biological control of weeds by insects are the control of alligator weed in Florida by the leaf and stem feeding flea beetle, *Agasicles* sp.; the puncture vine in the western United States by two species of beetles, *Microlarinus* spp., a seed-infesting weevil and a stem and crown mining weevil; and a poisonous rangeland weed, tansy ragwort, *Senecio jacobaea,* in the western United States by the cinnabar moth, *Tyria jacobaea.* Important precautions must be taken in research associated with such biological control. Prior to the movement of phytophagous insects from one country or area to another as introduced species the specific insect needs to be ruled out as a possible pest on other important plants in the new area (Andres and Goeden 1971).

Wilson (1969) pointed out that the notion of using plant pathogenic organisms to control weeds is about as old as the science of plant pathology but it has met strong resistance because of the inherent dangers of introducing new pathogenic organisms into an area—the introduced pathogen may have a wide host range that would allow it to become a disease on an important crop plant. Plant pathogens probably play an important role in nature in the reduction of some weed populations, but this phase of plant pathology has received little attention and has no significant practical control use so far (Wilson 1969; Goeden et al. 1974). However, in 1974 a committee of the American Phytopathological Society was established to investigate the desirability of a new subject matter committee in the area of biological control of weeds with plant pathogens (James Tammen 1975, pers. commun.).

There have been a number of partial successes in controlling weeds with plant pathogens. The feasibility of this approach has been proven and each year sees expanded activity. Effective plant pathogens will have at least three advantages over chemical herbicides: they can be specific on the weed to be controlled, the residue and toxicity problems will be eliminated, and there will be no accumulation of herbicide residues in the soil and groundwater (Wilson 1969). However, some plant pathogens may produce potent mycotoxins and may be carcinogenic.

Wilson (1969) cites several examples of research in biological control of weeds by plant pathogens. In Hawaii, a destructive *Fusarium* disease of the prickly pear cactus, *Opuntia megacantha,* has been found. In the western United States the dwarf mistletoe, *Arceuthobium* spp., is the major pathogen of important forest conifers. Three fungal parasites of the mistletoe hold some promise for control—*Septogloeum gillii, Wallrothiella arceuthobii,* and *Colletotrichum gloeosporioides*—but do not yet control it. In Russia, there is a report of control of dodder by a species of *Alternaria.* In Arkansas and Oklahoma there is a report of control of the persimmon tree in pastures by the persimmon wilt organism, *Cephalosporium diospyri.*

Biological control methods for parasitic higher plants such as the dodders, broom rapes, witchweed, and other phanerogamic parasites are important. Research should be initiated to find control measures among plant disease pathogens, insects, etc.; since these parasitic plants belong to specialized plant families, the possibility of finding disease organisms and insects specific to these plants is good (Sankaran and Rao 1966; NAS 1968c). As an example, Tucker and Phillips (1974) have isolated a fungus, *Phytophthora citrophthora,* from roots and stems of dying strangler vines of the milkweed family, *Morrenia odorata,* a major weed of citrus in Florida. This fungus appears to be pathogenic and lethal only to the strangler vine and shows promise in biological control.

Inman (1971) reported in a field plot study quite effective control of curly dock, *Rumex crispus,* by infection with the Rumex rust, *Uromyces rumicis.* There was severe reduction in root stock vigor and seed production. Only 43 percent of the curly dock plants resumed growth the next spring as compared with 95 percent in the control plots. The use of a plant pathogen to control northern joint vetch, an important weed in the rice crop in some parts of the world, has been reported by Shaw (1974a). A recent survey by Templeton et al. (1979) summarized weed control to date with mycoherbicides.

An unexplored area of biological control of weeds is the combined use of insects, bacteria, and/or fungi. A team approach would be appropriate for this effort (Wilson 1969; Baker and Cook 1974).

For aquatic weeds, no biological controls by plant disease organisms have been reported. This area needs cooperative research among the concerned disciplines (Zettler and Freeman 1972). Some dramatic controls have been seen in nature. Blue-green algal blooms have been partially controlled by the blue-green algal virus (L-1). In 1966 and 1967 the northeast disease of Eurasian water milfoil, *Myriophyllum spicatum,* dramatically reduced the populations of blue-green algae in the upper Chesapeake Bay. This disease is believed to be caused by a virus but confirmation is needed. In India the water hyacinth has a thread blight that shows some promise as a biological control. Disease epidemics in phytoplankton populations are caused by pathogenic aquatic fungi and are apparently quite common. Populations have been reduced dramatically by attacks of aquatic fungi, especially chytrids (Wilson 1969).

Animal Pests

An interesting report on the natural biological control of the water snail, *Ampullaria lineata,* in rice is given by Feakin (1970). These snails occur in South America, mainly in Brazil, in large numbers and eat the plumules of the sprouting rice plant. They are so damaging in some cases that it is necessary to replant the rice. The snail is eaten and quite well controlled locally by the snail hawk, a bird whose presence in rice fields is encouraged. Other examples of bird control of insects are given in Chap. 14. Many feel that these examples constitute biological control.

12

Biological Control by Antagonism

Antagonism, Synergism, and Stasis

 Many potentially toxic materials synthesized by plants, microorganisms, and other pest species appear likely to be associated with plant disease or pest control. These materials are complex and the nomenclature, developed by workers in biological as well as chemical disciplines, is confusing and at times conflicting. A great deal of research is being conducted in these fields now, most of it independently. However, even though the evolving picture seems murky, this area will probably prove to be at the heart of our understanding of the nature of resistance and immunity.

Many would not characterize these branches of biochemical research as a part of biological control; others insist that they will be at the heart of future biological control. This attitude is summarized by Apple (1974):

> The traditional concept of biological control involved the action of parasites, predators, and pathogens in reducing the population density of another organism (mostly insects, etc.). Since this traditional concept involved only insects, it must be broadened in the context of an integrated pest management program to include such phenomena as antibiosis, competition, lysis and cross protection as biological control methods for plant pathogens.

To plant pathologists this whole area, including all the products produced by the various competing plants and microorganisms in the soil, is generally described under the term *antagonism*. Snyder (1960) summarized the importance of antagonism:

> One is left to conclude that the total antagonism potential of a soil upon which the plant pathologist may draw is enormous. The soil abounds with powerful antagonists which compete with, parasitize or poison plant pathogens. These antagonists are selective for the pathogens they antagonize. They are selective for the kind of organic materials on which they thrive and they are antagonized in turn by other elements of the flora of the soil even as

they antagonize. The opportunities for playing one soil organism against another to man's advantage are there and only await man's cleverness in dealing with antagonists.

Kilgore and Doutt (1967) defined antagonism "as the sum total of the unfavorable influences which one organism exerts against another. In such a broad sense the activity of an antagonist may include physical destruction, parasitism, antibiotic secretions, and more subtle forms of attrition or competition for nutrients and space."

Neither the exact nature nor the mechanisms of action of most antagonisms are fully understood but information suggests that these phenomena hold tremendous promise for the future as effective means of controlling soil-borne plant pathogens (Kilgore and Doutt 1967). McNew (1966) said that "there are almost unlimited possibilities of controlling the severe destruction from soil inhabiting pathogens once the forces operative in the soil, especially near the roots and root hairs, are better understood. The forces involved in the rhizosphere are complex, but progress in the past two decades offers much promise."

In addition to antagonistic forces in the soil there are the forces operating between plants and microorganisms, including the animals and microfauna of the soil, which predispose to coexistence as well as synergism. Consequently, the biochemical forces involved, depending on the balance of the various metabolites produced by microflora and microfauna, may be neutral, antagonistic, synergistic, or static.

One fairly common soil phenomenon is known as stasis—fungistasis if fungi are involved or bacteriostasis if bacteria are involved. In some cases of fungistasis or mycostasis the spores of fungi do not germinate so long as they remain in the soil in spite of favorable conditions of temperature and moisture because of unknown inhibitory factors. In other cases the hyphae stop growing, are retarded, or are terminated by unknown conditions in the soil environment. The dynamic phenomena of fungistasis can theoretically be explained as stimulatory forces that are balanced by inhibitory forces. These could be either biotic or abiotic. Fungistasis does not occur in all soils and is usually more pronounced at the surface than in the subsoil. By 1964 at least 53 genera and 116 species of fungi had been recorded as being affected by soil fungistasis (Meyer 1972).

Any factor that reduces soil biological activity will reduce the level of fungistasis (Meyer 1972; Watson and Ford 1972). Meyer thinks the most likely explanation for fungistasis is that not enough sources of energy are available for the germination of spores in the soil. Watson and Ford (1972) think that inhibitors in the soil, both biotic and abiotic and probably including pH, induce and maintain fungistatic conditions. The phenomenon of stasis is potentially very important in plant disease control.

Winter (1948) concluded that fungistatic materials in the soil were more important than nutrients in limiting fungus growth, and numerous studies since have emphasized the importance of fungistasis in inhibiting spore germination. One of the major problems in the physiology of spore germination in the rhizosphere is the difficulty of measuring the roles of fungistasis versus nutrition and the effect of plant root exudates on these phenomena (Schroth and Hildebrand 1964).

Antagonism, as far as pathogens are concerned, is the equivalent of reducing virulence. Synergism, by contrast, is the result of the interaction of two or more pathogens that enhance virulence. Synergistic phenomena exist when the combined effects of two or more diseases are greater than the sum of their independent effects. Synergistic phenomena are common but are not discussed further because they are not thus far associated with practical control.

The microorganisms and organisms making up the microflora and microfauna of the soil are in fierce competition. Thus far it has not been possible to utilize or control this activity. This area is one of the most promising for successful biological control of plant diseases and soil pests. This competition exists between fungi and bacteria and other microorganisms and also between nematode species, insect species, and all other microfloral and microfaunal soil constituents. The soil is so complex that thus far it has not been possible to add any competitive species to it for plant disease or pest control.

Nematodes of different species compete in the soil. Whether a given nematode is a serious pest of plants depends on factors such as the host present, the initial populations of the pest species and other nematode species, the soil type, the relative reproductive rates of the nematode species present, and other environmental factors that may be significant in nematode populations. Any advantage that one nematode species may have over another is apt to change with the planting of a new crop or any major change in the environment, either artificial or natural (NAS 1968b).

Similar relationships between other microfaunal and microfloral species in the soil are present, but information is fragmentary and no practical control techniques via the introduction of particular species have been developed. Control practices that appear to be useful in the control of harmful soil microflora and microfauna have all been empirical.

Plant Exudates and Diseases

The work of Snyder (1960) and his associates in California on the effects of plant exudates on saprophytic and pathogenic activities of *Fusarium solani* f. sp. *phaseoli* demonstrates the ways in which exudates influence the survival, reproduction, and development of various microorganisms. These phenomena are extremely complex. Other plant exudates affect other microflora and microfauna in equally complex ways. Most studies of the effects of plant exudates on disease development have been done in the laboratory because it has been impossible thus far to study them in the natural environment. Perhaps an artificial laboratory habitat where conditions approximate those of nature can be developed. Many laboratory studies have produced conflicting and questionable results and are probably not an accurate reflection of what really occurs in nature (Schroth and Hildebrand 1964).

Extensive surveys of plants for the presence of exudates and other antimicrobial substances in root sap have shown that these materials are widespread and exert a selective effect on the microflora in the soil (Schroth and Hildebrand 1964). It should be expected that higher plants might produce many inhibitory substances, since they have the innate chemical capacity to exclude most parasitic microorganisms from entry. Many inhibiting substances exuded into the soil environment may accumulate in the soil and remain active for some time (Burges and Raw 1967).

Rovira (1965) concluded that root exudates play an important role in the establishment and maintenance of rhizosphere populations of microorganisms around young plants and that this action is often quite specific. He feels that research will eventually lead to the development of some basic principles useful in the biological control of root pathogens of plants.

Several examples of the effectiveness of plant root exudates and plant leaf exudates are in the literature. When cabbage is sowed in combination with onions, garlic, beets, or radishes, the infection of cabbage seedlings by *Pellicularia filamentosa* is reduced. This effect is also noted when onions or garlic have been grown as the preceding crop (Lavroka 1962). Gladiolus produces a root exudate that stimulates the germination of the fungus *Sclerotium cepivorum;* in the field the number of sclerotia are greatly decreased in soils planted to gladiolus (Tichelaar 1961). The juices of the garlic plant, *Allium sativum,* and the solvent extracts of commercial garlic powder are characterized by strong bactericidal and fungicidal properties. Both gram-positive and gram-negative plant pathogenic organisms are destroyed. One to 20 percent aqueous garlic sprays controlled the following diseases under greenhouse conditions: downy mildew of cucumber, downy mildew of radish, cucumber scab, bean rust, bean anthracnose, early blight of tomato, brown rot of stone fruits, angular leaf spot of cucumber, and bacterial blight of beans. A garlic dust controlled both bean rust and downy mildew of cucumber (Ark and Thompson 1959).

One case in which normal tissue from plants contains powerful inhibitory phenolic compounds correlated with disease resistance is that of onion smudge (Walker 1969; Robert Scheffer 1975, pers. commun.). This may be unusual in nature because the dead outer colored onion scales of the plant are involved in this resistance. White onions do not have it.

It may eventually be possible to spray natural exudates that are toxic to pathogens on the foliage. The exudates would translocate to the underground parts of the plant and be exuded through the roots into the rhizosphere. For example, application of urea, polymyxin, triiodobenzoic acid, and chloramphenicol to several plants increased root exudates significantly. Spraying gibberellin on red kidney bean plants produced a root exudate that made the beans more susceptible to one isolate of *Rhizoctonia solani*. The exudates of these plants showed many more carbohydrate substances than the exudates of untreated plants and the increase in severity of the disease was attributed to changes in exudates from the roots. If a practical technique for spraying leaves to alter root exudates is developed, it will be a revolutionary mechanism for the control of soil-borne plant diseases. More research is needed in this general area (Schroth and Hildebrand 1964).

Kushner and Harvey (1962) demonstrated that phytocides (antibacterial substances) were present in the foliage extracts of ten species of conifers and eight species of deciduous trees; they also showed that the same antibacterial substances were in the insects feeding on these plants. With these materials they were able to inhibit the growth of the two bacteria, *Bacillus thuringiensis* and *B. cereus*. It has also been shown that these phytocides protect insects against these bacterial diseases and that they have a wide range of properties that can inhibit a number of other bacteria. Just how these materials are related to plant root exudates is not known but certainly somewhat the same phenomena are involved. These phenomena are potentially important for the control of plant diseases and for the possible control of other pests.

Other plant exudates function as stimulants. For example, the exudation of nutrients from cracked seeds stimulates the germination of plant disease fungus organisms such as members of the genera *Pythium* and *Rhizoctonia* (NAS 1968*b*). These exudates have not been used in disease control but deserve study.

Root Exudates and Nematodes

Some root exudates, after leaching into the soil, are toxic to certain plant parasitic nematodes. When the French or African marigold is grown in soil infested with the lesion nematode, *Pratylenchus* spp., the number of nematodes in the roots of susceptible host plants is reduced and the populations are generally reduced. Marigold plants have also reduced populations of the stunt nematode, *Tylenchorhynchus dubius*. Some other nematodes are not affected. Three compounds of an a-terthienyl type toxic to some nematodes have been identified as root exudates from marigold (NAS 1968*b*).

In Holland, tulips and daffodils have been grown immediately after marigolds for many years. Recently, commercial nursery workers have discovered that interplanting marigolds improves growth of some other plants. Marigolds have reduced populations of *Meloidogyne, Pratylenchus,* and some other nematode genera. The soil surrounding marigold plants becomes toxic and adjacent plants are at least partially protected (Rohde 1972).

Asparagus, *Asparagus officinalis,* contains a glycoside in the roots, stems, and leaves that is highly toxic to the nematode, *Trichodorus christiei,* and several others. It may explain the apparent resistance of asparagus to this nematode. Populations of *T. christiei* die quickly in the asparagus root zone. The toxic materials may also spread through the soil and protect adjacent susceptible plants (Rohde 1972).

Nematodes may be repelled or attracted by root exudates of other plants. Some plant extracts that are toxic to nematodes are believed to be related to plant resistance but so far none has been shown to be the sole mechanism of resistance in nature (NAS 1968*b*; Rohde 1972).

Several phenols, for example, p-cresol and a catechin found in the cyst wall itself, have been shown to inhibit hatching in cyst nematodes in the laboratory. Under natural conditions these materials have not been shown to influence nematode hatch even though they are common constituents of plants, especially injured plants. Plants that contain nematode toxins are attacked and often injured by nematodes but nematode development is quickly retarded and populations are rapidly reduced. Many of the compounds from plants used in human and animal medicines that are toxic to animal parasitic nematodes are phenols, similar to the phenols that appear to be related to disease resistance in plants (Rohde 1972).

Encysted nematode eggs can remain dormant for a number of years; many require specific root exudates from plants to act as hatching factors. The isolation and characterization of these hatching factors could lead to the control of many nematode pests. If, for example, the hatching factors could be manufactured cheaply enough to be used in soil broadcasts over infested soil when no food supply is available, eggs could be induced to hatch and the emerging larvae would starve. Since the materials used are normal soil constituents, ecological damage from the use of these synthetic hatching factors is unlikely (Sondheimer and Simeone 1970).

Nematodes develop normally but very slowly in particular plants. The reason is not now known but it has potential for practical control of nematode populations (Rohde 1972).

Allelopathic Materials

Many exudates of plants that seem to function primarily against higher plants are known as allelopathic materials. Numerous toxic compounds excreted into the soil by growing plants damage other higher plants growing nearby and may play a role in some so-called soil sickness problems (Meyer 1972). These allelopathic inhibitors or substances certainly affect the dynamics and the composition of plant communities and probably are involved in the phenomenon of plant succession (Whittaker 1970). Most of the allelopathics found so far are phenolic compounds, terpenoids, nitriles, and alkaloids. Many appear to have no metabolic significance in plants but may be defenses against competing plants and possibly animals and may be of considerable evolutionary significance. Allelopathy is widespread in nature although usually inconspicuous in plant communities. Other similar or perhaps identical materials are called "secondary plant substances" (Fraenkel 1959).

The first allelopathic chemical described is attributed to Davis (1928), who reported that walnut trees inhibit the growth of several understory species. For example, many broad-leaved herbs, shrubs, and broom sedge are essentially excluded. Others, such as Kentucky bluegrass or black raspberry, are tolerated or even favored and may form the ground cover. The active chemical in walnut trees, juglone, has been described (Brooks 1951; Bode 1958; Sondheimer and Simeone 1970).

Muller et al. (1964) studied several examples of allelopathy from the soft chaparral community in southern California. In this low shrub land a mint, *Salvia leucophylla,* and a sagebrush, *Artemisia californica,* dominate the plant community. The soft chaparral shrubs tend to invade the grasslands in this region. Inhibition appears to be associated with allelopathic chemicals, probably some terpenes produced by the shrubs. Under experimental conditions the terpenes cineole and camphor have an inhibitory effect on germination and seedling growth of some grasses and other plants of the chaparral communities. It is believed that these terpenes accumulate in the soil during the dry summer season and inhibit the germination of annual plant seeds when rains arrive in the spring (Muller et al. 1968; Sondheimer and Simeone 1970).

Some plants from dry climates that produce or are suspected of producing allelopathic inhibitors are from the genera *Parthenium, Encelia, Hordeum, Eucalyptus, Larrea, Myrtus,* and *Tridodia* (Went 1970).

A new biological control of weeds that might eventually make even selective herbicide use unnecessary has been reported by Putnam and Duke of Michigan State and Cornell universities, respectively (Allelopathy 1975). Certain breeding lines of cucumber restrain or limit the growth of weeds (millet and mustard) in their midst and root leachates from these cucumber lines inhibit the growth of mustard seedlings markedly. An inherited character like this could give crop plants a strong competitive advantage over certain weeds.

Although allelopathic materials inhibit other plants, it is surprising that their strongest inhibition is against their own seedlings. Went (1970) explained it by the following hypothesis.

> In arid climates the amount of water limits plant movement. Occasionally a heavy rain will replenish the soil water supply which normally would result in the vigorous growth of all shrubs. If this were all above ground growth, the root system in the following drought period might not be adequate to supply enough water to the tops. Therefore, a mechanism by which the plant restricts its own growth under occasional favorable conditions would be of distinct advantage. In the desert adequate root growth should always precede top growth. The root inhibitor mechanism seems to insure this, for in the greenhouse, with plenty of water to leach out the inhibitor, growth of the desert shrubs is rapid.

Allelopathic plant exudates may be stimulatory as well as inhibitory to higher plants. Examples are found among the phanaerogamic parasites of plants, e.g., the genera *Striga* and *Orobanche*. Their seeds germinate only when in the immediate area of host plant roots, which contain a germination stimulant (Went 1970).

The area of inhibitory and stimulatory allelopathic substances produced by plants may have considerable potential in weed control as well as in the control of phanaerogamic parasites of plants (Crafts and Robbins 1962). Theoretically, it ought to be possible to use any inhibitory or stimulatory material that is of evolutionary advantage to one plant as a control of another plant or animal that in nature has been conceived of as an enemy. There may be some practical empirical use of such phenomena in agriculture in the use of trap and catch crops to control pests such as nematodes and phanaerogamic parasites.

A review by Putnam and Duke (1978) deals with the practical possibilities of allelopathic materials and a text was written by Rice (1974).

Antibiotics

Antibiotics are known to be extremely important in the soil in the inhibition and control of competing species, but the details of this inhibition and control for the most part are not known. Antibiotics are toxins or strong inhibitory substances secreted by microorganisms that function primarily against other microorganisms (Meyer 1972).

The antibiotic phenomena perhaps should include all aspects of the use of microorganisms or their by-products in the control of pests or diseases;

microbial control is often applied rather narrowly to only insects and mites. In the future these all will be included within a widening concept. At the moment, however, it is appropriate to discuss antibiotics here.

The importance of antibiosis in nature is summarized by Jackson (1965):

> A consideration of all the evidence we now have must convince us that antibiosis, in one form or another, plays a key role in the ecology of soil microorganisms, being perhaps second in importance only to competition for nutrients. Increased knowledge of the interrelations and dynamics of the rhizosphere population will lead to increasing possibilities for the biological control of root diseases through antibiosis.

Antibiotics have not been used successfully in the soil in plant pathology but have been widely tested on plants for systemic prevention and eradication of plant diseases. Three antibiotics, streptomycin, griseofulvin, and cycloheximide, have been quite promising with bacterial diseases. Bean plants have been protected from halo blight by streptomycin, and fire blight of apples and pears has been controlled systemically by agrimycin (NAS 1968a).

Vidaver (1976) discussed the use of bacteriocins—antibiotic materials produced by certain strains of bacteria and active against other strains or closely related species—that have some possibility as control agents against specific bacterial plant diseases. She urged more research to develop them and make them economically competitive and practical.

At least 25 bacterial diseases and about 50 fungal diseases have been partially controlled by antibiotics (Arnon 1972). However, none have been effective when artificially introduced into the soil.

Symptoms of aster yellows (a mycoplasma disease) have been suppressed by chloramphenicol tetracycline and chlortetracycline but not by penicillin when used as a spray. Since antibiotics are not effective against virus diseases, Davis et al. (1968) argued that aster yellows was caused by a mycoplasma or bedsonialike organism rather than by a virus.

Most antifungal antibiotics are produced by *Streptomyces* spp. The best of these, the cycloheximides (Actidione), have functioned as systemic antifungal antibiotics and chemotherapeutants. The only disadvantage of the Actidione materials is their tendency to be phytotoxic.

Antibiosis and Antagonisms in the Soil

Although it is reasonably certain that antibiosis is very important in the soil, it has been difficult to prove. Meyer (1972) thinks that most research on antibiotics in the soil has been worth little, since most of the work has been done with sterilized soil into which the antibiotics or the organisms that produce antibiotics were introduced. Pramer in 1965 (quoted by Meyer 1972) summarized the problem as follows:

> Only rarely will the proportion of antibiotic-producing organisms in a natural soil be high enough to produce detectable quantities of antibiotics even after enrichment. There is in fact a complete lack of convincing evidence to support the thesis that antibiosis produced under natural conditions can exert a significant and general effect in soils. Even though practical antibiosis has not been demonstrated under completely controlled conditions in the soil and where supposedly utilized in control has been based upon empirical observations, the potential . . . is exceedingly important.

Organic matter and its decomposition are used empirically in the control of various plant diseases even though little is known about what actually happens during decomposition. Adequate empirical knowledge is available to make use of organic and compost materials, which are of great value in agriculture for many reasons other than plant disease control. The many interlocking, often apparently conflicting, phenomena occurring in the soil during organic decomposition are so complex that they have with few exceptions remained a mystery.

Evidence proves that the decomposition of organic matter in the soil produces compounds that may be favorable or unfavorable in their effects on various plants and microorganisms. However, under field conditions it has not been possible to study the effectiveness of these various decomposition products separately. Patrick et al. (1964) summarized these difficulties:

> As with all soil problems much more is unknown than is known. . . . We are dealing with dynamic systems where all effects are transitory, where production, transformation and destruction go hand in hand. Under such conditions direct observations are difficult at best, and often cannot be made with known techniques.

There is evidence that some of the toxins produced during the decay of plant residues or produced by living roots explain the poor growth of corn in stubble mulch farming and the poor growth during the first season after harvesting in the tropical forest. The water extracts of these soils are very active inhibitors of root development. Several toxic organic compounds have been isolated from these extracts, for example, coumarin, vanillin, salicylic aldehyde, cinnamic acid, and other materials derived from the degradation of ligninlike materials (Meyer 1972). Meyer reported that corky root rot of lettuce appears to be caused by substances coming from decomposing plant tissues and that aqueous extracts of crop residues have caused the death of root meristems, inhibited the germination of seeds, and killed roots.

McNew (1972) thinks the antibiosis of plant pathogens in the soil via organic matter decay contributes greatly to their suppression and gives illustrations. Plant tissues added to soils have been shown to help suppress the Texas root rot fungus, *Phymatotrichum omnivorum,* and sugars added to the soil to stimulate bacterial antagonisms have helped suppress the strawberry root rot complex.

Wellman (1972) thinks that antibiotic effects appear to be operating in many tropical soils. He reports supposed antibiotic effects that result in many unexpected reductions in plant disease severity and feels that the so-called hyperparasites plus other antibiotic effects deserve expanded research.

It is recognized in the tropics that antibiotics produced by bacteria are inhibitors of *Fusarium oxysporum* f. sp. *coffeae.* This disease is more severe when shade or leafy mulches are removed. One of the best controls of the coffee fusarial wilt as well as the *Meloidogyne* spp. nematodes is replanting shade trees for the coffee plants and increasing the amount of weed and grassy mulch materials used around them (Wellman 1972).

There have been several reports of the reduction of population levels of plant pathogenic nematodes after the addition of organic manures to the soil. Without question the activity of microorganisms following these treatments increases greatly, and reduction in nematode populations have been assumed to be correlated with the buildup of organisms that destroy nematodes. However, even though organic manuring is used widely and effectively, the actual reasons for the population drops are not known (NAS 1968*b*). The population drops indicate that the antagonistic and antibiotic factors in the soil function not only against plants and microorganisms but also against the microfauna of the soil.

Phytotoxicity from antibiotics occurs rarely. Patulin, an antibiotic produced by *Penicillium expansum* and *P. patulum,* was named as a possible cause of apple soil sickness by Borner in 1963 (reported by Meyer 1972). Patulin also has been reported as a possible source of plant toxicity in stubble mulching by Norstadt and McCalla in 1969 (Meyer 1972). However, phytotoxicity is not a common result of antibiotics in the soil.

Mycorrhizae

Mycorrhizae are important to the growth of many plants. A large number of ectomycorrhizal fungi produce antibiotics inhibitory to bacteria. The test organisms usually have been *Staphylococcus aureus* and *Escherichia coli.* It is not known whether these antibiotics are also inhibitory to the feeder root diseases of plants, most of which are caused by fungi. A result of antibiotics inhibitory to bacteria may be a selective influence on the development of particular bacterial populations in a root zone (Marx 1972).

The mycorrhizal fungal mantle creates a complex environment. It appears to be a mechanical barrier to pathogen penetration, but root cortex cells that are surrounded by the Hartig net also are resistant to certain pathogens. This suggests a chemical function originating from the host (Marx 1972). Roots that bear ectotrophic mycorrhizae may be less susceptible to root pathogens than nonmycorrhizal roots. The means of resistance may be mechanical protection, competition, antibiosis, or a combination (Meyer 1972).

An antibiotic mechanism of resistance appears to function in some mycorrhizal situations. Normally susceptible roots that grow adjacent to antibiotic-producing ectomycorrhizae become resistant to attacks by certain pathogenic fungi. It is known that mycorrhizae support a microbial population that is different both quantitatively and qualitatively from populations of nonmycorrhizal roots and nonrhizosphere soils. Probably these mycorrhizae have a marked effect on certain microorganisms, on the characteristic microbial competition that develops, and possibly on root pathogens. Apparently many pathogens are not attracted to ectomycorrhizae as they are to nonmycorrhizal roots. These phenomena show the possibility of utilizing ectomycorrhizae in the biological control of pathogens of feeder roots (Marx 1972).

Mycorrhizae are essential for many plants. This fact is illustrated by failures in attempts to grow trees in formerly treeless areas. All attempts to grow pine in Puerto Rico were unsuccessful until appropriate mycorrhizae were introduced with the trees. The reasons that mycorrhizae aid tree growth and often are required for it are not clear. Most workers ascribe it to mycorrhizal aid in improving nutrition and in the plant's use of carbohydrates. Other workers believe that delicate root tissues are protected by the fungus symbiont from attack by various parasitic fungi. Other benefits are the known antibiotic action of some mycorrhizal symbionts possibly working with other soil fungi. Also, mycorrhizae furnish a physical barrier to pathogens and pests (Zak 1964).

Phytotoxins and Similar Materials

Microorganisms produce many metabolites in vitro that can be classified broadly as toxins, enzymes, antibiotics, and growth factors and other metabolites that appear to be biologically inactive in low concentrations. In some cases the conditions for production are well known but the biochemical reasons for most of them remain unknown. Their behavior in vitro often, perhaps usually, appears to be quite different from that in vivo. In nature the study of their ecological significance is difficult (Meyer 1972).

Toxins (specifically, phytotoxins) are materials produced by microorganisms that affect higher plants adversely (Meyer 1972). The term toxin has been broken down by Wood et al. (1972) into several subheadings, but in all likelihood no logic will emerge in the effort to designate each type of toxin precisely until each can be classified chemically and controlled biologically as a known chemical. A. E. Dimond made the following statement in 1970 (Wood et al. 1972): "Is it [even] worthwhile to attempt to define the word toxin at this point?"

Many examples of phytotoxic substances occur and most have not been described. Some toxic materials are produced by microorganisms near the affected plant and cause necrosis without any physical contact between the host and the pathogen; e.g., a necrosis induced by *Rhizoctonia solani* on the roots of Chippewa soybean seedlings was reported by Wyllie in 1962 (Meyer 1972). Oxalic acid produced by *Aspergillus niger* causes necrosis in some plants and is the cause of the crown rot of peanut seedlings as reported by Gibson in 1953 (Meyer 1972). Meyer gives another example that was the result of research by Ylimaki in 1967. Some species of the fungus genus *Marasmius* produce HCN, which damages the crown tissues of several plants and predisposes them to invasion by other fungi. Some metabolites produced by fungi induce albinism in seedlings. For example, *A. flavus* produces albinism in citrus seedlings and *Alternaria tenuis* inhibits chlorophyll formation in citrus seedlings and other plants (Meyer 1972).

The role of toxins in pathogenesis for most disease-host situations is not clear. In certain cases more than one toxin seems to be produced by a given microorganism, but the relative importance of toxins in pathogenicity is unclear (Meyer 1972).

A few phytotoxins have been studied over a period of time and are quite well understood. They are the host-specific plant toxins that are defined as metabolic products of pathogenic microorganisms and are toxic only to the host of a particular pathogen. The three host-specific toxins found thus far have been produced by *Helminthosporium victoriae*, *Alternaria kikuchiana*, and *Periconia circinata*. These materials are highly toxic to their hosts but not to other living organisms. They produce all the symptoms of the diseases caused by the three respective pathogenic organisms (Pringle and Scheffer 1964).

Host-specific toxins have been used by plant breeders. The host-specific toxin from *Helminthosporium victoriae* has been used in Florida to screen for resistance to the fungus (Robert Scheffer 1975, pers. commun.). The toxin from *Periconia circinata* has been used in breeding for resistance to the milo disease of sorghum, incited by *P. circinata* (Scheffer and Yoder 1972). This research was done by Shertz and Tai in 1969 (Scheffer 1975). Recently, Steiner in Hawaii, working for the Hawaiian Sugar Planters' Association, has used the host-specific toxin from the organism *Helminthosporium sacchari* in screening for resistance in sugarcane. This breeding technique has not been utilized with phytotoxins that do not appear to be host-specific (Scheffer 1975).

Phytoalexins and Related Materials

Different chemical substances or mechanical injuries may produce a host reaction in the form of a reaction metabolite. In these cases the acquired resistance of the plant does not appear to be related entirely to a pathogen but seems to be host specific. A typical example is pisatin, which is induced only in peas by mechanical, chemical, or biological injuries (Kuc 1972). Often several substances may be produced by the host in response to infection or injury, and the resistance response of the plant tends to develop early, creating an unsatisfactory environment for the pathogen or invader. In certain cases, materials synthesized by the plant in response to infection may make a disease worse. For example, ipomeamarone, which has been reported as responsible for the resistance of sweet potatoes to the fungus *Ceratocystis fimbriata,* may act as a vivatoxin that damages and kills sweet potato root tissues (Kuc 1972).

Another class of materials, probably closely related or identical to those just discussed, arises after infection by a microorganism and produces an altered metabolism in the infected plant tissues. These materials are known as phytoalexins (Wood et al. 1972). Phytoalexins are defined by Muller in 1956 (Cruickshank 1965) as "antibiotics that are produced as the result of the interaction of two metabolic systems, host and parasite, and that inhibit the growth of microorganisms pathogenic to plants." This concept has been expanded somewhat by Kuc (1972), who thinks "the term phytoalexins should serve as an umbrella under which chemical compounds contributing to disease resistance can be classified whether they are formed in response to injury, physiological stimuli, the presence of infectious agents or the products of such agents." Kuc's point is that the metabolic products are formed in response to a given agency or pathogen. When this broader definition is used, pisatin (described by Kuc originally in 1966), which forms in pea plants in response to injuries, can be classified as a phytoalexin. In sweet potato, infection, injury, or treatment with chemical agents can lead to the development of several phytoalexins—caffeic acid, scopoletin, esculetin, chlorogenic acid, isochlorogenic acid, umbelliferone, and ipomeamarone (Kuc 1972).

By contrast, Robert Scheffer (1975, pers. commun.) indicated that phytoalexins by definition are produced in response to a pathogen that penetrates the cuticle of a host. According to available data little or no phytoalexin would be found in the undisturbed tissue prior to invasion by the pathogen. Whether one uses the broader interpretation of Kuc or the narrower interpretation of Scheffer and others, phytoalexins always occur in response to a pathogen or possibly an injury or other stimulus.

Van der Plank (1975) has a different concept; he thinks of phytoalexins as "chemical inhibitors synthesized in the host plant" and discusses the phytoalexins and their possible relationships to vertical resistance in plants. He says, "We see phytoalexins and hypersensitivity as providing preformed resistance, which is resistance present before invasion by the pathogen it resists. This is directly opposed to the theory of phytoalexins and hypersensitivity as responses to the pathogen they must provide resistance against."

Some examples of phytoalexins produced in response to pathogenic microorganisms follow. A group of phytoalexins that has been studied in the Irish or white potato occurs in response to infection with the potato late blight fungus, *Phytophthora infestans*. The phytoalexins produced are rishitin, solanidine, scopoline, chlorogenic and caffeic acids, and others. Phytoalexins from cotton, alfalfa, red clover, and other plants have been produced in response to disease organisms and injuries. In the broad bean, *Vicia faba*, phytoalexins have been developed in response to inoculations with two fungus pathogens, *Botrytis cinerae* and *B. fabae* (Kuc 1972). But Scheffer (1975) reminds us that none of the toxins known to be involved in plant disease development are known to be inducers of phytoalexins.

Both Cruickshank (1965) and Kuc (1972) believe that phytoalexins are involved with disease resistance and probably with immunity. Kuc (1972) included disease resistance as an important component in phytoalexins. He suggested:

> The final proof for the role of the phytoalexin in immunity or varietal resistance must be based on tissue normally used by the infectious agent for entrance and development. . . . Induced plant protection is a tool in studying mechanisms for disease resistance and its application for practical control of disease also deserves much more attention and support. Expression of genetic information (biochemically) is the key to disease resistance.

Kuc (1979) has summarized these ideas and others in an article on biochemicals and their relationship to plant protection.

Cruickshank (1965) expressed his position as follows:

> The basic postulates of the phytoalexin theory have been confirmed and there appears good grounds for considering that pisatin plays a primary role in the disease reaction not only of the pod tissues, but also of the leaves, stems and roots of *Pisum sativum*. At first glance the occurrence of phytoalexins may appear to have little relevance as a factor determining the behavior of plant pathogens in the soil. If, however, the phenomenon of immunity, in which pisatin appears to be involved, is considered, then compounds of this type are extremely important and may in fact be primary factors in biological control.

By contrast, Robert Scheffer (1975, pers. commun.) does not think that there is sufficient evidence as yet concerning phytoalexins and their possible role in disease resistance and immunity:

None of the phytoalexins are of practical use at this time. Probably none will be useful to the plant breeder in the near future. There has been much work on 6-methoxy benzoaxolinone as it is related to the corn borer, but this compound does not qualify as a phytoalexin according to current concepts. This work, however, might be of practical significance in breeding for insect resistance. In spite of all the work on phytoalexins I would say that disease resistance in general as it is related to phytoalexins is not understood at this time.

These phenomena are complex and potentially important. Whether phytoalexins can be used by breeders and are actually involved in plant disease resistance and immunity is possible but not yet known.

Other Toxins; Related Materials from Arthropods

Responses of plants to wounding and feeding by insects may or may not be comparable to phytoalexins. For example, while feeding, the adult Colorado potato beetle and larvae wound the leaves of potato and tomato plants, inducing a rapid accumulation of a potent proteinase inhibitor throughout the plant tissues exposed to the air. The same response is achieved from mechanical wounding of the leaves, as is the case of some phytoalexins (Kuc 1972). This accumulation of a powerful inhibitor of major intestinal proteinases of animals and its rapid synthesis in response to wounds of leaves is probably a defense mechanism in plants. Its value in biological pest control and its relationship to other plant responses such as phytoalexins should be studied. Many other examples occur in plants in response to the feeding of insects (Green and Ryan 1972).

Another phenomenon that is not understood is the tremendous inhibition of growth produced in many plants by the feeding of red spiders. It is completely out of proportion to the number of spiders that are feeding. Apparently the red spider injects powerful growth inhibitors, probably into the plant phloem. This type of plant response is significant. These materials should be compared biochemically with other metabolic materials, such as phytoalexins, that are synthesized in response to outside forces working against higher plants. There are many other examples of this phenomenon among insects and other mites (Went 1970).

Soil insects that produce materials deleterious to other living organisms are reported. For example, a hemipterous insect that lives on banana roots is able to reduce the local soil population of the causal organism of the Panama disease of banana, *Fusarium oxysporum* f. sp. *cubense* (Burges and Raw 1967).

The significance of many defensive chemical substances in arthropods is unknown. Most of these substances are compounds that were initially discovered in higher plants. Their presence and particularly their significance in plants continues to be a matter of controversy. Some feel that these "secondary plant substances" do not play a role in the fundamental biochemical processes of the plants and consequently are superfluous. Others consider these substances to be defensive for the plant. The fact that plants possess materials that are known to be defensive in other organisms might be considered circumstantial evidence in support of the notion that they are also defensive in plants, utilized in adaptive evolution. Most of these secondary plant substances have never been screened systematically for toxicity, repellency, or other defensive characteristics. In cases where they resemble or are identical to defensive factors of arthropods, they should be checked. A likely supposition is that the defensive action might be somewhat similar in plants (Sondheimer and Simeone 1970).

Eisner in 1964 (Sondheimer and Simeone 1970) made such a study with the catnip plant. This plant contains nepetalactone, which excites cats. Similar materials produced by insects were found to be potent repellents. One might justifiably argue that this indicates its true adaptive significance in plants. More studies are needed of repellent and toxic materials that are normal constituents of both plants and insects.

One of these materials, discussed in detail in Chap. 5, is the so-called paper factor, which was first isolated in several American conifers and is also known to be present in insects. It is the active material in juvenile hormones in insects. These materials and other pheromones are important in specific cases of insect control. The paper factor or juvenile hormone, a normal component in several American fir trees, is felt to be an adaptive defense mechanism against insects and accounts for the frequent immunity of these trees to a wide variety of insects in nature. Again, cooperative research among entomologists, plant pathologists, plant breeders, and biochemists is very important.

The thousands of secondary plant products, alkaloids (over 4000), terpenes, and phenolics must include some that are associated with plant resistance to insects, herbivores, and plant diseases (Levin 1976). Much more research is needed on the biochemical nature of plant resistance.

In summary, it may eventually be possible, when we know the details of the biochemical nature of resistance and immunity, to give plants a biochemical treatment to confer a high level of resistance or immunity. The union of those who spray plants with chemicals and those who insist that crop breeding for resistance is the only desirable goal would combine the two most effective control techniques now utilized in plant protection.

13

Plant Resistance

 Many are sure that the best plant protection for the future will be found in plant resistance (Frankel and Bennett 1970). There are some very important advantages. Genetics controls all the characteristics of a plant— whether agronomic, horticultural, or pest management related. Susceptibility, resistance, and immunity factors are involved in almost all phenomena that affect plants. For example, we are discovering excellent plant resistance characteristics to air pollution problems. When a plant is bred for a desired characteristic, the chosen characteristic normally will persist for long periods if guarded in a careful breeding program. This pattern of resistance or immunity becomes an automatic control built into the seed or propagule and is the simplest and the least expensive plant protection technique available. The research is expensive and usually time consuming, but the ultimate cost to the grower will be no greater than the cost of the seed or propagule. It is no wonder that outstanding plants have been enthusiastically received by growers all over the world.

Resistance or immunity to pests and plant diseases is as old as each of the evolving plants. Plant diseases and insect problems have been important for thousands of years. During this period of time selection (artificial and natural) in crop plants has produced highly heterozygous and heterogeneous populations with enhanced adaptability to local environments and usually some resistance and immunity to many pests and diseases (E. Smith 1972).

Relatively poor tillage and fertilizer practices of traditional and primitive agriculture have caused the evolution of plants vigorous enough to survive and produce under relatively poor growing conditions and also less susceptible to local pests and diseases. For example, in Indonesia more than 600 Bulu rice varieties are grown. Simple selection techniques used by growers for thousands of years have developed plants adapted to a specific region and typically resistant and/or tolerant to local pests and diseases (R. Smith 1972).

185

Jennings (1976) has emphasized the importance of saving the many specific types of resistance selected over thousands of years that are represented by thousands of traditional rice (and other crop) varieties. For example, more than 30,000 different kinds of rice have been collected at the International Rice Research Institute in the Philippines.

One of the principal reasons for the success of modern agriculture is the widespread use of high-yielding, pest- and disease-resistant crop varieties. They have been developed, along with agronomically and horticulturally acceptable characteristics, as a result of cooperative plant breeding efforts of the past 75 years. At present about 75 percent of the total acreage in agricultural production in the United States is planted with resistant varieties. In alfalfa and small grains, 95–98 percent of the acreage grown is planted with varieties resistant to one or more plant diseases (Thurston 1971).

Breeding for Resistance

Plant pathologists and nematologists (who until recently were trained as plant pathologists) have always emphasized the importance of plant breeding. Many plant pathologists are convinced that plant breeding is the most significant type of biological control. The following statement is characteristic of many plant pathologists who have spent their lives in developing cooperative plant breeding programs with agronomists.

> The public pressure to get pesticides out of the environment will no doubt bring about some governmental action that is not supported by facts. There is a big push for biological control of pests. Current literature is lopsidedly concerned with insects and weeds. It is almost as though breeding for resistance to pathogenic organisms were not biological control. For the individual interested in controlling crop diseases by genetic means . . . practices the epitome of biological control and he should be a front runner in the environmental protection phase of his profession. . . . The time is ripe for a new surge of emphasis on breeding disease resistant cultivars to meet the challenge of environmental protection by biological control of plant disease. [Roane 1973]

Recently, there has also been a heartening development of interest in the production of plants resistant to insects and mites. Only a few entomologists were interested in this phase in the past.

Many workers in plant protection are disturbed by the fact that plant breeding is primarily the function of agronomists and horticulturists. Although plant resistance to pests and diseases is important, the most important goals of breeding have always been yield, quality, adaptability, vigor, and the like. To be most productive, a crop breeding program should be a cooperative one in which the program leader is an agronomist or horticulturalist. Plant protection breeders (whether pathologists, entomologists, or nematologists) should work in cooperation with agronomists and horticulturalists; this usually means a secondary but necessary role for the plant protection breeder.

Outstanding breeding programs have usually been cooperative. The people involved have in the long run been rewarded by the development of great varieties that have persisted over many years. Cooperative breeding programs were the most important factor in the Green Revolution.

There have been outstanding cooperative breeding programs in maize and small grains in the United States. Many have been largely voluntary or informal, but they have produced outstanding crop varieties with the agronomic and many of the resistance characteristics sought. Some private seed companies have also had outstanding plant breeding programs. One of the best has been the breeding of sugarcane in Hawaii (Mangelsdorf 1953). In this formal-industry, cooperative breeding program, plant breeders were teamed with workers in every other relevant discipline to develop the best possible sugarcane varieties. Warner (1953) said,

> The objective of sugarcane breeding in Hawaii reduced to its simplest terms is to produce for each environmental condition canes which give maximum yield of sugar per acre month at minimum cost. To a plant breeder this means the producing of new combinations of genes which interact with their environment, including the agronomic system under which they are grown, in such a way as to give increased yields. In the last analysis, plant breeding as a science is nothing more than accelerated and directed evolution.

Some characteristics selected in the sugarcane breeding program in Hawaii were (1) general suitability to an area; (2) sugar content (sucrose); (3) growing power or vigor, including adequate stooling; (4) freedom from tasseling and other disqualifying features; (5) stalk toughness, which allows no detrimental lodging or breaking; (6) hardness or avoidance of softness that makes cane more susceptible to borers and rats; (7) juiciness; (8) leaf system arrangement; (9) drought resistance; (10) disease resistance; and (11) insect and borer resistance. Complete records of seedling growth at the same and different locations were kept (Mangelsdorf 1953). These characteristics are quite similar to the characteristics sought in other plant species. It must be noted that most of them have little or nothing to do with plant protection—they are associated with yield, quality, vigor, and adaptability, the primary characteristics that cause growers to select a specific variety. Growers normally think of protection characteristics last unless they have a bad disease or pest problem. It appears inevitable that resistance characteristics will be put at the bottom of the priority list by plant breeders unless they are faced with a severe disease or pest situation. It is a reflection of the relative importance of disease and pest problems in the development of varieties acceptable to the grower.

Some other genetic problems are involved in plant protection—problems associated with resistance of insects to pesticides and other chemicals and the genetic variations of pathogens, insects, nematodes, and other pests that make them either more or less potent troublemakers for specific crop plants. As yet we have not been able to control the populations of pathogens, insects, mites, nematodes, and other crop pests through genetics or to utilize genetics creatively to alter them except in a very few cases.

Although much plant breeding ignores the needs of plant protection, it will increasingly emphasize a complete crop package that includes yield, quality, adaptability, vigor, and pest and disease resistance. New programs sponsored by international foundations and large private and/or industrial agricultural corporations include formal cooperative breeding programs working toward the whole package. For example, the International Rice Research Institute in the Philippines has released rice varieties that are resistant to five major pests, including both diseases and insects (Brady 1974).

Breeding work is a continual process, since sooner or later pests and disease organisms evolve that overcome much of the resistance bred into specific cultivars, a problem that has been the bane of all plant breeders. Early plant breeding was primarily devoted to single gene breeding. This can be illustrated by the development of wheat varieties resistant to rust. The average useful life for most rust resistant varieties has been about 5 years. They succumb to races of rust that have evolved or have become more significant because of the virtual elimination of other races by a new resistant crop cultivar.

Continuous single gene breeding efforts have been necessary also for crown rust of oats, Hessian fly of wheat, powdery mildew of barley, *Cladosporium* leaf mold, tobacco mosaic virus on tomato, golden nematode, and late blight of potato. In each case the life of the developed resistant varieties has been relatively short (Day 1972). However, there have been cultivars with single gene resistance, the so-called vertical type, that have remained resistant for many years—for example, the wheat cultivars that have been resistant to soil-borne wheat mosaic virus since the 1930s.

The plants with monogenic (single gene) resistance have been associated with the development of the huge so-called monocultures of plants and are usually the products of large breeding programs. This has been true of maize and of all the small grain varieties (cultivars). They have virtually driven the traditional varieties, characterized by heterogeneity and heterozygosity, out of existence. The new varieties have been higher yielding and of better quality but have usually had a narrower gene base, which has made them susceptible to disasters. In 1970 in the United States an epiphytotic of the southern corn leaf blight occurred on 90 percent of the U.S. maize acreage. Almost all major U.S. maize varieties had a common source of susceptibility to the southern corn leaf blight, and in 1970 corn blight caused a greater economic loss on a single crop in a single year than any similar agent known in the history of agriculture (Hooker 1974*a*, 1974*b*).

The new Mexican wheat varieties so widely acclaimed as a part of the Green Revolution and planted throughout Asia from India to Turkey also have a single gene base for some characters. A change in the races of wheat rust to a race of rust capable of attacking these wheats might be as disastrous as the southern corn leaf blight outbreak in the United States in 1970.

Critics of the Green Revolution who have urged a return to traditional varieties forget that these varieties were not particularly productive and lacked many of the other excellent characteristics shared by the newer varieties. Since they were not grown on such large acreages, a disaster for one of the traditional varieties (which occurred frequently) did not affect too many farmers. By contrast, the new varieties now are grown on millions of acres and are subject to widespread disaster when successfully attacked by a disease or pest.

Norman Borlaug's reply to the critics of huge monocultures should be pondered. He says, "It is far better for mankind to be struggling with new problems caused by abundance rather than with the old problems of famine" (E. Smith 1972; R. Smith 1972).

The story of the rubber tree illustrates what can happen when a wild plant, formerly widely dispersed in nature, is grown in large acreages under monocultivation. In the Amazon region in its native jungle habitat there are usually about six rubber trees, *Hevea braziliensis,* per acre. Each tree is separated from other rubber trees by many other trees, which are barriers to the wind-borne spores of the South American leaf blight caused by *Dothidella ulei.* This fungus disease did very little damage when rubber was collected from wild jungle trees, but when the rubber tree was developed as a cultivated crop on huge plantations the South American leaf blight became a very serious problem and virtually eliminated thousands of acres of rubber trees in Latin America (Thurston 1971).

These problems remind plant breeders that breeding for disease and pest resistance is a perennial problem, a continuous function (Shurtleff et al. 1972). It emphasizes the importance of inserting genetic diversity into plant breeding schemes. Great plant diversity occurs in nature and considerable diversity is found in the traditional varieties. In new breeding programs every effort needs to be made, not only in the tropics where several major disasters have occurred but also in the temperate zone where relatively few have occurred, to insert genetic diversity into plant breeding programs; broadly based multigenic (so-called horizontal) resistance needs more emphasis. When possible it would be wise to combine broadly based multigenic types of resistance with narrowly based monogenic (vertical) types (Thurston 1971).

Monogenic types of resistance have been less troublesome when many varieties, each representing a different gene for resistance, have been used. Consequently, a distinction must be made between the widespread and continuous planting of one particular genotype and the use of several genotypes. The use of one genotype as a basis for all resistance in a huge area is usually doomed to disaster, as has already been documented in the case of the southern corn leaf blight outbreak of 1970. However, when new varieties that include new genotypes are frequently introduced, the different genotypes may be intermixed over wide areas and grown successfully over many years.

Another possibility is the combination of various isogenic or single gene lines in blended or synthetic varieties that differ only in their resistance to a specific disease. They may be blended in different ratios and planted as mixed populations. In preparing these blends, the harvesting time and physical characteristics of each variety must be considered carefully. This possibility in the past would have been a breeder's nightmare but it now has potential, particularly for small grains (NAS 1968a).

Not only in developed countries and in larger plantations have problems associated with an isogenic (vertical) gene base arisen. An interesting case is discussed by Ren-jong Chiu. In 1973 three new Indica-type rice varieties were introduced into Taiwan. Chianung Sen 6 was resistant to bacterial leaf blight; Chianung Sen 11 was resistant to brown plant hopper; Chianung Sen 8 was not resistant to a particular pest but was characterized by high yield and high grain quality. All three varieties were very cold sensitive and the latter two were susceptible to bacterial leaf blight. In areas planted to Chianung Sen 11 the brown plant hopper population became extremely high. The bacterial leaf blight was so bad on the two susceptible varieties that "Kresek"-type symptoms, common in other areas of southeast Asia, were seen in Taiwan for the first time. Rice blast disease epidemics appeared where the new varieties were grown. Such problems suggested that the new varieties had too narrow a genetic base where resistance was concerned. In Taiwan, it is now recognized that to develop varieties resistant to only one disease or one insect is hazardous. When possible, the base of resistance will be broadened to include several diseases and several insects, a difficult but necessary task (Chiu 1974, pers. commun.).

Breeding results from plants with narrow isogenic (vertical) resistance are more dramatic and immediate than from plants with multigenic (horizontal) resistance. Multigenic resistance usually achieves a reasonably satisfactory field tolerance but is not as outstanding in the short run as monogenic resistance. However, many insist it will be much more helpful in the long run (Day 1972).

Van der Plank (1963) coined the term *horizontal resistance* to describe multigenic resistance, which is reasonably effective against all races of a pathogen. This resistance has also been described as uniform resistance, field resistance, tolerance, mature plant resistance, generalized resistance, and nonspecific resistance (Day 1972). The mechanisms involved in horizontal resistance are not as well understood as those of vertical resistance. The responses are likely to be varied. They also tend to be stable and continuously effective against all forms of a pathogen, even though at a lower level (Van der Plank 1963; Day 1972).

Wellman (1972) emphasized the importance of both types of resistance in the tropics and believes that resistance is potentially the most important plant disease control measure, particularly for the small farmer. Even though horizontal resistance may be harder to develop and not quite as effective as vertical resistance, its importance lies in its permanence. By contrast, Wellman pointed out that vertical or single gene resistance (also called monogenic, isogenic, or specific), although outstanding and relatively easy to isolate and manipulate, is less valuable because resistance usually will not continue over a long period of time.

The use of the multiline in introducing variability into a group of isogenic lines was first suggested by Norman Borlaug and Browning and Frey in 1969 (Browning and Frey 1969; Day 1972). A multiline cultivar is made up of a collection of lines called isolines that are nearly isogenic except that they may possess different genes for vertical resistance. Each line is produced by introducing resistance by backcrossing into a parent variety that is common to all the isolines. The multiline varieties can be changed as rapidly as available component lines are produced. The rationale is that no super pathogenic race that would be equally pathogenic on all component lines will ever develop. Cultivars that have up to ten component isolines have been released in Iowa (Day 1972).

The same general principles could be used to develop "heterolines" that might be resistant to one disease such as stem rust and also to other pests and pathogens. This process, although very time consuming, would produce groups of varieties that could be expected to last for a long time. The question the plant breeder always must ask is how much reintroduction of genetic variability and diversity can occur while maintaining acceptable quality, yield, vigor, and resistance (Day 1972).

Another type of resistance that is not often used in practical breeding programs is the hypersensitive reaction. In this case the host reponse to the pest or pathogen is localized death of a small amount of plant tissue and death, or at least limited growth, of the plant pathogen or pest. Such hypersensitive reactions are quite common with plant viruses and bacteria. Some fungi and insects also cause this type of reaction in specific plant hosts (Stevenson 1970; Day 1972). The hypersensitive reaction in tobacco to tobacco mosaic virus is being used for field control of TMV in Taiwan.

The available information shows that most plant resistance depends on physiological or biochemical plant differences. In some instances toxic substances are released by resistant plants, reducing pathogen or pest activities. Since single gene resistance seems to be quite common, it is probable that, biochemically, resistance depends on one or at most very few enzymes and the metabolic pathways and compounds they control. There is usually a continuous gradation between resistant and susceptible host plants, as can be seen in most plant disease nurseries. This phenomenon can best be explained by slight changes and gradations in the enzyme systems involved in the resistance patterns (Rohde 1960).

Resistance and immunity to plant diseases, insects, and other pests is the norm in nature. Susceptibility is the exception (Wellman 1972). He reminds us that "normally resistance is a common feature in nature, more than susceptibility. Most plants are resistant to most organisms. Only specialized parasites attack." Baker and Cook (1974) also pointed this out, noting that most pathogens are restricted to a few host species and sometimes to only one. We seldom ask why an oak tree does not get club root of cabbage or why a sycamore tree does not get Dutch elm disease, but these questions should be asked; when answered, resistance and particularly immunity will be understood and complete control of a pest or a plant disease will be possible.

The host range of the typical plant pathogen and of most pests is usually limited. Some rare weedlike pathogens, parasites, and pests have very wide host ranges. Some insects feed on a wide variety of hosts, but they also tend to be the exception. Most insects have strong preferences and some are limited to a single species of plant. The fundamental questions that must be asked and answered are: (1) Why is immunity so common in nature? (2) How is it controlled genetically and physiologically? (3) Can it be applied chemically (therapeutically) to a plant or created by either genetic or chemical means?

The possibility that we might, by a spray or other topical application, confer immunity or high resistance on a plant by utilizing the natural immunity or resistance factors found in other plants is exciting. It is being done in a limited way in a few cases. For example, Corden and Dimond (1959) increased the resistance of tomato plants to tomato wilt, *Fusarium oxysporum* f. sp. *lycopersici,* by the use of several naphthalene-substituted aliphatic compounds (growth-regulating substances). Of those used, 1 naphthaleneacetic acid produced the greatest resistance. Researchers consider the use of growth regulators to confer resistance on plants an important possibility (they might be applied somewhat as fungicides or herbicides are applied). This possibility is suggested (NAS 1968*a*):

> Indirect approaches to chemotherapy involve increasing the resistance of the host or otherwise changing the metabolism of the host so that it is no longer a suitable substrate for the pathogen. Some growth regulators appear to act in this manner. Thus one therapeutic approach would be to use compounds that produce changes in susceptible plants so that they are similar to plants having genetic resistance to diseases, where the resistance is known to have a chemical basis.

More information on the genesis of biotoxins is needed, as these phenomena may be related to the nature of disease resistance. Van der Plank (1975) argued that phytoalexins and hypersensitivity may provide preformed resistance (resistance present prior to the invasion of a particular pathogen in plants. (See discussion of phytoalexins in Chap. 12.) More complete explanations of resistance phenomena would be of great benefit in devising techniques for fast screening of large populations for resistance. Knowledge of the interactions and relationships between disease resistance phenomena and underlying biochemical processes would lead to more rapid incorporation of biochemical resistance against diseases or pests into a single crop variety or group of varieties. The needs are summarized in the following statement (NAS 1968*a*):

> New and improved breeding techniques are needed to reduce the time required for developing and testing resistant varieties, most notably in the case of perennials or woody crops. Keys to progress along these lines are increased information on the biochemical basis for resistance in plants and the factors that govern host specificity in pathogens.

McNew (1972) summarized the new approaches to breeding for resistance that are necessary in the plant protection disciplines. Resistance to diseases and pests should be given primary consideration in research funding. Each crop, seed bank, and breeding stock must be catalogued for resistance to all its known pests and diseases and their biotypes. Coupled with this is need for expanded storage facilities in seed banks and more room for maintenance of breeding stocks.

Breeding programs should be built around three relatively new concepts, according to McNew (1972). (1) Breeders should direct their efforts to seeking multigenic sources of resistance wherever possible. The monogenic resistance of the past is too easily broken down by new strains or biotypes. (2) The fundamental bases of resistance and immunity need to be determined by prolonged, intensive physical and biochemical research. We must be able to determine why a crop is resistant or immune and to manipulate the physical or biochemical factors that control resistance or immunity.

(3) We must learn how to introduce synthetic genes into the crop with the skills of molecular biology. The desired nucleotide chains would be synthesized as small fragments of DNA and RNA, which would be incorporated into the genetic structure of plants being bred.

Hedin (1977) summarizes knowledge of the biochemical nature of plant resistance and emphasizes the importance of this type of research.

Diseases

Disease resistant cultivars provide the simplest, most effective, and most economic means of controlling plant diseases. In low value per acre crops such as small grains, disease resistance is one of the few sensible approaches. Chemicals have always been too expensive. If it were not for resistance, some crops could not be grown in certain areas. Success stories in plant breeding for disease resistance are legion. Some of the most dramatic and important successes have been with rusts, smuts, and viruses of cereals; wilt-resistant crucifers, cucurbits, cotton, and tomatoes; mosaic-resistant beans; and sugar beets resistant to the curly top virus (Univ. Calif. 1972c). Resistance or field tolerance to *Fusarium* wilt, generally severe in the southeastern states and the upper Mississippi River delta areas of the United States, and satisfactory tolerance levels against *Verticillium* wilt have been bred into cotton varieties (Falcon and Smith 1973). Both *Fusarium* wilt of tomato and cabbage yellows (a *Fusarium* wilt disease) may be controlled by the use of resistant varieties.

Outstanding control of bunt or stinking smut of wheat was achieved using resistant varieties. This disease has almost disappeared from the Great Plains of the United States where it once was severe. In Europe black wart of potato has been successfully controlled by resistance. An apparently unique type of resistance is associated with several phenolic substances that occur only in the outer colored leaf scales of colored onions. These scales are antibiotic to at least two fungi, *Botrytis allii,* which causes gray-mold neck rot of onion, and *Colletrotrichum circinans,* which causes onion smudge. Certain phenolic substances have been isolated that resist these fungus diseases (Walker 1969). (See Chap. 12.)

Many diseases cannot be controlled yet by plant resistance. Plant breeders have been struggling to improve resistance to *Erysiphe graminis,* powdery mildew of cereals and grasses, for many years. Their work has been complicated by pathogenic specialization—many races of the fungus have been described and a complex resistance pattern is present. This disease is very easy to control by dusting with sulfur or spraying with Karathane, but on small grains such chemical treatments are usually too expensive to consider (Walker 1969). Several other plant diseases are too complicated thus far to control by plant resistance, and progress has been discouraging. Prolonged efforts to control wheat streak mosaic virus have only resulted in a relatively unsatisfactory field tolerance (horizontal resistance). The resistance pattern of this disease is multigenic (Swarup et al. 1956).

Several diseases associated with air pollution eventually will be controlled by plant breeding techniques. For example, as mentioned before, in response to industrial stack gases one tree may be symptomless, a neighbor may be dead, and others on the same acre may display a wide range of distinctive foliage symptoms. A single clonal line response to air pollution will typically be uniform. This wide range of sensitivity is characteristic of different plants representing different genotypes in response to air pollution and efforts to develop resistant varieties are now in progress (NAS 1968a).

There have been new developments in multiple disease-resistant lines of a few crop plants. The multiple disease-resistant lines of sorghums are good examples (Rosenow and Fredericksen 1979). High levels of resistance (to at least 12 diseases) in various combinations exist in several sorghum lines developed in Texas.

Nematodes

Resistance has been one of the most important ways of controlling nematode diseases of plants. More than 150 crop varieties in 17 major crops are resistant to one of three species of the ten most distinctive known nematodes (Good 1972b). Breeding efforts have therefore been only partially successful, since more than one nematode generally attacks a given crop. Efforts to develop multiple resistance patterns in new varieties, including resistance to several plant soil diseases, are needed. Some progress has been made with tobacco, soybeans, cotton, and alfalfa (Good 1972b).

Thus far plant breeders working with nematologists have developed nematode-resistant varieties in cotton, lespedeza, cowpeas, lima beans, soybeans, tobacco, tomatoes, peppers, grapes, and peaches. They have developed root stocks resistant to root-knot nematodes; potatoes resistant to the golden nematode; barley resistant to cereal root nematode; alfalfa and clover resistant to stem nematode; citrus root stalks resistant to citrus nematode; maize resistant to stunt nematode; soybeans resistant to soybean cyst nematode; alfalfa, oats, and barley varieties resistant to stem nematodes; and soybeans, lima beans, and cotton resistant to root-knot nematode (NAS 1968b). Figure 13.1 illustrates resistance found in soybeans to the soybean cyst nematode.

Few plants are immune to nematode attack, but resistance has been found in both cultivated and wild species. Thus resistance is known to be widely dispersed in nature and potentially important in nematode control.

Resistant plants may have either mechanical or chemical mechanisms

Fig. 13.1. Resistance in the soybean plant to the soybean cyst nematode, *Heterodera glycines*. Center: Susceptible soybean variety Hill. Sides: Resistant variety Dyer. (Courtesy J. M. Good)

to resist the entry and feeding of nematode larvae. The resistance may restrict penetration or inhibit reproduction after penetration. Breeding for resistance to nematodes must be done in conjunction with breeding for resistance to other pathogens and also in relation to the critical considerations of yield, quality, vigor, and other important agronomic and horticultural characters. Successful breeding programs have typically been cooperative programs between plant breeders, nematologists, and sometimes other plant protection personnel (Moore 1960). Both vertical and horizontal resistance to nematodes are present, just as with plant diseases (Kehr 1966).

Many problems are associated with achieving a long lasting solution. Resistant plants take many years to develop even when a good source of resistance is available. Often the resistant plants have undesirable agronomic or horticultural characteristics or are susceptible to other diseases or nematodes. Also, new biotypes of nematodes tend to appear after a few years that attack plants formerly resistant. In spite of these problems, developing plant resistance is the best practical approach to nematode control (Univ. Calif. 1972*b*).

A major difficulty in breeding for nematode resistance is raising large quantities of uniform, viable nematodes for inoculum (NAS 1968*b*).

Nematode-resistant varieties are often more effective when combined with desirable rotations and nematicides can be used as a supplementary control with low or medium levels of resistance (Good 1972*b*).

Arthropods

Genetic resistance is infrequently used for controlling insect and mite populations. Little is known about the attraction of an insect to its host and what the chemical bases for resistance are (Apple 1974). Painter (1951), one of the original proponents of insect resistance in plants, believed that this lack of knowledge could be partially explained by the lack of training in genetics received by most entomologists. He emphasized the potential importance of plant resistance to insect control:

> In contrast to the use of insecticides, where results are sudden and there is decreasing effectiveness unless reapplied, insect resistant varieties are more permanent and cumulative in effectiveness. This is especially true of low levels of insect resistance, which have not received the attention they deserve. The use of insect resistant varieties should be of increasing value around the world particularly in the coming development of integrated insect control.

The advantages of insect-resistant plant varieties include no insecticidal residues; no contamination of the environment; no harm to beneficial insects; little or no disturbance to the delicate balance between destructive insects and their natural enemies; minimum production costs; simplicity of use; and compatibility with other biological, chemical, and cultural control methods (Falcon and Smith 1973). Breeding insect-resistant crop plants is a complicated and slow process. The research involves plant breeding, insect and plant physiology, insect behavior studies, insect and plant morphology, and often a combination of insect and plant genetics. In plants resistant to insects cases of both vertical and horizontal resistance are found.

Many plant protection specialists have feared the development of new insect biotypes that could attack and feed on resistant plant varieties, but only 13 such plant-insect relationships in Hessian fly representing possibly new biotypes are known. They have occurred where resistance has been vertical. In cases where insect resistance had a complex multigene base no difficulties with new biotypes have occurred (Painter 1966). For example, certain grape phylloxera strains produce galls only on the leaves of resistant grape varieties. The larvae of certain biotypes of the Hessian fly, *Mayetiola destructor,* will survive and reproduce on the stems of certain resistant wheat varieties and seem to neutralize the usual defense of the plant. These are examples of vertical resistance and the insect biotypes developing are the equivalent of races or new biotypes of plant disease organisms. There is a range in other factors such as differences in attractiveness and suitability of different cultivars as food plants or sites for oviposition for insects. Many of these characteristics function in the same fashion as horizontal resistance in plant diseases (Day 1972).

The level of control achieved by host plant resistance as measured by yield has been much more effective than control by insecticides in the grape phylloxera, the wooly apple aphid, and the Hessian fly on wheat (Painter 1951, 1958). The value of Hessian fly resistance in 1969 was estimated at $238 million by Luginbill (1969). During 1969 over 9 million acres of resistant wheat (16 percent of the total acreage) was grown in the United States. In 13 states where Hessian fly damage is potentially great, over 50 percent of the acreage was planted to resistant wheats.

Host plant resistance is especially valuable for crops with a small profit margin—the unit value of the crop per acre is small and the acreage large. It is increasingly valuable in the developing world where individual land-holdings are too small to permit the economical use of insecticides, or where growers are not able to obtain insecticides or are not familiar with their use (Painter 1951).

Before the genetic nature of plant resistance to insect attack can be controlled in many cases we need to understand the mechanism of insect attraction to preferred hosts. Then it may be possible to manipulate genetically the chemical signals utilized by the plant to attract or repel insects for effective population management tools (Apple 1974). It is not known now whether vertical or horizontal types of resistance are involved.

Many populations of insect pests are altered after the introduction of a new host crop cultivar, demonstrating the importance of genetics in regulating insect pest populations. The genetic constitution of crop plants is changed constantly to improve yield and quality and this change also occasionally produces major changes in particular insect pest populations (Pathak 1970).

The final resistance developed to a pest may be vertical (monogenic) and not permanent, although it is likely to last longer than some detractors have indicated. It may also leave the plant completely unprotected from another important pest. The newly selected and bred varieties need to be tested for resistance to less severe pests and plant diseases of economic importance. Plant protection specialists must work constantly with plant breeders in developing new resistant varieties (Falcon and Smith 1973).

Although it has usually taken many years to develop varieties resistant to insect pests, such resistance has been surprisingly stable. Resistance to grape phylloxera in Europe has been successful for over 90 years. Resistance of wheat varieties to the Hessian fly, *Mayetiola destructor,* and the wheat stem sawfly, *Cephus cinctus,* are also examples of prolonged stability of insect resistance in crop plants (Pathak 1970). As indicated earlier, new biotypes that attack resistant plants appear quite infrequently in insects, possibly because of their complex physiology and probably because insect resistance in plants is more often multigenic than monogenic. There has been more stability in the characteristics of resistant plants than expected (Pathak 1970). Only six biotypes of the Hessian fly, four of the corn leaf aphid, *Rhopalosiphum maidis,* and three of the greenbug, *Schizaphis graminum,* have appeared and been described on wheat (Painter 1966).

By 1951 breeding for insect resistance to plants had been proved useful in such crops as potatoes, cotton, sorghum, maize, and wheat (Painter 1951). Successful results in breeding for insect resistance have been reported recently. At the International Rice Research Institute, after 10 years of research, resistance has been combined in specific rice varieties against several insect species. Certain varieties are now resistant to the striped rice borer (five species) in the genera *Chilo, Tryporyza, Chilotraea,* and *Sesamia.* Resistance is outstanding against *Chilo suppressalis.* Resistance is also present to *Nephotettix virescens,* the vector of several virus diseases (leaf-yellowing, tungro, yellow dwarf, and penyakat merah); the rice green leaf-hopper, *N. impicticepts;* and the brown plant hopper, *Nilaparvata lugens* (Pathak 1971).

The Hawaiian Sugar Planters' Association has sponsored coordinated plant breeding research on sugarcane for many years. In the 1930s some studies were made on rind hardness in relation to resistance to the beetle borer or weevil, *Rhabdoscelus obscurus.* This type of breeding was also done in Australia where *Rhabdoscelus* was a problem. A positive correlation has been found between rind hardness and resistance to these borers and many excellent resistant varieties have been produced. The program of the Hawaiian Sugar Planters' Association has always included breeding for insect resistance, resistance to plant diseases, and any other factors that could realistically be included (Asher Ota 1975, pers. commun.).

Various types of resistance need to be considered in developing plant resistance to insects. Some varieties of plants encourage egg-laying; others do not (Painter 1936). Chinch bugs raised on seedlings laid about 18 times as many eggs on Dwarf Yellow milo, a variety of grain sorghum, than on Atlas sorgo, a variety of forage sorghum, and about 25 times as many eggs on Manchuria barley than on Kanred wheat (Dahms et al. 1936). In a South African study of the relationship of hosts to the bollworm, *Heliothis armigera,* Parsons et al. (1938) found that larvae bred on a purplish flowered chick-pea, *Cicer arietinum,* developed into small, lightweight pupae and small moths that produced few eggs; those reared on the ordinary white flowered chick-pea developed large and prolific larvae that survived well. The chick-pea is one source of the bollworms that infest cotton and influences bollworm populations on cotton.

Eichmann and Webster (1940), in a study on the relationship of the pea aphid populations to alfalfa and canning peas, showed that severe infestations of the canning pea crop were derived from alfalfa, and they suggested the use of resistant varieties of alfalfa for the control of pea aphids on peas. In Kansas such studies have resulted in the isolation of several strains of alfalfa that are much more resistant to the pea aphid than the variety Ladak (Dahms and Painter 1940). Much progress has been made to control the pea aphid on the two crops by the use of outstanding resistant varieties in alfalfa. It can be seen from these examples that resistant varieties of critical alternate hosts of certain insects are very important for plant resistance (Painter 1951).

Low levels of resistance to insects in various crop plants are valuable and should not be ignored. Crops with only moderate to low resistance normally do not allow levels of insect populations as high as crops with less or no resistance, so lesser amounts of insecticides are needed for control. This combination of moderate or low levels of resistance with smaller quantities of insecticides is very useful in integrated insect control programs (Painter 1968).

All maize varieties that have been studied can be destroyed by huge populations of grasshoppers in epidemic years. However, in other years certain varieties show significantly higher resistance to grasshoppers than others. This moderate to low level resistance is very useful when combined with insecticides, because smaller quantities of insecticides are required. When grasshopper populations are relatively low, crops with a low level of resistance can be grown without any insecticides at all (Brunson and Painter 1938). The value of low levels of plant resistance was also emphasized by Fowden G. Maxwell (1975, pers. commun.): "The greatest use of insect resistant varieties in the future will undoubtedly be as one component part of a pest management system for a crop. In this type of management system the value of low levels of resistance will be greatly enhanced."

Low or moderate levels of plant resistance to insects are also significant in pasture grasses and soil conservation plants. All plants utilized in conservation and forage programs should be tested against the more important insect species that attack them, particularly plants that serve as alternate hosts to important crop insect pests. If they discourage large populations of important crop pest insects, they become useful in partial control of the insect on a crop plant grown nearby. Even low levels of plant resistance mean that the grasses and conservation species survive much better under the attack of insect pest species and will not be killed outright except when population levels are very high. Considerable information on native grasses and other conservation species with low levels of resistance is now available; more is needed. This type of information needs to be considered carefully by entomologists (Hays and Johnston 1925; Jones 1939).

Other important considerations in breeding programs can confer the equivalence of resistance to a new crop plant although the plant itself is actually not resistant. For example, cotton breeders have shown that the boll weevil can be partially controlled by the development of rapid fruiting varieties that circumvent or avoid boll weevil attack because of their early maturity (Falcon and Smith 1973). In Texas short season, early maturing cotton varieties that set fruit early in the season have been developed so that the cotton bolls often escape late season insect attacks or are no longer palatable to late season insects (Walker et al. 1978). In Africa cotton varieties have been bred to have a dense coating of long hairs on the undersurface of the leaves to make them less accessible to egg-laying by jassids—a practical type of mechanical resistance (Falcon and Smith 1973).

Prior to 1940 the wheat jointworm, *Harmolita tritici,* did considerable damage in Kansas. It is almost unknown now; the development of early maturing wheats in Kansas (largely for other reasons) solved the problem. At present wheat jointworms are found only in Kharkof and Turkey wheats and other late maturing varieties, usually in county demonstration plots that are near a grassy field border in which the native hosts of the jointworms are abundant (H. W. Somsen 1975, pers. commun.).

The field of genetics in relation to insect management and control has received much greater attention in recent years. Many severe insect problems should eventually be resolved with genetic techniques (Hoy and McKelvey 1979).

Weeds

No breeding work has been done with weeds, since the primary goal in weed control is the destruction of weeds. However, crop plants with increased resistance to herbicides have been bred. For example, there are wheat mutations with increased seedling resistance to the herbicide terbutryn, and there are mutants of certain tomato varieties with increased resistance to diphenamid. Such mutations may provide a good tool for breeding crop cultivars with resistance to certain herbicides that are useful in weed control but potentially phytotoxic to a given crop (Pinthus et al. 1972). The Hawaiian commercial sugarcane breeding program now screens all new varieties for herbicide tolerance before they are released to member companies. Several good varieties have been driven out of production primarily because of their susceptibility to antiphotosynthetic herbicides (Robert Osgood 1974, pers. commun.).

Combined Resistance

Plant resistance to insects often is combined with resistance to diseases and with other control techniques, both cultural and chemical. Low or moderate levels of resistance to insects and plant diseases can be combined with other control procedures to achieve adequate control and may permit use of smaller amounts of insecticides. Combining control programs with resistance is increasingly important.

A significant case of control of both insects and plant diseases appeared with the development of the new rice variety IR-8 by the International Rice Research Institute in the Philippines. Since the advent of IR-8, which is highly resistant to the rice green leafhopper, the incidence of this pest has decreased sharply. Since this insect is the vector of tungro disease of rice, the virus has also become much less prevalent. IR-8 in field trials typically develops about one-quarter as much tungro virus as other rice varieties that are similarly susceptible (Bae and Pathak 1968; Pathak 1970).

In Colombia, South America, IR-8 is resistant to rice delphacid, *Sogatodes orizicola,* but is susceptible to the hoja blanca virus disease transmitted by the same insect. In field plantings IR-8 remains virtually virus-free, while other varieties susceptible to the virus and to the rice delphacid become seriously infected with both the virus and the delphacid (Jennings and Pineda 1970).

The rice variety IR-20 developed by the International Rice Research Institute is the most widely grown improved variety in the Philippines, Vietnam, and Bangladesh and is becoming popular in several other countries. It displays varying degrees of resistance to the striped borer; the green leafhopper; rice blast disease; bacterial leaf streak disease; bacterial leaf blight disease; and six different soil problems—aerobic acid soils, aerobic neutral soils, iron toxicity, phosphorus deficiency, zinc deficiency, and reduction products. It has a reasonably good field resistance to the tungro virus and the grassy stunt virus, two severe virus diseases of rice. The variety, however, is susceptible to the brown plant hopper (Pathak et al. 1973). It is the result of probably the best cooperative breeding program ever developed and includes outstanding agronomic characteristics and resistance to insects, plant diseases, and abiotic crop production problems common to Asian rice fields and elsewhere. IR-20 also is high yielding with excellent grain quality and enormous vigor and adaptability (Pathak 1970).

In Texas considerable progress has been made in the development of cotton varieties that are resistant to several of the important cotton insect pests and diseases. Excellent resistance to bacterial blight of cotton and good levels of resistance to *Verticillium* wilt are now available (Huffaker 1974).

The Hawaiian Sugar Planters' Association sugarcane breeding program breeds for outstanding agronomic characteristics in new sugarcane varieties, horizontal and vertical resistance to six diseases, resistance to all the important known insect pests, and the effects of herbicides on the cane. The result is a group of varieties so outstanding that no insecticides have been necessary for many years. Only one fungicide, benomyl (Benlate), is used on seed pieces. Several herbicides are used routinely for the control of weeds (Robert Osgood 1974, pers. commun.).

Many combination control programs utilize resistant varieties. Excellent combination control measures used against Hessian fly on wheat are (1) late sowing in the fall, (2) destruction of volunteer wheat, (3) destruction or plowing under of stubble, and (4) resistant varieties. Excellent, consistent combination control measures for the wheat stem sawfly are (1) plowing under stubble in the fall, (2) crop rotation with an immune crop, and (3) growing solid stem varieties resistant to the insect (Metcalf et al. 1951).

There are also combinations of nematode and root disease control that owe their principal effectiveness to resistant varieties. The inheritance patterns of some combinations of this sort are known, but in most cases the details of the nature of resistance are not known. Nematode-fungus complexes and their relationships to resistance have only recently been considered by plant geneticists. Important potentials for a team approach to combined nematode and soil-borne disease control by plant resistance are present (Van Gundy 1972).

Some maize hybrids are now resistant to the root lesion nematode, corn rootworm, and stalk rot. One of these hybrids is shown in Fig. 13.2.

Root-knot nematodes alone damage cotton badly; in the presence of other microorganisms and particularly in the presence of the *Fusarium* wilt organism, *Fusarium oxysporum* f. sp. *vasinfectum,* they are much more severe. The nematodes predispose the cotton plants to infection or perhaps furnish ideal infection courts for the fungus. In such cases it is important to breed for resistance to all organisms present in a complex and particularly for nematode resistance, since nematodes appear to predispose plants to this type of soil disease (NAS 1968*b*).

Many possibilities to be exploited in combined resistance programs against various pests and plant diseases have been described by Russell (1978).

Germ Plasm Storage

A major problem associated with the development of effective long-range cooperative plant breeding programs is long-term storage of germ plasm— diverse seed stocks that contain genes from nature or genes manipulated and in a sense captured via breeding programs. It seems impossible to maintain all the seed and breeding stocks that should be kept for long-term consideration. Traditional or primitive varieties of crop plants as well as wild plants need to be stored. Individual plant breeders cannot maintain large and diverse nurseries of seed and planting stocks and irreplaceable seed and breeding stocks have been discarded because of the lack of time, funds, and nursery space. New, well-financed seed and breeding stock storage banks

Fig. 13.2. Combined plant resistance in a maize hybrid to root lesion nematode, corn rootworm, and stalk rot. Right: Susceptible hybrid. Left: Resistant hybrid. (Courtesy Malcolm Shurtleff)

and nurseries are needed, in which seed and breeding stocks can be kept indefinitely for use by plant breeders from all over the world. It must be done on a national or an international scale to be successful. We dare not discard the plant diversity that nature has evolved in thousands of ecological niches throughout the earth.

In the United States the North Central Plant Introduction Station and several other regional stations store seed and breeding stocks, and there are a number of centers in other parts of the world. Many more are needed.

Type-culture Centers

A closely related matter is the need for many more state, national, and international centers for type-cultures and maintenance of disease and pest species of all types. They are needed for pathogenic microorganisms (i.e., bacteria, fungi, and mycoplasmas), nonorganisms (i.e., viruses), and various pest animals (i.e., nematodes, insects, mites, and their biotypes).

Research workers gradually accumulate important cultures from past research that, because of lack of time and funds, cannot be maintained properly. They need to be shifted to state, national, or international centers for preservation and maintenance and made available to other researchers who need to study, use, or compare them with local collections. Such culture, disease, and pest maintenance and preservation centers are particularly valuable for screening plant collections for resistance to pests and plant diseases.

14

Vertebrate Pests

 Control of vertebrate pests has often been, ignored by people in plant protection. Agronomists and horticulturists probably have dealt more with vertebrate pests than individuals in plant protection. Growers often have severe problems with vertebrate pests. Zoologists, veterinarians, and physicians have been interested in vertebrate pests as related to public health more than as related to food production. Consequently, researchers in vertebrate pest control are people with a variety of backgrounds, usually people confronted with severe vertebrate pest problems in a specific location.

Many controls have been developed to solve problems of rodents but they have all been disappointing. Even the rodenticide warfarin leaves much to be desired. Rodents are intelligent and reproduce with amazing rapidity. When they are eliminated in a small area new populations move in quickly to take their places.

We have no endangered species in any of the major pest groups. Certainly, the major pest rodents seem to adapt well to every effort to destroy them. (Also, no hue and cry has arisen concerning possible endangered species among insect pests that are being destroyed.)

It appears that rodenticides and other vertebrate biocides are most effective when used in conjunction with other methods, such as control of weeds, cultural controls, and in some cases fungicides. It is worthwhile to discuss the control of vertebrate pests as it relates to cooperative and interdisciplinary plant protection procedures that might be developed.

Few fungicides or plant pathological materials have been useful in destroying or repelling vertebrate pests. In one case fungicides have functioned effectively as repellents to deer and big game. The fungicides zinc dimethyl dithiocarbamate (ZAC) cyclohexyl amine complex and TMTD-Ibis (dimethyl-thiocarbamoyl disulfide) protect young orchard trees from deer without destroying the deer (NAS 1970).

A book on the subject of vertebrate pest control was written by Jackson and Marsh (1977).

Rodents

Rodent control has been difficult in the wet tropics. Living conditions for rodents are sometimes improved by cover crops and certain favored foods. Thus growers may actually create preferred rodent habitats. Cutting forests and permitting extensive overgrazing of rangelands also tend to develop favored habitats and to create rodent migration patterns deleterious to crops (NAS 1970).

On the other hand, small rodent and mammal populations are often eliminated by constant or repeated disturbance of their habitats by cultivation in maize and wheat fields and by minimizing or eliminating fence rows and border areas. Their necessary cover is destroyed repeatedly. This cultural control is generally more effective than any known chemical method. Robert Osgood (1974, pers. commun.) of the Hawaiian Sugar Planters' Association has emphasized the importance of altering the habitat to control rats in sugarcane. He also stresses the importance of good weed control at the edges of cane fields. The favored habitat is destroyed in wide bands around the cane fields to discourage rat entrance into fields.

A recently developed rodenticide, Bromadiolene, appears to be very effective against several species of rats, ground squirrels, pocket gophers, and deer mice (Marsh and Howard 1979). Only time will tell how effective it remains. (Warfarin also was expected to solve the rat problem.)

Feakin (1970) summarized problems associated with rodent control in rice. They are characteristic of most tropical situations:

Lasting control cannot be achieved by killing the rodent. Reinfestation always occurs sooner or later through reproduction among the survivors or through immigration. There is a tendency for some methods, particularly poisons, to become less effective with continual use. There are several important ways in which damage to rice can be reduced without killing the rodents concerned. Weed control both within the crop and along the bunds and dykes separating fields has an important limiting effect on rat population. The clearance of bush or swamp close to rice fields also limits the number of rodents by reducing sources of food and cover during periods of the year when no rice is available. Further reduction in alternative food sources for rodents can be achieved by encouraging a monocultural system in areas particularly suited to rice. Maintaining the water levels in rice fields may prevent rodent damage to germinating seed and reduce damage at other times. Harvesting before the rice is fully ripe saves grain that might be lost from shattering and also allows less grain to fall to the ground for rodents to pick up. Poison control can be conducted best in the off season when remaining rodents are confined to relatively small areas where food is scarce rather than when they are widely dispersed among the crop.

Rats have been so difficult to control in peanuts that the crop has been abandoned in many islands of the South Pacific (Brady 1974). Since the advent of no-tillage maize production in the U.S. Corn Belt, field mice have become a serious problem in some areas (B. D. Blair 1979, pers. commun.).

It is apparent that rodent control, to be effective, must be developed along interdisciplinary lines. Cultural and weed control techniques, particularly, need to be combined with the standard chemical poisons for effective control.

Large Animals

In the tropics there are locally important cases of plant destruction by large vertebrates such as elephants and various species of ruminants. These special cases are not discussed in detail here. Most of them must be solved by furnishing alternative food supplies, adequate barriers, or similar techniques that do not actually destroy the animal but keep it from destroying food crops. Poisons are not the answer; all these animals are valuable creatures and some are actually endangered species. The losses sustained by the local farmers, however, are often very great and serious thought and effort must go into developing adequate control methods. Research in the development and utilization of repellents to keep the animals from feeding on plants being protected is important. Insecticides or fungicides that could also serve as repellents for vertebrate pests (both large and small) would be an added bonus.

Birds

Birds, particularly migratory birds, are destructive in various parts of the world. For example, the quella bird, a small sparrow-sized bird found in vast numbers in parts of Africa, holds the power of life or death over large numbers of small farmers—and no effective control is known (Brady 1974).

Birds can easily fly away, are brighter than many animals, and are more difficult to discourage and kill. Again, research in the development of chemical repellents is important. Few effective bird repellents are available and none are used extensively, although some insecticidal and fungicidal sprays may discourage bird feeding temporarily. Few good chemical control methods for birds are available to protect crop plants. It seems strange that relatively little effort has gone into the development of bird repellents when one considers the enormous crop losses caused by birds in many parts of the world.

Mesural applied to portions of a cornfield effectively controls redwinged blackbirds, and it is also useful on cherries and plums. A variety of noisemakers, some having explosive devices, are used with varying success. They are used in pecan orchards to reduce crow damage and are used widely to reduce blackbird damage on a variety of crops (B. D. Blair 1979, pers. commun.).

The best control methods designed so far for birds are built around cultural procedures, weather factors and climate, various agronomic procedures, and some resistant varieties. Emphasis is needed in consideration of varieties resistant to birds. For example, a maize (corn) resistant to bird attack has been developed in New Jersey and Delaware (Buckley and Cottam 1966). Maize planted near marshlands in these states normally gets twice as much bird damage as maize planted elsewhere (however, soybeans can be planted near the marshes satisfactorily). The resistant maize has a tight husk that extends beyond the tip of the ear. In several New Jersey townships all farmers changed to the resistant maize in 1964 and had much less damage. Birds are often fussy about food and the development of unattractive varieties presents good control possibilities. A high tannin milo sorghum with sharp awns has been quite effective in bird control (NAS 1970).

Another genetic mechanism helpful in controlling birds is the use of quickly ripening grain varieties that reduce the period of exposure to attack (NAS 1970). There are several such varieties of rice in Arkansas (Buckley and Cottam 1966).

Weather conditions influence bird damage to crops. During severe winter weather grain losses from birds increase, particularly in storage areas, and crops still in the field when migrating birds move through during severe weather suffer great losses. Bird feces contamination occurs in feedlots and storage areas during severe weather when birds remain feeding in protected areas (NAS 1970). Bird sanctuaries or refuges with good cover and adequate food reduce crop losses tremendously (Buckley and Cottam 1966). It is often desirable to plant, just for the birds, a few rows of preferred foods such as sorghums and millets near the larger bird habitats to protect crops from bird losses. This practice has been quite effective in some cases.

Cultural methods, such as use of several crop varieties, the method or time of planting, and time of harvesting crops, are often helpful (Buckley and Cottam 1966). In each case the pests' times of arrival and departure in the spring and fall must be considered. Planting can occur either before or after the birds move north. Seed planted deep is much less likely to be discovered by birds and often reduces the loss of sprouted seed. Plants seeded underwater, such as rice, are protected from birds until the seedlings have emerged. Another successful technique is to plant crops that mature when the birds' natural or preferred foods are abundant (NAS 1970). Any cultural practices that make crops less available to birds will reduce damage. The techniques vary with the species because of different feeding habits, foods, and migration times and patterns.

Harvesting techniques are often important (Buckley and Cottam 1966). For example, maize growers who use artificial dryers can harvest their crop earlier and greatly reduce bird damage; also, much less grain is shattered and (as a plant pathological control bonus) much less mold develops.

Peanuts dried in the open in shocks are available to birds for weeks. Use of artificial dryers virtually eliminates bird losses and also the labor and cost of shocking. Use of quick drying systems for crops is an excellent bird control procedure and has many other benefits, such as reduction in the growth of fungi on seeds (Buckley and Cottam 1966).

Vertebrates as Pest Controls

Birds and many other vertebrates (such as toads, snakes, skunks, shrews, moles, and even fish) are valuable to agriculture as ardent consumers of insects. In fact, they are often very valuable in insect control, as are chickens and other domestic fowl in specific situations. Growers should be made aware of this. Research can help growers decide whether their value in insect control exceeds losses caused by their destruction of food. This trade-off must be considered particularly as it relates to migrating birds. Metcalf et al. (1951) summarized the value of birds:

> Birds, particularly young birds, may eat their weight in insects each day. Even those species which are largely grain feeders such as the blackbirds and English sparrows will feed mainly on insects when they are in large numbers and easy to obtain. While birds cannot be expected to become sufficiently abundant in any thickly settled farming area for us to depend upon them alone to prevent insect damage they are of great value in insect control. Most birds earn many times over the fruits and berries they take from our orchards and gardens. They are worth all the protection we can afford them.

More than half of the food that birds eat is reported to be insects, and among the vertebrates birds are the most effective enemies of insects.

Some vertebrates, but no birds as far as known, have been carried from country to country for the purpose of controlling insects. The giant toad of Mexico, Central America, and South America has brought the white grubs destructive to sugarcane in Puerto Rico under control. The giant toad has also been introduced into Hawaii, the Philippines, and the West Indies for insect control (Metcalf et al. 1951).

Many small mammals such as moles, skunks, and shrews feed extensively on insects and destroy large numbers of soil insects, especially larvae. Ground squirrels eat large numbers of white grubs and other soil insects as a small part of their diet.

Some species of salamanders, snakes, and newts eat largely insects and are quite useful in local insect control. The toad's food is made up almost entirely of insects. It is one of our most valuable small vertebrates in field and garden. In 24 hours an actively feeding toad fills its stomach about four times with insects (Metcalf et al. 1951).

In addition to the cat and occasionally the dog, several species of snakes are extremely efficient in destroying rodents, a fact which unfortunately is often unknown or ignored by farmers and the general public.

Geese are used in various places in the world in certain crops on small fields or plots in the control of weeds.

15

Integrated Control

Concepts of Pest Management

Entomologists have been under pressure to develop new methods of insect and arthropod control because of the problems associated with the use of insecticides. The new arthropod control methods have been called "pest management" or "integrated pest management" (or "control"). Although they often have been regarded as synonymous, they are not.

Pest management is the broader term. It includes all possible approaches toward control of arthropods and many other pests, ranging from a single-component control method such as spraying insecticides to the most sophisticated combination of control mechanisms used in a systems approach. Pest management, then, is a general term that applies to any type of pest population manipulation; it attempts to consider the social, environmental, and economic needs of the grower and of people in general (FAO 1973*b*). This point of view has become even broader and more inclusive recently (NAS 1975*a*).

Integrated pest management (*control*) is a pest management system—a combination of arthropod and other pest control procedures. It is usually a systems approach to pest management within the context of a particular environment, taking into account the population dynamics of a particular pest species. It attempts to use all the known suitable techniques of control to maintain the particular pest population at a level below that which causes economically important injury to the crop. Integrated control depends to a great extent on an understanding of population dynamics of pests and of potential pests, the ecology and the economics of a given cropping system, the potential predators and parasites, and the effects on the environment of particular pesticides. It includes not only the pest management systems approach but all attempts to use combinations of controls in an integrated way on a given pest (FAO 1973*b*). Apple (1974) and others have favored the term "integrated pest management" rather than "integrated pest control"

211

because they feel the true goal of this research is to manage pest populations rather than to control or eliminate them.

Another term, not often used, is *supervised control*. It is often an integrated type of pest management built around the use of a minimum amount of pesticide under the direction of a specialist. It emphasizes the minimum use of the right kind and amount of pesticide based on an assessment of the pest population density and its potential for crop damage. It considers ecological implications and natural enemies and attempts to apply the pesticide at an ideal time in a minimum but adequate amount. The amount of pesticides used is hoped to cause minimal undesirable side effects in the environment. Supervised control is an essential part (but only a part) of many integrated pest control systems (FAO 1973b).

The term *integrated control* actually dates back at least to 1954 in the work of Smith and Allen (1954). The basic ideas of integrated control of insects are well over 100 years old and were advocated by several early entomologists who recognized that economic entomology and arthropod control should have an ecological base (R. Smith 1972). A classic early example of integrated control and probably the first use of insect scouts occurred in Arkansas in 1925 (Lincoln, no date). Smith and Hagen (1959) first emphasized modern integrated control and pointed out that it was a combination of biological and chemical control methods. The chemical control was to be used only when necessary in a way that would cause as little disruption as possible to the biological control techniques available.

Pickett and MacPhee (1965) indicated that integrated control should keep arthropod populations below economic tolerance levels by using environmental resistance supplemented with the use of selective pesticides when pest population levels become too high. They felt that the aim of integrated control was to increase the environmental resistance as much as possible to reach a balance of maximum stability under a given set of environmental conditions. Environmental factors controlling population movements and levels of noxious arthropods that should be manipulated, if possible, are:

1. Climate
2. Natural enemies
3. Condition of the host plant
4. Cultural measures used in growing the crop
5. Technical control measures used in growing the crop

Some of these can be manipulated; others cannot. In the case of climate, it is possible to avoid severe climates or alter cropping patterns and concentrate on more favorable environments for arthropod control.

Smith and Van den Bosch (1967) expanded the concept of integrated pest control:

> Integrated control is a pest population management system that utilizes all suitable techniques either to reduce pest populations and maintain them at levels below those causing economic injury or to so manipulate the populations that they are prevented from causing such injury. Integrated control achieves this ideal by harmonizing techniques in an organized way, by making the techniques compatible and by blending them into a multifaceted flexible system. Practical experience and logic have shown that we must in the final analysis integrate not only chemical and biological control but all procedures and techniques into a single pattern aimed at profitable production and minimum damage of the common environment.

This system has an ecological base and is built around many management techniques, both natural and manipulated.

Lawson (1966) summarized the advantages of integrated control:

> Almost always achieving control in this way has involved manipulating insecticide treatments so that populations of parasites and predators occurring naturally would be conserved to reduce populations of the pest insect. Compared with the unrestricted use of insecticides, such programs have several advantages. The most important of these are:
> 1. The total quantity of insecticides required is reduced so that the crop contains less toxic residues and there is less contamination of the environment.
> 2. Development of resistance in the host (pest) population may be delayed or prevented.
> 3. Conservation of natural enemies tends to prevent the host (pest) from increasing rapidly or outbreaks of other phytophagous insects from developing.
> 4. The total cost of control may be reduced considerably.

Note that Lawson considered chemical insecticides and biological controls but did not mention cultural controls via manipulation of the crop or plant resistance to insects.

By 1972 a much broader concept, including more control techniques, had developed, and is summarized (USGPO 1972):

> Integrated pest management is an approach which maximizes natural controls of pest populations. An analysis of potential pest problems must be made. Based upon knowledge of each pest and its environment and its natural enemies, farming practices are modified (such as changes in planting and harvesting schedules) to affect the potential pests adversely and to aid natural enemies of the pests. If available, seed which has been bred to resist the pests should be planted. Once these preventive measures are taken, the fields are monitored to determine the levels of the pests, their natural enemies and important environmental factors. Only when the threshold level at which signifi-

cant crop damage from the pest is likely to be exceeded should suppressive measures be taken. If these measures are required, then the most suitable technique or combination of techniques such as biological controls, use of pest specific diseases, and even selective use of pesticides must be chosen to control a pest while causing minimum disruption of its natural enemies. This approach differs markedly from the traditional application of pesticides on a fixed schedule. In general, use of the integrated pest management approach should lead to greatly reduced environmental contamination from pesticide use and to many fewer problems with pest resistance and secondary outbreaks while maintaining or improving our current ability to prevent pest damage.

In a discussion of integrated pest management (Glass 1975), plant breeding for resistance to insects is given primary emphasis for the first time and the use of pesticides is deemphasized somewhat. Included in the group of pests considered as possibilities for integrated control are insects, rodents, nematodes, weeds, and plant pathogens. Other areas included are biological controls, cultural controls, autocidal controls, pesticides, insect attractants and repellents, growth regulators, quarantine, and eradication. The many abiotic problems that afflict plants are excluded probably because they are of primary concern to plant pathologists, agronomists, and horticulturists.

Another 1975 work emphasized the fact that the concept of integrated pest control is constantly expanding and becoming more inclusive. It listed the areas mentioned above, again excluded all discussion of abiotic maladies (NAS 1975), and recommended biological and chemical controls after all possible agronomic and plant resistance control techniques had been used.

By 1970, as Huffaker (1970) pointed out, the procedural manual for establishing an integrated control program for cotton pests included not only standard biological controls by predators and parasites but also the development of scouting and trapping programs with supervised control, an analysis of economic injury levels of each pest species, an attempt to manage the agroecosystem from an ecological point of view, the role and use of any microbial controls of the pest or pests, possible use of selective pesticides or possibly a selective use of pesticides, the role and use of cultural or agronomic control techniques, and use of plant varieties resistant to the pests.

As Huffaker (1970) stressed, such integrated programs of control develop gradually: "In much of this work it is necessary to develop the integrated control program in step by step modifications of an existing, previously rather unilateral pesticide program." He emphasized doing the best one can each year with any modifications that are made in existing control programs and gradually evolving an integrated control program for the situation.

Several people have emphasized, however, that in an integrated control program chemical pesticides must remain at the center (NAS 1969):

> Each control technique (in integrated control) has a potential role to play in concert and harmony with the others and a major technique such as the use of pesticides can be the very heart and core of integrated systems. Chemical pesticides will continue to be one of the most dependable weapons of the entomologist for the foreseeable future. There are many pest problems for which the use of chemicals provides the only acceptable solutions. . . . The use of pesticides for pest control is not an ecological sin. When their use is approached from the sound base of ecological principles, chemical pesticides provide dependable and valuable tools for the biologists. This use is indispensable to modern society.

Very few integrated control programs have developed into a practical approach for controlling pests. Several problems probably account for this. The first is emphasized by Good (1974*b*):

> Growers must become convinced and have confidence that integrated pest management practices are an improvement over previous methods of managing pests. Accurate information and consultation must be provided growers so that they can make management decisions based on knowledge of pest densities and the economic benefits of alternate control decisions. Accurate records must be maintained not only of pest populations but also of weather, soil and crop conditions, dates and amounts of pesticide applied, other production inputs, and assessment of yield and quality in order to determine the economic benefits to growers. Methods of monitoring pests must be effective and accurate, [and] the pest control decisions must be made in relation to probable losses so that the potential for damage can be predicted and treatment needs [can] be determined for maximum effectiveness and compatibility with other farm operations.

The basic question of economics must be solved before integrated control programs will be accepted routinely on a large scale.

Huffaker and Smith (1972) emphasized a point made also by Corbet (1971) that the principal constraints on integrated control come from the extreme pressures on arable land and the complete interdependence of economics and agriculture. The goals in crop production have been to achieve optimum or maximum short-term yield by exploiting fossil fuel energy resources. Modern insecticides have been part of a subsidy that includes fossil fuels. Corbet feels that as long as short-term yields are foremost in the farmer's mind the chances of utilizing integrated control techniques are minimal. However, when the goals of integrated controls become more important through political and social pressures for a cleaner environment, the trend will gradually move toward developing the more reasonable practices of integrated control. Insect resistance and other insecticide-induced problems that deny the achievement of short-term control objectives will tend to force a change in the direction of integrated pest control. Corbet and also Huffaker and Smith emphasized that integrated control techniques will have to be utilized eventually to safeguard the environment and solve several other agricultural problems created by the excessive use of insecticides. Burges and Hussey (1971) emphasized another problem—the scarcity of selective chemicals and the frequent necessity of using a wide-spectrum chemical material in as selective a manner as possible.

A number of human factors are associated with the adoption of integrated pest control systems (FAO 1971). The special characteristics of cropping systems and of individual farmers must be considered. There are questions of mixed versus monoculture cropping, types of plants being grown, size of planting, dispersion of plants, patterns of planting, general education of the populace, technological levels of the country or the agricultural system, problems of land tenure, and the psychological and cultural characteristics of individual growers. A dedicated group of consultants (such as extension people) with knowledge of integrated control techniques is necessary for success. The type of local government and the political climate of a country also may determine whether integrated programs can be used. By 1979, integrated pest management (IPM) projects were initiated in all states in the United States and two territories. Greatest opportunities appeared to be in the area of systems research involving management of insects, diseases, nematodes, and varietal methods of control (Good 1979).

Campbell (1972) pointed out that integrated control programs will be subject to change periodically as conditions change. He emphasized that "much of the value of a management system should lie in its ability to inform the decision maker that it is becoming obsolescent, and to provide explicit mechanisms for self-renewal."

Pathak and Dyck (1973) think simple systems of integrated pest control in the tropics are a necessity:

> In spite of the serious yield losses inflicted on the rice crop in tropical Asia by insect pests, most of it is either left unprotected from pest damage or receives only partial protection. It is doubtful if farmers . . . would adopt sophisticated or intensive pest control practices in the near future. What is needed at present is a simple combination of different methods of control which, even though not highly efficient, should be inexpensive and relatively nonhazardous. Pesticides would only be used as needed, when available.

R. Smith (1972) also stressed the importance of a broad ecological approach to pest control in the less developed countries in the tropical and subtropical world. The biotic elements of population regulation are often dominant in biological regulation. For example, well-established biotic controls of a number of pests of tropical plants—coconuts, tea, rubber, cotton, oil palm, and citrus—are often revealed when disrupted by the introduction of chemical pesticides. In certain crops such as rice and cabbage the biotic controls do not seem to be adequate but biological control agents have given at least partial control. The plant pest specialist must combine these natural and partial controls with other measures such as resistant plant varieties, agronomic or cultural controls, and necessary chemical controls for what is hoped to be a sound economic protection system. Integrated control systems can often be developed from a virtually undisturbed base, since few or no chemical pesticides have been used.

Huffaker (1971) also mentioned the possibility of utilizing integrated pest control effectively and quickly in the developing countries of the tropics:

> There is cause to look at the pest control procedures in many tropical crops, for integrated techniques can often be developed without the prior need for highly sophisticated, time consuming and expensive ecological studies (notwithstanding their ultimate desirability) to give far more effective as well as cheaper results.

Huffaker thinks that integrated control is not only a possibility but eventually a virtual necessity in the perennial plantation crops.

J. Lawrence Apple (1975, pers. commun.) discussed an activity that has contributed to the emergence of integrated pest management—the Pest Management and Related Environmental Protection contract directed by Ray Smith and funded by USAID through the University of California at Berkeley. Through this project integrated pest management teams have been sent to many areas of the world in an attempt to make scientists and government officials in the United States and in developing countries aware of the need to improve pest management programs as a part of overall agricultural development. Apple thinks that this program has been very effective.

The general prognosis for the eventual use of integrated control in the developing world appears to be excellent. Integrated control probably will be developed and utilized on a large scale in the developed world also in the foreseeable future. Integrated pest management (IPM) is reviewed by Smith and Pimental (1978) and in the book edited by Apple and Smith (1976).

Arthropods

Probably the oldest attempt at integrated control was begun in Arkansas in the boll weevil scouting program that began in 1925 (Boyer et al. 1962; Lincoln et al. 1963). It has always included agronomic, cultural, weather, and environmental information; the possibilities for use of biological control; a survey of insects present; population estimates; and a recommendation for insecticide use. Recently it has added information on weeds and plant diseases. This program started with one scout, James Horsefall (a plant pathologist), who was then a student at the University of Arkansas. It now has over 150 summer scouts and is carried out on a statewide basis as an extension sponsored program throughout the cotton growing areas.

Other examples of integrated control that began long before the name was coined are given by Metcalf et al. (1951). (Remember that these measures were developed before the advent of DDT and other synthetic organic insecticides.) The tobacco flea beetle was controlled in seedbeds by a combination of cultural practices and insecticide treatments. The tobacco budworm was controlled by the destruction of crop trash and fall plowing in combination with poison bait. The tobacco hornworm was controlled by handpicking the worms when labor was inexpensive, by fall and winter plowing to destroy stubble and stalks, and by insecticides when necessary.

Lawson (1966) gave some examples of specific integrated control measures. Two flies, the oriental fruit fly, *Dacus dorsalis,* and the melon fly, *D. cucurbitae,* were eradicated from several locations in the Marianas islands by a combination of male-sterile insects, attractants, and appropriate insecticides when necessary. In North Carolina a great reduction in tobacco hornworms, *Protoparce sexta,* has been achieved by a combination of light traps, a chemosterilant and sex attractant in the light trap, and cultural control techniques.

Ganyard and Ellis (1972) reported a tobacco extension pest management pilot project in North Carolina in which a systems approach is being attempted. The data procured and a computer printout with the best available data and recommendations are sent to farmers and county agents. The goals and techniques are summarized:

> The immediate goal of the pilot project is to establish a more ecologically, economically, and socially acceptable system for protecting tobacco from insect pests. Four principles are being integrated on an area wide basis to achieve this goal.
> 1. Maximum natural suppression of pests by beneficial species.
> 2. Application of selected insecticides made only when pest population levels exceed the economic threshold (as determined by weekly scouting or survey).
> 3. Effective sucker control through properly timed application of chemicals.
> 4. Early thorough stalk destruction, to reduce late season insect food supply and hence check buildup of over wintering pest populations.
> This approach provides an effective area wide pressure on the general pest population while avoiding undue suppression of beneficial species.

Insect control problems on maize are extremely complex, as emphasized in a maize insect workshop (Huber 1972). Entomologists at the workshop developed nine recommendations for integrated insect control on maize:

1. Early planting—beneficial except in the case of the European corn borer.

2. Use of the best possible adapted or resistant plant varieties with optimum fertilization.

3. Emphasis on pheromone research for possible control of the European corn borer.

4. Careful control of irrigation—particularly important for control of the European corn borer and the corn rootworm.

5. Early harvesting of all late planted maize plus consistent use of dryers whenever possible—emphasized for partial control of the corn rootworm and European corn borer.

6. Use of crop rotation with soybeans and possibly with alfalfa—use of grasses in the rotation should be avoided, since many grasses encourage the development of pest insects and function as alternate hosts.

7. Use of minimum tillage planting systems despite some unfavorable results for insect (and disease) control. It was felt that agronomic, economic, and soil conservation benefits in favor of minimum tillage were of great significance. (Specific positive factors were increased water retention, decreased fertilizer and pesticide runoff, and overall environmental benefits.)

8. Development as soon as possible of accurate economic threshold levels for all maize insect pests.

9. Continued use of chemical pesticides only when absolutely essential. It was felt that there was no realistic way to eliminate these at present and still maintain necessary levels of production.

Petty (1972) (reporting on Illinois maize insect recommendations) suggested several other important factors. He stressed the maintenance of parasite and predator levels for maize insects and the encouragement of any insect diseases present (he pointed out that Illinois insect control in maize in recent years has been remarkably good). He suggested insecticide seed treatments on maize and recommended the use of insecticides for the control of corn rootworm and the European corn borer and insecticide baits for the control of cutworms until adequate biological or cultural controls are developed for these three insects.

Olkowski et al. (1974) reported success in an integrated program aimed at controlling all important insect pests on urban trees with minimal use of insecticides. It is a combination of cultural, physical, microbial, and biological control procedures combined with selective use of insecticides.

Costs and environmental contamination have been reduced and citizen complaints have been nearly eliminated.

Pathak (1969) and Pathak and Dyck (1973) reported outstanding success in integrated control of rice insects in the tropics. They used a combination of insect-resistant plant varieties, insecticides, and sex attractants for the control of several rice insects and diseases. Much emphasis was placed on the development of combination resistant varieties at the International Rice Research Institute in the Philippines. They reported selection IR-532-E-576 as resistant to borers; tolerant to green leafhoppers and brown plant hoppers; and partially resistant to the tungro virus, bacterial leaf blight, bacterial leaf streak, and several local races of blast disease. Hybrids are being developed with very high resistance to the tungro virus, bacterial leaf blight, bacterial leaf streak, and several local races of blast disease. Also, hybrids being developed with very high resistance to the green leafhopper and the brown plant hopper should help control the two viruses, grassy stunt and tungro, that are transmitted by these insects. The insecticides used were usually either benzene hexachloride (BHC) or Diazinon (dimpylate) in the paddy water. Adding the insecticide to the paddy water eliminates the contact toxicity that destroys predators and parasites when leaf spray techniques are utilized and leaves the predators and parasites available on the plants for biological control. The introduction of other predators and parasites for biological control has been attempted but without much success.

A sex attractant (pheromone), produced by young females, has been isolated for rice stem borer males. The males are attracted and captured in traps and then are chemically sterilized by food sterilants. The sterile males are released and the result is the laying of unfertilized eggs, resulting in about a 50 percent reduction in stem borer populations (Pathak and Dyck 1973). The combination of these procedures on rice has made it possible to use much less insecticide than formerly. This program illustrates a creative use of integrated control techniques on one of the world's most important crops. Biodegradable insecticides are also used to minimize environmental pollution and insecticides are utilized as a root coat in the transplanting of young rice plants. Root coat treatments are quite effective in protecting the crop from rice gall midge and whorl maggot and are nonthreatening to predators and parasites. Cultural practices being evaluated are stubble management (believed to reduce pest populations) and systematic roguing of plants infected by virus diseases (to minimize inoculum sources). The net result of these efforts is adequate control of rice insects and some diseases with fewer insecticidal treatments; lower costs; and less damage to parasites, predators, and the environment (Pathak and Dyck 1973).

An integrated control program started in 1971 was aimed particularly at the 130 species of insects that occur on the 40 vegetables grown in Taiwan (Yen 1971). Chemicals previously used were not providing satisfactory control of the insects, and all the familiar problems associated with excessive amounts of insecticides had developed in vegetable production areas. Three species of the 54 natural insect enemies that are known on the island are being reared and released. These species include a parasitic wasp, *Apanteles plutellae,* a disease of insects caused by *Bacillus thuringiensis* (the bacterium is released along with some of the bacterial products), and the granulosis virus of insects. Also, a nematode called DD-136 that feeds on insects has been grown and released.

The release of these enemies of vegetable insects will be combined with spray schedules and results will be carefully analyzed. It is hoped that far fewer applications of insecticides will be needed. A concentrated effort is being made to control the diamondback moth, *Plutella xylostella,* one of the most serious insect pests of crucifers in Taiwan. Although mass-rearing techniques and liberation of the larval parasites have been beset with many problems, the efforts are continuing (Chin et al. 1974).

Integrated control programs are being initiated in other countries in the developing world. For example, in Thailand under an FAO–United Nations Development Programme an integrated control program on cotton pests has been initiated for the same reasons that it was initiated earlier in the United States (Deema et al. 1974).

Weeds

Until the advent of large-scale use of herbicides weed control was essentially integrated. Growers utilized weed control mechanisms in all possible combinations. These included preplanting cultivation, postplanting cultivation, weed-free seed, burning of debris, mowing of weeds prior to seed production, and other techniques routinely used to achieve the best possible weed control. With the advent of chemical herbicides in technologically advanced countries, growers have become somewhat careless concerning other types of weed control. Even though the earlier combination methods and some present-day controls (which sometimes include all known combinations) have never been classified as such, they are the equivalent of integrated control programs.

The best weed control is often the use of two or more different sequences or combinations of controls. A combination of tillage and herbicide use is common. Planting a crop as early as possible to give it a competitive advantage over certain weeds is often followed by cultivation and use of herbicides. The principal objective is to achieve effective weed control as inexpensively as possible. When weeds that serve as alternate hosts for other crop pests and diseases are controlled, the procedure becomes a part of the integrated control of these other diseases and pests (Upchurch 1975).

Diseases

In plant pathology the terms *pest management* and *integrated pest control* have seldom been used, but integrated control has been a standard practice. This situation is summarized in the following statement (Univ. Calif. 1972*c*):

> The terms "integrated pest management" and "biological control" are frequently heard these days and plant pathologists are often asked whether these concepts have application in the field of plant disease control. The truth of the matter is that the principles of integrated disease management and biological control have been an integral part of plant pathology for decades. For the most part plant diseases are controlled by prevention, not cure. In essence, this means that appropriate measures are taken before the disease develops, not after an outbreak has occurred.

Apple (1974) emphasized that integrated pest management in its broadest interpretation, which includes entomology, plant pathology, nematology, weed science, and the like, has not been implemented anywhere. Such total agroecosystem management has been considered only in descriptive and predictive models. However, Apple reported that there have been a number of examples of partial integrated pest management. He felt that the perspective of plant protection specialists and agronomists has been broadened and interdisciplinary communication and action has been fostered by integrated pest control efforts; there should be interdisciplinary management integration that embraces all classes of pests (including plant diseases) that effect the agroecosystem. He recommended that natural populations of disease organisms and pests be contained by natural regulating mechanisms such as parasites, predators, diseases, competition, food supply, and hostile environments. He points out that his enthusiasms are not widely shared: "Integrated pest management is rapidly gaining acceptance as the integrating science of crop protection, but there are many who still scoff at the approach as impractical and redundant."

"Squirt gun" pathology alone has seldom been used for major crop areas. For major grain and forage crops, cultural controls and resistant plant varieties are the primary mechanisms for control and fungicides have been used only rarely. In fact, the equivalent of integrated control has been practiced. Spray schedules have become routine only on fruit crops and some vegetables and ornamentals, such as apples, peaches, potatoes, and fruit and vegetable crops that require a cosmetic control of disease for an acceptable quality product. The integrated control approach in plant pathology should not be difficult to combine with the technique that is of recent importance in entomology. However, some new concepts should be added to plant pathology—the principles of ecology and systems analysis as they relate to disease control.

Although many plant pathologists would quarrel with some of Apple's ideas, few would quarrel with the importance of management tactics being ecologically based to utilize efficiently all population-regulating mechanisms—whether they function against insects, plant disease organisms, or other pest populations. The notion that management tactics should be a part of an integrated systems approach, recognizing not only the needs of the crop but also the problems of economics and environmental quality, would be acceptable to most plant pathologists (although usually impossible to carry out at this time). It is also clear that cooperative integrated pest management systems need to be developed for an area rather than for an individual grower or farm. Regional control programs of pests and diseases will become increasingly significant, particularly in areas where a given crop is of major importance (Apple 1974).

When we compare integrated control programs for insects with those in plant pathology, we find some slight differences (H. Smith 1973). Cultural control techniques, including environmental controls that can be manipulated, can be utilized routinely for both insects and plant diseases. One of the problems with plant resistance to insects is that new insect strains with capability of attacking the resistant host keep evolving, e.g., new Hessian fly strains that attack resistant wheat. Plant pathologists must face this problem constantly, too, as new plant disease strains arise. Quite often, too, resistant plants prove to be unacceptable agronomically. Biological controls in plant pathology are usually antagonistic factors in the soil and are generally more difficult to manipulate than are those in entomology. Antagonistic microorganisms, metabolites (such as antibiotics), and so forth are often used in plant disease control, but less is known concerning them than is known concerning predators and parasites of insects.

Insecticide use in entomology can be based on a reasonably certain knowledge of economic threshold levels of insect and mite populations and routine insect and mite surveys and monitoring. In plant pathology, population counts of microorganisms in the field are impossible and would not be meaningful in relation to epiphytotic outbreaks of disease. Other factors, such as environmental quality and relative resistance of available hosts, must be taken into consideration. Most chemical control or spraying in plant pathology has until recently been preventive rather than therapeutic.

The diagnosis of plant diseases and identification of disease organisms are usually more complex than the identification of pest insects. Scouts are not as useful and must be better trained for plant pathology than for entomology. For plant disease scouting a well-trained college graduate is required; whereas for entomology high school graduates can be trained as effective scouts during a summer scouting program. In recent years, though, some states, e.g., Ohio, have used scouts with less training successfully. These scouts are trained and supervised by county agricultural agents (advisors) or other specialists. They collect and send what appear to be plant disease samples to a central clinic for identification. There is no national disease survey in plant pathology; accurate surveys are difficult, costly, and time consuming. Some states, e.g., Ohio, have statewide plant disease surveys. By contrast, national and state surveys for insects and mites have been going on for over a quarter of a century, are relatively easy to conduct, and are reasonably accurate. However, some feel that national and state insect surveys are of little value in integrated pest management (B. D. Blair 1979, pers. commun.).

Although many differences and difficulties exist and many variables make the problems of the two disciplines quite different, it is possible and helpful to develop integrated control programs with available knowledge concerning insects and plant diseases on a given crop instead of waiting until all the necessary data are available (H. Smith 1973).

Chiarappa (1974) has emphasized the importance of what he calls *supervised plant disease control* in plant pathology. It involves the use of fungicide chemicals. From his simulation model Chiarappa concludes that stem rust of wheat can be controlled with chemicals but that it is impractical and uneconomic to do so at this time. However, the model that concerns the late blight of potato shows that this crop-disease combination is suited to supervised plant disease control, since it satisfies all the economic and biological requirements of the model system. Chiarappa indicated that only a small number of plant diseases fulfill all the economic, biological, and managerial criteria essential for profitable use of supervised plant disease control. Most of these diseases are foliar or fruit diseases of high value crops, for which forecasting systems and methods of disease appraisal have been developed.

It will be helpful to illustrate some of the complex problems associated with controlling plant diseases and to discuss some examples of integrated control. The potato is a good starting point. The potato plant has 18 known virus diseases, 6 bacterial diseases, 46 fungus diseases, 5 nematode diseases, at least 39 nonparasitic maladies, and 10 parasitic seed plants that attack it. Of course these diseases do not all occur in any one place or at any one time on a given potato crop. There are diseases of the soil, of the air, and of seed pieces and diseases that are preharvest, are postharvest, or occur primarily in storage. Some are controlled entirely by weather phenomena (NAS 1968a).

The complexity of the integrated control program necessary for potato late blight, a classic plant disease (NAS 1968a; Walker 1969), incited by *Phytophthora infestans,* is surprising. During the winter sanitary measures are very important—the potato dump piles that serve as the first sources of spring inoculum should be destroyed. Resistant varieties are grown in dry areas where late blight ordinarily does not develop. Spray schedules vary in different environments and with different varieties; in the wet, cooler areas where the climate is favorable for late blight a complex protective fungicidal spray schedule is followed. A late blight forecasting service for the wetter areas facilitates timely applications of sprays and often recommends fewer applications, saving time and money while giving more efficient protection. The foliage is often killed in mature plants before digging by flame throwers, herbicides, or mechanical vine beaters to reduce inoculum at harvest-time. Injuries to potatoes are avoided and careful sorting eliminates infected tubers. At harvesttime tuber contamination is minimized by watching surrounding fields and by destroying sources of inoculum. Finally, elaborate storage and shipping techniques make certain that the potato crop gets to the consumer in the best possible condition. Even with all these efforts, control of this disease may not be complete.

In many areas integrated practices, largely cultural, are being used successfully by bean growers in the control of *Fusarium* root rot. They include seed treatment to eliminate seed-borne inoculum, well-prepared seedbeds followed by shallow planting, avoidance if possible of prolonged periods of excessive soil moisture, rotation of a cereal crop such as barley with beans, sanitation measures after harvest to avoid reinfestation of the soil with the causal organisms, avoidance of seed coat cracking through extreme care in harvesting, seed cleaning to eliminate accumulated dust that carries inoculum, and fertilization practices based on a knowledge of the disease and the nitrogen requirements of the fungus (NAS 1968a).

Several other diseases have been controlled by a similar integrated system for a number of years. The *Diplodia* disease of maize, incited by *Diplodia maydis,* is controlled by a combination of fungicides, cultural methods, and plant resistance. The seed is treated with a fungicide (often Captan); a suitable rotation system and careful sanitation are also helpful in partially controlling the disease. Inbred and hybrid lines of maize are available that differ markedly in their resistance to the crown rot and stalk rot phases of the disease. It is particularly important to avoid susceptible hybrids where *Diplodia* disease is a problem (Walker 1969).

Bean anthracnose, incited by *Colletotrichum lindemuthianum,* is controlled by monitoring the seed sources, using resistant varieties, and various cultural techniques. Western grown bean seed that is free of the inciting organism is used as seed. Only resistant varieties are planted. Sanitation measures are used to eliminate overwintering plant debris and two- and three-year rotations are recommended. It is important in wetter areas to cultivate the vines only when they are dry, particularly if the disease is present. The combination of these procedures gives quite good control.

Ergot of grains and grasses, incited by *Claviceps purpurea,* is controlled by using ergot-free seed, destroying or mowing any susceptible native grasses that are on the headlands or border areas of the crop, and rotating with legumes or other nonsusceptible hosts (Walker 1969).

Gray-mold neck rot of onion, incited by *Botrytis allii,* is well controlled by a series of integrated steps. The colored resistant varieties of onions are used in preference to the white. If the blast phase of the disease develops on the foliage, carbamate sprays that also protect the onions against ozone damage are used. The onion tops are allowed to mature and die back well before harvest. At harvesttime bruises are kept to a minimum by extreme care. When the onions are cured, they are aerated as soon as possible. Warm air is forced through by a ventilation system until all the freshly sorted onions are dry. Then the crop is stored at slightly above 0°C at a relative humidity of 64 percent (Walker 1969).

Tobacco mosaic on tomatoes is a virus disease, difficult to control, but by a combination of seed control and cultural practices it can be done. The seed is either produced by greenhouse tomato growers in the United States, England, and elsewhere or treated with 10 percent trisodium phosphate for 10 minutes. Since the disease is spread very easily by mechanical means, infested soil is avoided; all plant refuse is eliminated by careful sanitation; all seedbeds are sterilized; and when transplanting, the hands are washed carefully or dipped in milk. Spraying the beds with milk in transplanting will often help control the disease. By combining all these techniques the disease has been controlled quite well (Walker 1969).

The Hoja blanca disease, a virus disease of rice, is transmitted by leafhoppers, *Sogatodes* spp. The combined use of resistant varieties and insecticides controls its vector. For example, in Louisiana, where a careful insecticide program was followed, the vector, *S. orizicola,* disappeared for 2 years after treatment in 1959 (Feakin 1970).

Soil-inhabiting fungi, particularly those with the capacity to survive as saprophytes in the soil, are difficult to control. A good example is the fungus, *Sclerotium rolfsii,* which has an extremely wide host range and can also maintain itself at quite high levels on crop refuse. The only reasonably satisfactory control has been a combination of cultural and sanitary practices, proper crop sequences, and the use of resistant varieties where available (Sun 1974).

To control transitory yellowing disease of rice, a severe virus disease in Taiwan, three methods are combined. It is very important to delay planting time for the second crop to avoid the time of peak density of the vector. Resistant cultivars such as Kaohsiung 21 are then planted. Finally, the rice plants are protected during growth and at critical times after transplanting with suitable insecticides such as Sevin. This combination of methods achieves good control (Chiu 1972).

A combination of control measures is used in several fungus root diseases in rubber plantations. The causal fungi are *Rigidoporus lignosus, Ganoderma pseudoferreum,* and *Pehllinus noxius.* The first methods used are a combination of cultural controls and herbicides. Following the felling of old rubber trees, the stumps are killed with 60 percent cacodylic acid; 2, 4, 5-T; or other herbicide and removed. Mechanical root cutters are used between the old trees and deep plowing in the interrow reduces the spread from any remaining infected trees. After clearing, the area is planted to a mixed stand of creeping legumes that affords good protection to the soil and helps to reduce future root disease losses, probably by enhanced direct antagonism of actinomycetes and possibly some other microorganisms. Collar protectant dressings around the bases of the trees protect against root diseases. Fungistatic treatments used are the chemical PCNB (quintozene), drazoxolan (PP-781), or others. Finally, all tree wounds are dressed with 20 percent Izal in a bitumen emulsion and any stumps remaining are either poisoned or painted with creosote to reduce stump infections (Lim 1972).

The tungro disease of rice, a destructive virus disease in the Philippines, is controlled by a combination of insecticides and the use of resistant cultivars. Carbaryl (Sevin) or some other suitable insecticide is used to partially control the vector, the green leafhopper, *Nephotettix impicticeps,* in the rice nurseries; it is also necessary to plant resistant rice cultivars (Feakin 1970).

Summarizing integrated control of plant diseases (NAS 1968*a*):

> The use of multiple disease control measures against a particular disease, as exemplified by [potato] late blight, is a general practice in plant disease control (and has been for many years). Where several important diseases occur on the same crop a combined or integrated multiple approach to disease control has been standard practice for many years and has always included such efforts as the use of resistant varieties and cultural controls.

In spite of integrated efforts of all known control methods, many plant diseases still are not controlled satisfactorily. An example is bacterial leaf blight of rice, incited by *Xanthomonas oryzae.* Various combined techniques have been used all over Asia from Japan to India, but no one has reported satisfactory, consistent control (Feakin 1970).

Nematodes

Integrated control procedures for nematodes have been closely associated with control procedures for many soil fungi. Before 1955 most nematologists were trained as zoologists but recently plant nematologists have been trained as plant pathologists, and the two disciplines have consequently developed hand in hand. Good (1975) pointed out that chemical methods are usually used against nematodes only when all other methods have failed. Many different kinds of nonchemical control methods have been developed and many have been integrated with those used against various soil fungi and other soil pests. Good (1972a) recommended further development of integrated approaches in nematode control programs and emphasized the importance of a systems approach. He also suggested that a definite control advantage exists where combinations of plant varieties resistant to nematodes are used with cultural control measures and perhaps a nematicide.

Good nematode control in tobacco has been achieved in North Carolina by integrated control methods. Crop rotation combined with resistant varieties and the use of nematicides when necessary have given much better control than any of the separate methods alone. Todd, as reported by Good (1972a, 1972b), in North Carolina has developed a unique program termed *system control* for some of the major nematode and soil disease problems in tobacco. The system uses various important principles of nematode and disease control in an integrated fashion: seed and field sanitation, destruction of crop residues immediately after harvest, crop rotations, resistant varieties when available, and the use of various types of pesticides when necessary. The choice of control combinations is made after determining the species composition and population of the nematodes and plant disease propagules.

Van Gundy (1972) reported a case in Mexico in which the lesion nematode disease of wheat was controlled by integrated methods, since chemical control alone was not economical. It was found that planting could be delayed until soil temperatures dropped to 15°C. Delayed planting combined with a nitrogen application at the time of first irrigation resulted in an insignificant crop loss. In addition, the use of resistant or tolerant wheat varieties (when available) and a crop rotation with either soybeans or cotton was recommended. Van Gundy suggested that "as plant pathologists and nematologists we need to approach the problem from the point of view that chemicals will only be used as a last resort to restore pathogen balance."

The root lesion nematode is a migratory endoparasite and control has been difficult. A combination of methods has been used. With perennial crops, clean nursery stock planted after a chemical soil treatment is quite effective. With annual crops, soil fumigation may be used with suitable crop rotation when the alternate nonhost crops are also profitable for the grower. Some success has been achieved in developing resistant varieties and root stocks, which are used when available (Univ. Calif. 1972b).

Stem and bulb nematodes are also migratory endoparasites that are difficult to control. Integrated methods have been developed (Univ. Calif. 1972*b*). On alfalfa and clover a combination of seed fumigation, crop rotations, and the use of resistant or immune varieties has given satisfactory control. On onion, fumigation of seed and the use of nematode-free planting stock combined with suitable crop rotations have been satisfactory. On garlic, suitable crop rotations have been combined with a hot-water treatment of the planting clones, 51.5°C (125°F) for 5 minutes in 1 percent formalin. On several other crops, a combination of soil or seed fumigation, nematode-free planting material, suitable crop rotation patterns, and resistant or tolerant varieties when available is recommended.

Root-knot nematodes on rice have been controlled by a combination of methods (Feakin 1970). If possible the soils are flooded for prolonged periods, followed or accompanied by destruction of alternate weed hosts. Rice-vegetable rotations are used. Rice cultivars resistant to root-knot nematodes are used when available. If absolutely necessary, the rice seedbeds are injected with a D-D mixture or with DBCP (Nemagon) 2 weeks before sowing. This combination of methods used after careful observation of nematode populations is giving satisfactory control. In Hawaii, nematodes on pineapple are controlled by a combination of the use of resistant varieties and soil fumigation, using either D-D (Dichloropropane-Dichloropene) or chloropicrin (Collins 1960; Wallace G. Sanford 1974, pers. commun.).

Prospects

Eventually it is hoped that more control procedures that are useful against more than one pest or disease may be combined with measures used against other diseases, insects, weeds, or nematodes. This approach would be ideal when possible and undoubtedly would be more economical. This has seldom been done. A good example is a maize pest control program in Ohio that includes wildlife pests, weeds, insects, diseases, and agronomic practices (B. D. Blair 1979, pers. commun.). Coordinated research is needed to achieve this complex type of control (NAS 1968*a*). It is also important to emphasize the need for an ecologically sound approach to newly integrated control programs (Smith et al. 1976).

The impression has been given by some people that integrated control occurs only when sophisticated computer programming, modeling, and systems analyses are used to analyze and predict proper control procedures. It has also been implied that careful monitoring by field scouts and a staff of sophisticated supervised control experts are necessary. These procedures, helpful and perhaps required in some difficult cases, are certainly not necessary in a great many cases. By empirical, adaptive field research techniques it is possible to develop integrated control programs for many (perhaps most) pests and plant diseases. In most parts of the world it is not realistic to wait until more sophisticated approaches can be used. Integrated control techniques must be utilized now on the most pragmatic level. Computer techniques should be used where equipment, trained personnel, and funding are available. The two approaches should be used simultaneously as conditions and possibilities permit.

Glass and Thurston (1978) have pointed out the importance of traditional farming methods that have been used to control weeds, pests, and diseases in the tropics. They include slash-and-burn agriculture, paddy rice culture methods, long crop rotations, polyculture and crop diversity, biological control, and selection of outstanding resistant plants. This combination has often achieved the equivalent of integrated control and usually represents the accumulated empirical knowledge of centuries of farming in a particular place. We would be wise to attempt to understand that accumulated knowledge and use it as a base for helping traditional agriculturalists improve their farming methods.

A book by Bottrell (1980) sponsored by the Council on Environmental Quality (U.S.A.) presents the most recent developments in integrated pest management. Huffaker (1979) has edited another book that gives detailed information on integrated pest control technology.

16

Cooperative, Combined Controls

 To growers, the combined adverse effects of plant diseases and pests and other crop problems (including weather, nutrition, etc.) often appear as a single, complex, interrelated problem opposing their efforts to grow healthy, high-yielding, quality crops. Research personnel who must separate these problems and work on them as individual entities tend to become so engrossed in a narrow research activity that the holistic aspect is, at least temporarily, forgotten. This is one reason why one group of research personnel occasionally develops control procedures or recommendations that are diametrically opposed to recommendations being made by other researchers working on other problems in the same crop. Many examples of this are given in Chap. 17.

Consider the various conditions that produce wilt in a plant. The field situation may be extremely complex. We would include the wilts associated with drought or any water loss, with feeding of various root insects, with parasitic plants such as *Striga* spp., with severe nematode infestations, and with severe wilt diseases such as bacterial and *Fusarium* wilts. To further complicate the situation, a wilt may occur as the result of two or more of these causes occurring simultaneously. Analyses of apparently simple plant troubles in the field are complex and require professionals with much field experience and considerable finesse for accurate diagnosis.

Growers need a body of plant protection information that can be used in coordinated or combined procedures. They need, if possible, to be able to control weeds at the same time they apply fertilizer or to control an insect at the same time they control a plant disease or perhaps to control nematodes at the same time they control soil diseases and insects. All necessary treatments for a given crop combined in a single effort would be ideal. It would be much cheaper and more efficient in the long run and probably would mean fewer adverse effects on the environment. There are examples of such combined control procedures but, considering all the plant protection research efforts to date, their number is not large.

One of the principal problems is the interdisciplinary and interdepartmental research, communication, and interaction for coordinated or combined control programs. Individual departments usually compete with other related departments for funding rather than cooperate in coordinated projects. This is also true of individual researchers, who often dominate a group of research personnel, obtain as much funding as possible, and build a small "kingdom," usually apart from other closely related disciplines. This procedure has advantages in sophisticated basic research problems, but in applied, adaptive research where problems that occur in the field must be faced, it is often counterproductive.

One of the principal reasons for the success of the combined Rockefeller-Ford Foundation and the Philippine government effort at the International Rice Research Institute is that a completely coordinated, cooperative effort on a single crop brought together the best minds available to attack the problems of crop production and management. Although individual research efforts have been encouraged, they are always coordinated with the larger interdisciplinary, coordinated approach to a given crop's production, improvement, and management problems; of course, plant protection is part of this effort. This approach to agricultural research is relatively rare, which is one reason why we have not solved many of the practical crop improvement, production, and protection problems.

Apple (1974) summarized this situation very well in the following statement:

> We have made considerable progess in recent years in effecting integration across crop protection disciplines, but the lack of interdisciplinary and interdepartmental communication and interaction remains as a principal deterrent to agroecosystem management. We can no longer permit each disciplinary group to pursue independently their research without regard to the impact of their actions on other components of the productive system. We are just beginning to recognize the negative interactions involving fungicides, insects, insecticides, disease organisms, agronomic practices, pest problems and so forth. Experiment station directors can do much to stimulate this type of integrated research through their project development and funding practices.

Another major problem in developing interdisciplinary research efforts to produce coordinated control techniques is the question of who will direct it. Strong, competent leadership is required and without it the effort usually collapses. A spirit of cooperation and selflessness is equally important.

Insecticides and Fungicides

Although successful interdisciplinary, combined control procedures are rare, they do exist. One of the oldest examples is the effort by plant pathologists and entomologists to combine spray programs for plant diseases and insects on deciduous fruits and some vegetables, particularly to control diseases and pests of apples and other fruits demanding a rather complicated and consistent spray schedule. In some eastern land-grant universities in the United States these spray programs have nearly always been cooperative. It is also true in some other areas of the world where sophisticated and consistent spray schedules have been necessary.

Occasionally the routine use of insecticides or fungicides results in an additional benefit that is the equivalent of a combined control procedure. For example, in the Philippines the use of cabaryl insecticides (Sevin) on seedling rice to control certain insects also controls the algae growing in rice and seedbeds (Feakin 1970). In some cases the application of benomyl (Benlate), a chemotherapeutic fungicide, to the soil that is nematode infested markedly benefits plant growth. It also reduces air pollution injury to leaves emerging early in the season. On shaded tobacco in Connecticut, benomyl fungicide has been shown to reduce ozone fleck by 63 percent (Taylor and Rich 1973).

In Taiwan farmers routinely combine fungicides with insecticides in regular schedules for the control of rice blast and sheath blight and (with insecticides such as organophosphates and carbamates) to control the insect vector, *Nephotettix* spp., of yellow dwarf (a mycoplasma) and transitory yellowing (a virus disease). The combination of fungicides and insecticides also is common for orchard fruits and some vegetables where a regular and usually rather complex spray schedule is required (Ren-jong Chiu 1974, pers. commun.).

It has long been known that sulfur and some of its derivatives are excellent miticides as well as fungicides. The susceptibility of red spiders to sulfur derivative sprays varies greatly and it is interesting that this variation seems to depend on the plants infested by the mites. For instance, red spiders are difficult to control on rose with various sulfur derivatives but are very effectively controlled on other plants (Compton and Kearns 1937).

It would be desirable if many insecticides and herbicides could be applied to the soil with fertilizer. Several experiments are being conducted at the International Rice Research Institute in the Philippines for applying fertilizer and insecticides together on and under the soil surface of rice fields. Efforts in this direction are also being made on other crops (S. H. Ou 1974, pers. commun.).

Some control of rodents has been achieved by insecticides, fungicides, and herbicides. Some ground spray formulations of the more toxic insecticides have been used on several crops, for example, seed alfalfa, to poison meadow mice. Useful mice repellents are contained in certain fungicides such as zinc dimethyl dithiocarbamate and tetramethyl thiuram disulfide. Treatments of seed with fungicides and occasionally with insecticides discourage the feeding activities of rodents and birds (NAS 1970). Herbicides applied around trees in young orchard or plantation crops for weed control have been effective in some areas in reducing rodent damage to the bark of the new plantings. Also, herbicide weed control around grain storage areas has often reduced rodent damage (W. R. Furtick 1975, pers. commun.).

Cooperative Programs with Plant Breeders

An excellent group of examples are the cooperative, usually voluntary plant breeding research programs for small grains and maize (corn) in the U.S. plains states. The Hard Red Winter Wheat Improvement Association and the Soft Red Winter Wheat Improvement Association have developed over many years as essentially informal cooperative research ventures and have produced most of the wheat cultivars grown in the plains states. Similar results have come from the outstanding spring wheat breeding program in which Canada and the United States have cooperated.

The cooperative rust research program is another example. Plant pathologists in Canada monitor stem rust each year and evaluate breeding program material for rust reaction. When additional or different sources of resistance are needed the plant pathologists inform the plant breeders, who try to breed the necessary resistance into new cultivars. By this technique stem rust has been kept under control for many years (Hooker 1974).

Another example, from maize, is the Ht type of resistance to the northern leaf blight, incited by *Helminthosporium turcicum*. This new type of resistance was discovered and transferred by backcrossing into about 30 inbred lines that have since been used in the seed industry by plant breeders to produce resistant hybrids. This disease has not caused any serious losses for a number of years (Hooker 1974).

Another recent example concerns the 1970 southern leaf blight epidemic of maize in the United States (Hooker 1974). He described the situation as follows:

> We had identified the new race T, and demonstrated that only cms-T cytoplasm corn was susceptible. When the epidemic came in 1970, a demonstration and interpretation of its cause was available on our research plots. The seed industry visited our plants and other meetings were held in the late summer of 1970. By September the correct decisions were made to bring the disease under control. This was by means of normal cytoplasm. Agronomists here at Illinois had collected a series of other cytoplasms for male sterility. I took those to the field and inoculated them with race T in the summer of 1970. Most were resistant and I made crosses onto these cytoplasms with the inbred lines most widely used by the seed corn industry. This F_1 seed was released in September 1970, and planted within a few days in Hawaii and Florida. Six generations of breeding, two years of performance testing and seed stocks have been increased since that time, all by the industry. A considerable

amount of hybrid seed (commercial) on one of these cytoplasms was produced this past summer, 1974.

This is also a good example of cooperation to achieve a coordinated control program between plant pathologists, plant breeders, and the seed industry.

J. C. Gilbert (1974, pers. commun.) described a situation in which the soil in Hawaii had become so heavily infested with various soil-borne tomato pathogens after 30 years of continuous cultivation of tomato that not even the most resistant tomato cultivars could survive. The following strategy made it possible to grow the most resistant tomato varieties again. Three crops of nematode-resistant soybeans were planted to lower the level of nematode infestation and the level of infestation of soil-borne diseases of tomatoes. The fruit of susceptible tomato cultivars that were planted in such soil was still destroyed rather rapidly, but multiple-resistant tomato varieties that were planted had sufficient resistance to produce a good crop. The level of soil-borne diseases and nematodes had been reduced enough to allow the resistance of the tomato varieties to become effective. This is an important lesson in how to get maximum use out of moderate disease resistance with a combination of crop rotation and resistant varieties.

An interesting example from industry of a successful cooperative program developed by plant breeders, plant pathologists, and weed scientists is the case of the sugarcane smut that recently appeared in Hawaii. The scientists of the Hawaii Sugar Planters' Association cooperated on a program of control of this so-called culmiculous smut, *Ustilago scitaminea.* The smut caused severe damage for several years. Fortunately several of the best varieties were resistant, and this germ plasm was immediately utilized in the breeding programs. When it was found that the smut survived between crops on the ratoons, the herbicides Tandex (Karbutilate) and paraquat (Weedol) were used successfully to eliminate the infected ratoon plants. The herbicides and a successful breeding program have achieved fine control of this introduced disease (Hawaiian Sugar Plant. Assoc. 1975, pers. commun). It also was found that the herbicide, Karbutilate, used under an emergency state label, can control the smut disease and several insect pests by destroying volunteer plants (Robert Osgood 1974, pers. commun.).

In Taiwan when disease resistance in the rice plant is combined with the use of fungicides and insecticides to control vectors of sheath blight, yellow dwarf, rice blast, and transitory yellowing, the effectiveness of the resistance seems to be very much enhanced. None of the major rice varieties is highly resistant to sheath blight but most are moderately resistant to rice blast and some have adequate field tolerance to transitory yellowing. This is another example of the value of moderate resistance combined with minimal amounts of pesticides (Ren-jong Chiu 1974, pers. commun.).

In Hawaii in the summer of 1970, disease-resistant plants saved a crop that had been seriously infested at an early age by the tomato pinworm. The plantings represented a variety of genetic lines of tomato, including various combinations of resistance and susceptibility to root-knot and tobacco mosaic virus. When the field was sprayed late with Diazinon (dimpylate) for tomato pinworm control, the breeding lines that combined resistance to several diseases and root-knot recovered from the pinworms, gradually made new growth, and developed a nearly normal crop. The tomato varieties that had little or no disease resistance did not recover from the serious leaf and stem damage caused by the tomato pinworm and died out completely. There was little doubt that the plant's ability to recover from serious injury was closely related to its resistance to root pathogens, root-knot nematode, and perhaps virus diseases also (J. C. Gilbert 1974, pers. commun.).

The control of mealybug wilt of pineapple requires the destruction of ant populations that bring in the mealybugs and nurture them. Destruction of the ant population and the mealybugs has been achieved by spraying or dusting the plants with insecticides—Diazinon has been used effectively to control the ants. This insecticide control used with resistant hybrids, such as the variety Cayenne, is even more effective (Collins 1960).

The International Rice Research Institute in the Philippines is seeking insect-resistant rice varieties that will make it possible to reduce the number of chemical applications necessary to control specific diseases and insect pests. Painter long ago (1951) predicted a trend toward the use of resistant varieties combined with minimal amounts of pesticidal chemicals. At that time there were only a few examples to illustrate this phenomenon. Swingle (1939) showed that the kill by lead arsenate of certain leaf-feeding insects varied from 0 to 98 percent, depending on the previous diet or hosts of the insect. Markos and Campbell (1943) studied the effects of the host plant on the calcium arsenate susceptibility of the southern armyworm. The mortality was high when the insect was fed on rhubarb and much lower when fed on soybeans, maize, or squash. Malenotti (1935) reported that the mortality from three different insecticides on the coccid, *Epidiaspis leperii,* was much lower on pear than on peach. Painter's prediction that such data eventually would prove to be extremely valuable in combining resistance with minimal doses of pesticides is now proving to be true. Continuing research in these areas will be productive.

Combined Weed and Pest Controls

Weed control often increases the efficiency of control of pests and plant diseases, since weeds harbor diseases, insects, and nematodes and serve as alternate hosts for plant disease vectors. Consequently, weed control is often one of the best and most economical control measures for plant diseases and pests (Crafts and Robbins 1962). On the other hand, weed control may spread diseases and pests. For example, in the southeastern United States the frequent cultivation of peanuts to control weeds shifts the soil onto the lower foliage levels of the crop and may result in increased incidence of the soil-rot fungus, incited by *Rhizoctonia solani,* and the southern blight fungus, incited by *Sclerotium rolfsii.* The use of herbicides to control weeds as a substitute for frequent cultivation has reduced the disease level. Also, weed control may cause a mass movement of certain insect species from preferred weed hosts to nearby crop plants (NAS 1968c).

Control of weeds helps to control the common bean blight, since the bacterium survives in several of the wild legumes. The causal organism of the blackleg of cabbage survives on several weeds in the sunflower family (Compositae), for example, the sow thistle and prickly lettuce. Control of the common sow thistle and prickly lettuce has sharply reduced the populations of bean thrips, greatly improving bean yields in the western United States. The curly top of sugar beets, a virus disease, is transmitted from its wild host plants to cultivated plants (particularly sugar beets) by the beet leafhopper, *Circulifer tenullus.* The important alternate hosts are desert plants, various saltbushes, and the Russian thistle. If such preferred weed hosts could be eliminated, some of the worst crop pests could be controlled quite well (Crafts and Robbins 1962).

The elimination of the common barberry, an alternate host, is quite effective in some parts of the world in controlling the stem rust of wheat, barley, oats, and certain grasses. In other areas where the summer or red spore stage is transported in vast numbers by air currents, barberry eradication has not been effective. This includes most of the major wheat-producing areas of the United States; in this case weed control has not resulted in the benefits anticipated (NAS 1968c).

The yellow spot, a virus disease of pineapple and a strain of tomato spotted wilt, is controlled by good management practices plus chemical sprays. Management practices include keeping the weed hosts of the vector, the onion thrips, *Thrips tabaci,* under control. The principal weed host is a small annual plant of the sunflower family, *Emelia sonchifolia.* Control has been quite effective where the weed hosts have been eliminated from fields and borders and has been even better when chemical spray programs have been used for the control of the thrips vector and other insects (Collins 1960; Wallace G. Sanford 1974, pers. commun.).

Herbicides may either increase, decrease, or not affect the incidence of various plant diseases, fungi, viruses, and nematodes. Herbicides belonging to different chemical groups may have a wide variety of effects. Other things being equal, priority should be given to herbicides that reduce, or at least do not enhance, disease incidence. Prior to release all herbicides should be screened concerning their reaction and interaction with relevant plant disease organisms and pests (Katan and Eshel 1973). Recent studies also suggest that there are interesting and involved interactions between soil microorganisms and herbicides. For example, simazine (Gesatop) and atrazine (Aatrex) stimulate several genera of fungi known to be antagonistic to certain root organisms, particularly *Fusarium* spp. In this case the overall beneficial effects of herbicides may extend far beyond routine weed control (NAS 1968c). Another example of partial control of a fungus with an herbicide is the suppression of root rot of peas, *Aphanomyces euteiches,* by dinitroaniline herbicides (Harvey et al. 1979).

Shaw (1964, 1974a) has emphasized a combination of technologies for managing the agroecosystem for better weed control. For example, he encouraged united, preventive weed control efforts not just on a field or farm but in an area or region with each region handled as a weed control unit in a directed total ecosystem approach. Crop production and plant protection principles and practices would be directed toward the control of weeds and all other pests. Shaw would include the use of multiple pest–resistant, high-yielding, well-adapted, highly competitive cultivars; good seedbed and seeding methods; weed- and pest-free crop seed; optimum fertilization and irrigation techniques; careful crop rotations; crop diversification; optimum plant spacing and populations; timely cultivations; careful harvesting methods that do not spread pests and weed seeds; field sanitation techniques; and chemical controls, if necessary. He suggests rotating herbicides for weed control when the same crop is grown continuously, and for best and safest results he recommends rotating both crop and herbicide. Other possibilities for consideration are sequential treatments, combination herbicide treatments, and herbicide mixtures. He suggests they should be combined with mechanical, cultural, and biological control methods for control of all weeds, pests, and diseases.

Combined Nematode and Pest Controls

Combination control measures for nematode infestations and their various combinations with soil-borne plant disease organisms, both fungal and bacterial, are effective. Nematodes alone do not rot roots, but they favor the entry of root rot organisms and create ideal infection courts for a variety of soil microorganisms (NAS 1968a). Many ordinarily weak bacterial and fungal root pathogens would not gain entrance unless a suitable infection court or port of entry was available by way of nematode feeding; then ordinarily weak pathogens can cause tremendous damage. Also, plants with nematode-damaged roots invaded by weak parasites are much more susceptible to cold and drought injuries and to nutrient deficiencies. There is also some evidence that fungal infections of roots increase the populations of nematodes in those roots (NAS 1968b).

In recent years many complicated interactions have been demonstrated between plant parasitic nematodes and soil-inhabiting pathogens, bacteria, fungi, and viruses. Certain crop varieties that were selected for resistance to

Fig. 16.1. Prospective strawberry land being fumigated in California; sheets of polyethylene film hold fumigant in the soil. (Courtesy Malcolm Shurtleff)

specific bacterial or fungal diseases have behaved very differently in fumigated nematode-infested soil as compared to untreated nematode-infested soil. The increases in growth and yield of these disease-resistant varieties in fumigated soils greatly exceeded those in nonfumigated soils (NAS 1968b). Also, in greenhouse tests plant pathogenic nematodes have greatly increased the severity of diseases caused by some bacteria and fungi in plants typically resistant to these diseases. Examples are the breakdown of resistance in tobacco varieties to the black shank fungus, *Phytophthora parasitica* var. *nicotianae,* and the Granville wilt bacterium, *Pseudomonas solanacearum,* and the collapse of several tomato and cotton varieties resistant to *Fusarium* wilts when grown in soil heavily infested with root-knot nematodes, *Meloidogyne* spp. The mechanisms that make these supposedly resistant plants susceptible to the diseases when attacked by a large number of nematodes are not understood.

A very good example of combined control of nematodes, *Verticillium* wilt and some other soil-borne diseases, and weed propagules in strawberries by a fumigant mixture, chloropicrin and methyl bromide, is given by Wilhelm and Paulus (1980) and shown in Fig. 16.1.

Other apparently synergistic relationships between nematodes and plant disease organisms occur. When the lesion nematode, *Pratylenchus penetrans,* is present in large numbers, the incidence and severity of eggplant wilt, incited by *Verticillium dahliae,* is greatly increased. Also, the number of nematodes inside the eggplant roots is increased significantly when the fungus is present—the fungus-infected roots are more readily invaded by the nematodes than noninfected roots. These relationships are not yet understood (NAS, 1968*b*).

J. C. Gilbert (1974, pers. commun.) has emphasized the use of resistant cultivars in combination with soil fumigants. He has found that combinations of soil fumigation, crop rotation, and genetic resistance benefit greatly the control of nematodes and several soil-borne fungus and bacterial diseases. It is also possible when using resistant cultivars to extend the intervals between soil fumigations so that less chemical materials are needed. By using the resistant crop and an immune rotation crop the root-knot nematodes tend to be starved out. For example, lettuce or cucumber, which has no nematode-resistant cultivars, should be followed by soil fumigation and then by a root-knot resistant crop to take care of the few nematodes that survive the fumigation. If the grower replanted immediately with a root-knot susceptible crop, the land could become reinfested within a year. If combinations of plant resistance to nematodes, fungi, and bacterial diseases are also present, the combination of soil fumigation, crop rotation, and the use of plant resistance is even more effective.

In the moist tropics nematodes and fungi are found in much greater abundance than in the temperate zones and may multiply with extreme rapidity. Again, the combination of nematodes with a fungus disease may make the fungus disease more severe. For example, *Fusarium*-resistant cotton varieties may be rendered susceptible by large numbers of root-attacking nematodes. Also, the *Fusarium* wilt of bananas is more severe in the presence of severe infestations of root-knot nematodes, *Meloidogyne* spp. Resistant tobacco varieties developed in nematode-free soil also become susceptible to the *Fusarium* wilt organism, *Fusarium oxysporum* f. sp. *nicotinae* when grown in fields heavily infested with root-knot nematodes. In many parts of the tropics fusarial wilts are more severe when occurring in combination with nematode infestations (Wellman 1972).

Chemical soil treatments that kill nematodes may reduce the incidence of certain soil-borne viruses, particularly those that are nematode borne or nematode transmitted (NAS 1968*b*). This is also true of the soil-borne wheat mosaic, which is a virus disease whose vector is a root-inhabiting soil fungus (Pacumbaba et al. 1968).

Another good example, from Indiana, is the control of strawberry nematodes and some soil-borne diseases, insects, and weeds by the soil fumigant vapam (N-869 A) introduced with irrigation water in a sprinkling

Fig. 16.2. A good strawberry crop due to combined control of nematodes and some diseases, insects, and weeds by vapam applied via spray irrigation water. (Courtesy Malcolm Shurtleff)

system. Figure 16.2 shows a healthy strawberry planting grown in 1977 after such a vapam treatment of a badly infested field in 1975.

Fumigants in Combination Controls

Some fumigant chemicals are valuable as general control agents. Examples are the volatile fumigants such as chloropicrin, which can be used as a temporary soil sterilant. It kills soil insects, nematodes, weeds, seeds, fungi, and bacteria; root rots are greatly reduced; and damping-off organisms are virtually eliminated. Such materials are particularly effective in greenhouse soils and have been used successfully on pineapples, eggplants, carrots, peppers, and tomatoes in the field (Crafts and Robbins 1962). Other general volatile soil fumigants are carbon bisulfide, tetrachloroethane, and methyl bromide.

A specific example is the control of root rots, wilts, nematodes, and

Fig. 16.3. Soil injection with Telone (mostly 1, 3-dichloropropene) for the control of nematodes and bacterial canker of peach. Soil under background tarp strips similarly treated with methyl bromide. (Courtesy W. H. English)

probably some insects and weed seeds in strawberry beds in California by soil fumigation with methyl-bromide-chloropicrin (Albert D. Paulus 1979, pers. commun.).

An interesting example of the simultaneous control of two organisms by the fumigant Telone (mostly 1, 3-Dichloropropene) is given by Lownsbery et al. (1977) (see Fig. 16.3). A nematode, *Macroposthonia xenoplax,* in some way increases the severity of the disease, bacterial canker of peach, incited by *Pseudomonas syringae.* Both may be controlled by the use of the single fumigant.

The toxic vapors from these materials often act as temporary soil sterilants and kill some plants, seeds, insects, rodents, and plant disease organisms. The fumigant gradually denatures, after which the soil can be used again to grow crops (NAS 1968c). These fumigants can also be used as outstanding herbicides to kill some deep-rooted perennial plants such as Russian knapweed and field bindweed. They can be employed as sterilants to eliminate fungi, insects, weed seeds, and rodents in nursery beds or areas where perennial trees, vines, or shrubs are being replanted.

Sterilization has another advantage: it often increases the availability of soil nutrients. Some fumigants after decomposition contribute chemicals that may act as either residual toxicants or soil amendments (NAS 1968c). Methods for using these valuable materials on a larger scale in the field need to be developed. The potential for combination control of many plant diseases, pests, and weeds is great.

Cultural Controls in Combinations

The combination of improved management with cultural control techniques is often valuable in achieving better plant protection. In turf grass culture, for instance, pesticides that control insects, diseases, and weeds are combined with proper irrigation, fertilization, and mowing techniques. In most cases pesticides are used only after other methods have failed (Turgeon et al. 1973).

Aster yellows, a mycoplasma disease, can be controlled on carrots and lettuce by the use of insecticides at frequent enough intervals to greatly reduce the leafhopper vector populations. A number of leafhopper species carry this mycoplasma. These insecticides are combined by commercial florists with growing of plants in frames covered with cloth that protects them from leafhoppers. This cultural technique (a barrier) combined with minimal use of insecticides achieves excellent control of the disease (Walker 1969).

On the Hilo coast in Hawaii the amount of herbicide needed for weed control in sugarcane is greatly reduced by deep plowing (18–20 inches), which buries many seeds so deep that they cannot reach the soil surface after germination. The weeds that do germinate are easily controlled by preemergence applications of herbicides followed by spot applications for the treatment of stubborn plant species. This type of weed control aids in at least partial control of certain insects and plant diseases that survive on these alternate weed hosts (Robert Osgood 1974, pers. commun.).

A novel and significant method of controlling diseases and pests, including weeds, has been tested in Israel (Katan 1979; Katan et al. 1976). Solar heating of the soil by mulching with transparent polyethylene sheets during hot seasons has effectively controlled fungus propagules, nematodes, and weeds (see Fig. 16.4). This method improves stands and plant growth, is less costly than fumigation, leaves no residues, and helps to preserve moisture in the soil. It has been used successfully with potatoes, eggplant, cotton, peanuts, and tomatoes. Jaacov Katan (1979, pers. commun.) reports successful control of many species of weeds and nine different pathogens on a wide variety of crops.

Fig. 16.4. Solar heating of soil in Israel by mulching with transparent polyethylene sheets during hot season. (Courtesy Jaacov Katan)

Other Examples

Many combinations of controls were discovered accidentally. An effort has been made by some plant protection personnel, usually in cooperation with agronomists and horticulturalists, to achieve coordinated combination controls.

The earliest efforts probably were carried out by industry in the large plantation crops such as sugarcane, pineapple, bananas, tea, and coffee and the cooperation was formal. People were obtained by the industry specifically to work cooperatively. The primary goals were high crop production, improvement, and management; the plant protection aspects of the program were subordinated to this goal. The programs of the Hawaiian Sugar Planters' Association and the Pineapple Research Institute have been particularly outstanding. Some equally fine programs in bananas, coffee, and tea in other parts of the world were developed. Note that plant resistance has long been considered of primary importance in these programs.

Possibly the most successfully coordinated, cooperative plant protection programs ever developed have appeared in large foundation-controlled institutions such as the International Rice Research Institute in the Philippines. Perhaps ten to a dozen similar institutions are now operating in various parts of the world. All are characterized by formal, coordinated, cooperative efforts by the individuals working on particular crops. Most research is coordinated around a given crop or a small number of closely related crops. For example, the International Crops Research Institute for the Semi-Arid Tropics near Hyderabad, India, concentrates on sorghum and its relatives. The primary goal in each institution is high crop production, improvement, and management. The plant protection researchers involved accept their supporting role within the context of the overall goal of producing the best possible crop. In both industrial and foundation-controlled institutions, researchers and all other personnel are hired with the understanding that their efforts will be cooperative and supportive of the larger overall goals of the total program. The success of such programs should encourage more such research organization throughout the world but most of the research done by plant protection personnel is still largely independent; uncoordinated; and divided into several, often competing, subdisciplines.

Some recent government-controlled programs in the United States and elsewhere have attempted better coordination and cooperation in research. Such institutions as the Northern Grain Insect Research Laboratory at Brookings, South Dakota, and several similar USDA institutions that have sprung up in recent years are of interest from the standpoint of coordinated, cooperative, goal-oriented research. Each institution has a specific goal or goals that for the most part are aimed at a group of interrelated, basic, practical problems in an area but not primarily at the achievement of outstanding crop production, improvement, and management in a specific crop. Such organizations achieve better coordination of research efforts than do most past efforts but typically are not as successful as foundation- or industry-supported research organizations.

Some states in the United States have developed cooperative, coordinated plant protection research efforts for specific crops built around outstanding crop production and management programs. One of these is the excellent program on peaches in Arkansas (O. J. Dickerson 1975, pers. commun.). All the problems associated with this crop are approached by a team of horticulturalists, entomologists, and plant pathologists. This approach has at times been followed in other states on crops such as apples, pears, and peaches—crops of economic significance that require a great deal of effort and usually chemical spray schedules to control plant diseases and crop pests. There is also a fine pecan program in Alabama (B. D. Blair 1979, pers. commun.).

The Hard Red Winter Wheat Improvement Association of the Great Plains states (mentioned earlier in the chapter) is an example of largely informal cooperation and mutual self-help within and between institutions and states. The primary controlling role for the organization has gone to agronomists, particularly wheat breeders. The federal government has been involved, as well as the land-grant universities at which hard red winter wheat breeding is done. Usually at least two meetings are held each year in which research plans and results are discussed. The primary goal again is outstanding crop production, improvement, and management and plant protection has been subordinate.

Similar efforts are characteristic of the soft red winter wheat program in the eastern plains states and the spring wheat program in the northern plains states and Canada. Such programs indicate that team effort without completely formal control is possible if personnel involved feel it is to their mutual advantage.

Another example of outstanding, largely informal, cooperative research is the cooperative research program on maize in the U.S. Corn Belt states, largely under the direction of personnel from the federal government (USDA), the University of Illinois, and Iowa State University.

Formal Programs

Some specific examples of large formal projects in different parts of the world are worth mention. Protection of cotton crops has been particularly troublesome. Cooperative efforts gradually have been developed to deal with this problem. In the fiscal years of 1972 and 1973, 39 pilot pest management projects on 15 crops were established in 29 states in the United States, with an emphasis on cotton. About $2 million in federal monies plus fiscal support by the states was involved. Each pilot project was established to operate for a 3-year period and involved cooperation of state and federal research agencies, regulatory agencies, and industry. These large applied research and demonstration programs required not only interest but planning, organization, support, and participation on the part of growers.

Fourteen projects dealt with cotton insects; 6 with insects and weeds on maize; 4 with insects and weeds on grain sorghum; 2 with diseases, weeds, nematodes, and insects on peanuts; 6 with pests of apples, pears, and citrus; 4 with insects on vegetables and potatoes; and 2 with insects on alfalfa; one project attempted an integrated management of all pests plus sucker control on tobacco. The total integrated pest management (IPM) program was described by Good (1973a, 1973b):

> The state pilot pest management programs now under way and those to be sponsored in the future by the USDA must accommodate in a harmonious system the entomologists' concept of insect management, the plant pathologists' concept of plant health, the nematologists' concept of population regulation and the weed scientists' view on total weed management on farms. This is necessary because management of farm units requires a systems approach to controlling a large array of pests, all of which can contribute to reduced yields and quality. Failure to control a single component complex often negates the benefits of other controls. In like manner control of one pest often

has inescapable effects on other pests. The objective of the pilot pest management projects is to establish multiple and alternate choice systems of pest control that are effective, economical and environmentally sound. The ultimate goal of these projects is to promote effective use of combinations of cultural, biological and chemical controls. This program is supported by not only research and extension personnel, both state and federal, but also regulatory personnel, industry, growers' organizations and individual farmers. If the integrated programs become accepted and if their value can be shown to the growers, it is expected that funding, particularly for non-professional costs to the growers, will be shifted to either growers' organizations or individual growers. The research function and the technical advisory function would be continued by public agencies or occasionally might be picked up by private pest management advisory organizations or individuals. Where possible computers are being utilized to construct models for crop protection and pest management that include whatever variables that are available such as pest populations, beneficial insects, agronomic practices, cropping histories, weather conditions and so forth. It is hoped that this information can be utilized to develop a systems approach to specific crops and the control of specific crop protection and pest management problems.

The first two IPM pilot projects were established in 1971 to control insects on tobacco in North Carolina and on cotton in Arizona. The first large integrated project initiated by the extension service was on cotton insect management in 1972 in 14 states. The goal was to achieve an improved, economic insect control. It was necessary to maintain yield and quality at least equal to the past, and control procedures had to be compatible with agronomic and other pest management practices. All the new environmental regulations had to be followed and growers helped plan and execute the projects individually and through their organizations. The results have been quite successful, with costs lower than for earlier control efforts. Residue analyses of pesticides used were made routinely and all the workers were checked regularly by health departments. It is hoped that plant diseases, nematodes, and weeds can be included in the program in the future (Good 1974c).

The projects on integrated control in cotton probably have been successful because of experience with insect scouting in most of the states and because of the enthusiastic cooperation of the growers, who contributed about $500,000 in 1972, $822,000 in 1973, and $1.2 million in 1974 on 868,000 acres of cotton. Growers paid the costs of the scouting service in 11 of the 14 states, and funds contributed by the growers were equal to approximately half of the funds contributed by state and federal governments. Net returns reported have been as high as $95 per acre above conventional insect control procedures (Good 1974d).

Since 1974 a great expansion of the program has occurred. By 1975 over 40 pilot IPM projects on 19 commodities had been conducted in 30 states. By 1976, the USDA extension service had provided funds to carry

out 52 pilot IPM projects in 33 states on 23 crops. By 1977, 230 private consultants were working with organized IPM projects; and 16 consulting
firms, 60 local growers' associations, and 10 registered cooperatives were
participating. In 1978 funds were made available to all states and protec-
torates to initiate pilot projects or to expand existing ones; there were 136
IPM demonstrations on most major crops in 47 states and the Virgin
Islands. In 1979 all states, Puerto Rico, and the Virgin Islands had IPM
programs on 45 crops.

In 1973 at least some projects involved more than the discipline of entomology. By 1977, about 85 percent of the total program was in entomology and the remaining 15 percent (in a few projects as much as 50 percent) was devoted to managing diseases, nematodes, and weeds.

As the programs have been accepted and their value proven, increasing
amounts of the costs have been assumed by the growers. Farmers pay all the
direct cost of field scouting and monitoring of population densities. Their
pest control decisions are based on the monitoring of pests and of beneficial
insects and the levels of weed, disease propagules, and nematode incidence.
The most appropriate control technology is used. When available, computers are used to construct simulation models based on pest populations,
beneficial insects, cropping history, agronomic practices, and soil and
weather conditions (Blair and Edwards 1979).

By 1979, about 800,000 acres were in extension-sponsored Cotton Insect Management Programs in 11 southern states. There were also 1.5
million acres of cotton in private consultant programs and 300,000 acres
handled by growers' associations. A great reduction in insecticide use, from
39 million pounds in 1972 to 18 million pounds in 1977, has occurred
(USDA 1979).

One of the largest cooperative research projects has been developed
largely through the influence of C. B. Huffaker (1974). In his words the
project was developed for the following purposes:

> As part of the International Biological Program (IBP) 19 universities,
> segments of the Agricultural Research Service, the Forest Service, and
> elements of private industry are joining together in a major effort to develop
> new re-oriented, expanded and closely coordinated research efforts seeking
> practical alternatives to the expensive use of broad spectrum toxic chemicals
> for control of certain insect pest complexes.

The research for this crop-centered program was done on five major
crops: alfalfa, pine, citrus, cotton, and soybeans. The project was funded
jointly by the National Science Foundation and the Environmental Protection Agency and was under the direction of entomologists Huffaker and
Ray F. Smith (Apple 1974). The project was predominantly conducted and
managed by entomologists, although a few plant pathologists, nematolo-

gists, weed scientists, and agronomists functioned in limited technical ways and on advisory committees. An important new development for entomologists was the cooperation with plant breeders to develop plants resistant to insects. People in computer science, systems analysis, toxicology, and environmental monitoring were also included. Even though this program could not be classified or developed into a completely cooperative program to include all the plant protection disciplines, it was a major step in the right direction.

Comments of plant pathologists officially involved with the Huffaker project have not been too reassuring. All the plant pathologists involved were contacted and several responses indicated that the program was aimed primarily at integrated insect control, a perfectly legitimate goal, and was controlled by entomologists. One plant pathologist said, "The entire Huffaker program is slanted toward integrated insect control. I happen to be involved by being a member of the so-called steering committee. . . . Nothing in the program thus far seems to concern plant pathology at all."

Another plant pathologist reported an attempt "to make more funds available for plant pathology research on pest management. Since this meeting we have been . . . invited to submit a new grant proposal in the area of disease management. . . . Until now essentially nothing has been done in plant pathology."

Several plant pathologists have defended the project. J. Lawrence Apple (1975, pers. commun.) made the following statement:

> The Huffaker Project . . . was conceived principally as an entomological project. . . . A few "outsiders" such as myself have been added to the Steering Committee. The principal function of the latter is to review annually project results and plans for the coming year. My observation is that the Huffaker project . . . has done more to stimulate Integrated Pest Management research and cognizance than any other single activity or event. It is unfortunate that it is restricted to insects, but that was the original premise. . . . The project will be phased out after two more years.

In defense of the Huffaker project J. M. Good (1975, pers. commun.), a nematologist who served on the overall steering committee, stated:

> In 1971 and 1972, when the Huffaker project was being formulated there was little interest and support of integrated pest management by other disciplines. Therefore, the entomologists proceeded to provide leadership in this area. They are to be commended by their foresight and now their willingness to broaden the base of integrated pest management.

Weed scientists were also asked to be involved in the Huffaker project but essentially have not been used. Several, in response to questions, indicated that it is an insect research program. One weed scientist involved in the project (W. C. Shaw 1975, pers. commun.) made the following comment:

> When Dr. Huffaker and his associates first proposed the integrated pest management program, some of the objectives seemed sufficiently broad to include other major classes of pests such as plant diseases, nematodes and weeds. . . . However, when the project was funded, apparently the interpretation of the research objectives was primarily limited to insects and their control.

The project was very ambitious and particularly important to entomologists at the time. It is hoped that eventually projects such as this can be developed by cooperating research personnel from all the plant protection disciplines with all disciplines having equal input.

The first large progress report of the Huffaker project (Huffaker 1974) included two small plant disease research reports concerning root rots on pine and the common leaf spot on alfalfa. Most of the other reports were associated with integrated insect control. It is clear that some effort was made to include other subdisciplines of plant protection.

W. C. Shaw (1975, pers. commun.) emphasized the technical difficulties encountered in developing large-scale cooperative projects:

> The differences between the pests, their hosts, competitors, and the ecological situations in which they exist are so different that it is often very difficult to identify lines of research that are mutually compatible with achievable worthwhile objectives. At first thought, it would seem simple to design an experiment to determine corn yield losses caused by weeds, diseases, nematodes, insects and other pests. Yet, I am not aware of a single successful experiment in which this objective has been achieved. We are attempting such an experiment at Tifton, Georgia, at the present time. The complexity of the base line data required as a standard for comparative purposes is so complex that I am doubtful that we will achieve the objectives that were established for this experiment. If you add additional and more complex variables, the chances of success seem to be lessened.

Huffaker (1975, pers. commun.) explains the constraints in developing this project:

> It is true that the breadth of scope of the originally designed project left room for inclusion of plant diseases, nematodes and weeds. When the program planning and budgeting got further under way, it was the vast majority's opinion (of the planners) that to include each of these areas in a fully joint effort would so dilute the effort among the disciplines that major headway would not be made on anything with the necessary dispatch. Consequently, it was decided, if it were not in fact rather presumed from the outset, that the main focus would be on insects and mites, but that where significant interactions existed (posing interaction problems) with weed problems, nematode problems or plant disease, some effort would have to be devoted to these

areas. . . . We believe that the principles, strategies and tactics we are employing do apply to integrated pest management in general, and that focusing on the insects has been both necessary (financially) and rewarding in helping to show the way for broader inter-disciplinary efforts. I would like to see such develop and hope that a leadership group for organizing such will emerge.

A large interdisciplinary project, supported by the Environmental Protection Agency, the National Science Foundation, and the USDA, that attempts to include all aspects of plant protection has been initiated (Ray Frisbie 1980, pers. commun.). Fifteen universities are cooperating and plant diseases, insects, nematodes, weeds, and other pests on four crops (alfalfa, apple, cotton, and soybean) are being considered, using a systems approach and integrated control. Three entomologists and one plant pathologist are the key organizers and an entomologist is the director. It is too early to say whether all disciplines involved will function on an equal basis.

Large formal interdisciplinary research programs are difficult to organize, develop, fund, and implement. Perhaps less ambitious projects should be encouraged at present. For example, people interested in reducing the quantities of pesticides used on a given crop could concentrate also on the use of moderately resistant plants and cultural or agronomic techniques that suppress a pest or group of pests and diseases and make it possible to use fewer pesticide applications in the control program. Such comparatively simple controls deserve more serious attention.

At Oklahoma State University an interesting peanut health program that centers on peanut production and management has been developed (R. V. Sturgeon 1974, pers. commun.). The program includes disease, weed, insect, and nematode control. A peanut production guide for Oklahoma growers has been developed that includes information for the production of healthy peanuts. The plant protection program is coordinated with crop improvement, management, production, irrigation, storage, and marketing efforts. It involves research and extension personnel; members of growers' organizations; and representatives of the plant protection disciplines—agronomists, plant breeders, agricultural engineers, soil scientists, and the like. This is essentially the approach used by the plantation industries and the international foundation-supported work discussed earlier.

All plant protection disciplines are combined in a research program on apples in New York State. This program involves the state Cooperative Extension Service, the state Agricultural Experiment Stations, the USDA Extension Service, the USDA Agricultural Research Service, and the Animal and Plant Health Inspection Service. The New York State Apple Pest Management Project, which has been in progress for several years, includes a data processing system via computer techniques and environmental monitoring of the effects of the various treatments on the environment.

Despite some early organizational and administrative problems, it is one of the best overall formal cooperative programs in the United States. This program, because of the importance of the apple crop in New York and the necessity of spraying schedules for both disease and insect control, may become a classic case of successful cooperative effort in integrated interdisciplinary control (Brann and Tette 1973; James E. Brann 1974; P. A. Arneson 1975; J. E. Hunter 1975, pers. commun.). Of course, the final test is the number of growers who use it successfully. This project does not yet appear to be completely coordinated with and subordinated to apple improvement, production, and management, although it may be the case in practice. It has not included weed problems and some other growers' problems (Tette et al. 1979). No coordinated plant protection program is going to be consistently successful that ignores its logically subservient relationship to total crop production and management.

In July 1977 a cooperative, interdisciplinary, 6-year experiment was initiated in Georgia. It is supported by a private foundation and includes agricultural engineering, agricultural economics, agronomy, entomology, horticulture, plant pathology, nematology, and weed science. Its title is Irrigated Multiple-Cropping Production Systems and all plant protection discipline problems are combined with all other production and management problems on each crop. Fifteen scientists from the different disciplines are involved. It appears to be organized well to achieve the long-term goals of growing several crops under irrigation using a systems approach (A. W. Johnson 1980, pers. commun.).

In Israel, an interesting cooperative approach to plant protection in citrus is described by Harpaz and Rosen (1971).

> The citrus board of Israel is the sole organization through which all of the citrus crop of the country is marketed, whether for export or local consumption. The board is empowered to collect certain levies imposed on the proceeds of citrus fruits sales and through its agrotechnical division the board finances research and development projects covering all aspects of citrus fruit production and marketing, among which pest control is the most prominent. The board is authorized to carry out pest control operations on citrus on a countrywide scale. It also acts as the major purchaser and distributor of insecticides and pesticides on behalf of the country's growers for reasons both of economy and quality control.

The achievements of this organization are impressive, particularly in plant protection. It has developed, for example, an effective program of biological control of the Florida red scale, *Chrysomphalus aonidum*. Note that the effort is centered on one crop and primary efforts are in production and management, with plant protection being a subordinate but necessary and important part of the total program.

Developing World

In India, coordinated research projects are being developed on different crops with national cooperative efforts and coordinated multidisciplinary research support. In the words of Vishnu Swarup (1974, pers. commun.),

> The main objective of such coordinated projects is to undertake research on various aspects of crop production including crop protection in different agroclimatic conditions of the country. In such projects a number of research centers participate in conducting the experiments in a coordinated manner. For each project there is a project coordinator for the vegetable crops program.

A. Appa Rao (1974, pers. commun.), Andhra Pradesh Agricultural University, Hyderabad, India, discussed a similar Indian program in more detail:

> We in India are placing much emphasis on integrated pest control and we are trying to translate this into action over large areas in what we call Operational Research Projects. Under such a program we take up 1,000 to 2,000 acres of continuous area belonging to many farmers in which a single crop is growing where the integrated pest control measures can be practiced. All the operations will be done by the farmers but under the supervision of the university scientists and the Department of Agriculture Extension workers.

This particular cooperative integrated control program includes all plant protection disciplines. Appa Rao listed ten pest-disease complexes on nine different crops in India that are being controlled by a combination of insecticides and fungicides. He also mentioned four crops on which a combined program controls either a pest, a disease, or a combination plus nutrient deficiency and lists the pesticides and specific nutrients that are used. At least three disciplines are coordinating crop protection programs on rice. Plant pathology, entomology, and agronomy are working on tungro, a virus disease of rice. Plant pathology, agronomy, and plant breeding programs are coordinated on the grassy shoot virus disease of sugarcane. Plant pathology and entomology are cooperating on the yellow mosaic of bhendi and tristeza of citrus, both virus diseases.

Cooperative Rice Pest Control Program—Taiwan

A cooperative program in plant protection is being developed in Taiwan. Some have thought the Taiwan program to be an integrated pest control program (Luh 1971), but it is far more: "Integrated rice production and integrated summer vegetable production are emphasized in Taiwan. This could be confused with integrated pest control. Actually, it is the equivalent of the International Rice Research Institute's 'Package of Practices,' also used in India.''

In other words, it is an effort in coordinated crop production and management that includes, in a supporting role, cooperative and coordinated efforts in plant protection. This is the ideal and proper way to move, and the Taiwan program is developing successfully. This cooperative rice pest control program is so outstanding that its description is quoted in its entirety as submitted by Ren-jong Chiu (1974, pers. commun.) of JCRR (now PACD), Taipei.

> For the past ten years, "cooperative rice pest control" has been a major program which signifies a great joint effort by the Joint Commission on Rural Reconstruction (JCRR), government agencies and rice growers to increase rice production. The principle of cooperative control was first tested in 1961 when the demonstration was first organized jointly by JCRR, Provincial Department of Agriculture and Forestry (PDAF) and Provincial Forestry Bureau (PFB) at 10 different townships to compare the effectiveness of pest control by team operations with what was done on the individual farm basis. In 1962, 62 more such teams were organized. The philosophy behind such a program is that unified operations to combat diseases and insect pests could more efficiently and thoroughly remove the infection or infestation sources, thereby augmenting the effect of each single operation. . . . The program has made this possible by channeling technical guidance from the various district agricultural improvement stations to farmers' teams through short training courses, discussion panels and other means.
>
> Except for 5 townships which entered the program as township-wide demonstration units, usually each team consists of 50 or more farmers who are farming in adjoining rice fields with a total area of 50–100 ha. This total area of rice fields constitutes a demonstration unit for the cooperative pest control to be practiced. Each team has a leader . . . who disseminates technical information from the government extension workers and coordinates all activities within the team. Application of pesticides is scheduled jointly by the team leader and township extension workers, with the assistance of PDAF and district agricultural improvement station technical personnel. To raise the knowledge level of the team leaders and selected members, PDAF sponsors short training courses once in each rice season. Frequent discussion sessions are also held within or among the teams. The first two years of demonstration of cooperative pest control indicates that rice yield from the demonstration fields could be elevated by 11 to 14 percent over those fields where pest control was organized but not well-coordinated.
>
> Encouraged by the above results, JCRR, PDAF and PFB jointly launched in 1964 a five-year program on cooperative rice pest control in which hsien/city governments also participated by providing matching funds. It was so planned that each year a certain number of townships are selected to set up demonstration teams of the size described above. Extension effort will follow in the next year such that the remaining rice farmers in the same townships are organized into extension teams, the number of which varies with the var-

ied rice acreage in each township. PDAF and PFB are responsible for organizing demonstration and extension teams, respectively. Subsidies were given to each participating township for the first two years of demonstration to cover the partial cost (about 50 percent) of sprayers and dusters purchased for the benefit of township extension workers, leaders and selected members of the cooperative pest control demonstration and extension teams. During the period of 1964–1968, a total of 321 demonstration teams and 2078 extension teams were organized in 303 townships. The following table [Table 16.1] gives the details:

The carrying out of the cooperative pest control program during the last ten-year period has produced the following desirable results:
1. An increased yield of rice per unit area (despite some climatic and cultural factors that combine to affect the level of disease and insect incidence). According to data collected during 1965–1966 by PDAF, the cooperative pest control demonstration fields averaged 11–13 percent higher yield over those in which rice growers conducted pest control on an individual farm basis and by their own judgment. To accompany this yield increase was an increased net profit of the same magnitude for those farmers participating in the program. The difference in these comparisons became narrower in later years as the non-participating farmers gradually learned to follow the same pattern of pest control as in the cooperative fields.
2. An elevated level of knowledge of rice pests for the township extension workers and farmers as well. This is one of the most significant achievements of the program in the long run.
3. An organizational basis on which to impose later in some selected townships the so-called "integrated demonstration program on improved rice cultivation techniques" for an even greater increase in rice yield.

Undoubtedly, such an extensive pest control program tends to encourage pesticide use, sometimes to an extent beyond the actual need. That Taiwan's rice growers in many major areas spend a sizable amount of money, about 20 percent of the cost of rice production, on controlling rice insects and diseases

Table 16.1.   A Summary of Data on Cooperative Rice Pest Control in Taiwan

| Year | Cumulative No. of Cooperative Pest Control Teams | | | No. of Participating Farmers | No. of Participating Townships | Rice Acreage Covered |
	Demonstration	Extension	Total			
Existing prior to 1964	72*	. . .	72*	. . .	72*	. . .
1964	221	160	381	35,793	111	33,799
1965	271	825	1106	124,013	161	112,002
1966	321	1335	1656	200,491	210	172,503
1967	321	1585	2082	254,814	276	218,213
1968	321	2078	2399	300,299	303	251,932

*Including 5 township-wide teams.

seems to attest to this undesirable side effect. Except in Japan where pesticide use in the rice field is even more extensive, Taiwan's farmers are not surpassed in pesticide expenses by their counterparts in any other rice growing countries of the world. To correct this trend may require more fundamental knowledge in the disease and insect ecology and sustained efforts for developing varieties with multiple resistance to major diseases and insects.

The present state of cooperative pest control activities differs somewhat from township to township. In those townships where the responsible extension personnel remain devoted to their work, the program is being continued with vigor. In others the interest in cooperative activities has gradually faded as a result of suspended government subsidy. This is so particularly under the present circumstance of a decreased profit for farmers from growing rice. One outgrowth from the program, unexpected at its start, has been the emergence of pesticide application as a private profession in many townships which previously benefited from the cooperative pest control program. Some of those who now provide this service had in the past received subsidies for purchasing dusters or sprayers. Although such development is not entirely undesirable, it was not so intended originally.

This type of program is useful in areas of the world where very small farms are typical. The organization of research and agricultural workers at the field level and the cooperation among the disciplines are equally outstanding. In this program is a constant realization that plant protection is a necessary but subservient part of the overall program of rice improvement, production, and management in Taiwan. It also emphasizes key problems—for example, the fact that necessary environmental and ecological data are not available. Yet without the data and without computer analyses, field analyses based on applied adaptive research techniques have produced an essentially applied systems approach to cooperative plant protection that is practical and quite effective. Sophisticated computerized systems analyses are not required for adequate integrated interdisciplinary control programs. Since computerized programs will not soon be available, this particular program is encouraging for workers who are concerned about coordinated programs of plant protection in the developing world.

Organizational Problems

Within specific educational and research institutions in the Western world the tendency has been to build theoretical research programs around outstanding individuals, but educational institutions often have difficulty attracting outstanding people into applied field research programs. Basic research in which an individual works independently is often more exciting, results are easier to measure, and results can be published more rapidly. Cooperative applied research programs need individuals who can yield to pressures and subordinate themselves to the larger goals of the overall projects.

One of the problems of administrators of research programs in land-grant or agricultural universities is encouraging and rewarding outstanding cooperative applied research. It is much more difficult to give credit for individual effort, there are usually fewer publications, and research is conducted more slowly in the field within nature's time frame.

A few institutions have been able to encourage independent researchers and also to develop outstanding practical cooperative projects within disciplines. The University of Wisconsin has been such an institution (Arthur Kelman 1975, pers. commun.). For example, in 1975 in the department of plant pathology 25 cooperative projects involved either two or three other departments. The horticulture department was involved with 9 projects, agronomy with 8, soils with 2, food science with 2, entomology with 3, forestry with 1, veterinary science with 1, dairy science with 1, and agricultural engineering with 1. In many institutions subdisciplines within plant protection seldom cooperate and rarely communicate from day to day.

Workers in field research face the difficult problem of trying to achieve a healthy crop on well-managed farmland. They know that nature is essentially complex but holistic. These people understand the need for cooperation and coordination. They know too that in the field all researchers quickly become humbled simply because nature is so complex and diverse—confusing even to the brightest mind. This sobering realization has been the stimulus for the development of most of the outstanding projects of cooperative research aimed at the achievement of coordinated control programs designed to solve complex plant protection problems.

17

Conflicting Recommendations

 The recommendations of one discipline in agricultural science may conflict with the recommendations of another—particularly the recommendations of agronomists and horticulturalists as opposed to those of the various plant protection disciplines. Growers usually consider the agronomic and horticultural recommendations first, unless plant protection problems happen to be severe. Growers' considerations hinge first on yield. Their second consideration is usually the least costly acceptable agronomic practice for achieving a high-yielding, high quality crop. The third consideration concerns the conservation and building of soil and the wise use of water and fertilizer. Soil conservation and protection generally hold higher priority for growers than any plant protection problem except the control of weeds, which is paramount. Often at the bottom of the priority list (depending on pest and disease problems) are insects, plant diseases, nematodes, or any combination that needs to be controlled. In spite of the low priority, however, growers often attempt to achieve some sort of insurance against all loss possibilities.

Because of this hierarchy of grower concerns and interests plant protection personnel must develop, if possible, economically acceptable control procedures that fit into the desired agronomic or horticultural practices and the best soil-building and conservation schemes. We cannot expect a complex, expensive recommendation to be followed unless the crop gives good return and pests and diseases are severe each year. If there is a conflict, plant protection personnel must develop new control techniques that fit into the acceptable pattern of economic agronomic practices and requirements.

More effort should be made to develop cooperative schemes that fulfill the needs of plant protection and do not run counter to other recommendations. Some of these problems are outlined below (FAO 1971):

> At the research and development stages there is, therefore, a special need for collaboration between scientists of the different disciplines. For example, collaboration with agronomists and soil chemists is essential where cultural prac-

tices and soil fertility affect pest incidence. Furthermore, since the basis for most forms of plant resistance to insects is often so sophisticated, plant breeding for resistance may need the collaboration of plant breeders, entomologists, behaviourists and physiologists. Before introducing new crop species or varieties to a specific agroecosystem their response to prevailing pest complexes should be determined as carefully as their response to climatic and soil conditions. Weed control with herbicides has profoundly affected the ecology of many agroecosystems but modern selective herbicides can now be used to adjust the weed species complex as well as the overall abundance of weeds. That collaboration with weed control specialists may prove valuable in integrated pest control programs is shown by the evidence that different weed species can variously act as a camouflage against colonizing insects, as a vital link in the maintenance of natural enemies, or conversely, as an undesirable source of the pest. In addition, the use of fungicides or other pest control chemicals by plant pathologists may greatly interfere with or eliminate the activity of natural enemies keeping a group of key insect pests under control or influence the rate of increase of pest populations.

Good (1972*a*, 1972*b*) emphasized that recommendations for the control of a specific pest or plant disease are often made without consideration for the management of other pest problems and important factors are often overlooked. Hooker (1974) reminds us that "changes in cultural practices, such as plant spacing, fertilizer application, tillage method or irrigation practice may contribute to environmental changes which increase plant disease incidence."

Often the management practices of modern agriculture increase the likelihood of severe plant disease outbreaks or insect attacks. For example, large-scale monocultures often have a narrow gene base for a given characteristic or set of characteristics and will occasionally suffer a rapid development of severe specific insect or plant disease problems. Forests that have only one or very few tree species also are excellent spots where specific insects and plant diseases can become very damaging.

Changes in irrigation and fertilizer practices can furnish more favorable habitats for insects and weeds. Pools of water often produce good reproduction sites for insects, and a combination of irrigation water and fertilizer provides the necessary nutrients for good crops and weed growth (USDA 1972*a*; USGPO 1972*b*). Fertilization tends to produce larger, more succulent crop plants that seem more susceptible to certain diseases and insects than plants grown at minimal nutritional levels; and irrigation in general favors the development of diseases and insect pests.

Tillage practices may favor or inhibit the development of diseases and insects, depending on the disease or pest involved. Cropping patterns too may stimulate an increase in or control of certain pests and plant diseases. High plant population densities tend to make the microenvironment somewhat wetter, favoring the development of more pests and diseases (Apple 1972).

Tillage and Agronomic Practices

Specific cases of conflicts in recommendations illustrate some of the serious problems that exist when conflicting recommendations are given.

Minimum tillage, a fairly recent development in technologically advanced countries, is an important agronomic and horticultural practice that has many agronomic advantages. It takes much less time, reduces tillage costs, and is an excellent mechanism for reducing wind and water erosion by maintaining a good ground cover.

But it has disadvantages; it essentially eliminates crop sanitation as a plant disease and pest control technique. Minimum tillage makes it much easier for plant pathogens and pests to overwinter and increases possibilities for early season infection and infestation on the next crop. It counters many recommendations concerning the control of plant diseases and insects. For example, the southern corn leaf blight organism survives in plant debris on the surface but will not survive when the plant debris is buried and overwinters underground (Burns 1973; Hooker 1974). The European corn borer has been partially controlled in the past by destruction or farm use of all crop residues and deep moldboard plowing techniques, and one of the recommended methods for grasshopper control in the United States is the destruction of eggs in the fall and winter by deep plowing or disking and thereby exposing the eggs to weather and to birds (Metcalf et al. 1951).

Farmers like to grow alfalfa in solid stands to facilitate irrigation and the use of farm machinery in harvesting. The pest control recommendation to strip-crop alfalfa is seldom practiced because strip cutting means modified irrigation techniques and considerably less efficient use of machinery (P. S. Messenger 1975, pers. commun.).

Weed Control

A number of conflicts exist in the area of weed control. For example, increased use of fertilizer or irrigation water also means more lush growth of weeds so that control is often difficult during the first few years of an irrigation program. When preemergence herbicides eliminate weed populations, insects are forced to move from the preferred weeds to the crop, aggravating the insect control problem on that crop (W. R. Furtick 1975, pers. commun.).

Entomologists interested in biological control often complain about herbicides killing all the weeds on which parasites and predators survive. A few alternate host weeds are needed in a crop to keep desirable parasites and predators going, particularly during the noncrop season. It is important in biological control to maintain at least low population levels of important insect species.

One example of this has occurred in Hawaii in the sugarcane industry. A weed, *Euphorbia* spp., is necessary for the survival of a particular predator on sugarcane. In recent years weed control has been so efficient that too few plants have remained for the preservation of satisfactory levels of the predator insect (Wallace Mitchell 1974, pers. commun.). The details of this problem are documented by Topham (1973). A dipterous parasite, *Lixophaga sphenophori,* was introduced into Hawaii to control the New Guinea sugarcane weevil, *Rhabdoscelus obscurus.* Two plants were excellent food sources for the adult fly—*E. heterophylla* and *E. geniculata.* Use of herbicides in the sugarcane plantations destroyed most of these weeds and left few spots for survival of the parasitic fly. The result was a great reduction in the parasitization of the New Guinea sugarcane weevil by the fly, a noticeable increase in the population of the weevil, and far more damage than, for example, 25 years ago. Many other plants that offer a routine source of food for the adult parasite are also killed with the herbicides used. Agronomists feel strongly that it is more important to have sugarcane fields free of weeds than to leave a few to function as alternate host plants for a parasite; and industry workers usually attempt to kill all weeds with herbicides and ignore the need for parasite and predator survival (Topham 1973).

Herbicides often are incompatible with other pesticides. For example, the herbicide MCPA (Methoxone) is not compatible with organic carbamate insecticides (M. D. Pathak 1974, pers. commun.), and there are many other examples of undesirable interactions between insecticidal and herbicidal sprays.

If weeds and grasses are not controlled, other problems develop. For example, when grasses grow abundantly in maize the armyworm tends to become a serious problem. The multitude of tiny larvae develop first on the grasses and then move to maize. Also, chinch bugs often kill foxtail grass and do not move to maize until all the foxtail is devoured (Petty 1972).

Weeds tend to become serious problems in fields where the crop stand is thin. Continuous cropping of maize is beneficial in insect control but may present serious problems in plant disease control—southern corn leaf blight and certain root rots tend to become more severe after continuous cropping. On the other hand continuous cropping of maize usually makes weed control much easier (Petty 1972).

Insect Control

Many entomological recommendations conflict with agronomic practices and recommendations. In the sandy land area of central Kansas, the stubble and debris of a maize crop are left on the soil surface to prevent wind erosion and to provide fodder. This practice, although an agronomic recommendation for the area, encourages the survival of several maize insect pests in the plant and leaf debris and protects overwintering larvae from low temperatures (Herbert Knutson 1974, pers. commun.).

The Hessian fly has been quite severe in the past in Kansas and some other plains states. Resistant wheat varieties have long been available but often are not grown because their flour is not of the best quality for bread. Consequently, late planting and control of volunteer wheat are recommended for good control of the Hessian fly. However, farmers want to use volunteer wheat for pasture, and they often plant early so they can get more early fall pasture. Hence, growers tend to ignore all Hessian fly control recommendations until the infestation becomes severe (H. W. Somsen 1975, pers. commun.).

In Montana in the 1930s, most of the wheat fields were planted in strips about 80–100 feet wide. This fallow system preserved and utilized the scarce moisture and reduced wind erosion. This pattern of farming is still often used. It was favorable for the development of the wheat stem sawfly, *Cephus cinctus,* which overwintered in wheat stubble and later flew to the nearest wheat field, seldom moving more than 300 feet into the field. Hence large, square fields had much less damage from the sawfly than narrow strips (H. W. Somsen 1975, pers. commun.).

In Illinois, entomologists used to recommend that maize be planted late to escape severe corn borer damage; by contrast, agronomists recommended early planting for maximum yields (Hooker 1974*b*). In the Coachella valley of California, irrigation practices that are best for the date palm have encouraged the development of huge populations of eye gnats, which are so abundant that it is virtually impossible for people to work without covering their faces. They are particularly annoying to golfers (John J. McKelvey, Jr., 1975, pers. commun.).

Fungicides normally do not kill insects or enhance their populations, but occasionally a recommendation for a fungicide will conflict with the recommendation of an entomologist. In India, Bordeaux mixture is used for preserving the finger rhizomes of turmeric for seed purposes; this use conflicts with the recommendation of the entomologists because it results in severe infestation by several scale insects (A. Appa Rao 1974, pers. commun.).

Quite often insecticide treatments destroy important predators and parasites. For example, the use of DDT or lead arsenate for the control of codling moth on apples also destroys the important lace wing predators, *Chrysopa* spp., and allows the mealybugs to become severe pests on apples. Also, since World War II the large-scale use of organic pesticides has altered predator populations and led to the development of pesticide resistance in insects and mites, and spider mites have become a major plant pest problem (Huffaker et al. 1970).

The use of chlorinated hydrocarbons and carbamates to control lygus

bugs on cotton in California has resulted in tremendous outbreaks of noc-
tuid defoliators of cotton (including the armyworm, the leaf perforator, the
bollworm) because of the destruction of the natural enemies of these pests
(P. S. Messenger 1975, pers. commun.). Many insecticides destroy insect
and mite predators. Acaricides designed to destroy mites also destroy many
mite predators of insects. Some fungicides, particularly those containing
sulfur, have a general detrimental effect on predacious mites and sometimes
also on insect predators of other insect pests (McMurtry et al. 1970).

Plant Breeding

A number of conflicts occur as a result of plant breeding changes. Often
plants with a high level of resistance have poor or unacceptable quality or
other undesirable agronomic characteristics. The breeding of resistant
plants is replete with examples of success in controlling one pest only to find
that the plant is very susceptible to other equally important pests.

Agronomists have tended to recommend the release and growth of
relatively few varieties of crops with a very narrow gene base and vertical
resistance, if present. By contrast, plant pathologists and entomologists
have tended to recommend more genetic diversity and horizontal resistance
and have not emphasized quality and yield sufficiently.

Several newly developed insect-resistant genotypes have displayed susceptibility to other pests. Some cotton genotypes with a high gossypol content are resistant to *Heliothis* spp; unfortunately, these lines are particularly
attractive to thrips whose populations are often increased fourfold on these
plants as compared to plants with a normal gossypol content. Glabrous cottons (smooth leaves and reduced leaf and stem hairs) provide unfavorable
oviposition sites and consequently are highly resistant to *Heliothis* spp. (the
bollworm–tobacco budworm complex) but are particularly attractive to the
cabbage looper, *Trichoplusia ni.* Likewise, glabrous cottons produce reduced populations of the cotton fleahopper, *Pseudatomoscelis seriatus,* but
are more susceptible to leafhoppers (M. J. Lukefahr 1975, pers. commun.).
The frego-bract type cotton bred for resistance to the boll weevil is very susceptible to attacks by several plant bugs in the family Miridae (P. L. Adkis-
son 1975, pers. commun.). The pubescent cottons have high levels of resistance to thrips and fleahoppers and substantial resistance to boll weevils.
However, these hairy types are particularly attractive to and preferred by
the cotton bollworm (Knox Walker 1975, pers. commun.).

Disease Control

Plant disease recommendations related to the recommendations of agronomists bring many examples of conflicts to mind. Agronomists have recommended high plant populations and high nitrogen fertility for maximum

yields of maize and other crops. These recommendations for maize have produced more severe stalk rot problems; and high plant populations in maize and other crops tend to increase the incidence of diseases associated with high humidity (Hooker 1974*b*).

Wheat streak mosaic is a virus disease transmitted by an eriophyid mite, *Aceria tulipae*. Recommendations for control of this disease include elimination of all volunteer wheat several weeks prior to planting and planting wheat late (after the mite has become quiescent for the winter). The volunteer wheat carries not only the oversummering virus but also the virus vector, the eriophyid mite. However, farmers in the U.S. Great Plains like to keep summer volunteer wheat for early fall pasture and often plant wheat as early as possible for early fall pasture; both practices encourage the development of wheat streak mosaic (Somsen and Sill 1970).

Plant pathologists have recommended low plant populations in maize for stalk rot control. Agronomists, by contrast, have recommended high plant populations for best yields. A compromise recommendation of an intermediate plant population has gradually evolved (John Schmidt 1974, pers. commun.).

In Taiwan a power transplanter of rice introduced in 1970 required that rice seedlings be grown under dry-land conditions. This practice favored a seedling disease that was never a problem in lowland or wet conditions, and it became very severe. The new cultural practice was in complete opposition to former plant protection methods. Fortunately, successful control measures have been found. They consist of a modification of the seedbed cultural pattern and the use of soil fungicides against the plant disease organisms (a complex) (Ren-jong Chiu 1974, pers. commun.).

In the United States the soybean plant is being increasingly infected with a complex of microbial pathogens. This problem is of sufficient importance to justify the use of fungicides or in some cases antibiotics for control. However, after fungicide use there is considerable evidence of destruction of some microbial pathogens that are important natural control agents of some major soybean insect pests. Such complex interrelationships emphasize the importance of an interdisciplinary approach to plant protection research (Huffaker 1974).

Herbicides occasionally increase disease problems. For example, root rot problems of peas and peanuts have been much more severe since a certain chemical herbicide has been used routinely for weed control (A. L. Hooker 1974, pers. commun.).

Nematode Control

Nematode control techniques also may work against the control techniques of other plant protection disciplines. For example, nematologists recommend Temik (aldicarb) to control *Rotylenchulus* spp. on cotton in Louisiana and this chemical has completely upset the program for insect control on cotton (O. J. Dickerson 1975, pers. commun.).

In India horticulturalists recommend intercropping grape with Giner to give more return per acre. This practice is not appreciated by plant protection personnel as it encourages a buildup in root-knot nematode populations. Horticulturalists also recommend that papaya be grown on the borders of grape vineyards. Again, this is discouraged by plant protection personnel because it encourages a rapid buildup of nematodes. In India, horticulturalists recommend dipping bunches of turmeric in a solution of gibberellic acid, but nematologists discourage it because it encourages a fast buildup of nematodes in the turmeric (A. Appa Rao 1974, pers. commun.).

Other Conflicts

Sometimes unwise laws conflict with pest control recommendations. For example, in California a law was passed that allows the growth of only one cotton varietal type. Over the years the result has been the increase of very severe pest problems on this crop. Rotation of different varieties, particularly those with varying patterns of resistance to the different pests, would have made this problem much less severe (Hooker 1974).

Many more examples of conflicts between recommendations of agronomists and horticulturalists and those of plant protection personnel could be given. It must be the goal of all concerned to reconcile these differences. Remember that solutions must fit into acceptable economic, agronomic, and conservation requirements without producing unacceptable environmental effects. This assignment is difficult; friendly and helpful cooperation between research workers in the relevant agricultural disciplines will be necessary to carry it out.

18

Conclusions

 The many natural and possible interrelationships among the several plant protection disciplines have been shown. Cooperative and combined efforts would often produce a more effective control system for a particular pest or disease (or combination) than independent efforts, and the cost of plant protection has increased so greatly that it has become imperative to achieve satisfactory control at less cost.

The problems arising from extensive use of pesticides accentuate the need for moving away from synthetic organic pesticides that do not denature quickly. We should utilize chemicals that are not dangerous to people, warm-blooded animals, and beneficial species of arthropods; and we need to build more control procedures into the cropping system or into the crop itself.

The development of cooperative, combined control approaches at the field level is difficult. In addition, complex sociological and political patterns that involve power and prestige work against interdisciplinary, integrated efforts. Researchers in the field of agriculture must be willing to be part of a cooperative undertaking that has not been given great personal prestige, unlike independent research that often results in more prestige, publications, promotions, and remuneration. There is also the difficult and as yet unsolved problem of achieving for agriculture a meaningful position and priority in the national plans of many of the developing countries. Such a situation makes it almost impossible to develop a long-term approach to agricultural improvement, to say nothing of plant protection improvement.

Although plant protection disciplines overlap, the training, the point of view, and the basic approach to control has been independent and often different. For example, in entomology the general approach has been to control arthropods after they appear and usually after they have achieved economically significant population levels. Preventive control has not been routine and in general has not been practiced except for a few cultural techniques that were used in some areas long before the advent of insec-

266

ticides. Because of the many agricultural and environmental problems that have been created by excessive use of insecticides, entomologists have begun to move away from insecticide use toward a multiple-faceted effort called pest management or integrated pest control. A few preventive controls such as plant resistance to insects are included, but therapeutic controls such as insecticides are used whenever integrated management techniques are not adequate. The biological controls recently emphasized are not new in entomology. Some of them are among the oldest methods used in that discipline but were neglected during the heyday of insecticides.

By contrast, in plant pathology the effort always has been toward preventing disease and maintaining plant health. It is usually impossible to ascertain precisely what constitutes an economic threshold level of a given disease propagule, since environment is as important in the development of a disease as the susceptibility of the potential host. Thus plant pathologists have been trained to think first of preventive controls, particularly of discovering or achieving disease resistance or immunity in plants (NAS 1968*b*).

In certain areas of plant pathology fungicides have been used routinely as preventive measures. (Examples are the routine spray schedules associated with pome and stone fruit crops, Irish potatoes, and some vegetable crops.) Only recently have practical therapeutic chemicals been developed and only a few plant diseases are now controlled by chemotherapeutic sprays. The use of fungicides and spray techniques in general has been reserved for diseases that are difficult to control or plants that need a cosmetic control. Most diseases that seriously infect plants cannot be overcome in an economically feasible way (NAS 1968*a*). Control efforts therefore have been aimed at eliminating or minimizing the inoculum source, preventing disease and its spread, or developing immune or resistant varieties of the crop.

Cultural control techniques have always been important in plant pathology, particularly in grain crops, and have usually been combined with plant resistance. For a few diseases, elimination of alternate hosts has been extremely significant; and such simple procedures as altering planting dates or roguing have proved to be very effective in certain cases. Exclusion (preventing the introduction of a pathogen into an area where it does not exist) is often the cheapest and best control method. It has been achieved in many ways—through plant quarantine and inspection systems; certification of planting stocks; and control of the movement of seed, plant parts, and soil. Simply moving the crop to areas where the disease does not exist (sometimes called *avoidance*) is particularly important in some parts of the world.

Sophisticated chemical control programs have been developed for certain high value plantation crops in the tropics, such as cacao, sugarcane, coffee, rubber seedlings, pineapple, and bananas; but chemicals have not been used widely, particularly on the small farms. The chemicals are costly and difficult to procure. Also, application equipment and technical expertise are lacking. Since their effective use depends very much on local rainfall, humidity, and temperature patterns, each country or area must work out its own solutions.

Until recently plant nematology has been part of plant pathology (most nematologists working with plant parasitic nematodes have been trained as plant pathologists) because many soil-borne diseases of plants caused by fungi are closely associated with plant nematodes. Also, many nematode controls, particularly fumigants, are also effective controls of soil fungi and other associated soil microorganisms that may be part of a causal complex. The diagnosis and understanding of the complex and its treatment are difficult (NAS 1968b). The most desirable form of nematode control would combine the encouragement of parasites and predators of nematodes, the physical manipulation of the soil to control nematode populations, and nematode-resistant plants. Minimal amounts of chemical soil treatments would then be used if absolutely necessary.

Nematologists, in general, have been more interested than entomologists in resistant plants and in cultural and physical control manipulations. Although many nematicides have been developed and some are very effective, until recently the tendency has been to use nematicides as a last resort (Good 1972a, 1972b). Plant nematologists are in a position between entomologists and plant pathologists. They typically have been more interested in plant resistance and nonchemical controls than entomologists but more inclined to use pesticides than plant pathologists. Nematologists, who work with sizable living organisms, can measure populations with reasonable accuracy and determine the agronomic threshold levels of certain nematode species; plant pathologists thus far have not been able to measure the effects of plant disease propagule populations.

Nematologists, like entomologists, are interested in such biological control techniques as utilizing natural enemies. However, natural enemies in the soil are difficult to study and control, usually very small, and typically not well understood. It is well known that maintaining high levels of organic matter, adding organic amendments, and using organic fertilizers reduce nematode populations to some extent and these techniques are used wherever possible. Also, such methods as flooding, fallowing, field and seedbed sanitation, various land preparation methods, crop rotation, and trap crops are common in nematode control. These practices encourage the growth of populations of soil organisms that are important in the biological control of nematodes (Good 1972a, 1972b).

Although weed science has only recently emerged from the provinces of agronomy and horticulture, control of weeds has been of primary importance in agriculture for thousands of years. Weeds are alternate hosts of many plant diseases, insect and mite vectors, and other arthropod pests. Weed control is by far the most important plant protection procedure for the farmer. Weeds are always a problem, whereas in a given year the effects of plant diseases and insects may be unimportant.

Herbicides have been the primary reason for the development of weed science as a separate discipline. Herbicide use is increasing more than the use of any other chemical control measure. The environmental effects of herbicides are minimal as compared to several of the important insecticides. Most herbicides are believed to break down rather quickly into innocuous materials and usually are not harmful to warm-blooded animals, although the speed of breakdown is questioned by some people (B. D. Blair 1979, pers. commun.).

Historically, preventing weed growth has been the most basic of all weed control methods. Prevention requires the use of weed-free seed and planting stocks; proper quarantine and plant regulation methods; often elaborate, preplanting tillage methods; mowing of weeds prior to seed production; flooding; shading; and smothering. A recently developed valuable shading and smothering technique is the use of black polyethylene strips along crop rows. It has become a standard practice in some large plantation industries, e.g., the pineapple. One weed control agent that is often forgotten is the crop itself. A crop that is growing vigorously and in sufficient density will eventually smother most annual weeds (USGPO 1972).

In the developed countries, weed control has changed dramatically with the advent of herbicides, but in most of the world (particularly in the developing world of the tropics) weed control techniques used are still prevention where possible and physical elimination where necessary. This state of affairs is likely to continue for some time in most of the developing world.

Interdisciplinary Efforts

It is increasingly clear that interdisciplinary efforts must be the central approach in solving the environmental, agricultural, and economic problems associated with the use of pesticides and economic constraints alone should push us in the direction of nonchemical control techniques. The use of pesticides has resulted in the development of resistance by many arthropods, and more resistance is noted each year among nematodes and even among some plant disease organisms. This trend will make it increasingly difficult to utilize broad-spectrum pesticides effectively. At the field level every practical problem associated with plant protection will push us toward maximum utilization of interdisciplinary efforts in the development of combined control methods that are cheap, practical, and do not contaminate the environment unduly. They must also be safe for warm-blooded animals and humans and protect desirable or useful arthropods and other species.

Because of the necessity of breaking down analytical research problems into their smallest components, it has been difficult to develop effective interdisciplinary research programs. Sir John Russell (1955) discussed the problems created by excessive specialization: "The modern danger is that specialists may lose touch one with the other and the subject may end up as it began; as a mass of facts of greater or less moment, out of which a clear and lucid system is yet to be framed." Russell felt that the dangers of specialization could be averted in the following way:

> Only by arranging regular meetings for the reading and discussion of papers and carefully planned conferences where subjects of special importance can be examined along very broad lines will it be possible to avoid an accumulation of a mass of apparently unrelated facts which cannot be utilized in a combined coherent way to understand a large system. The advent of the modern computer and the possibilities of systems analysis certainly have not arrived too soon. A concerted effort needs to be made by a new breed of cooperative researchers to bring together the mass of data in the various disciplines into a coherent, meaningful whole and to express the possible knowledge in a new approach to a system of crop protection and pest management controls which take into consideration the complexities of the environment and the problems of its contamination as well as the ecological details of not only the crop being grown but the various plant disease organisms and pests which feed upon it and must be controlled.

Huffaker (1974) felt that cooperative efforts must embrace a wide spectrum of tactics for entomologists and urged other plant protection personnel to consider them also. These tactics are:

1. Establishment of realistic economic thresholds for remedial action for a given pest or plant disease.

2. Development of plant breeding techniques suitable for developing new crop varieties resistant to all the pests and plant diseases attacking a given crop.

3. Use of parasites; predators; various insect pathogens; conventional biological control techniques; and unconventional techniques such as antagonism and antibiosis, particularly within the plant pathological field.

4. Development of more economic, selective use of pesticides, insecticides, fungicides, nematicides, etc., in modified control programs that use less chemical material and are combined with other control methods.

5. Development of new types of cultural control techniques for all crop protection and pest management problems.

6. Development of the new important biological chemicals, such as

pheromones, for monitoring pest populations and as direct control procedures, where possible.

7. Improvement of all monitoring and forecasting techniques and the development of life-cycle tables for all crop pests and plant diseases in the hope that a system of prediction through the use of models may be made available.

In particular, it is necessary to bring outside specialists, such as systems analysts, ecologists, economists, plant physiologists, biochemists, and soil scientists, into cooperative research programs. Of course agronomists and horticulturalists should have primary roles. The research of plant protection scientists must be subservient to the larger needs of crop improvement, production, and management as well as those of a protected and improved environment. Unfortunately, this important principle has been forgotten or resisted far too often.

The cheapest possible control, of course, is immunity. Much more emphasis in routine breeding programs should be placed on resistance to various plant diseases and pests combined with the even more important characters controlling yield, quality and vigor, and the examination of plants from the standpoint of the biochemical nature of immunity and resistance. The whole area of allelopathic materials, phytoalexins, plant host–specific toxins and other toxins, antibiotics, and all types of antagonisms that are the result of metabolites produced by plants or microorganisms needs more study from the perspective of plant immunity or resistance. The ideal might be to spray a plant with a material that confers resistance or even immunity to a specific plant disease or pest, combining chemical and biological control.

Cooperative research is essential. The plant breeder must be the coordinator of this team approach. Painter (1951) prophetically summarized this need in the following quotation:

In plant breeding the pursuit of any one genetic character such as insect resistance, without continual attention to all others, may quickly make a plant strain of little use. So many facets are involved that there is an important requirement for team research. Formal written agreements can facilitate such teamwork and may be administrative necessities. But real success depends on sharing work as well as credit, and on the true meeting of minds in the field plot, the laboratory or greenhouse as well as about the conference table. The workers require a broad biological background with particularly an understanding of the problems and possibilities in the other's field of work.

This quotation summarizes the basic problems associated with the development of team research in plant breeding and also the basic problem of achieving a broad enough background to understand the attitudes and approaches of other disciplines. The problem here is also one of convincing persons in one discipline that the work being done in other disciplines is equally important, equally complex, and in the long run equally significant.

The problem of good administration is the development of inter-disciplinary research aimed at programs of cooperative and integrated plant disease and pest control. Administrators need to be aware of the extreme importance of cooperative research, its cost, its long-term significance, and the necessity of long-term support, since these goals can only be accomplished over many years of concentrated effort by teams working together closely. In the long run it probably requires what O. J. Dickerson (1975, pers. commun.) suggests is the most important ingredient: "a very strong and capable administrator who is willing to take the bull by the horns and knock some heads together."

Forced cooperation may be necessary but often has not been too fruitful. The most exciting team efforts have been built around informal efforts where individuals were willing and anxious to develop a team approach to a problem that could not be solved by individuals working alone. Outstanding examples of team research are those controlled by plantation industries such as sugarcane, pineapple, banana, etc., or by large private foundations through institutions such as the International Rice Research Institute in the Philippines. Such international institutions have made it a point to hire individuals who were willing and anxious to work in cooperative, coordinated research teams attempting to solve important field problems in a specific crop. It is no accident that they have had such outstanding success.

The analytical research specialist is the basis for the accumulation of basic data that can eventually be brought together in a systems approach to solve problems in the field. This research role always will be significant and basic in agricultural research. The two areas should always be in dynamic tension. The approaches to research—basic and applied, analytic and synthetic, disciplinary and interdisciplinary—are like two sides of the same coin and must be given equal importance. Achieving a proper balance between basic and applied research has always been difficult. Some technique has to be discovered for giving adequate and equivalent prestige, power, and pay to individuals who are willing to bury themselves and lose their identity in cooperative, interdisciplinary research. These individuals often receive much less credit and in the minds of their peers are often felt to be involved in less significant research. A positive, forceful approach must somehow rectify the errors of the past that have tended to downgrade the significance of applied research and upgrade or overemphasize the importance of basic research. Logically these two should have equivalent status. Solving this problem should be one of the most important goals of research administrators in agriculture.

Crop Production, Improvement, and Management

The most important aspect of plant protection is actually intertwined with crop improvement, production, and management. Hooker (1974) said,

> The plant science research worker in state experiment stations and federal laboratories must not lose contact with the crop and the way farmers grow it. He simply cannot become wholly academic and isolate himself from agriculture. Continued emphasis is needed on research with application to production, so that yields can be improved and stabilized.

Nusbaum and Ferris (1973) emphasized the same point for entomologists:

> Because the cropping system is the dominant feature of agroecosystems, it is the foundation upon which integrated pest management systems rest. A well designed crop rotation experiment (by an agronomist) may provide material for analytical study not only of nematode populations but also of other soil pathogens, soil insects and weeds. This emphasizes the interdisciplinary nature of pest management, especially where different kinds of pests interact with each other and with a given management practice.

Thurston (1971) expressed this point of view for plant pathologists:

> Plant disease control cannot focus only on the pathogen or the damage it causes. It has to be integrated with the entire package of management practices in agriculture, especially those related to insect and weed control. The object of these practices is the production of maximum yields consistent with sound ecological principles which maintain or result in a wholesome environment.

In the developed world the role of plant protection as a part of overall crop production will continue to become more sophisticated but it will still be a secondary consideration.

In the developing countries plant protection is much more difficult. Wellman (1968) noted that the temperate zones have many more publications, scientists, and facilities than the tropics but the tropics have far more crop species, diseases, and pests. In a comparison of the number of diseases on plants, Wellman estimated that there are 32 important diseases of tomato in the temperate zones and 50–278 in the tropics, depending on the area and the time of year. On cabbage, 9 important diseases are found in Wisconsin; Wellman has counted 18–36 in the American tropics. On citrus, in the United States about 50 diseases are considered to be of importance; whereas in the West Indies and in South America Wellman reported approximately 250. Remember that these diseases are occurring on a few large plantations and millions of small farms in the tropics and remember also the scarcity of scientific personnel, libraries, equipment, scientific facilities, administrative support, teaching, extension, and especially money.

Ivan C. Buddenhagen (1975, pers. commun.) outlined the problems of plant protection in the developing world:

> If the basic research and knowledge in ecology and epidemiology necessary to make "pest management" more rational seem to be inadequate in the temperate countries (advanced) this inadequacy is magnified a hundred or thousand fold in most tropical countries. . . . Expenditures toward "pest management" or "crop protection" action programs will automatically result in increased spraying of pesticides, in spite of known desirability of the pure theoretical concept of "pest management," while at the same time lip service will be given to this concept. This has already happened in India. In most underdeveloped tropical countries . . . the major concern of an administrator . . . will be in maintaining or enlarging his organization and its budget in tight competition with many other agencies. Seen as support in this struggle are ever-increased numbers of acres sprayed, helicopters bought and increased state-supported purchase of pesticides. If crop yields go up such activities can take partial credit whether deserved or not. The slow accretion of important biological-ecological-epidemiological information will not sell easily.

Paddock (1967) expressed the problem in these words:

> New or imaginative disease control methods specifically designed for the needs of the developing world are badly needed. . . . The question asked here is whether or not plant pathologists have sufficiently studied alternate methods of disease control specifically adapted to the developing nations. . . . Efforts to date to find imaginative solutions for the agricultural problems of the hungry world have been largely by individuals. . . . A few symposia have been held but the professional societies have not otherwise recognized the need for demonstrating leadership in this area. . . . If plant pathologists and other professional associates organized their skills and the necessary support for those skills, loss from plant diseases might well be reduced and their consequences minimized. If the plant pathologist cannot do this today, then perhaps some modern equivalent of the Irish famine may force him to do so in the future.

In tropical areas that have used high-yielding plant varieties, the problems developing are similar to the problems found in the more advanced countries. R. Smith (1972) discusses this situation:

> The new high-yielding plant varieties of the "green revolution" require reliable water management and increased use of fertilizers to express their yield potential. The combination of water, fertilizer and new plant variety produces a different micro-environment and a different plant environment in the rice paddies and other grain fields. As a result the plant protection problems in these modified ecosystems have changed. For example, in rice, plant hoppers and leaf hoppers have increased in importance as pests and the virus diseases which these insects transmit have increased to serious proportions

(i.e., the serious outbreaks recently of tungro virus in the Philippines). Rice gall midge has increased in parts of Indonesia, India and Sri Lanka and the rice stem borer species complex has changed in several areas. In Sri Lanka, the paddy leaf roller (*Marasmia bilinealis*) formerly mainly a pest in shaded areas, has assumed a new significance correlated with the higher use of fertilizer and the new rice varieties. In general rice leaf blast has become much more important and rice blast less important.

The problems of plant protection for the small farmers of the developing world are complex and usually unsolvable. These farmers could not afford to buy fertilizers or appropriate pesticides if they were available. They have not been instructed in the use of these materials (with the exception of such rapidly advancing countries as Taiwan) and for the most part are not convinced that the new techniques are better than the old because of the lack of demonstration farms or plots. Lack of agricultural advisory personnel is another serious weakness.

Even the improved seeds being developed by most international agencies are cultivars that require good water control, fertilization, and pest control techniques. These practices would be impossible for most small farmers even if they understood and wanted to use them. However, if cultivars could be developed that would produce a larger, more vigorous crop despite inadequate fertilization, water management, and pest control, they would be a tremendous boon to the small farmers of the developing world.

Most farmers of the developing world need an approach to plant protection problems that is less costly and almost automatic. This approach has received inadequate attention. Ivan C. Buddenhagen (1975, pers. commun.) summarized these problems and needs:

> In my view the most basic need at least in food crops in the tropics is to further develop the concept and practice that pest management is, first and foremost, the integration of the epidemiological pathologist, the ecological entomologist and the crop production man with the practicing breeder who is breeding the next major food source for the pests. . . . Secondly, I would back epidemiological and ecological crop production oriented research areas, extremely difficult in the tropics. Thirdly, I would attempt to develop agricultural education in these two directions and to so educate the very best young men, thoroughly, wherever in the world it may be possible, with this emphasis so that they can return and carry the zeal for such an approach to crop improvement in the tropics.

> I believe it would be useful to ask ourselves what we are really trying to do under the term "pest management." . . . We are really concerned then with overall *crop production* practices and especially for food crops with *crop improvement (the breeding of new varieties)*. The real need then is to sleuth the intricacies responsible for the differences between *yield potential* and *actual yield,* to design research which would lead to practices to reduce this difference and to design new varieties which would have less difference between

276   P L A N T   P R O T E C T I O N

yield potential and *actual yield* naturally without doing anything else. I believe that to develop "pest management" only as a practitioneering operation for "the management of pest populations" as a separate entity from *crop production* and *crop improvement* and from *basic ecological research* is to depart from the most basic need of agricultural improvement in the tropics.

Buddenhagen emphasizes a basic rift between the more sophisticated approach to plant protection in the developed countries and the approaches needed in the developing world. In the technologically advanced countries, coordinated, combined programs that use cultural controls, plant resistance, biological controls, and any other natural controls can be combined, when necessary, with minimum chemical controls in a sophisticated package utilizing a computerized systems approach.

The vast numbers of small farmers in the developing world need simple types of cultural and biological control practices. Cooperatives eventually might be developed in which certain biological control techniques or minimal use of chemicals can be used on a relatively large-scale basis as in Taiwan. But in most parts of the developing world, even this is not possible now. Immediate research efforts for the small farmer need to be built around crop improvement, production, and management practices that are simple, cheap and, where possible, essentially automatic.

Need for better plant protection techniques will continue. Because of burgeoning world population, need for increased crop production is obvious. The opportunities are legion for brilliant efforts in cooperative, interdisciplinary research to achieve combined, coordinated, and integrated control programs in plant protection. Whether these opportunities and problems will be approached and solved creatively and unselfishly by interdisciplinary research teams is a question that only the future can answer. One can only hope that the necessary solutions will appear in time to help solve the staggering food problems of a burgeoning humanity. Alas, the prognosis at this time is not too hopeful.

REFERENCES CITED

Advani, Shyam B., and Robert C. Koestler. 1979. Microencapsulated insecticides. Abstr. 319. IX Int. Congr. Plant Prot., Washington, D.C.

Allelopathy: Biological weed control. 1975. *Phytopathol. News* 9 (2):8.

Altieri, Miguel A., and W. H. Whitcomb. 1979. Manipulation of insect populations through weed management, Pap. 121, Abstr. Pap. IX Int. Congr. Plant Prot., Washington, D.C.

Altman, Jack, and C. Lee Campbell. 1977. Effect of herbicides on plant diseases. *Annu. Rev. Plant Pathol.* 15:361-85.

Andres, L. A., and R. D. Goeden. 1971. The biological control of weeds by introduced natural enemies. In *Biological Control,* C. B. Huffaker, ed., pp. 143-64. Plenum Publ., New York.

Apple, J. L. 1972. Intensified pest management needs of developing nations. *Bioscience* 22:461-64.

Apple, J. Lawrence. 1974. Integrated pest management: The status of research and academic programs. Paper presented at annual meeting of Agric. Res. Inst., 15 Oct. 1974. Denver, Colo.

Apple, J. Lawrence, and Ray F. Smith, eds. 1976. *Integrated Pest Management.* Plenum Publ., New York.

Ark, Peter A., and James P. Thompson, 1959. Control of certain diseases of plants with antibiotics from garlic, *Allium sativum* L. *Plant Dis. Rep.* 43:276-82.

Arnon, I. 1972. *Crop Production in Dry Regions: Background and Principles.* Barnes and Noble, New York.

Austin-Bourke, P. M. 1970. Use of weather information in the prediction of plant disease epiphytotics. *Annu. Rev. Phytopathol.* 8:345-70.

Bae, S. H., and M. D. Pathak. 1968. Common leafhopper-plant hopper populations and incidence of tungro virus in diazinon-treated and untreated rice plots. *J. Econ. Entomol.* 62:772-75.

Baker, Kenneth F., and R. James Cook. 1974. *Biological Control of Plant Pathogens.* W. H. Freeman, San Francisco.

Baker, K. F., and W. C. Snyder, eds. 1965. *Ecology of Soil-borne Plant Pathogens: Prelude to Biological Control.* Univ. California Press, Berkeley.

Baker, Ralph. 1975. Survey on biological control concepts. *Phytopathol. News* 9 (8):2-3.

Beirne, B. P. 1967. Biological control and its potential. *World Rev. Pest Control* 6(1):7-20.

Benedek, Paul, 1979. A national system of plant protection forecasting and its role in integrated pest management in Hungary. Pap. 637, Abstr. Pap. IX Int. Congr. Plant Prot., Washington, D.C.

Benz, George, 1971. Synergism of micro-organisms and chemical insecticides. In *Microbial Control of Insects and Mites,* H. D. Burges and N. W. Hussey, eds., pp. 327-55. Academic Press, New York.

Beroza, Morton, ed. 1970. *Chemicals Controlling Insect Behavior.* Academic Press, New York.

Biehn, W. L., and A. E. Dimond. 1971. Prophylactic action of benomyl against Dutch elm disease. *Plant Dis. Rep.* 55:179-82.

Blair, B. D., and C. R. Edwards. 1979. The development of integrated pest management programs in the United States. Sci. and Educ. Adm., Ext. USDA, Washington, D.C.

Bleiholder, H., and F. R. Rittig. 1979. Remote sensing as an aid for the evaluation of plant protection trials. Pap. 535, Abstr. Pap. IX Int. Congr. Plant Prot., Washington, D.C.

Bode, H. R. 1958. Beitrage zur Kenntnis allelopathischer Erscheinugen bei einigen Juglandaceen. *Planta* 51:440–80.

Borlaug, N. E. 1965. Wheat, rust and people. *Phytopathology* 55:1088–98.

Bottrell, Dale G. 1980. *Integrated Pest Management.* Counc. Environ. Qual., Supt. Doc., USGPO, Washington, D.C.

Boyer, W. P.; L. O. Warren; and Charles Lincoln. 1962. Cotton insect scouting in Arkansas. Exp. Stn. Bull. 656. Univ. Arkansas, Fayetteville.

Bradshaw, A. D. 1976. Pollution and evolution. In *Effects of Air Pollutants on Plants,* T. A. Mansfield, ed., pp. 135–57. Cambridge Univ. Press.

Brady, Jane E. 1974. Experts for pest control to increase world's food. *New York Times,* 28 Oct. 1974.

Brann, James L., Jr., and James P. Tette. 1973. New York State Apple Pest Management Project, annual report. Mimeogr. Coop. Ext. Serv. and Agric. Exp. Stns. with Agric. Res. Serv., Ithaca.

Brooks, M. G. 1951. Effect of black walnut trees and their products on other vegetation. Agric. Exp. Stn. Bull. 347. West Virginia Univ. Morgantown.

Browning, J. A. 1977. Proposal for a national plant health system. Remarks before U.S. Senate Agric. Comm., 31 Oct. 1977.

Browning, J. A., and K. J. Frey. 1969. Multiline cultivars as a means of disease control. *Annu. Rev. Phytopathol.* 7:355–82.

Brunson, A. M., and R. H. Painter. 1938. Differential feeding of grasshoppers on corn and sorghums. *Am. Soc. Agron. J.* 30:334–36.

Buckley, J. L., and C. Cottam. 1966. An ounce of prevention. In *Birds in Our Lives,* A. Stefferud, ed., pp. 454–59. U.S. Dep. Inter., USGPO, Washington, D.C.

Bunting, A. H. 1972. Ecology of agriculture in the world of today and tomorrow. In *Pest Control Strategies for the Future,* pp. 18–35. Div. Biol. Agric., Natl. Counc. National Academy of Sciences, Washington, D.C.

Burges, A., and F. Raw. 1967. *Soil Biology.* Academic Press, New York.

Burges, H. D. 1971. Possibilities of pest resistance to microbial control agents. In *Microbial Control of Insects and Mites,* H. D. Burges and N. W. Hussey, eds., pp. 445–57. Academic Press, New York.

Burges, H. D., and N. W. Hussey, eds. 1971. *Microbial Control of Insects and Mites.* Academic Press, New York.

Burke, D. W. 1965. Fusarium root rot of beans and behavior of the pathogen in different soils. *Phytopathology* 55:1122–26.

Burns, Edward E. 1973. Will conservation tillage increase the incidence of plant disease? *Ill. Res.* 15:8–9.

Byerly, T. C. 1972. Preventive practices and effective pest management. In *Pest Control Strategies for the Future,* pp. 341–51. Div. Biol. Agric., Nat. Res. Counc. National Academy of Sciences, Washington, D.C.

Campbell, Robert W. 1972. The conceptual organization of research and development necessary for future pest management. In *Pest Management for the 21st Century,* R. W. Stark and A. R. Gittens, eds., pp. 23–38. Nat. Resour. Ser. 2. Idaho Res. Found. Moscow.

Certain groups of nematodes attack only insects. 1979. *IPM Pract.,* vol. 1, no. 12.

Chant, D. A. 1966. Research need for integrated control. In *Proceedings of the FAO Symposium on Integrated Pest Control, III.* pp. 103–10. FAO, United Nations, Rome.

Cheng, W. Y., and C. B. Chen. 1962. Preliminary studies on green muscardine fungus. Rep. Taiwan Sugar Exp. Stn. 29:67–76, Taipei.

Chiarappa, L. 1974. Possibility of supervised plant disease control in pest management sytems. FAO Plant Prot. Bull. 22:65–68.

Chin, Shui-chen; Ching-chin Chien; Ken-ching Chou; Liang-chuan Chang; and Shui-chou Chiu. 1974. Mass production and field liberation of a larval parasite (*Apanteles plutellae*) of the diamond-back moth. *J. Taiwan Agric. Res.* 23 (1):56–57.

Chiu, Ren-jong. 1972. Transitory yellowing of rice: A virus disease occurring in Taiwan. Paper presented at Southeast Asia Reg. Symp. Trop. Plant Dis. 11-15 Sept. 1972. Jogjakarta, Indones.

Christie, J. R. 1960. Biological control: Predacious nematodes. In *Nematology,* J. N. Sasser and W. R. Jenkins, eds., pp. 466-68. Univ. North Carolina Press, Chapel Hill.

Civerolo, E. L., and H. L. Keil. 1969. Inhibition of bacterial spot of peach foliage by *Xanthomonas pruni* bacteriophage. *Phytopathology* 59:1966-67.

Colhoun, John. 1973. Effects of environmental factors on plant disease. *Annu. Rev. Phytopathol.* 11:343-64.

Collins, J. L. 1960. *The Pineapple.* Interscience, New York.

Colwell, Robert N. 1973. Remote sensing as an aid to the management of earth resources. *Am. Sci.* 61:175-83.

Compton, C. C., and C. W. Kearns. 1937. Improved control of red spider on greenhouse crops with sulphur and cyclohexylamine derivatives. *J. Econ. Entomol.* 30:512-21.

Corbet, P. S. 1971. Pest management: Objectives and prospects on a global scale. In *Concepts of Pest Management,* R. L. Rabb and F. E. Guthrie, eds., pp. 71-79. North Carolina State Univ. Press, Raleigh.

Corden, Malcolm E., and A. E. Dimond. 1959. The effect of growth regulating substances on disease resistance and plant growth. *Phytopathology* 49:68-72.

Crafts, Alden S., and Wilfred W. Robbins. 1962. *Weed Control,* 3d ed. McGraw-Hill, New York.

Cruickshank, I. A. M. 1965. Pisatin studies: The relation of phytoalexins to disease reaction in plants. In *Ecology of Soil-borne Plant Pathogens: Prelude to Biological Control,* K. F. Baker and W. C. Snyder, eds., pp. 325-36. Univ. California Press, Berkeley.

Dahms, R. G., and R. H. Painter. 1940. Rate of reproduction of the pea aphid on different alfalfa plants. *J. Econ. Entomol.* 33:482-85.

Dahms, R. G.; R. O. Snelling; and F. A. Fenton. 1936. Effect of different varieties of sorghum on biology of the chinch bug. *J. Econ. Entomol.* 28:160-61.

Danthanarayana, W. 1967. Tea entomology in perspective. *Tea Q.* 38:153-77.

Davis, E. F. 1928. The toxic principle of *Juglans nigra* as identified with synthetic juglone and its toxic effects on tomato and alfalfa plants (abstr.). *Am. J. Bot.* 15:620.

Davis, F. S.; J. R. Wayland; M. G. Merkle. 1971. Ultrahigh-frequency electromagnetic fields for weed control: Phytotoxicity and selectivity. *Science* 173 (3996):535-37.

Davis, Robert E.; Robert F. Whitcomb; and Russell L. Steere. 1968. Remission of aster yellows disease by antibiotics. *Science* 161 (3843):793-94.

Day, P. R. 1972. Crop resistance to pests and pathogens. In *Pest Control Strategies for the Future,* pp. 257-71. Div. Biol. Agric., Natl. Res. Counc. National Academy of Sciences, Washington, D.C.

DeBach, Paul, ed. 1964. *Biological Control of Insect Pests and Weeds.* Reinhold Publ., New York.

DeBach, Paul, and C. B. Huffaker. 1971. Experimental techniques for evaluation of the effectiveness of natural enemies. In *Biological Control,* C. B. Huffaker, ed., pp. 113-40. Plenum Publ., New York.

Deema, P.; S. Thongdeetaa; T. Hongtrakula; T. Oonchitrawattana; Y. Singhasenee; and Paul Lippold. 1974. Integrated control of cotton pests in Thailand. Plant Prot. Serv., Tech. Bull. 23 UNDP 8/FAO THA 68/526. Dep. Agric., Minist. Agric. Coop., Bangkok.

Dekker, J. 1976. Acquired resistance to fungicides. *Annu. Rev. Phytopathol.* 14:405-28.

Dethier, V. G. 1970. Chemical interactions between plants and insects. In *Chemical Ecology,* E. Sondheimer and J. B. Simeone, eds., pp. 83-102. Academic Press, New York.

Dubey, H. D. 1970. A nitrogen deficiency disease of sugarcane probably caused by repeated pesticide applications. *Phytopathology* 60:485-87.

Duddington, C. L. 1960. Biological control: Predacious fungi. In *Nematology,* J. N. Sasser and W. R. Jenkins, eds., pp. 461-65. Univ. North Carolina Press, Chapel Hill.

Dukes, P. D. 1970. The influence of crop rotations, crop sequences within rotations, and fallowing on black shank of flue-cured tobacco (abstr.). *Phytopathology* 60:583.

Edwards, Cline A. 1970. *Persistent Pesticides in the Environment.* CRC Press, Chemical Rubber Co., Cleveland, Ohio.

Eichmann, R. D., and R. L. Webster. 1940. The influence of alfalfa on the abundance of the pea aphid on peas grown for canning in southeastern Washington. Agric. Exp. Stn. Bull. 389. Washington State Univ., Pullman.

Eisner, T. 1964. Catnip: Its *raison d'être*. *Science* 146:1318–20.

Elton, C. S. 1958. *The Ecology of Invasions by Animals and Plants*. Methuen, London.

Ennis, William B., Jr.; Warren C. Shaw; Loran L. Danielson; Dayton L. Klingman; and Francis L. Timmons. 1963. Impact of chemical weed control on farm management practices. *Adv. Agron.* 15:161–210.

Erwin, Donald C. 1973. Systemic fungicides: Disease control, translocation, and mode of action. *Annu. Rev. Phytopathol.* 11:389–422.

Fadeev, Y. 1979. Control of spider mite populations resistant to pesticides. Pap. 614, Abstr. Pap. IX Int. Congr. Plant Prot., Washington, D.C.

Falcon, Louis A., and Ray F. Smith. 1973. Guidelines for integrated control of cotton insect pests. FAO, United Nations, Rome.

FAO (Food and Agricultural Organization). 1968. Report of 2d session of FAO panel of experts on integrated pest control. Meet. Rep. P./1968/M/3. United Nations, Rome.

———. 1971. Report of 3d session of FAO panel of experts on integrated pest control. Meet. Rep. AGP: 1970/M/7. United Nations, Rome.

———. 1973*a*. The use of viruses for the control of insect pests and disease vectors. FAO Agric. Stud. 91, or WHO Tech. Rep. Ser. 531. United Nations, Rome.

———. 1973*b*. Report of 4th session of FAO panel of experts on integrated pest control. Meet. Rep. AGP: 173/M/5. United Nations, Rome.

———. 1973*c*. Pesticide residues in food. Report of 1972 joint meeting of FAO working party of experts on pesticide residues and WHO expert committee on pesticide residues. FAO Agric. Stud. 90, or WHO Tech. Rep. Ser. 525. United Nations, Rome.

———. 1973*d*. Pesticides and the environment: The position of FAO. WS/C7537/E/11/73/2/1000. United Nations, Rome.

Farkas, A., and A. Amman. 1940. The action of diphenyl on penicillium and diplodia molds. *Palestine J. Bot. Jerusalem Ser.* 2:38–45.

Fawcett, C. H., and D. M. Spencer. 1970. Plant chemotherapy with natural products. *Annu. Rev. Phytopathol.* 8:403–18.

Feakin, Susan D., ed. 1970. Pest control in rice: PANS manual 3. Cent. Overseas Res., Foreign Common. Off., Overseas Dev. Adm., London.

Fellows, Hurley, and Webster H. Sill, Jr. 1955. Predicting wheat streak mosaic epiphytotics in winter wheat. *Plant Dis. Rep.* 39:291–95.

Ferron, P. 1978. Biological control of insect pests by entomogenous fungi. *Annu. Rev. Entomol.* 23:409–42.

First natural virus insecticide registered by EPA. 1976. *Phytopathol. News* 10(5):9.

Fraenkel, G. S. 1959. The *raison d'être* of secondary plant substances. *Science* 129:1466–70.

Frankel, O. H., and E. Bennet, eds. 1970. *Genetic Resources in Plants: Their Exploration and Conservation*. Davis, Philadelphia.

Galston, A. W. 1971. Some implications of the widespread use of herbicides. *Bioscience* 21:891–92.

Ganyard, Milton C., Jr., and H. C. Ellis. 1972. Tobacco pest management pilot project. North Carolina State Univ. and Ext. Serv., USDA, Raleigh.

Ganyard, M. C.; J. R. Bradley, Jr.; and J. R. Brazzel. 1978. Wide-area field test of diflubenzuron for control of an indigenous boll weevil population. *J. Econ. Entomol.* 71:785–88.

Ganyard, M. C.; J. R. Bradley, Jr.; F. J. Boyd; and J. R. Brazzel. 1977. Field evaluation of diflubenzuron (Dimilin) for control of boll weevil reproduction. *J. Econ. Entomol.* 70:347–50.

Garrett, S. D. 1965. Toward biological control of soil-borne plant pathogens. In *Ecology of Soil-borne Pathogens: Prelude to Biological Control*, K. F. Baker and W. C. Snyder, eds., pp. 4–17. Univ. California Press, Berkeley.

Georgopoulos, S. G. 1969. The problem of fungicide resistance. *Bioscience* 19:971–73.

Glass, Edward H., coord. 1975. Integrated pest management: Rationale, potential, needs, and implementation. Entomol. Soc. Am. Spec. Publ. 75-2.

Glass, Edward H., and H. David Thurston. 1978. Traditional and modern crop protection in perspective. *Bioscience* 28:109–15.

Goeden, R. D.; L. A. Andres; T. E. Freeman; P. Harris; R. L. Pienkowski; and C. R. Walker. 1974. Present status of projects on the biological control of weeds with insects and plant pathogens in the United States and Canada. *Weed Sci.* 22:490–95.

Good, J. M. 1968. Relation of plant parasitic nematodes to soil management practices. In *Tropical Nematology,* G. C. Smart, Jr., and V. G. Perry, eds., pp. 113–38. Univ. Florida Press, Gainesville.

_____. 1972*a*. Bionomics and integrated control of plant parasitic nematodes. *J. Environ. Qual.* 1 (4):382–86.

_____. 1972*b*. Management of plant parasitic nematode populations. Proc. Annu. Tall Timbers Conf. Ecol. Anim. Control Habitat Manage., 24–25 Feb. 1972. USDA, Beltsville, Md.

_____. 1973*a*. Evolution of pest management programs. Symposium paper presented at annual meeting of Entomol. Soc. Am. 26–30 Nov. 1973, Dallas, Tex.

_____. 1973*b*. Pilot programs for integrated pest management in the United States. Paper presented at US-USSR Pest Manage. Conf., 10–18 Sept. 1973, Kiev.

_____. 1974*a*. Pest management practical implementation: Importance of grower acceptance. Paper presented at annual meeting of Entomol. Soc. Am., 1–5 Dec. 1974, Minneapolis.

_____. 1974*b*. Integrated pest management programs. Paper presented at Pest Manage. Symp., annual meeting of Weed Sci. Soc. Am., 12–14 Feb. 1974, Las Vegas, Nev.

_____. 1974*c*. Extension emphasis and results from cotton pest management projects. Report to Beltwide Cotton Prod. Mech. Conf., 9–10 Jan. 1974, Dallas, Tex.

_____. 1974*d*. Pilot pest management projects. Statement prepared 1 Feb. 1974, Ext. Serv., USDA, Washington, D.C.

_____. 1974*e*. The role of extension specialists and private consultants in pest management programs. Paper read at Corn Grain Sorghum Pest Manage. Workshop, 17–19 Apr. 1974, Lincoln, Neb.

_____. 1979. IPM and weed science. Paper presented at Northeast. Weed Sci. Soc., 3 Jan. 1979, Boston, Mass.

Green, T. R., and C. A. Ryan. 1972. Wound-induced proteinase inhibitor in plant leaves: A possible defense mechanism against insects. *Science* 175 (4023):776–77.

Grinstein, A.; J. Katan; A. Abdul Razik; O. Zeydan; and Y. Elad. 1979. Control of *Sclerotium rolfsii* and weeds in peanuts by solar heating of the soil. *Plant Dis. Rep.* 63:1056–59.

The growing furor over acid rain. 1979. *U.S. News & World Report,* 19 Nov. 1979.

Guengerich, H. W. , and D. F. Millikan. 1964. Heat therapy as a method for obtaining virus-free clones of apple. *Plant Dis. Rep.* 48:343.

Gustafson, Magnus. 1971. Microbial control of aphids and scale insects. In *Microbial Control of Insects and Mites,* H. D. Burges and N. W. Hussey, eds., pp. 375–86. Academic Press, New York.

Hardison, John R. 1976. Fire and flame for plant disease control. *Annu. Rev. Phytopathol.* 14:355–79.

Harpaz, Isaac, and David Rosen. 1971. Development of integrated control programs for crop pests in Israel. In *Biological Control,* C. B. Huffaker, ed., pp. 458–68. Plenum Publ., New York.

Harvey, Robert G.; John R. Teasdale; and Donald J. Hagedorn. 1979. Suppression of common root rot in peas with dinitroaniline herbicides. Pap. 173, Abstr. Pap. IX Int. Congr. Plant Prot., Washington, D.C.

Hassall, K. A. 1969. *World Crop Protection. Vol. 2, Pesticides.* CRC Press, Chemical Rubber Co., Cleveland, Ohio.

Hayes, D. K. 1970. Photoperiod manipulation of insect diapause: A method of pest control? *Science* 196 (943):382–83.

Hayes, W. P., and Johnston, C. O. 1925. The reaction of certain grasses to chinch bug attack. *J. Agric. Res.* 31:575–83.

Heagle, Allen S. 1973. Interactions between air pollutants and plant parasites. *Annu. Rev. Phytopathol.* 11:365–88.

Hebard, F. V., and G. J. Griffen. 1979. Implications of chestnut blight incidence in recently clearcut forests and mature forests to biological control of blight with hypovirulent strains of *Endothia parasitica.* Pap. 161, Abstr. Pap. IX Int. Congr. Plant Prot., Washington, D.C.

Hedin, Paul A., ed. 1977. *Host Plant Resistance to Pests.* ACS Symp. 62. Am. Chem. Soc., Washington, D.C.

Hodek, I. 1970. Coccinellids and the modern pest management. *Bioscience* 20:543-52.

Hooker, A. L. 1974. Epidemics, vulnerability, plant health, and research. In Paul A. Funk recognition program 1973. Spec. Publ. 30, pp. 35-62. Coll. Agric., Univ. Illinois, Urbana-Champaign.

Horsfall, James G. 1972. Selective chemicals for plant disease control. In *Pest Control Strategies for the Future,* pp. 216-25. Div. Biol. Agric., Natl. Res. Counc. National Academy of Sciences, Washington, D.C.

Hoy, Marjorie A. 1979. Genetics of biological control agents. Pap. 354, Abstr. Pap. IX Int. Congr. Plant Prot., Washington, D.C.

Hoy, Marjorie A., and John J. McKelvey. 1979. Genetics in relation to insect management. Rockefeller Found. Conf., 31 Mar.-5 Apr. 1978, Bellagio, Italy. Rockefeller Found., New York.

Hsiao, Ting H., and Catherine Hsiao. 1973. Benomyl: A novel drug for controlling a microsporidian disease of the alfalfa weevil. *J. Invertebr. Pathol.* 22:303-4.

Huber, Roger T. 1972. Corn workshop summary. In *Implementing Practical Pest Management Strategies,* pp. 116-19. Proc. Natl. Ext. Insect Pest Manage. Workshop. Purdue Univ., Lafayette, Ind.

Huffaker, C. B. 1970. Summary of a pest management conference: A critique. In *Concepts of Pest Management. Conference Proceedings,* North Carolina State Univ. Press, Raleigh.

Huffaker, C. B., ed. 1971. *Biological Control.* Plenum Publ., New York.

Huffaker, C. B., 1974. *Integrated Pest Management: The Principles, Strategies, and Tactics of Pest Population Regulation and Control in Major Crop Ecosystems.* Vol. 2. *Detailed Institution Submittals.* Int. Cent. Biol. Control. Univ. California, Berkeley.

Huffaker, Carl B. 1979. *New Technologies of Pest Control.* Wiley, New York.

Huffaker, Carl B., and P. S. Messenger, eds. 1976. *Theory and Practice of Biological Control.* Academic Press, New York.

Huffaker, C. B., and R. F. Smith. 1972. Future Techniques of Pest Management. In *Pest Management for the 21st Century,* R. W. Stark and A. R. Gittens, eds., pp. 49-72. Nat. Resour. Ser. 2. Idaho Res. Found., Moscow.

Huffaker, C. B.; M. Van de Vrie; and J. A. McMurtry. 1970. II. Tetranychid populations and their possible control by predators: An evaluation. *Hilgardia* 40:391-458.

Inman, R. E. 1971. A preliminary evaluation of *Rumex* rust as a biological control agent for curly dock. *Phytopathology* 61:102-7.

Ishii, S., and C. Hirano. 1959. Effect of fertilizers on the growth of the larvae of the rice stem borer. I. Growth response of the larvae to rice plants cultured in different nitrogen level soils. *Japanese Appl. Entomol. Zool.* 2:198-202.

Jackson, R. M. 1965. Antibiosis and fungistasis of soil microorganisms. In *Ecology of Soil-Borne Plant Pathogens: Prelude to Biological Control,* K. F. Baker and W. C. Snyder, eds., pp. 363-73. Univ. California Press, Berkeley.

Jackson, W. B., and R. E. Marsh. 1977. *Test Methods for Vertebrate Pest Control and Management Materials.* Am. Soc. Test. Mater., Philadelphia.

Jacobsen, Martin. 1972. *Insect Sex Pheromones.* Academic Press, New York.

James, W. C. 1973. Development of a model for estimating crop losses due to late blight of potato caused by *Phytophthora infestans.* Abstr. 0588. Second Int. Congr. Plant Pathol., Minneapolis.

Janick, Jules; Robert W. Schery; Frank W. Woods; and Vernon W. Ruttan. 1969. *Plant Science: An Introduction to World Crops.* W. H. Freeman, San Francisco.

Jennings, P. R. 1976. The amplification of agricultural production. *Sci. Am.* 235:180-94.

Jennings, P. R., and A. Pineda. 1970. *Sogatodes orizicola* resistance in rice varieites. Mimeogr. Cent. Int. Agric. Trop., Palmira, Colombia.

Johnson, Julius E. 1971. The public health implications of widespread use of the phenoxy herbicides and picloram. *Bioscience* 21:899-905.

Jones, E. T. 1939. Grasses of the tribe Hordeae as hosts of the Hessian fly. *J. Econ. Entomol.* 32:505-10.

Kalyuga, M. V. 1968. Combined use of microbiological preparations in pest control. *Entomol. Rev.* 47:274-76.

Katan, Jaacov. 1979. Solar heating of the soil and other economical environmentally safe methods of controlling soil-borne pathogens, weeds, and pests for increasing food production. Pap. 344, Abstr. Pap. IX Int. Congr. Plant Prot., Washington, D.C.

Katan, J., and Y. Eshel. 1973. Interaction between herbicides and plant pathogens. Francis A. Gunther and J. D. Gunther, eds. *Residue Rev.* 45:145-77.

Katan, J.; A. Greenberger; H. Alan; and A. Grinstein. 1976. Solar heating by polethylene mulching for the control of diseases caused by soil-borne pathogens. *Phytopathology* 6:683-88.

Katznelson, H. 1965. Nature and importance of the rhizosphere. In *Ecology of Soil-Borne Plant Pathogens: Prelude to Biological Control,* K. F. Baker and W. C. Snyder, eds., pp. 187-209. Univ. California Press, Berkeley.

Kehr, A. E. 1966. Current status and opportunities for the control of nematodes by plant breeding. In *Pest Control by Chemical, Biological, Genetic, and Physical Means,* E. F. Knipling, ed., pp. 126-38. Publ. 33-110. USDA, Washington, D.C.

Kennedy, M. V., ed. 1978. *Disposal and Decontamination of Pesticides.* Am. Chem. Soc., Washington, D.C.

Kilgore, Wendell W., and Richard L. Doutt, eds. 1967. *Pest Control.* Academic Press, New York.

Knipling, E. F. 1972. Sterilization and other genetic techniques. In *Pest Control Strategies for the Future,* pp. 272-87. Div. Biol. Agric., Natl. Res. Counc. National Academy of Sciences, Washington, D.C.

Kommedahl, T.; C. E. Windels; G. Sarbini; and H. B. Wiley. 1979. Status of biological seed treatment to control root diseases in four crops. Pap. 588, Abstr. Pap. IX Int. Congr. Plant Prot., Washington, D.C.

Krieg, Aloysius. 1971. Interactions between pathogens. In *Microbial Control of Insects and Mites,* H. D. Burges and N. W. Hussey, eds., pp. 459-67. Academic Press, New York.

Kuc, J. 1972. Phytoalexins. *Annu. Rev. Phytopathol.* 10:207-32.

Kuc, Joseph. 1979. Biochemicals and plant protection. Proc., Opening Sess. Plenary Sess. Symp. IX Int. Congr. Plant Prot., Washington, D.C.

Kushner, D. J., and G. T. Harvey. 1962. Antibacterial substances in leaves: Their possible role in insect resistance to disease. *J. Insect Pathol.* 4:155-84.

Lavroka, K. G. 1962. Plant secretions and possibilities of their practical utilization (trans.). *Ref. Zh. Biol.* 14:V119.

Lawson, F. R. 1966. Integrating control of pest populations in large areas. In *Proceedings of the FAO Symposium on Integrated Pest Control,* pp. 27-46. FAO, United Nations, Rome.

Lester, E. 1976. Plant pathology and plant protection. *Med. Fac. Landbouwwet. Rijksuniv. Gent.* 41/2.

Levin, Donald A. 1976. The chemical defenses of plants to pathogens and herbivores. *Annu. Rev. Ecol. Syst.* 7:121-59.

Likens, G. E., and F. H. Bormann. 1974. Acid rain: A serious regional environmental problem. *Science* 184 (4142):1176-79.

Lim, T. M. 1972. Recent progress in research and control of root diseases of hevea in Malaysia. Paper presented at Southeast Asia Reg. Symp. Crop Prot., Jogjakarta, Indones. Rubber Res. Inst., Malaysia, Kuala Lumpur.

Lincoln, Charles. (No date.) Integrated insect management systems: Integrated insect control in the mid-South. Symp. Dev. Optimum Crop Prod. Syst. Mid-South. Spec. Rep. 67. Agric. Exp. Stn., Univ. Arkansas, Fayetteville.

Lincoln, Charles; Grover C. Dowell; W. P. Boyer; and Robert C. Hunter. 1963. The point sample method of scouting for boll weevil. Agric. Exp. Stn. Bull. 666. Univ. Arkansas, Fayetteville.

Lipa, Jerzy J. 1971. Microbial control of mites and ticks. In *Microbial Control of Insects and*

Mites, H. D. Burges and N. W. Hussey, eds., pp. 357–73. Academic Press, New York.

Lopez-Rosa, Julio H., and Elvin G. Boneta-Garcia. 1979. Control of sigatoka (*Mycosphaerella musicola*) via natural shade. Pap. 883, Abstr. Pap. IX Int. Congr. Plant Prot., Washington, D.C.

Lownsbery, B. F.; H. English; G. R. Noel; and F. J. Schick. 1977. Influence of nemaguard and lovell rootstocks and *Macroposthonia xenoplax* on bacterial canker of peach. *J. Nematol.* 9:221–24.

Luginbill, P., Jr. 1969. Developing resistant plants: The ideal method of controlling insects. Prod. Res. Rep. III. USDA, Washington, D.C.

Luh, C. L., ed. 1971. Better crop production: Problems and solutions. PID activities. Plant Ind. Ser. 30. Plant Ind. Div., Joint Comm. Rural Reconstr., Taipei, Taiwan.

Lysenko, O., and M. Kucera. 1971. Micro-organisms as sources of new insecticidal chemicals: Toxins. In *Microbial Control of Insects and Mites,* H. D. Burges and N. W. Hussey, eds., pp. 205–27. Academic Press, New York.

McEwen, F. L. 1978. Food production: The challenge for pesticides. *Bioscience* 28:773–77.

MacFarlane, I. 1952. Factors affecting the survival of *Plasmodiophora brassicae* Wor. in the soil and its assessment by a host test. *Ann. Appl. Biol.* 39:239–56.

McLaughlin, Roy E. 1971. Use of protozoans for microbial control of insects. In *Microbial Control of Insects and Mites,* H. D. Burges and N. W. Hussey, eds., pp. 151–72. Academic Press, New York.

McMurtry, J. A.; C. B. Huffaker; and M. Van de Vrie. 1970. I. Tetranychid enemies: Their biological characters and the impact of spray practices. *Hilgardia* 40:331–90.

McNew, G. L. 1966. Progress in the battle against plant disease. In Scientific *Aspects of Pest Control.* Publ. 1402. Natl. Res. Counc. National Academy of Sciences, Washington, D.C.

McNew, George L. 1972. Concept of pest management. In *Pest Control Strategies for the Future,* pp. 119–33. Div. Biol. Agric., Natl. Res. Counc. National Academy of Sciences, Washington, D.C.

Malenotti, E. 1935. *Agricultural Methods against Insects.* Agricoltori, Rome.

Mangelsdorf, A. J. 1953. Sugar cane breeding in Hawaii. Part II. 1921–52. In *Hawaiian Planters' Record,* L. D. Baver and Lydia C. Nickerson, eds. pp. 101–37, vol. 54, no. 3. Exp. Stn. Hawaiian Sugar Plant. Assoc., Honolulu.

Manning, W. J., and P. M. Vardaro. 1973. Suppression of oxidant air pollution injury on bean plants by systemic fungicides under field conditions (abstr.). *Phytopathology* 63:204.

Mansfield, T. A., ed. 1976. *Effects of Air Pollutants on Plants.* Cambridge Univ. Press.

Markos, B. G., and F. L. Campbell. 1943. Effect of host plant on the susceptibility of the southern army worm (*Laphygma eridania* Cram) to calcium arsenate. *J. Econ. Entomol.* 36:662–65.

Marsh, Rex E., and Walter E. Howard. 1979. Bromadiolone: A promising rodenticide for plant protection. Pap. 485, Abstr. Pap. IX Int. Congr. Plant Prot., Washington, D.C.

Marx, Donald H. 1972. Ectomycorrhizae as biological deterrents to pathogenic root infections. *Annu. Rev. Phytopathol.* 10:429–54.

Matsumura, Fumio; G. Mallory Boush; and Tomomasa Misato. 1972. *Environmental Toxicology of Pesticides.* Academic Press, New York.

Mazzone, H. M.; R. A. Lautenschlager; and J. D. Podgwaite. 1979. Viruses as regulators of forest pest insects. Pap. 208, Abstr. Pap. IX Int. Congr. Plant Prot., Washington, D.C.

Messenger, P. S. 1970. Bioclimatic inputs to biological control and pest management programs. In *Concepts of Pest Management. Conference Proceedings,* pp. 84–102. North Carolina State Univ. Press, Raleigh.

Metcalf, C. L.; W. P. Flint; and R. L. Metcalf. 1951. *Destructive and Useful Insects.* McGraw-Hill, New York.

Metcalf, Robert L. 1972a. Development of selective and biodegradable insecticides. In *Pest Control Strategies for the Future,* pp. 137–55. Div. Biol. Agric., Natl. Res. Counc. National Academy of Sciences, Washington, D.C.

――――. 1972b. Selective use of pesticides in pest management. In *Implementing Practical Pest Management Strategies,* pp. 41–91. Proc. Natl. Ext. Pest Manage. Workshop. Purdue Univ., Lafayette, Ind.

Meyer, J. A. 1972. The ecological significance of toxin production by microorganisms. In *Phytotoxins in Plant Diseases,* R. K. S. Wood, A. Ballio, and A. Graniti, eds., pp. 331–45. Academic Press, New York.

Moore, E. L. 1960. Some problems and progress in the breeding and selection of plants for nematode resistance. In *Nematology,* J. N. Sasser and W. R. Jenkins, eds., pp. 454–60. Univ. North Carolina Press, Chapel Hill.

Moyer, J. H.; H. Cole; and N. L. LaCasse. 1974. Reduction of ozone injury on *Poa annua* by benomyl and thiophanate. *Plant Dis. Rep.* 58:41–44.

Mrak, E. 1969. Report of secretary's commission on pesticides and their relationship to environmental health. U.S. Dep. Health, Educ. Welfare. USGPO, Washington, D.C.

Muller, C. H.; W. H. Muller; and B. L. Haines. 1964. Volatile growth inhibitors produced by aromatic shrubs. *Science* 143:471–73.

Muller, W. H.; F. Lorber; and B. Haley. 1968. Volatile growth inhibitors produced by *Salvia leucophylla*: Effect on seedling growth and respiration. Bull. Torrey Bot. Club 95:415–22.

Naegele, John A., ed. 1973. Air pollution damage to vegetation. Adv. Chem. Ser. 122. Am. Chem. Soc., Washington, D.C.

Nakashima, M. J., and B. A. Croft. 1974. Toxicity of benomyl to the life stages of *Amblyseius fallacis. J. Econ. Entomol.* 67:675–77.

NAS (National Academy of Sciences). 1968*a*. Principles of plant and animal pest control. Vol. I. Plant disease development and control. Publ. 1596. Natl. Res. Counc. Washington, D.C.

_____. 1968*b*. Principles of plant and animal pest control. Vol. 4. Control of plant-parasitic nematodes. Natl. Res. Counc. Washington, D.C.

_____. 1968*c*. Principles of plant and animal pest control. Vol. 2. Weed control. Publ. 1597. Natl. Res. Counc. Washington, D.C.

_____. 1969. Insect-pest management and control. Publ. 1695. Natl. Res. Counc. Washington, D.C.

_____. 1970. Principles of plant and animal pest control. Vol. 5. Vertebrate pests: Problems and control. Natl. Res. Counc. Washington, D.C.

_____. 1975. Pest control: An assessment of present and alternative strategies. Vol. 1. Contemporary pest control practices and prospects. Natl. Res. Counc. Washington, D.C.

Nusbaum, C. J., and Howard Ferris. 1973. The role of cropping systems in nematode population management. *Annu. Rev. Phytopathol.* 11:423–40.

Okabe, Norio, and Masao Goto. 1963. Bacteriophages of plant pathogens. *Annu. Rev. Phytopathol.* 1:397–418.

Olkowski, W.; C. Pinnock; W. Toney; G. Mosher; W. Neasbitt; R. Van den Bosch; and H. Olkowski. 1974. An integrated insect control program for street trees. *Calif. Agric.* 28:3–4.

Ordish, George, and David Dufour. 1969. Economic bases for protection against plant diseases. *Annu. Rev. Phytopathol.* 7:31–50.

Organic farming being researched. 1979. *IPM Pract.,* vol. 1. no. 11.

Pacumbaba, R. P.; E. A. Addison; W. H. Sill, Jr.; and O. J. Dickerson. 1968. Effect of soil fumigation on incidence of soil-borne wheat mosaic and wheat yield. *Plant Dis. Rep.* 52:559–62.

Paddock, William C. 1967. Phytopathology in a hungry world. *Annu. Rev. Phytopathol.* 5:375–90.

Painter, R. H. 1936. The food of insects and its relation to resistance of plants to insect attack. *Am. Nat.* 70:547–66.

_____. 1951. *Insect Resistance in Crop Plants.* Macmillan, New York.

_____. 1958. Resistance of plants to insects. *Annu. Rev. Entomol.* 3:267–90.

_____. 1966. Lessons to be learned from past experience in breeding plants for insect resistance. In *Breeding Pest Resistant Trees,* pp. 349–66. Proc. NATO and NSF Symp. Pergamon Press, New York.

Painter, Reginald H. 1968. *Insect Resistance in Crop Plants,* 2d ed. Univ. Press Kansas, Lawrence.

Palm, Charles E. 1972. The role of the land-grant universities in developing and implementing pest management programs. In *Implementing Practical Pest Management Strategies,* pp.

201-6. Proc. Natl. Ext. Insect Pest Manage. Workshop. Purdue Univ., Lafayette, Ind.

Palti, J. 1979. Plant protection benefits from trickle irrigation. Pap. 872, Abstr. Pap. IX Int. Congr. Plant Prot., Washington, D.C.

Parris, G. K. 1968. Automobile exhaust fumes cause dieback of redbud. *Plant Dis. Rep.* 52:744.

Parsons, F. S.; H. Hutchinson; and J. Marshall. 1938. Progress reports from experiment stations, Barberton, South Africa. In Empire cotton growing corp., Rep. Exp. Stn. 1936-37, pp. 26-32.

Pathak, M. D. 1969. Integrated control of rice stem borers, leafhoppers, and planthoppers. Paper presented at International Seminar on Integrated Pest Control, 20-24 Jan. 1969, New Delhi, India.

———. 1970. Genetics of plants in pest management. In *Concepts of Pest Management. Conference Proceedings,* pp. 138-57. North Carolina State Univ. Press, Raleigh.

———. 1971. Resistance to insect pests in rice varieties (suppl.). *Oryza* 8 (2):135-44.

Pathak, M. D., and V. A. Dyck. 1973. Developing an integrated method of rice insect pest control. *PANS* 19:534-44.

Pathak, M. D.; H. M. Beachell; and Fausto Andres. 1973. IR-20, a pest- and disease-resistant high yielding rice variety. Int. Rice Comm. Newsl. 22(3):1-8.

Patrick, Z. A.; T. A. Toussoun; and L. W. Koch. 1964. Effect of crop-residue decomposition products on plant roots. *Annu. Rev. Phytopathol.* 2:267-92.

Peregrine, W. T. H.; Kassim bin Ahmad; and Bakti bin Yunton. 1974. Some observations on leaf scald *Rhynchosporium oryzae* (Hashioka and Yokogi) in Brunei. *PANS* 20:177-80.

Perkins, R. C. L., and O. H. Swezey. 1924. The introduction in Hawaii of insects that attack lantana. Hawaii Sugar Plant. Assoc. Exp. Stn. Bull. Entomol. Ser. 16. Honolulu.

Petty, H. B. 1972. Corn insect pest management. In *Implementing Practical Pest Management Strategies.* pp. 107-15. Proc. Nat. Ext. Insect Pest Manage. Workshop. Purdue Univ., Lafayette, Ind.

Phillips, D. V., and J. W. Todd. 1979. Identification and evaluation of potentially beneficial pesticide interactions in soybean production. Pap. 72, Abstr. Pap. IX Int. Congr. Plant Prot., Washington, D.C.

Phillips, Shirley H., and H. M. Young. 1973. *No Tillage Farming.* Thomson Publ., Fresno, Calif.

Pickett, A. D., and A. W. MacPhee. 1965. Twenty years experience with integrated control programs in Nova Scotia apple orchards. In *Proceedings XII International Congress of Entomology.* London.

Pimental, David. 1970. Training in pest management and the "systems approach" to control. In *Concepts of Pest Management. Conference Proceedings,* pp. 209-26. North Carolina State Univ. Press, Raleigh.

Pinthus, M. J.; Y. Eshel; and Y. Shehori. 1972. Field and vegetable crop mutants with increased resistance to herbicides. *Science* 177 (4050):712-16.

Poinar, George O., Jr. 1971. Use of nematodes for microbial control of insects. In *Microbial Control of Insects and Mites,* H. D. Burges and N. W. Hussey, eds., pp. 181-203. Academic Press, New York.

Poucher, Charles; H. W. Ford; R. F. Suit; and E. P. DuCharme. 1967. Burrowing nematode in citrus. Bull. 7. Fla. Dep. Agric., Div. Plant Ind., Gainesville.

Prasad, N., and R. Mankau. 1970. Control of nematode populations with a sporozoan endoparasite (abstr.). *Phytopathology* 60:1536-37.

Pringle, Ross B., and Robert P. Scheffer. 1964. Host-specific plant toxins. *Annu. Rev. Phytopathol.* 2:133-56.

Proverbs, M. D. 1969. Induced sterilization and control of insects. *Annu. Rev. Entomol.* 14:81-102.

Putnam, Alan R., and William B. Duke. 1978. Allelopathy in agroecosystems. *Annu. Rev. Phytopathol.* 16:431-51.

Putwain, Phillip D., and Roy J. Holliday. 1979. Herbicide resistance in weeds. Pap. 353, Abstr. Pap. IX Int. Congr. Plant Prot., Washington, D.C.

Rice, Elroy L. 1974. *Allelopathy.* Academic Press, New York.

Rich, Saul. 1964. Ozone damage to plants. *Annu. Rev. Phytopathol.* 2:253-66.

Richardson, L. T. 1957. Effect of insecticides and herbicides applied to soil on the development of plant diseases. I. The seedling disease of barley caused by *Helminthosporium sativum* P. K. and B. *Canadian J. Plant. Sci.* 37:196-204.

Richardson, Lloyd T. 1959. Effect of insecticides and herbicides applied to soil on the development of plant diseases. II. Early blight and fusarium wilt of tomato. *Canadian J. Plant Sci.* 39:30-38.

———. 1970. Effects of atrazine on growth response of soil fungi. *Canadian J. Plant Sci.* 50:594-96.

Ridgway, R. L., and S. B. Vinson, eds. 1977. *Biological Control by Augmentation of Natural Enemies.* Plenum Publ., New York.

Roane, Curtis W. 1973. Trends in breeding for disease resistance in crops. *Annu. Rev. Phytopathol.* 11:463-86.

Roberts, Donald W., and William G. Yendol. 1971. Use of fungi for microbial control of insects. In *Microbial Control of Insects and Mites,* H. D. Burges and N. W. Hussey, eds., pp. 125-49. Academic Press, New York.

Rohde, R. A. 1960. Mechanisms of resistance to plant-parasitic nematodes. In *Nematology,* J. N. Sasser and W. R. Jenkins, eds., pp. 447-53. Univ. North Carolina Press, Chapel Hill.

Rohde, Richard A. 1972. Expression of resistance in plants to nematodes. *Annu. Rev. Phytopathol.* 10:233-52.

Rosenow, D. T., and R. A. Fredericksen. 1979. Development of multiple disease resistant sorghums. Pap. 579, Abstr. Pap. IX Int. Congr. Plant Prot., Washington, D.C.

Rotem, J., and J. Palti. 1969. Irrigation and plant diseases. *Annu. Rev. Phytopathol.* 7:267-88.

Rovira, A. D. 1965. Plant root exudates and their influence upon soil microorganisms. In *Ecology of Soil-borne Plant Pathogens: Prelude to Biological Control,* K. F. Baker and W. C. Snyder, eds., pp. 170-84. Univ. California Press, Berkeley.

Russell, E. John. 1955. The changing problems of applied biology. *Ann. Appl. Biol.* 42:8-21.

Russell, G. E. 1978. *Plant Breeding for Pest and Disease Resistance.* Butterworths, Woburn, Mass.

Sabrosky, C. W. 1955. The interrelations of biological control and taxonomy. *J. Econ. Entomol.* 48:710-14.

Sankaran, T., and V. P. Rao. 1966. Insects attacking witchweed (*Striga*) in India. Commonw. Inst. Biol. Control Tech. Bull. 7:63-73.

Scheffer, Robert P., and Olin C. Yoder. 1972. Host-specific toxins and selective toxicity. In *Phytotoxins in Plant Diseases,* R. K. S. Wood, A. Ballio, and A. Graniti, eds., pp. 251-72. Academic Press, New York.

Scher, Herbert B., ed. 1977. *Controlled Release Pesticides.* ACS Symp. 53. Am. Chem. Soc., Washington, D.C.

Schroeder, W. T., and R. Providenti. 1969. Resistance to benomyl in powdery mildew of cucurbits. *Plant Dis. Rep.* 53:271-75.

Schroth, Milton N., and D. C. Hildebrand. 1964. Influence of plant exudates on root infecting fungi. *Annu. Rev. Phytopathol.* 2:101-32.

Seem, R. C.; H. Cole, J; and N. L. Lacasse. 1972. Suppression of ozone injury to *Phaseolus vulgaris* 'Pinto III' with triarimol and its monochlorophenyl cyclohexyl analogue. *Plant Dis. Rep.* 56:386-90.

Sharvelle, Eric G. 1961. *The Nature and Uses of Modern Fungicides.* Burgess, Minneapolis.

Shaw, Warren C. 1964. Weed science-revolution in agricultural technology. *Weed Sci.* 12:153-62.

Shaw, W. C. 1973. Weed control technology for agroecosystems management. Paper presented at Symp. Ecol. Agric. Prod., 10-17 July 1973, Univ. Tennessee, Knoxville.

———. 1974a. Total farm weed control concepts for pest management. Paper presented at Symp. Weed Science Phase of Pest Management. Annual meeting of Weed Sci. Soc. Am., 12-14 Feb. 1974, Las Vegas, Nev.

———. 1974b. Need for controlled release technology in the use of agricultural chemicals. Paper presented at Symp. Controlled Release of Pesticides, 16-18 Sept. 1974, Univ. Akron, Akron, Ohio.

Shurtleff, M. C.; Dwight Powell; E. E. Burns; and J. B. Sinclair. 1972. Modern fungicides and their uses. Circ. 1002 (rev. 1/72). Dept. Plant Pathol., Univ. Illinois, Urbana-Champaign.

Shurtleff, M. C., and H. B. Petty. (No date.) Problems of mixing pesticides. Circ. 1004. Dept. Plant Pathol., Univ. Illinois, Urbana-Champaign.

Sill, Webster H., Jr. 1978. *The Plant Protection Disciplines.* Halsted Press, New York.

Simons, J. N. 1957. Effects of insecticides and physical barriers on field spread of pepper vein-banding mosaic virus. *Phytopathology* 47:139-45.

Smirnoff, W. A. 1979. Results of treatments with *Bacillus thuringiensis* against the spruce bud-worm. Pap. 916, Abstr. Pap. IX Int. Congr. Plant Prot., Washington, D.C.

Smith, Edward H. 1972. Implementing pest control strategies. In *Pest Control Strategies for the Future,* pp. 44-68. Div. Biol. Agric., Natl. Res. Counc. National Academy of Sciences, Washington, D.C.

Smith, E. H., and David Pimental. 1978. *Pest Control Strategies.* Academic Press, New York.

Smith, Harlan. 1973. An analysis of insect pest management principles and how they might be applied to control plant diseases. Mimeogr. USDA Ext. Serv., Beltsville, Md.

Smith, Harlan E. 1976. Potentials of crop health. *Phytopathol. News* 10 (2):5.

Smith, R. F. 1969. The new and old in pest control. *Proc. Acad. Naz. Linci,* Rome. 366 (128):21-30.

Smith, Ray F. 1970. Pesticides: Their use and limitations in pest management. In *Concepts of Pest Management Conference Proceedings,* pp. 103-18. North Carolina State Univ. Press, Raleigh.

_____. 1972. The impact of the Green Revolution on plant protection in tropical and sub-tropical areas. Bull. Entomol. Soc. Am. 18:7-14.

Smith, Ray F., and William W. Allen. 1954. Insect control and the balance of nature. *Sci. Am.* 190:38-42.

Smith, Ray F., and Kenneth S. Hagen. 1959. Integrated control programs in the future of biological control. *J. Econ. Entomol.* 52:1106-8.

Smith, Ray F., and Robert Van den Bosch. 1967. Integrated control. In *Pest Control,* Wendell W. Kilgore and Richard L. Doutt, eds., pp. 295-340. Academic Press, New York.

Smith, R. F.; J. L. Apple; and D. G. Bottrell. 1976. The origins of pest management concepts for agricultural crops. In *Integrated Pest Management,* J. L. Apple and R. F. Smith, eds., pp. 1-16. Plenum Publ., New York.

Snyder, W. C. 1960. Antagonism as a plant disease control principle. In *Biological and Chemical Control of Plant and Animal Pests,* pp. 127-36. Am. Assoc. Advan. Sci., Washington, D.C.

Somsen, H. W., and W. H. Sill, Jr. 1970. The wheat curl mite, *Aceria tulipae* Keifer, in relation to epidemiology and control of wheat streak mosaic. Res. Pub. 162. Agric. Exp. Stn., Kansas State Univ., Manhattan.

Sondheimer, Ernest, and John B. Simeone, eds. 1970. *Chemical Ecology.* Academic Press, New York.

Spedding, C. R. W. 1975. *The Biology of Agricultural Systems.* Academic Press, New York.

Stairs, Gordon R. 1971. Use of viruses for microbial control of insects. In *Microbial Control of Insects and Mites,* H. D. Burges and N. W. Hussey, eds., pp. 97-124. Academic Press, New York.

Stark, R. W., and Ray F. Smith, 1971. Systems analysis and pest management. In *Biological Control,* C. B. Huffaker, ed., pp. 331-45. Plenum Publ., New York.

Steinhaus, E. A. 1951. Possible use of *Bacillus thuringiensis* Berliner as an aid in the biological control of the alfalfa caterpillar. *Hilgardia* 20:359-81.

Stevenson, A. B. 1970. Strains of the grape *Phylloxera* in Ontario with different effects on the foliage of certain grape cultivars. *J. Econ. Entomol.* 63:135-38.

Strickland, A. H. 1970. Some economic principles of pest management. In *Concepts of Pest Mangement, Conference Proceedings,* pp. 30-44. North Carolina State Univ. Press, Raleigh.

Sturgeon, R. V., Jr. 1974. Plant health programs. *Phytopathol. News* 8 (3):5-6.

Sun, M. H. 1974. Cropping system to minimize various crop damages from diseases, insects, and weeds. PID-C-363. Plant Ind. Div. Joint Comm. Rural Reconstr., Taipei, Taiwan.

Swarup, Vishnu; Elizabeth U. McCracken; Webster H. Sill, Jr.; and John W. Schmidt. 1956. A cytogenetical analysis of reactions to wheat streak mosaic virus in certain agrotricum hybrids. *Agron. J.* 48:374-79.

Swingle, M. C. 1939. The effect of previous diet on the toxic action of lead arsenate to a leaf feeding insect. *J. Econ. Entomol.* 32:884.

Szkolnik, Michael, and J. D. Gilpatrick. 1969. Apparent resistance of *Venturia inaequalis* to Dodine in New York apple orchards. *Plant Dis. Rep.* 53:861-64.

Sztenjnberg, Abraham. 1979. Biological control of powdery mildews by *Ampelomyces quisqualis.* Pap. 159, Abstr. Pap. IX Int. Congr. Plant Prot., Washington, D.C.

Talekar, N. S., and J. S. Chen. 1979. Persistence of some insecticides in cultivated soil in the tropics. Abstr. Pap. IX Int. Congr. Plant Prot., Washington, D.C.

Tamaki, George; Lee Fox; and B. A. Butt. 1979. Ecology of the green peach aphid as a vector of beet western yellows virus of sugarbeets. USDA Tech. Bull. 1599. Washington, D.C.

Taylor, G. S., and S. Rich. 1973. Ozone fleck on tobacco reduced by benomyl and carboxin in soil (abstr.). *Phytopathology* 63:208.

Templeton, George E.; David O. TeBeast; and Roy J. Smith, Jr. 1979. Biological weed control with mycoherbicides. *Annu. Rev. Phytopathol.* 17:301-10.

Tette, J. P.; E. H. Glass; D. Bruno; and D. Way. 1979. New York tree fruit pest management project, 1973-78. N.Y. Food Life Sci. Bull. 81.

Thurston, H. David. 1971. Managing plant diseases: An overview. Paper read at SEADAG Rural Dev. panel seminar on Research Needs on Crop Protection Systems at Kasetsart Univ., 1-3 Nov. 1971, Bangkok.

Tichelaar, G. M. 1961. The influence of gladiolus on the germination of sclerotia on *Sclerotium cepivorum. Tijdschr. Plantez.* 67:290-95.

Topham, Marshall R. 1973. Influence of adult food source plants on the New Guinea sugarcane weevil parasite, *Lixophage sphenophori* (Villeneuve). Master's thesis, Univ. Hawaii, Honolulu.

Toussoun, T. A.; W. Menzinger; and R. S. Smith, Jr. 1969. Role of conifer litter in ecology of *fusarium*: Stimulation of germination in soil. *Phytopathology* 59:1396-99.

Tucker, David, and Richard Phillips. 1974. The strangler vine: A major weed pest in Florida citrus groves. *Weeds Today* 5 (4):6-8.

Turgeon, A. J.; M. C. Shurtleff; and R. Randall. 1973. Turfgrass pest control. Circ. 1076. Agric. Ext. Serv., Univ. Illinois, Urbana-Champaign.

University of California. 1972a. Defoliation and other harvest-aid practices. In Study Guide for Agricultural Pest Control Advisers. Div. Agric. Sci., Berkeley.

_____. 1972b. Nematodes and nematicides. In Study Guide for Agricultural Pest Control Advisers. Div. Agric. Sci., Berkeley.

_____. 1972c. Plant diseases. In Study Guide for Agricultural Pest Control Advisers. Div. Agric. Sci., Berkeley.

Upchurch, R. P. 1975. Biological, chemical, and other factors influencing strategies for selective weed control. In *Pesticide Selectivity,* J. C. Street, ed., pp. 11-20. Marcel Dekker, New York.

USDA. 1957. Insect control by seed treatment. Agric. Res. Feb. 1957, p. 10.

_____. 1972. *Implementing Practical Pest Management Strategies.* Proc. Natl. Ext. Insect Pest Manage. Workshop. Purdue Univ., Lafayette, Ind.

_____. 1979. Cotton insect management programs, 1972-79. SEA Ext. Washington, D.C.

USGPO. 1972. Integrated pest management. Stock 4111-0010. Counc. Environ. Qual., Supt. Doc. Washington, D.C.

Van der Plank, J. E. 1963. *Plant Diseases: Epidemics and Control.* Academic Press, New York.

_____. 1972. Basic principles of ecosystems analysis. In *Pest Control Strategies for the Future,* pp. 109-18. Div. Biol. Agric., Nat. Res. Counc. National Academy of Sciences, Washington, D.C.

_____. 1975. *Principles of Plant Infection.* Academic Press, New York.

Van Gundy, S. D. 1972. Nonchemical control of nematodes and root-infecting fungi. In *Pest Control Strategies for the Future,* pp. 317-29. Div. Biol. Agric., Natl. Res. Counc. National Academy of Sciences, Washington, D.C.

Varley, G. C., and G. R. Gradwell. 1971. The use of models and life tables in assessing the role of natural enemies. In *Biological Control,* C. B. Huffaker, ed., pp. 93–112. Plenum Publ., New York.

Vidaver, Anne K. 1976. Prospects for control of phytopathogenic bacteria by bacteriophages and bacteriocins. *Annu. Rev. Phytopathol.* 14:451–65.

Waggoner, Paul E. 1965. Microclimate and plant disease. *Annu. Rev. Phytopathol.* 3:103–26.

Waggoner, P. E., and J. G. Horsfall. 1969. EPIDEM: A simulator of plant disease written for a computer. Agric. Exp. Stn. Bull. 698. Univ. Connecticut, New Haven.

Waggoner, P E.; J. G. Horsfall; and R. J. Lukens. 1972. EPIMAY: A simulator of southern corn leaf blight. Agric. Exp. Stn. Bull. 729. Univ. Connecticut, New Haven.

Walker, J. C. 1969. *Plant Pathology,* 3d ed. McGraw-Hill, New York.

Walker, J. K.; R. E. Frisbie; and G. A. Niles. 1978. A change in perspective: Heliothis in short-season cottons in Texas. Bull. Entomol. Soc. Am. 24:385–91.

Wang, Z. N., and L. S. Leu. 1974. Entomogenous fungi on sugarcane pests in Taiwan. Proc. 15 Congr. Int. Soc. Sugar Cane Tech., Joint Comm. Rural Reconst., Taipei, Taiwan.

Warner, John N. 1953. The evolution of a philosophy on sugarcane breeding in Hawaii. In *Hawaiian Planters' Record,* L. D. Baver and Lydia C. Nickerson, eds., pp. 139–62. vol. 54, no. 3. Exp. Stn. Hawaiian Sugar Plant. Assoc., Honolulu.

Watson, Andrew G., and Eugene J. Ford. 1972. Soil fungistasis: A reappraisal. *Annu. Rev. Phytopathol.* 10:327–48.

Watson, David L., and A.W.A. Brown. 1977. *Pesticide Management and Insecticide Resistance.* Academic Press, New York.

Way, M. J. 1979. Significance of diversity in agroecosystems. Proc., Opening Sess. Plenary Sess. Symp. IX Int. Congr. Plant Prot., Washington, D.C.

Weber, J. B.; S. B. Weed; and T. J. Sheets. 1972. Pesticides: How they move and react in the soil. *Crops Soils* 25:14–17.

Webster, R. K.; J. M. Ogawa; and Elaine Bose. 1970. Tolerance of *Botrytis cinerea* to 2, 6-dichloro-4-nitroaniline. *Phytopathology* 60:1489–92.

Weed Control Manual. 1979. Meister Publ., Willoughby, Ohio.

Wellman, F. L. 1968. More diseases on crops in the tropics than in the temperate zone. *Ceiba* 14:17–28.

———. 1972. *Tropical American Plant Diseases.* Scarecrow Press, Metuchen, N.J.

Went, F. W. 1970. Plants and the chemical environment. In *Chemical Ecology,* Ernest Sondheimer and John B. Simeone, eds., pp. 71–82. Academic Press, New York.

Westing, Arthur H. 1971. Ecological effects of military defoliation on the forests of South Vietnam. *Bioscience* 21:893–98.

Whittaker, R. H. 1970. The biochemical ecology of higher plants. In *Chemical Ecology,* Ernest Sondheimer and John B. Simeone, eds., pp. 43–70. Academic Press, New York.

Whitten, M. J. 1970. Genetics of pests in their management. In *Concepts of Pest Management. Conf. Proceedings,* pp. 119–37. North Carolina State Univ. Press, Raleigh.

———. 1971. Insect control by genetic manipulation of natural populations. *Science* 171 (3972):682–84.

Wilcke, H. L. 1972. The role of the food industry in solving pest control problems. In *Pest Control Strategies for the Future,* pp. 69–76. Div. Biol. Agric., Natl. Res. Counc. National Academy of Sciences, Washington, D.C.

Wilhelm, Stephan, and Albert O. Paulus. 1980. How soil fumigation benefits the California strawberry industry. *Plant Dis.* 64:265–70.

Williams, Carroll M. 1970. Hormonal interactions between plants and insects. In *Chemical Ecology,* E. Sondheimer and J. B. Simeone, eds., pp. 103–32. Academic Press, New York.

Williams, L. E., and A. F. Schmitthenner. 1962. Effects of crop rotation on soil fungus populations. *Phytopathology* 52:241–47.

Willison, R. S. 1963. Ionizing radiation for the control of plant pathogens: A review. Canadian Plant Dis. Surv. 43:39–53.

Wilson, C. L. 1969. Use of plant pathogens in weed control. *Annu. Rev. Phytopathol.* 7:411–34.

Winter, A. G. 1948. Untersuchungen uber die Beziehungen zwischen *Ophiobolus graminis* und anderen Organismen mit Hilfe der Aufwuchsplatten Methode. *Arch. Mikrobiol.* 41:240–70.

Wood, David L., ed. 1970. *Control of Insect Behavior by Natural Products.* Academic Press, New York.

Wood, David L.; Robert M. Silverstein; and Minoru Nakajima. 1969. Pest control. *Science* 164 (3876):203–10.

Wood, R. K. S.; A. Ballio; and A. Graniti, eds. 1972. *Phytotoxins in Plant Diseases.* Academic Press, New York.

Yarwood, C. E. 1968. Tillage and plant diseases. *Bioscience* 18:27–30.

_____. 1970. Man-made plant diseases. *Science* 168:218–20.

Yen, David F. 1971. Integrated control of vegetable insects. In *Better Crop Production: Problems and Solutions.* PID activities. PID-SC-070, Dec. 1971. Joint Comm. Rural Reconstr., Taipei, Taiwan.

Young, H. C., Jr.; J. M. Prescott; and F. E. Saari. 1978. Role of disease monitoring in preventing epidemics. *Annu. Rev. Phytopathol.* 16:263–85.

Zadoks, J. C. 1971. Systems analysis and the dynamics of epidemics. *Phytopathology* 61:600–610.

Zak, Bratislau. 1964. Role of mycorrhizae in root disease. *Annu. Rev. Phytopathol.* 2:377–92.

Zentmyer, George A. 1963. Biological control of *Phytophthora* root rot of avocado with alfalfa meal. *Phytopathology* 53:1383–87.

Zettler, F. W., and T. E. Freeman. 1972. Plant pathogens as biocontrols of aquatic weeds. *Annu. Rev. Phytopathol.* 10:455–70.

Zweig, Gunter, ed. 1963. *Analytical Methods of Pesticides, Plant Growth Regulators, and Food Additives.* Vol. I. *Principles, Methods, and General Applications.* Academic Press, New York.

OTHER USEFUL REFERENCES

Adams, M. W.; A. H. Ellingboe; and E. C. Rossman. 1971. Biological uniformity and disease epidemics. *Bioscience* 21:7067-70.

Boudreau, Gordon W. 1975. *How to Win the War with Pest Birds.* Wildlife Technology, Hollister, Calif.

Brader, L. 1974. Integrated control in the Netherlands. EPPO Bull. 4 (3):319-28.

―――. 1979. Integrated pest control in the developing world. *Annu. Rev. Entomol.* 24:225-54.

Chiu, Ren-jong. 1969. Two major field programs on rice pest control. PID-SC-028, 18 Aug. 1969. Plant Ind. Div., Joint Comm. Rural Reconstr., Taipei, Taiwan.

Edwards, C. A., ed. 1973. *Environmental Pollution by Pesticides.* Plenum Publ., New York.

Garrett, S. D. 1956. *Biology of Root-Infecting Fungi.* Cambridge Univ. Press.

Herbicide Handbook, 3d ed. 1974. Weed Sci. Soc. Am. Champaign, Ill.

Kiritani, Keizi. 1979. Pest management in rice. *Annu. Rev. Entomol.* 24:279-312.

Lambert, Michel, ed. 1973. Weed control in the South Pacific. South Pacific Comm. Handb. 10, Noumea, New Caledonia.

McFarlane, N. R., ed. 1977. Crop protection agents: Their biological evaluation. Proc. Int. Conf. Eval. Biol. Act., 16-18 Apr. 1974. Wageningen, Netherlands.

Mortensen, Ernest, and Erwin T. Bullard. 1968. *Handbook of Tropical and Sub-Tropical Horticulture,* rev. U.S. State Dep., USAID, Washington, D.C.

Ranney, C. D. 1972. Multiple cotton seed treatments: Effects on germination, seedling growth, and survival. *Crop Sci.* 12:346-50.

Roberts, Daniel A. 1978. *Fundamentals of Plant Pest Control.* W. H. Freeman, San Francisco.

Sanderson, M. W. 1939. Crop replacement in relation to grasshopper abundance. *J. Econ. Entomol.* 23:484-86.

Stakman, E. C.; Richard Bradfield; and Paul C. Mangelsdorf. 1967. *Campaigns against Hunger.* Harvard Univ. Press, Cambridge, Mass.

Stapley, J. H., and F. C. H. Gayner. 1969. *World Crop Protection.* Vol. I. *Pests and Diseases.* CRC Press, Chemical Rubber Co., Cleveland, Ohio.

Sweetman, Harvey L. 1936. *The Biological Control of Insects.* Comstock Publ., Ithaca, New York.

Thurston, H. David. 1973. Threatening plant diseases. *Annu. Rev. Phytopathol.* 10:27-52.

Wright, R. P. 1910. Rotation of farm crops. In *The Cyclopedia of British Agriculture,* vol. 10, pp. 147-50. Gresham Publ., London.

INDEX

Abiotic controls, 134–39
Abiotic maladies, 4, 18, 105, 131–34, 214
Agroecosystem, 37–38, 222, 238, 271
Air pollution, 131–33, 185, 195, 233
American Phytopathological Society, 144, 165
Anoxia, 123
Antagonism
  allelopathic materials in, 174–75
  antibiosis in, 176–78
  antibiotics in, 175–76
  in cultural control, 114
  defined, 168–69
  exudates in, 170–73
  mycorrhizae in, 178–79
  phytoalexins in, 181–83
  phytotoxins in, 179–81
  plant toxins in, 183
Arthropods, 28, 146–57, 183–84, 197–201. *See also* Insects

Bactericide, 68–69, 81
Biocide, 49. *See also* Pesticide
Biological control
  by antagonism, 168–84
  defined, 140
  by disease, 157–61, 223
  diversity and, 40–41
  of insects, 15, 146–57
  in integrated control, 214
  of nematodes, 161-64
  plant breeding as, 186
  pros and cons, 141–42
  of weeds, 17, 164-67
Birds, 208–10
Breeding, 12, 201, 273
  cooperative, 196–97, 234–36
  for resistance, 186–94, 199, 214, 263

Certification, seed and nursery, 21–24
Chemicals. *See also* DDT; Fungicide
  in biological control, 141
  bird control by, 208
  in chemotherapy, 71–73
  compatibility, 80–90
  controlled-release, 76–77
  degradation, 85–86, 89

in disease control, 68–69
harvest-aid, 70–71
hormonal, 61–63. *See also* Pheromones
insect control by, 49–66, 93. *See also* Insecticide
in integrated control, 214–15
multiuse, 74
for natural control, 61–64
nematode control by, 23, 99. *See also* Nematicide
phytotoxic, 10, 81, 82–84, 90, 119, 176, 201
residue, 84–90
resistance, 10, 56–57, 61
safety of, 51, 82, 84, 86, 88
selective, 59, 80, 216
synergism and, 61, 145, 154
systemic, for insects, 24
vector control by, 67–68
Chemotherapy, 71–73
Computers, 29, 42–48, 229–30, 251, 256
Controls, cooperative
  cultural, 242–43
  in developing nations, 253
  fumigants in, 241–42
  with insecticides and fungicides, 232–34
  of nematodes and pests, 238–41
  plant breeding programs in, 234–36
  problems of, 231–32, 256–57
  programs, 244–57
  in Taiwan, 253–56
  with weeds and pests, 236–38
Council on Environmental Quality (U.S.A.), 230
Cropping patterns, 100–102
Crop rotation, 92, 94–100, 238
Cultural control, 91–114, 214, 242–43
  of birds, 209
  by cropping techniques, 100–114
  crop rotation as, 94–100
  of disease, 93, 95, 223
  of insects, 94–95
  of pink bollworm, 93
  of rodents, 207
  of weeds, 100

DDT, 9, 16, 49, 52, 54, 55, 58, 61, 154
  residues, 85, 86, 88

293